Australian Studies

Urban Planning in Australia: Critical Readings

Titles in the **Australian Studies** series are:

Drinking and Alcoholism in Australia, by Margaret Sargent
The Military and Australia's Defence, edited by F. A. Mediansky
The Australian Urban System, by I. H. Burnley
Beyond the City, edited by Margaret Bowman
An Issue of People, by Robert Birrell and Tanya Birrell
Family Violence in Australia, edited by Carol O'Donnell and Jan Craney
The Australian City, by R. J. Stimson
Power, Privilege and Prestige, by Ann Daniel
Immigrants and the Media, by Naomi Rosh White and Peter B. White
Living together in Australia, by S. Sarantakos
Australian Urban Politics, by J. Halligan and C. Paris
Unemployment in the Eighties, edited by Robert Castle and John Mangan
Australian Women and the Political System, edited by Marian Simms
Choices About Children, by Victor J. Callan
Immigration and Ethnicity in the 1980s, edited by Ian Burnley, Sol Encel and Grant McCall
Work, Leisure and Technology, edited by Robert Castle, Donald Lewis and John Mangan
Urban Planning in Australia: Critical Readings, edited by J. Brian McLoughlin and Margo Huxley

Australian Studies

Urban Planning in Australia: Critical Readings

Edited by J. Brian McLoughlin and Margo Huxley

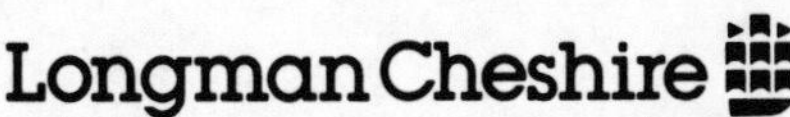

Longman Cheshire Pty Limited
Longman House
Kings Gardens
95 Coventry Street
Melbourne 3205 Australia

Offices in Sydney, Brisbane, Adelaide
and Perth. Associated companies, branches,
and representatives throughout the world.

First published 1986

Set in 10/11 Baskerville Roman (Linotron 202)
Printed in Malaysia
by Mun Sun Press Sdn. Bhd., Shah Alam, Selangor.

National Library of Australia
Cataloguing-in-Publication data

Urban planning in Australia.

Bibliography.
Includes index.
ISBN 0 582 71153 3.

1. City planning – Australia – Addresses, essays,
lectures. I. McLoughlin, J. Brian (John Brian). II. Huxley, Margo. (Series:
Australian studies).

307'.12'0994

Contents

Contributors

Ian Alexander, Senior Lecturer in the Department of Urban and Regional Planning at the Western Australian Institute of Technology, Perth

Carolyn Allport, Senior Lecturer in the School of History, Philosophy and Politics at Macquarie University, Sydney

Blair Badcock, Senior Lecturer in Geography at the University of Adelaide

Clive Beed, Senior Lecturer in the Economics Faculty at the University of Melbourne.

Mike Berry, Senior Lecturer in the Faculty of Humanities and Social Sciences at the Royal Melbourne Institute of Technology

Ray Bunker, Principal Lecturer in Town Planning at the South Australian Institute of Technology, Adelaide

Maurie Daly, McCaughey Professor of Geography at the University of Sydney

Clive Forster, Senior Lecturer in Geography at the School of Social Sciences at Flinders University of South Australia, Adelaide

Bob Graham, Consultant planner and former Member for Denison in the Tasmanian House of Representatives, Hobart

Elizabeth Harman, Senior Lecturer in the School of Social Inquiry at Murdoch University, Perth

Ron Horvath, Research Fellow in Geography at the University of Sydney

Margo Huxley, Research Fellow in the School of Environmental Planning at the University of Melbourne

Jim Kemeny, Research Fellow at the Swedish National Building Research Institute, Stockholm

Ross King, Senior Lecturer in the School of Environmental Planning at the University of Melbourne

Bill Logan, Head of Urban Studies at the Footscray Institute of Technology, Melbourne

Toni Logan, Senior Lecturer in the School of Environmental Planning at the University of Melbourne

Brian McLoughlin, Professor of Town and Regional Planning in the School of Environmental Planning at the University of Melbourne

Chris Maher, Senior Lecturer in Geography at Monash University, Melbourne

Max Neutze, Professor and Director of the Urban Research Unit at the Australian National University, Canberra

Chris Paris, Senior Research Fellow in the Urban Research Unit at the Australian National University, Canberra

Frank Stilwell, Associate Professor in the Department of Economics at the University of Sydney

Hugh Stretton, Reader in the History Department at the University of Adelaide

David Tait, Senior Research Fellow in the Social Welfare Research Centre at the University of New South Wales, Sydney

Peter Williams, Assistant Director (Education and Research) at the Institute of Housing in London

Acknowledgements

First and foremost, we wish to thank the authors of the individual chapters who responded so positively to the initial idea of this reader and who were unfailingly polite in the face of persistent calls for their copy. Our thanks also go to the various publishers and editors who granted their permission to reproduce material based on earlier publications.

We also thank Neil Ryan, Elizabeth Watson and their colleagues at Longman Cheshire for their encouragement, patience and helpfulness throughout the complex process of producing a set of readings.

Our colleagues in the School of Environmental Planning at the University of Melbourne, and many others in the diversified and vital 'invisible college' of urban social scientists and planners which exists throughout Australia, but especially in Melbourne, have been a source of constant inspiration and support. We are most grateful to Roz Edmond for the peace and quiet of 'Lakeview' at Daylesford which helped the final editing.

All those who have edited a collection such as this will know that its production involves a kind of masochism, the pain of which is greatly eased by a good secretary. Beulah Dickson has not only been the ideal support system in every way; she has also shown a personal enthusiasm for this project far beyond the call of duty. On occasions she has had the willing help of Dorothy Bugg and Morag Van Der Zee.

Editors' note

Despite all their best efforts, the editors have unfortunately been unable to expunge all traces of the gender bias of the English language. With a number of exceptions, where editorial amendment did not result in excessive clumsiness, we have left pronouns, etc. as written by the original authors.

Introduction

Chapter 1
Urban planning in Australia

Brian McLoughlin

Many writers have remarked that, despite Australia's extraordinary degree of urbanisation, it is only in the last ten years or so that social scientists have shown much interest in urban phenomena (see, for example, Halligan and Paris 1984:1; and Berry 1984:Chapter 1). Much of the corpus of writing until the early-to-middle 1970s was descriptive and empirical and did not reflect the more theoretical and analytical discourse which was by then growing rapidly in Europe and North America. In particular, there has been a distinct lack of interest in describing and analysing the theory, practice and outcomes of Australian town planning (as noted in Huxley and McLoughlin 1985).

How can we account for this surprising neglect of urban planning issues? One reason may well be the relatively recent introduction of formal town planning. Unlike say Britain and North America, statutory controls over the use and development of land were almost unheard of in the inter-war period. It was only in the 1950s and 1960s that formal controls became at all common, and indeed even then legislation was often permissive rather than mandatory. In Victoria, for example, the 1944 Act did not require municipalities to prepare schemes and the first Melbourne Metropolitan Planning Scheme, produced in 1954, was not approved until 1968 (T. Logan 1981:8). Central Perth still does not have an approved statutory planning scheme (Alexander 1985).

A second reason for this neglect may be the lack of significant urban government in Australia (Halligan and Paris 1984:Chapter 1) when compared with similar advanced societies. Whereas American, and especially British, urban governments are relatively powerful, having large incomes and highly politicised responsibilities for such services as housing, education and personal welfare, Australian municipalities by and large have been limited in their functions to the 'three Rs'—roads, rates and rubbish. Therefore, the questions of service delivery and struggles over 'collective consumption' which result in highly-charged debates elsewhere (see for example, Saunders 1981; Dunleavy 1980) have hardly ever occurred in Australia, or have been temporary and localised (see for example, W. Logan 1985; Mullins 1977, 1979*b*) with the exception of the 'green bans' alliances between building workers and (mainly) middle-class residents in the early 1970s (Roddewig 1978; Jakubowicz 1984). Most planning, other than bureaucratically routine permit-issuing, has been carried out at State level and, until quite recently, by somewhat opaque quangos such as the Melbourne and Metropolitan Board of Works. New South Wales did not have a State department explicitly charged with planning until 1980. In Victoria, although there had been a Town and Country Planning Board since 1944 and a (separate) Ministry for Planning since 1973, it was not until 1980 that an integrated ministry was set up. So, planning in Australia has not been particularly significant (for example, in terms of social and political conflict) or visible.

A third possible explanation for the lack of social-scientific attention is that Australian planning seems rather technocratic and unself-conscious. Its ethics and its methods have been imported, almost entirely from the United Kingdom (see for example, Power 1970; Stretton 1976; Sandercock 1983*a*; McLoughlin 1983*a*). Moreover Australia has never experienced the high summer of planning such as occurred in Britain in the decade 1965–75, associated with powerful authorities and the forceful combination of ministerial direction and closely-related academic research. The relative looseness of the academic/policy connection in Australia (with the notable exception of the Department of Urban and Regional Development under the Whitlam Labor administration of 1972–75) meant that planning itself has not been subjected to widespread critical scrutiny.

However, we have the impression that Australian urban planning and the issues with which it deals are changing in ways that will bring planning into wider debates on social and economic policy. As a result of 'quality-of-life' issues, crystallised in the 'green bans' and more diffusely expressed in concerns over residential amenity (for example, restrictive flat codes) in the 1970s, town planning agencies, especially as formal organs of State governments, became much more prominent (Low and Power 1984). Public dissatisfaction with planning practice, for instance as carried out by largely unaccountable quangos like the MMBW, led to the introduction of ministerially, and to some extent locally, accountable procedures. The *NSW Environmental Planning and Assessment Act of 1979* and the taking-over of the MMBW's planning powers by the Victorian Ministry for Planning and Environment can be seen in part as the results of these public (and State) concerns over the conduct of planning.

Ironically, the economic climate which gave rise to these concerns has changed, and the effects of economic recession are becoming felt at the time when the planning structures, policies and processes of the 1970s are being consolidated at State government level. The effects of global restructuring on Australia's economy and on urban areas are becoming evident here in ways sadly familiar to many communities in the older industrial regions of the northern hemisphere. Increasingly, in their attempts to ensure investment and to protect jobs, (for example, the Victorian government's Economic Strategy Statement; Victoria 1984) governments may be pushed to reduce social and welfare expenditure and to by-pass environmental controls and conservation measures. Administrative and legislative reforms for Ministerial accountability and co-ordination have the effect of increasing centralisation of control which can lead to attenuation of public participation processes (Berry and Huxley 1985). Such strategies will bring the contradictions of planning policy and practice into sharper focus and make more urgent the critique and debate which is gathering momentum (for example, Alexander 1981*a*; 1981*b*; Graham 1981*b*, and Chapter 13 of this volume; Kilmartin, Huxley and McLoughlin 1985).

We came to see the need for a book on Australian urban planning when we carried out a large-scale review of the wider urban studies literature (Huxley and McLoughlin 1985). Our work showed clearly that Australia has now achieved an international reputation in this field, especially in work carried out within a broad political economy perspective; however, as noted above, the number of publications specifically dealing with urban planning is relatively insignificant.

Our bibliographic work had revealed that there were indeed a number of good books and collections on urban issues. For example, there is a comprehensive literature on Australian urbanisation in general (for example, Burnley 1980; Neutze 1977, 1981; M. Logan et al. 1981; Berry 1984), on urban policy in general (for example, Stretton 1970, 1974, 1975, 1976, 1978; Neutze 1978), on specific planning systems (for example, Harris and Dixon 1978; T. Logan 1981) and on particular issues such as equity (for example, Troy 1981), urban government (for example, Parkin 1982), or 'social movements' (for example, Mullins 1977, 1979*b*) and urban politics (Halligan and Paris 1984). We were also aware of the often-expressed view (for example, Stretton 1972; Apps 1973*a*; Pahl 1973; Stilwell and Hardwick 1973) that Australian planning practice, and especially theory, need critical evaluation along the lines pioneered by writers such as Hall and his colleagues (1973) and Reade (1982) and we were conscious of the need for a 'reappraisal' inspired by scholars like Scott and Roweis (1977). But we found little if any work which had the specific aim of seeking to relate Australian urban planning to the process of urbanisation and to locate planning within the wider socio-political framework. In addition, we discovered through our network of colleagues and friends, that there were one or two important pieces of work which were either unpublished (for example, Ross King's work presented as Chapter 18 of this collection) or circulated in ephemeral form (for example, Ian Alexander's piece which appears as Chapter 8). The time seemed ripe for much of this material to be brought together and presented in such a way as both to reflect and to contribute to the Australian achievement so far.

The book is aimed at a wide and heterogeneous readership which includes practitioners in various branches of public policy-making, private-sector practice, scholars and students across the broad field of the urban social sciences. It will be especially useful for advanced undergraduate and postgraduate students in geography, economics, sociology, politics, urban and regional planning and urban studies.

This book (which we hope will be the first in a series) is therefore trying to serve a number of closely-related aims. First, it puts between one set of covers some of the best material we have found, for the benefit of Australian students, scholars and practitioners. Second, we hope it will inspire local scholars to set about the much-needed critical study of Australian urban planning. Third, we hope in particular that it will encourage scholars in traditional planning schools to participate with vigour in such an enterprise and to draw together the somewhat separated fields of urban studies and planning. Such work will serve two important and related purposes. First, it will add to the growing body of internationally comparative literature which is already revealing the broad similarities which characterise urbanisation under capitalism in the more 'advanced' societies. But it will also help to reveal how different historical paths of economic, social and urban development have led to very *different* forms of the state in general and its urban planning functions in particular, especially in Australia.

Our selection of readings attempts to place government policies in a broader context while retaining a general orientation towards the spatial and social outcomes of planning policies and practices. The contributions reflect the most important debates within the field of urban studies; for example, over the conception of the state and of planning, the dialectic between social processes and spatial forms, issues of territorial and social justice, strategies for intervention, and so on. Interesting examples of such debates are provided by Neutze and Paris/Williams on planning, Horvath, Graham, Forster and Allport on social and spatial inequalities and Kemeny and Stretton on private home-ownership. The overall approach of the editors is one of urban and regional political economy in a broad sense. We adopt this position because, in our view, it raises the most important and interesting questions in a consistent, integrated and socio-historical way. Moreover, at present, the various strands of urban political economy hold out the promise of considerable explanatory power.

A good example of the application of a political economy critique to urban planning is the important paper by Scott and Roweis (1977). Like them, we seek to relate urban planning practice and its social and spatial effects to the dynamic interplay between the processes of urbanisation and the evolving role of the state. As editors, we have made our selection of contributions on the basis that we are not so much concerned with 'abstract normative principles as to what planning *ought* in ideal circumstances to be' but rather with 'what planning actually *is* and *does*' (Scott and Roweis 1977:1097). This viewpoint is reflected in the organisation of the book.

We believe it is necessary to begin with an understanding of the broad historical and spatial condition of the Australian urban process.

Thus Section I sets out the background of the evolution and the present nature of urban development in Australia and its economic, demographic, social and spatial characteristics. Chris Maher's contribution (Chapter 2) emphasises recent demographic and geographical changes and is complemented by Mike Berry's analysis, in Chapter 3, of the economic forces which have driven urban development during the 'long boom' from 1946–73 and in the subsequent recession.

In recent years, economic, social and urban changes have called for increasing and more complex forms of state involvement and intervention which include various kinds of urban and regional planning. Much of the urban studies literature is concerned with analysing some important contradictions in the state's role, such as between the need to sustain the conditions for profitable private investment (for example, by collective provision of infrastructure) on the one hand, and the need for 'social expenditures' on health, welfare, education and so forth on the other. These contradictions can be seen as inherent in the state's position in capitalist society, embedded as it is in the primary contradiction between capital and labour.

A particularly interesting contradiction in the state's role concerns the 'urban land nexus' (Scott 1980) and this is of considerable importance in understanding modern urban planning. In market societies like Australia, the urban development process is a complex outcome of a myriad largely private investment (or disinvestment) decisions. These give rise to endemic conflicts over locational advantages. The state, and especially its urban planning arm, is called upon to mediate day-by-day to seek some resolutions of these conflicts, while at the same time ensuring the preconditions for continuing profitable investment and taking into the area of public responsibility as many of the negative (or unprofitable) consequences as possible.

Therefore, Section II is devoted to two views of the role of the state in relation to urban issues in contemporary Australia. Frank Stilwell's contribution (Chapter 4) addresses the types of issues raised by Scott and deals with their dynamics at a variety of geographical scales, from that of the whole country, to individual States and metropolitan regions. He gives empirical illustrations of the contradictions and dilemmas faced by various levels of government in seeking to cope with the more localised effects of economic restructuring. Elizabeth Harman, in Chapter 5, analyses in detail the urban effects of the boom-and-bust phenomenon of mineral resource development in Western Australia and the roles played by the State government in relation to large multinational corporations.

Following an overall logic of locating urban planning within the role of the state and urbanisation within the historical dynamics of particular societies, Section III is devoted to the contrasting views of how we might conceptualise present-day urban planning in Australia. In Chapter 6, Max Neutze is at pains to clear up some of the confusions which often arise in discussions by practitioners and academics who too often fail to distinguish between planning and implementation and the different levels of analysis—ideological, political, operational and technical—which are necessary. In Chapter 7, Chris Paris and Peter Williams point to the limited, but nevertheless significant effects of town planning and remind us that 'it involves relationships and processes which must be analysed in action, rather than discussed in a static and universal framework'.

The stage is now set for a specific examination (in Section IV) of the nature of urban planning in Australia today. Since economic growth during the 'long boom' appeared to be largely unproblematic until the mid-1970s, the focus of urban planning has been concentrated on the management of suburban expansion. Such consideration as was given to industrial location, labour markets, etc., mainly took the form of concerns with 'decentralisation' and 'regionalism' (especially during the 'Whitlam era'), both of which were by-products of concerns with metropolitan size and the negative 'externalities' of urban sprawl (M. Logan et al. 1975, 1981). The emphasis in this and following sections of the book, therefore, is very much in line with the substantive practice of Australian planning until the 1980s. It may be predicted that, as the effects of economic recession become more acutely visible, planning will turn increasingly to the problems of production (and future readings may reflect this change).

Ian Alexander's contribution (Chapter 8) is one of the very few broad overviews of Australian practice in 'land use and transport planning' and which we are happy to publish here for the first time. Because of the political, economic and social dominance in Australian life of its State capitals and their metropolitan regions, much Australian planning has been related to them as a whole or to various areas within them, taking the form of the management of the spatial or land use consequences of sustained growth, and hence with the physical form of their large urban areas. Bill Logan, in Chapter 9, looks at the politics involved in the various attempts to manage 'the shape of Melbourne'. Latterly, Australian planners have not confined their attention merely to *shape* on their plans but also to the configuration of land uses and densities. In particular, they have sought to impose some kind of internally coherent pattern of 'central places'—the CBD and suburban nodes—in attempting 'urban consolidation' and resisting suburban sprawl; some of these initiatives are discussed by Ray Bunker in Chapter 10. Such metropolis-wide strategies have implications for the plans, policies and development-control powers of local planners as shown by Toni Logan in Chapter 11.

The next part of the book, Section V, concentrates on some important associated and consequent aspects of planning, especially in terms of spatial and social justice and equity. Our selections attempt to reflect at least two essential elements of debate in the political economy and urban studies literature—how are inequalities produced and how are they distributed within the Australian urban process, including the role of the state and planning? In Chapter 12, Ron Horvath and David Tait illustrate the spatial and social characteristics of the Sydney metropolitan area by reference to their work on the 1980 *Social Atlas*. This original piece shows, graphically and often dramatically, the very large disparities in real incomes and 'life-chances' which characterise most modern western cities. Bob Graham in a complementary sense argues, in Chapter 13, that such inequalities may well be 'basic' to land use planning. His argument is therefore in line with one of the major strands of political economy, namely, that in modern capitalism, the state's productive and allocative roles are in contradiction and are *necessarily* (albeit unintentionally or unconsciously) inegalitarian and usually regressive in their effects.

Another enduring debate, both in conventional urban studies and in its more recent critical developments, is that concerning the casual links between social structure and process on the one hand and spatial development and form on the other. In other words, can we interpret spatial distributions of inequality (as shown in Chapter 12) as inhering in places? Or, should we rather see these as merely the geographical prints of deeper and more fundamental social structures? This debate is well illustrated in the case of unemployment in Adelaide by Clive Forster in Chapter 14.

In Chapter 15, Carolyn Allport's contribution exemplifies the development in urban studies of the feminist critique of both conventional *and* critical research. Feminist writing has argued that both academic urban studies and planning policies in practice, especially concerning suburban life and development, have consistently ignored the significance of suburbia as a locale for productive activities, the work and life-patterns of women, and has pointed to the inadequacies of conventional ideas about housing design, subdivision, standards and the like (for example, Hayden 1982, 1984; E. Harman 1983; Pringle 1983). Carolyn Allport's chapter examines the ways in which initiatives for the amelioration of the effects of low-density suburbia on the lives of women have met with little success, in part because they have been based on explicitly 'sexist' assumptions.

This leads us conveniently to a consideration of housing in Section VI. Here, the contributions link together the huge importance of housing, especially in Australia, with the wider urban land nexus. Two of our contributors illustrate the fruitful debate between differing points of view. Some writers like Jim Kemeny (Chapter 16) firmly believe in the essentially regressive nature of private owner-occupation, while others, like Hugh Stretton (Chapter 17), hold out considerable hope for much more humane opportunities within privately-owned suburban areas. Most work on housing in Australia clearly shows how, under the present system of taxes, mortgage structuring, subsidies and land development, the private housing market consistently shifts massive amounts of wealth from poorer to richer households, from tenants to landlords and from market entrants to established owners. Ross King (Chapter 18) demonstrates these regressive tendencies and indicates the role of planning in exacerbating them. In Chapter 19, Maurie Daly illustrates, with a wealth of empirical detail, how CBD boom-and-bust cycles are driven by the intersecting agencies of financiers, land speculators and public servants and the effects that land-price escalation had on the Sydney housing market.

In Section VII, contributors consider what planning can and should do. However, unlike much conventional planning theory, with its uncritically normative position, these authors offer their prescriptions in the light of a prior understanding of urbanisation and planning. Here again, we share with Scott and Roweis the feeling that we must move 'beyond innocence and despair'. For, if conventional planning theory 'interposes identifiable barriers to a global understanding of the real universe of urban planning activities . . . it is in the fullest sense of the term, an ideology', (Scott and Roweis 1977:1117). Like them, we wish to avoid the chronic dilemma of 'that eternal alternation between a purely subjective optimism (as we put our faith in the ideology) and a purely subjective pessimism (as we put our faith in the naked facts . . .' (loc. cit.). In Chapter 20, Clive Beed examines in detail the relationships between the urban development process, past and present planning policies and spatial and social equity. Using metropolitan Melbourne as his empirical base he shows how planning policies for 'consolidation', 'nodes' and so forth have been neither well-founded in theory nor effective in practice and speculates on the possibility of new forms of community control over land use and development. Blair Badcock's contribution, in Chapter 21, complements Beed's work by concentrating on the need for 'new forms of state intervention' including national economic planning, job creation, and new forms of urban and regional development planning, all against a backcloth of very much lower labour demand, motor fuel shortages and an ageing population.

Finally, in Chapter 22, Margo Huxley attempts to draw together and reflect on the material presented in the book in the light of the most important debates in urban social theory. In doing so, she also offers suggested further reading for those students who wish to undertake more advanced studies.

Section I:
Background

Chapter 2
Australian urban character: pattern and process

Chris Maher

Introduction

The character of a nation's settlement system is the complex product of historical, environmental, economic and socio-cultural forces. The development of urban functions results in a physical imprint on the landscape, the existence of which, while imposing certain conditions and constraints on the nature of further change, is itself continually responding to an ever-evolving context, particularly in the economic, demographic, and political spheres.

That the product of the forces of urban development as they have evolved over the past 150 years in Australia is distinctive, is beyond doubt. On the one hand, the nation is characterised by a degree of concentration of the population into urban, and more particularly into a small number of large metropolitan areas, which is matched by no other developed nation. On the other, these points of population concentration are themselves more internally dispersed than almost any other metropolitan regions in the world. The twin features of concentration at the national level, but dispersal at the local scale, and the implications which these features hold for the population, underlies many of the issues which will be confronted in this book.

The purpose of this chapter is to provide a description and interpretation of the current character of Australian urban development, through an account of the conditions under which such development has occurred; an evaluation of the current status of the urban environment, with particular reference to some of the implications which this contains; and an assessment of the manner in which recent changes are likely to affect that environment in the long run.

The background to Australian urban development

In many ways the white settlement of Australia, and the subsequent urban pattern, is typical of that which emerged in many new world countries in the nineteenth century. The emergence of capitalism which encouraged the development of resources for export back to the old world, the imposition of colonial administration, and the gradual extension of settlement into lands previously occupied on an extensive basis by indigenous peoples, which occurred in Australia soon after the advent of white colonisation, is similar to the experience of countries of the new world. Common features include the absence of pre-existing permanent settlement, the dependent status of the fledgling colonies, and the strong orientation of economic activity from points of contact in the new nation toward the colonial power. At the same time, the settlement pattern has also been affected by factors somewhat unique to Australia; factors such as the particular resource base, and the conditions of the local environment.

The initial settlement

Although Australia was first seen only as a depository for the undesirables of British society, the resource potential soon became apparent. Wool, wheat and gold all provided substantial stimuli for the development of the countryside and thus for the investment in infrastructure to enable the exploitation of those resources. Much of this investment went into the establishment of urban facilities through which the goods and investment could be channelled.

The timing of development proved crucial to the spatial expression of settlement. Although white settlement in Australia dates back to 1788, the development of large urban areas did not take place until the middle of the nineteenth century. As a result the urban pattern that has evolved in Australia is a classic illustration of the spatial imprint of post-1800 capitalism, (McCarty 1978; Jackson 1977; M. Logan et al. 1981) complicated by a fragmented political system, and implanted in a harsh and constraining physical environment which limited settlement to a few widely-separated regions (Whitelaw and Maher (forthcoming)).

Driven largely by the demands of an external power, the economy of the country, and thus the spatial expression of development, began and has continued to grow in a very distinctive manner. This is reflected both in the degree to which the settlement system of Australia has been responsive to external influences throughout the period of its development, and in the physical expression of development which has been brought about (Maher 1985).

The local environment was characterised by vast distances, and by conditions suitable for settlement in only a relatively narrow coastal zone. Superimposed upon that were the general conditions of economic potential and emerging administrative structures based on the initial colonial configuration. The result in terms of the settlement pattern was a system which focused on very few sites. Each of the emerging locations quickly dominated the commercial, administrative, and distributive sectors for the surrounding territory and each tended to develop somewhat separately from the rest. The degree of independence exhibited by the initial colonies meant that each developed a substantially-separate settlement system centred on, and dominated by, the port-city and administrative capital. This separate development was enhanced by such measures as the establishment of customs posts between the colonies, and by the introduction of different rail gauges.

The overall result in terms of the settlement pattern has been a marked degree of primacy being exhibited by each capital city within its own State. This is evidenced in the manner in which the proportion of each State's population has increasingly concentrated into the major metropolitan area (Table 2.1). The occurrence of such dominance prompted Rose (1966) to argue that although at a national level there was very little evidence of primacy in the distribution of settlement sizes, the situation for each State was the more appropriate pattern to observe and that these did exhibit an extreme primacy which Rose argued was in fact the 'normal' state.

Table 2.1 Capital city as proportion of State population, 1851–1981

	NSW	Vic.	Qld	SA	WA	Tas.
1851	28	38	—	28	—	—
1861	27	23	20	28	33	28
1871	27	26	13	27	—	25
1881	30	31	14	33	30	23
1891	35	41	24	37	32	22
1901	37	40	24	39	33	20
1911	47	45	23	41	38	21
1921	49	51	28	50	47	25
1933	51	54	32	54	39	27
1947	55	60	37	59	54	30
1954	54	62	39	61	54	31
1961	55	65	41	61	57	33
1971	59	71	44	69	62	33
1976	58	68	44	69	64	33
1981	56	67	41	69	64	31

Sources: 1851–1911, Logan et al. 1981; 1921–61, Bunker 1965; 1971–81, Australian Bureau of Statistics (ABS), *Persons and Dwellings in Local Government Areas and Urban Centres*.

Industrialisation and immigration

Federation at the turn of the century saw the creation of a national identity for Australia, although the heritage of the separateness of development which had been a characteristic up to that point has in many ways remained. The new Federal government gradually moved to establish its authority, and although interrupted by a world war and a major depression, strove to broaden the economic base of the entire nation. With a growing population creating larger markets, with some impediments to interstate trade being removed, and with the adoption of a nation-wide protectionist policy, industrialisation was begun in earnest. Again, because of the existing infrastructure, the population concentrations already in place, and the focus of transport facilities, the development of manufacturing added to the existing urban dominance. The majority of manufacturing was established in the metropolitan areas of New South Wales, Victoria and South Australia, and it was in these areas that the degree of metropolitan dominance grew to the greatest extent.

The peak of metropolitan dominance coincided with the long economic boom which followed the Second World War. Much of the growth which occurred in this period was associated with industrialisation (M. Logan et al. 1981). The growth in the manufacturing sector was largely engendered by domestic tariff policy, by import control, and by growing local demand arising from a rapidly-expanding population (Linge 1979). Even in this period of development and consolidation, the local economy was still very much influenced by external events. Overseas investment in manufacturing, and particularly the establishment of some of the very large international firms in the automobile and petrochemical areas, continued the tradition of external sources of expertise and finance which had been apparent since the beginning of economic development. In the 1950s much of the investment which was brought in by these and other firms was oriented toward import-substituting manufacturing activity (Adrian and Stimson 1984) and concentrated very much on Sydney and Melbourne. Only later, with economic downturn and structural change apparent, has there been a change from this pattern of concentration of investment and economic activity (Stilwell 1980).

Associated with the post-war recovery and industrialisation of the Australian economy, a further input was of great importance in the growth and character of the Australian population: that of immigration. Although immigration was important from the time of first white settlement, the period following the Second World War saw the greatest influx of migrants. During the 1950s and 1960s, the migrant intake was oriented predominantly toward supplying a labour force for the burgeoning industrial economy. In 1981, 20.6 per cent of the country's resident population had been born overseas; between 1947 and 1971, 42 per cent of population growth was directly attributable to external sources (Burnley 1976:24); and one third of the net gain in the period 1976–81 was likewise attributable (Australian Council on Population and Ethnic Affairs 1983). Even these figures greatly underestimate the impact which such movements have had. The migrants, many of whom have been of child-bearing age, have contributed further to population growth through adding to the natural increase. Burnley (1976) estimated that if the children of migrants were added to the immigration figures, then 60 per cent of the population rise between 1947 and 1971 could be attributed to this source.

More significantly, in terms of the character of urban Australia, the immigrants have shown a marked tendency to agglomerate in urban rather than rural areas. While approximately 60 per cent of the total population of Australia in 1981 resided in the eleven largest urban areas (those over 100 000) these areas contained in excess of 80 per cent of recent migrants (Australian Department of Immigration and Ethnic Affairs 1985).

Thus the development of manufacturing and its associated demands for labour in the post-war period was very influential in the manner in which population concentration occurred. Each State sought to achieve a widely-based industrial structure, although the costs of such an exercise were often never revealed or even considered (Linge 1979). Some attempt was made in most cases to diminish the effect of over-concentration in the metropolitan areas through incentives to locate elsewhere, although with few exceptions (notably Canberra and Albury-Wodonga) these were not very successful.

The background to the evolution of the urban system in Australia has therefore been tied very closely to economic development. The initial mercantilist functions of the major cities were soon supplemented by administrative and manufacturing roles, creating a strong impetus for growth. The fact that the functions centralised so rapidly, and also that there were few alternative sites for development, meant the emergence of a very top-heavy urban hierarchy. Unlike many more mature societies whose urban development was characterised by an urban system where the size distribution of settlements was arranged in a somewhat pyramidal manner, in which there existed a relationship between settlement size and frequency of occurrence of units in that size class, and whose balance between urban and rural populations was somewhat evenly distributed Australia developed a very different profile. Apart from the existence of a small number of large centres, there were few other centres of consequence which emerged. The pattern of urban development at the system level thus has been (at least until recently) characterised by a high and increasing degree of concentration, a point which is taken up later.

The dispersed urban form

At the same time that population concentration in metropolitan areas has been the major feature of urban development at the State and national scale, within these agglomerations a dispersed and socially-differentiated urban landscape was quickly established. The characteristic suburban nature of Australian cities, which has been most prominent since the end of the Second World War, had its genesis much earlier. Almost from the beginning, urban residents made use of the seemingly abundant space to create a sprawling form of development. Urban historians have pointed to the early significance of suburban development in Australia, arguing for example, that.. 'the history of Australian cities is peculiarly the history of the suburbs' (Davison 1970:169), and

> In a new land the bulk of a city could be suburbs, could indeed be little else. And most of the growth of cities in this new land took place after the nineteenth-century revolution in transport which suburbanized even old world cities. In Australia the suburbs started on a clean slate. (Fry 1978:32)

The predominance of suburban development has been attributed to three basic factors. The first was the fact of Australian cities having their origins as commercial centres created for the facilitation of trade between the new territory and the mother country (McCarty 1978). This distinguished them from traditional cities in that they were unencumbered by the constraining form of previous development and from industrial cities which were dominated by the predominant form of productive activity. The result was a form of development which was a direct reflection of the characteristics, wants, needs and affluence of a society which was made up of a 'large and fairly dispersed middle class, merging in to a working class that also exhibited a wider range of social attitudes and economic circumstances than was to be found in industrial cities' (McCarty 1978:19).

The second was the relationship between population growth and the development of transport technology. The density of urban development is governed primarily by ease of access to locations of activity. Where transport was confined to animate modes, the ability for extensive development remained limited. With the introduction of inanimate sources of power, and tracked forms of transport, the ability to extend the spatial range of development grew rapidly. That the availability of this technology coincided largely with the period within which urban concentration was occurring has considerable significance for the manner in which the urban population has tended to spread at what are, in relative terms, very low densities.

A third element in the establishment of urban character, was the attitudes of the population to space and to housing. Many had come from the urban society of England where space was precious and housing difficult to obtain. Faced with the seemingly unlimited extent of land in the new country, development extended much further much earlier than had been experienced in previous urban development. The detached house, with its attendant privacy and space became a norm for most Australian households. That, together with the cheapness of the land on the outskirts, particularly after there was massive investment in suburban railway networks, encouraged the outward movement of a large cross-section of the population. At the same time, the possibility of home ownership, often through self-help, and later through substantial governmental assistance and encouragement, was also more achievable than it had been in the old country. Ownership, although often initially associated with fairly minimal facilities, soon became a route to capital accumulation. Social mobility became inextricably linked with housing and thus with geographical mobility.

The nexus of suburban development and the great Australian dream of home ownership was forged very early in Australia's history.

The other particular feature of urban development from the beginning was the manner in which elements of social stratification in terms of status, power and wealth were translated into a spatial differentiation of neighbourhoods. Although Australian society was supposedly free of the rigid class system of Britain, the Australian city had a '... high degree of social mobility and defined its social classes principally in terms of actual wealth, ... however recently acquired' (McCarty 1978:19).

The variations in wealth created broad distinctions of the population through variations in access to real income (Harvey 1973), compounded by the vigorous manipulation of the ownership and control of property which has been termed a 'national hobby' (Sandercock 1979), resulted in the creation of very obvious spatial divisions on social and economic criteria. In particular there was a marked distinction between the houses of the middle class, built of permanent materials such as brick or stone, with ample land, and in relatively desirable locations away from the damaging effects of smell, dirt and noise which frequently accompanied nineteenth century urban development, and those of the working class, which were built on much smaller sites at much greater density, predominantly built of timber, and often in locations which frequently suffered poor drainage, and lower amenity in general. Barrett's (1971) account of the inner suburbs of Melbourne is a good exposition of the manner in which the initial conditions can play a crucial role in the subsequent character of development.

The initial nature of development, because it involves large-scale investment in physical facilities, has a major effect on subsequent processes and outcomes. At both the national and the local scale, the manner in which locations become established and the character which they assume, provide a long-lasting imprint on the landscape. Current urban character is very much a product of what has gone on before. Over time however, changes do occur, in response to general social, economic and political forces. It is to the current character of urban Australia, and the current forces of change, to which this chapter now turns.

The present situation: character and trends

Urban outcomes in terms of the distribution, function and character of areas at the national or local scale, are only a snap-shot view of the product of processes continually acting to modify the physical imprint on the landscape. In recent years there have been some marked changes in the social and economic climate within which urban development occurs, and these are having an impact at both the system and at the local level.

System level trends

The conditions under which the Australian urban system has evolved, and particularly those conditions which created the degree of metropolitan concentration described above, have undergone considerable change more recently. The metropolitan concentration of population was based largely on a pattern of development which had emphasised industrial growth through the protection of the manufacturing sector, while maintaining the traditional commercial, distributive, and administrative control functions governing rural enterprise. Through sustained economic growth, full employment, high population growth-rates and a steady investment in physical and social facilities, metropolitan dominance has continued to expand at least until the early 1970s. Table 2.2 shows the extent of population concentration in urban centres of various size-classes, and how this has altered between 1961 and 1981. Of particular interest in this table, is the fact that concentration in the major urban areas (those in excess of 100 000 people) peaked in New South Wales, Victoria, and South Australia in 1971. In the other three States, the peak occurred in 1976. In all cases however, there has been a slight decline in the level of concentration by 1981. The explanation for this must be sought in the changing conditions within which urbanisation has been occurring in recent years.

Table 2.2 Distribution of State and territory population in urban hierarchy, 1961–81

	Year	NSW	Vic.	Qld	SA	WA	Tas.	NT	ACT	Australia
Major urban	1961	65.4	65.3	40.9	60.7	57.0	33.1	—	—	58.8
	1966	67.1	68.7([a])	43.2	66.7	59.8	32.2	—	—	61.4
	1971	69.1([b])	71.7	44.8	69.0	62.3	33.3	—	97.8	64.5
	1976	67.9([c])	71.1	48.4([c])	68.9	63.9	32.6	—	98.4	64.6
	1981	65.9	70.6	47.0	68.7	63.5	30.7	—	99.0	63.5
Other urban	1961	19.7	19.5	35.0	18.1	16.2	37.3	39.5	95.9	22.9
	1966	19.3	16.8([a])	33.2	15.7	15.9	38.1	53.4	96.1	21.5
	1971	19.5([b])	16.1	34.6	15.6	19.2	40.9	64.1	—	21.1
	1976	20.8([c])	16.7	31.8([c])	16.0	19.6	42.3	66.4	—	21.4
	1981	22.2	17.4	32.2	16.1	20.8	44.5	74.2	—	22.2
Rural	1961	14.9	15.2	24.1	21.2	26.8	29.6	60.5	4.1	18.3
	1966	13.6	14.5	23.6	17.6	24.3	29.7	46.6	3.9	17.1
	1971	11.4	12.3	20.6	15.4	18.5	25.8	35.9	2.2	14.4
	1976	11.3	12.2	19.8	15.1	16.5	25.1	33.6	1.6	14.0
	1981	11.9	12.0	20.8	15.2	15.7	24.8	25.8	1.0	14.3

a) Affected by Geelong classified as major urban for first time.
b) Affected by Queanbeyan classified as part of urban Canberra for first time.
c) Affected by Gold Coast (part) classified as major urban for first time.

Source: Australian Council on Population and Ethnic Affairs 1983:14

In the past ten years both economic and demographic conditions have changed markedly. The long economic boom of the 1950s and 1960s has been replaced by the deepest recession the country has experienced since the 1930s. Associated economic conditions of high inflation and the realignment of international currencies have engendered a process of structural change which is having an impact on the nature of economic endeavour (Stilwell 1980; Linge and McKay 1981; Daly 1984) and thus on the distribution of Australia's population. The best indicator of such change is the manner in which the composition of the Australian workforce has changed over time. In particular there has been a marked shift since the Second World War, first from primary to secondary, and more recently from secondary to tertiary and quaternary activity. The proportion of the workforce in rural industries has fallen from 15.6 per cent in 1947 (Linge 1979) to only 6 per cent in 1981; manufacturing, which reached a peak in 1954 at 27.7 per cent and maintained that level through to 1966, had dropped to 17.7 per cent by 1981; mining and quarrying has remained stable at around 1.5 per cent; while all other activity has increased from 57.7 per cent to 74.9 per cent. These structural changes are being evidenced through substantial shifts of activity both at the national and at the local level. The implication is that there will be a growing differentiation between system members as specialisation increasingly takes place. The earlier regionally based urban systems of Australia are now increasingly national and in some cases even international.

At the same time there have been important changes in the demography of Australia. Birthrates have fallen, the population is ageing, and both the rate and composition of immigration streams have varied substantially from previous periods (Australian Department of Immigration and Ethnic Affairs 1985). These changed conditions affect the whole population but tend to be most marked within major urban areas. With smaller families, and a growing proportion of the aged for whom a metropolitan location is less essential than for those dependent on employment, growth rates through natural increase will inevitably fall.

Changes in the growth rates of the major metropolitan areas in the post-war period can be seen in Table 2.3. In that period there has been a consistent decline in the annual rate of growth at a national level. However it is at the level of individual urban areas that the uneven spatial impacts of such processes are most apparent. Apart from Canberra, which is clearly in a category of its own as far as growth rates are concerned, there have been some very significant changes in urban population trends. Overall there has been a consistent decline in the rate of growth in all centres — a decline which is more significant when taken in conjunction with rates of increase at the national scale which, while themselves decreasing, have not dropped so sharply.

The areas which have undergone the most drastic changes are the provincial industrial centres of Newcastle, Wollongong, and Geelong. In the latest period, Hobart is doing particularly badly, having actually lost population, while Adelaide has dropped from a situation of the greatest increase (excluding Canberra) between 1961 and 1966, to having one of the lower rates between 1976 and 1981. Sydney and Melbourne are also well down in terms of population increase, although both have improved in the latest period in relation to the previous five years. Of the major State capitals, Perth is the only one to have maintained an increase in excess of 2 per cent, with even Brisbane dropping to just over 1 per cent. On the other hand the late inclusion of the Gold Coast in the figures shows the extent to which some specialised areas are able to capture a large share of the growth.

Table 2.3 Growth rates of major cities, 1947–81

	1947–54	1954–61	1961–66	1966–71	1971–76	1976–81
Sydney	3.3	2.3	2.3	2.2	0.3	0.8
Melbourne	3.1	3.3	2.0	2.6	0.7	0.8
Brisbane	3.2	3.0	2.9	2.7	1.8	1.1
Adelaide	3.4	2.8	4.3	2.1	1.2	0.6
Perth	3.6	2.7	3.5	5.1	2.8	2.0
Newcastle	4.9	2.3	2.3	1.4	0.1	0.6
Canberra	9.2	10.4	10.4	8.8	7.6	2.3
Wollongong	5.4	5.4	4.2	2.8	1.2	0.8
Gold Coast	n.a.	n.a.	n.a.	6.9	9.4	7.9
Hobart	3.1	2.8	0.6	1.6	0.3	–0.5
Geelong	4.6	3.4	2.8	1.8	1.2	0.5

Source: Australian Department of Immigration and Ethnic Affairs 1985

The population trends enumerated above are in fact evidence that there is something of a turnaround occurring in the nature of population distribution both between urban areas, and among urban and rural regions. Much of the redistribution is occurring through the mechanism of internal migration and is from the capital city statistical division to the 'rest of State'—a term used to describe the non-metropolitan settlement component made up of smaller urban areas, as well as rural regions. While the magnitude of the net migration loss from the cities is not great, it does represent a dramatic reversal of earlier trends. The magnitude of the net changes and the manner in which these have changed over the past three intercensal periods is portrayed in Table 2.4.

Clearly there have been considerable changes in recent years in the manner in which the population has been distributed via the mechanism of internal migration. In the earliest period for which information is available (1966–71) the areas which were undergoing the greatest net gains in population were the metropolitan areas of Perth, Brisbane and Canberra, while the most significant losses were from the 'rest of State' components of South Australia, Victoria and Tasmania. In the later periods however, the net losses have tended to concentrate in the largest metropolitan areas of Sydney and Melbourne while many of the gains have been experienced by the non-metropolitan areas of Queensland and New South Wales. Even 'rest of State' Victoria, which was undergoing a very substantial loss between 1966 and 1971, has improved to the extent that there was a very small net gain between 1976 and 1981.

The reasons for the changes in internal migration patterns are very complex. Hugo and Smailes (1985) identified eight possible explanations which can be summarised generally into economic, demographic, life-style, political and technological factors. Within the economic category, shifts in population distribution have been related to structural change, economic recession, the occurrence of the resources boom, and the dis-economies of scale resulting from the over-concentration which has occurred. In demographic terms, the changing age structure of the population, falling birth rates and the growing proportion of a retired population have been seen to underly a lessening of the importance of workplace location. This can be linked with changes in lifestyle which have resulted in an expressed preference for environmental amenities such as a sunny climate and coastal living as are represented in coastal Queensland and northern New South Wales. Politically, there have been quite sustained attempts on the part of various governments to encourage a decentralisation of population away from the major metropolitan areas. The final element, technology, has obviously lessened the constraints of distance both by improved transport and the ability to substitute communication for the need for travel and hence lowering the need for proximity. Among other things this has allowed the dispersal of population beyond the official boundaries of metropolitan areas, and thus into the 'rest of State' area despite the fact that activity patterns of this element of the population are still very much oriented to the metropolis.

Table 2.4 Net internal migration by capital city/rest of State, 1966–71 to 1976–81

	1966–71	**1971–76**	**1976–81**
Sydney	–10323	–70802	–57894
NSW	–9746	–3101	33639
Melbourne	9836	–30765	–55507
Vic.	–36684	–7967	58
Brisbane	17532	37478	28548
Qld	–2144	27922	54926
Adelaide	–1564	14323	–3667
SA	–15301	–8132	–11121
Perth	27713	32975	18554
WA	–5149	–13368	–8097
Hobart	322	2572	–2440
Tas.	–7132	–6591	–2136
Darwin	5422	183	7533
NT	3394	–1082	–3072
ACT	23824	26355	644

Source: ABS unpublished tabulations.

Metropolitan character

Individual urban areas are being affected and are responding in quite different ways to the types of changes described above. As well as the forces being reflected in a process of reorientation at the system level, the character and role of the individual system members is altering, with important implications for their future development. The different conditions are reflected in elements such as population mobility and suburbanisation, population growth and composition, and the functional character of the area as reflected in the nature of the workforce. The end result is that the general opportunity structure provided to residents through the nature of the urban environment itself changes, contributing to variations in the welfare of individuals and households of different status levels (Badcock 1984).

Population mobility and suburbanisation

One of the most distinctive characteristics of Australian metropolitan development has been the rate and extent of suburbanisation, both of population and of economic activity (Maher 1982*a*). The result has been a very extensive and low-density development, the nature of which has been premised on high personal mobility through rising car-ownership and relatively cheap energy costs; the price of new land being kept within the reach of a wide range of the population; and a housing policy which has consistently encouraged both home ownership and the development of new, over the rehabilitation of existing, dwelling stock. Changes in energy costs, inflation which has affected both the costs of land and the costs of building, more stringent requirements for the serving of residential allotments, and a reappraisal of the attractiveness of inner-suburban living and investment have all had an effect on the manner in which population redistribution and consequent changes in characteristics are occurring within individual areas (King 1980; Maher 1982*b*; W. Logan 1985; Mullins 1982). Yet while there are clearly changes occurring in the character of population composition in various areas of individual cities, there is little evidence that the demands for outer-suburban living have diminished.

An example of the extent to which population suburbanisation has remained significant over a sustained period of time is evidenced in the figures showing the relative growth-rates of inner, middle, and outer zones in Melbourne (Maher 1982*a*). Table 2.5 highlights the consistent loss of population from the inner areas, even in the latest period when gentrification has been apparent; the gradual transition of the middle zone from a situation of gain to one of quite substantial loss; and the sustained growth of the outer suburbs.

Table 2.5 Population change by zone: Melbourne 1947–81

		Inner	Middle	Outer
1947–54	(1)	−32995	133043	147755
	(2)	− 1.3	2.2	9.4
1954–61	(1)	−29119	137427	287322
	(2)	− 1.3	2.0	9.7
1961–66	(1)	−1288	25037	222229
	(2)	− 0.1	0.5	6.5
1966–71	(1)	−6284	18109	260832
	(2)	− 0.4	0.3	5.6
1971–76	(1)	−48013	−88846	237450
	(2)	− 3.3	− 1.7	4.0
1976–81	(1)	−14538	−44290	177604
	(2)	− 1.1	− 0.9	2.5

1) Absolute population change.
2) Annual average percentage change.

Source: Maher 1984: viii.

The changing population distribution within Melbourne is symptomatic of the continued de-concentration of areas occurring within all metropolitan areas in Australia. Much of the differential growth and decline is the result of the redistribution of population through the means of intra-urban mobility—the manner in which households alter their location within an urban area in response to changing needs or conditions particularly with respect to the supply and location of housing. That this movement is predominantly outward, and has continued to exhibit this pattern despite quite significant changes which have occurred in locational preferences and in the costs of energy, has been clearly documented (Maher 1984; Maher, Goodman and Savage 1985). Again, while there have been some changes in the direction and rate of mobility flows, the strength of the suburbanising move still outweighs other trends.

Increasingly, the suburbs are taking on a significance, not just in the population numbers they are attracting, but also in the range and complexity of other functional roles. Suburban development is assuming a large number of the functions traditionally provided by the central city. These include an employment-provision role, and a servicing role. The current development of metropolitan structure is very much one which entails the role of the suburbs more closely approximating that of the central city in terms of the range and diversity of activities available, a range which is sufficient to make the suburban areas much more nearly self-contained (O'Connor and Maher 1979).

There are important implications contained within the fact that suburbs are becoming functionally more akin to the central city of course. In particular, the complexity and functional diversity mean that the suburbs themselves are now subject to many of the same processes and problems as the inner city. However, added to these are the locational attributes of the suburbs where accessibility has been subordinated to the requirements of space and where there are considerable demands on the mobility of the population. Some of the greatest problems are experienced among those groups for which mobility is most difficult, and particularly those not having access to an automobile (King 1980). Thus considerable difficulties are experienced, for example, among youth, especially in relation to their employment prospects (Maher et al. 1981). In addition, the difficulties and costs of providing services for the outer areas are becoming a growing concern. In the early stages of post-war suburbanisation, little forward planning was carried out, leaving newly-developing areas devoid of many necessary public services. Increasing governmental regulation of the location, timing and infrastructural provisions have improved that situation, but added greatly to the initial costs of development. Concerns with the magnitude of these costs, and how to distribute them equitably throughout the community, have brought a recent concern for urban consolidation to the fore (Bunker 1985; Chapter 10 of this volume).

The changing functional role of the cities

Suburbanisation and spatial change are products of a wide variety of other changes in the context of metropolitan development. One of the major changes affecting individual cities, as it is the urban system as a whole, is that of structural change. The effect of economic restructuring, as it affects urban development, can be seen at two scales. The first is in terms of the changes which are occurring in the nature of the workforce in each of the metropolitan areas. The second is in the location and nature of economic activity within each of the metropolitan areas.

The overall changes are best represented in terms of the changes which are occurring in the nature of activity pursued by the workforce. The major industry groups used by the Australian Bureau of Statistics, while somewhat gross in the level of detail they represent, can still be used to show the shifts in emphasis which are occurring within the economy. In that individual urban areas are responding differently to these changes, the impact on urban character can also be shown. The impact on the workforce composition is represented in Table 2.6.

The table highlights a number of trends which have occurred in 1971–81, that period which most closely approximates the changed economic environment, and for which data are available. There has been a general growth of the workforce in this period, despite severe problems of unemployment. However, both the location, and the nature of this growth has been quite uneven.

Table 2.6 Change in the industry composition of the workforce: Australian metropolitan areas, 1971–81

		Sydney	Melbourne	Brisbane	Adelaide	Perth	Hobart	Darwin	ACT	Newcastle	Wollongong	Geelong
Agriculture	(1)	–8.8	–7.5	1.5	–6.7	25.8	10.2	35.3	77.6	–10.4	–23.7	–6.4
	(2)	0.7	0.8	1.1	1.1	1.8	1.5	1.1	0.6	1.2	0.7	1.1
Mining	(1)	12.1	–30.3	20.1	36.4	52.4	–2.9	–8.7	66.7	22.1	21.2	–23.9
	(2)	0.4	0.2	0.7	0.5	1.2	0.2	0.9	0.2	4.9	6.4	0.2
Manufacturing	(1)	–18.1	–9.7	–2.0	–14.4	7.2	–23.4	54.3	3.7	–11.5	0.1	–4.1
	(2)	20.3	25.0	16.2	20.7	15.0	13.0	4.9	3.6	23.9	34.3	31.1
Elec etc.	(1)	20.6	39.5	44.6	6.1	78.3	1.2	164.9	67.0	47.6	40.7	22.2
	(2)	2.0	1.8	1.7	1.8	1.6	3.1	2.7	0.7	3.3	2.5	1.5
Construction	(1)	–7.2	–9.7	3.9	–10.5	10.3	–1.3	24.0	–21.0	27.8	–12.7	–0.4
	(2)	5.9	5.3	7.0	5.7	7.8	7.1	9.2	5.1	7.5	5.7	6.4
Wholesale &	(1)	5.4	3.9	12.2	4.3	19.5	6.6	65.8	59.5	2.6	12.7	5.8
retail	(2)	18.3	17.7	20.3	19.6	20.1	17.9	14.5	12.9	15.7	13.1	16.7
Transport &	(1)	18.6	14.3	30.6	9.1	23.8	–2.0	17.8	72.6	13.0	23.3	19.4
storage	(2)	5.9	5.0	6.1	4.3	5.4	4.1	5.4	2.7	5.4	5.1	4.6
Communications	(1)	18.0	21.6	41.9	21.9	27.7	17.4	80.4	62.7	23.2	32.0	50.4
	(2)	2.2	2.1	2.6	2.0	2.0	2.8	2.5	1.6	1.4	1.2	1.7
Finance &	(1)	39.7	32.9	52.8	33.7	69.8	32.7	134.9	100.5	55.6	46.6	40.7
business services	(2)	11.7	9.4	10.0	8.4	10.6	8.6	7.2	7.6	6.6	5.6	5.9
Public administration &	(1)	8.7	19.0	10.8	34.4	9.3	15.4	54.5	58.7	7.8	47.8	57.5
Defence	(2)	5.2	5.3	6.5	5.6	4.8	8.0	17.8	32.6	3.7	2.5	3.3
Community	(1)	57.3	62.6	70.4	58.2	90.1	62.5	151.3	102.1	57.2	80.7	61.1
Service	(2)	14.3	14.9	16.2	19.3	18.1	20.9	17.7	22.4	14.1	12.2	16.1
Entertainment	(1)	14.7	13.8	29.0	19.2	34.8	40.2	67.7	52.7	16.3	17.8	20.0
recreation	(2)	5.5	4.5	5.0	5.3	5.6	7.4	5.8	5.9	4.9	4.3	4.3
Other &	(1)	93.5	82.3	123.1	113.4	114.4	91.7	173.2	126.0	224.2	170.5	115.7
not stated	(2)	7.7	8.0	6.5	5.7	5.8	5.4	10.4	4.3	7.5	6.4	7.1
Change in total workforce		16.2	13.5	25.8	13.7	35.0	15.6	75.4	59.8	18.0	19.5	17.1

1) Percentage change between 1971 and 1981.
2) Percentage of workforce in industry category, 1981

Source: ABS Census of Population and Dwelling Units.

The greatest proportional growth of the workforce has occurred in Darwin and the ACT. Of the older State capitals, both Perth and Brisbane show markedly higher rates than any others, while Melbourne and Adelaide had the lowest growth performance. This latter fact may be related to the performance of manufacturing industry, as both cities had relatively high proportions of such activity in 1981, and it is manufacturing which has undergone the greatest declines in the period. However, the smaller cities of Newcastle, Wollongong and Geelong have all performed better than Adelaide and Melbourne, despite also having very high levels of manufacturing industry. It is possible that their performance will show a considerable deterioration after 1981 however, as the process of structural change has had more opportunity to have a spatial impact.

While manufacturing, and to some extent construction, showed a decline over most of the cities, two sectors which grew at very rapid rates were finance and business services, and community services. Growth in the community services area was relatively evenly distributed across all cities, although ACT has a much higher proportion of its workforce in this sector than does anywhere else. On the other hand, finance and business services are distributed relatively unevenly, and have shown very different growth rates across the eleven cities. Sydney, which had the highest proportion of its workforce in this industry, had a solid growth of nearly 40 per cent. Perth, Canberra and Darwin both grew much faster, but still do not have the concentration that Sydney does. Again, Melbourne, Adelaide, and Hobart have the lowest increase in this sector. The dominance of Sydney in the area of recent financial roles, and the implications for the national and international roles of Sydney and Melbourne, is a theme which Daly (1984) has elaborated.

The implications of the workforce changes are very significant in terms of the future growth and development of the individual cities, and in their relationships with each other and with the outside world. The two areas which are of greatest importance are the decline in manufacturing activity and the growth in the financial and business services sector. Of the areas which have been the manufacturing heartland of the country, declines in this sector have been much more marked in Sydney and Adelaide than in Melbourne or in the smaller manufacturing-based cities of Newcastle and Wollongong. However, whereas Sydney is clearly specialising increasingly in the quaternary business-service sector to a much greater degree, Adelaide has not been able to compensate for these losses. Melbourne on the other hand, while not able to compete with Sydney in the development of the quaternary-sector functions, does seem to be gaining a degree of specialism in the manufacturing sector.

Population composition

A further significant component of population growth and urban character has been in the nature of the population characteristics, and particularly the role which the distribution of the overseas-born plays in each of the major cities. As argued above, the process of industrialisation in the post-war period was made possible both by immigrant labour, and by the demand effects of population growth which again related strongly to the extent of immigration. Despite changing conditions and policies, the importance of immigration for urban development and growth has remained undiminished.

One of the major impacts of immigration is the manner in which the migrants have shown a preference first for urban rather than rural areas, and second for some urban areas over others. Perth has the highest component of its population born overseas, but the real significance of the process can be seen in Sydney and Melbourne, where population growth has for some time been based solely on the fact that these areas are dominant destinations for the incoming population (Maher 1982*a*). In fact if it were not for the overseas-born, both Sydney and Melbourne would have suffered population declines. Evidence of this in recent years is contained in Table 2.7.

Table 2.7 Components of migration and population change: capital cities, 1975–76 and 1980–81

	Net internal migration		**Overseas immigrants**		**Overseas born residents < 5 yrs (% all overseas born)**	
	1975–76	**1980–81**	**1975–76**	**1980–81**	**1976**	**1981**
Sydney	–16420	–28203	45294	58647	15.8	18.6
Melbourne	–14542	–13900	34724	40233	12.0	13.0
Brisbane	6966	10851	11715	17690	16.8	19.6
Adelaide	3736	–2437	10484	10964	11.7	8.6
Perth	11281	3866	15245	21023	17.3	15.7
Hobart	27	–1969	1651	1339	12.2	10.9
ACT	3561	–1096	4780	4605	15.7	13.2

Source: ABS Unpublished Matrix Tapes, Matrix 14, 1976; Matrix 184, 1981 and Australian Department of Immigration and Ethnic Affairs 1985:10

Table 2.7 demonstrates a number of features of the current role of immigration in the capital cities of Australia. Apart from its importance in promoting the growth of Sydney and Melbourne, the later period also shows a net internal loss of population from Adelaide, Hobart and the ACT. For all but Hobart, the replacement by overseas migrants is more than sufficient to make up the shortfall, but for the southernmost city, not only has there been a net move away through internal migrants, but there has been a fall in the level of immigrants.

Further significance of Table 2.7 can be found in the last two columns which show the relative distribution of the most recent migrants. This illustrates the manner in which there are changes occurring in the distribution of this element of the population, both in response to changing economic and social conditions, and also because of variations which have occurred in the nature of immigration itself. In the period represented in the table, there was a shift away from the traditional sources of Britain, Ireland, and Europe, towards those from Asia, Oceania, and the Middle East. The preference of New Zealanders in particular, but also other groups, for New South Wales and Queensland have altered the nature of the distribution of the overseas-born recently, and thus their impact on growth and population composition. Clearly the future impact of immigration will depend on both government policy with regard to intake levels and selection criteria, and on the continued movement of New Zealanders across the Tasman. This source has slowed dramatically since 1981 and thus the figures above could be something of a temporary aberration. However, they represent another facet of the way in which individual urban areas are a product of what has occurred before, and the current social, economic and political context within which further development takes place.

Conclusions

The aim of this chapter has been to examine the nature of urban development in Australia. The course of such development clearly has considerable implications for the living environment of a large proportion of Australians. To comprehend the dynamic basis of such processes, an understanding of the way in which the urban character has evolved, and the nature of forces to which it responds, is essential.

Literature in urban studies over the past ten years has devoted a great deal of attention to two elements of the urban process: the first is the implications of processes and outcomes, particularly as they are instrumental in affecting distribution or redistribution among groups variously placed in terms of access to all the resources necessary to provide adequate life chances; the second is in terms of attempting to understand the background to the evolving urban character by interpreting both the processes and the outcomes within a broader context which takes into account particularly the economic and social context of development.

The former has stimulated interest and concern, with a growing appreciation of the fact that space is not a neutral medium, but one which contains a range of resources which contribute particular standards of living, but which also acts as a mechanism through which these resources are differentially available to individuals, groups, or classes on the basis of their existing command over resources. The nature of, and changes in the form and process of development, it is increasingly being acknowledged, can and does act as a resource distributor, whereby those who are able, can act to take advantage in some way of the changed conditions in a manner which will improve their command over these resources. Thus the conditions and trends identified above, in terms of metropolitan concentration, suburbanisation, gentrification, economic restructuring and so on, are all outcomes which will further impinge on the already unequal and inequitable distribution of resources. It is important that these results and implications be understood.

Interest in the latter has been stimulated by the rather dramatic changes which have occurred in both the level of economic growth and in the degree of restructuring of economic processes in an attempt to cope with recessionary pressures. That the current economic context has wrought such changes has also brought about an interest in the effects of economic cycles on urban development as it has occurred in the past. A good deal of reinterpretation is now underway as to reasons which might underly many of the features of urban patterns which have often been taken for granted. In a situation of such rapidly-changing conditions as we are faced with currently however, little can be taken for granted. Only by careful research at both a theoretical and empirical level can an improved comprehension of both the processes and effects of urbanisation be achieved.

Chapter 3
Corporate accumulation and the corporate city: Australia in recession

Mike Berry

Introduction

Australian history, since white settlement, has been roughly coterminous with the era of industrial capitalism on the global scale. The development of the country, including its shape 'on the ground', has been determined as part of the uneven spatial and temporal rhythms of world capitalism through four successive periods (long waves) of expansion and decline. As reflected in Australia, these periods can be roughly characterised as colonial, commercial, industrial and corporate phases of dependent development (Berry 1983*a*:15–33; 1984). In the corporate mode of domination during the post-war period, far-reaching transformations in the form and spatial organisation of global capital accumulation have wrought significant changes in the pattern and pace of Australian urbanisation, producing the 'corporate city'.

The long boom in the Western economies which lasted from 1945 until the late 1960s was fuelled by several factors: huge pools of labour produced by demobilised service personnel and refugees; supplies of cheap raw materials from 'colonial' countries, the reconstruction of multinational trade under United States hegemony; the electronic and cybernetic technological revolutions (Mandel 1975). Within this changing global system Australia moved from dependence on British to dependence on United States capital during the 1960s. Large increases in net capital inflow (Beresford and Kerr 1980; Boehm 1979) began to result in steadily increasing foreign ownership of Australian manufacturing, especially through the agency of the transnational corporations (TNCs). These various changes intensified metropolitan concentration in south-eastern Australia and caused significant changes in the form and functions of the capital cities.

In the previous chapter, Chris Maher outlined the changing form and character of Australian cities, particularly the urban growth that occurred during the economic boom after the Second World War. This chapter examines the changes that have occurred since the 1960s, in the context of the latest phase of global corporate accumulation.

Based on Berry M. (1984) 'The Political Economy of Australian Urbanisation' Chapter 4 *Progress in Planning*, Vol. 22(1), by kind permission of Pergamon Press.

Crisis and Restructuring

In the late 1960s the long upswing turned down. Average profit rates began to fall as workers in the advanced capitalist countries continued to win substantial wage rises at the same time as the initial wave of technological innovation in production methods slowed (Mandel 1975:132). This tendency was reinforced, first, by the reversal of falling commodity prices for Third World exports and, second, by the breakdown in the international monetary system and consequent interruption to world trade caused by the collapse of the United States dollar as the international currency.

Falling profit rates and the build-up of idle capital in the capitalist centre encouraged capital increasingly to switch between sectors and across space in search of more profitable outlets. Thus, the central-city property booms — expressed, above all, in the rush to erect high-rise office towers and, more generally, by the process euphemistically termed, 'urban renewal' — which occurred in many American, Australian and British cities in the late 1960s and early 1970s illustrate the switch of capital into the built environment (Massey and Catalano 1978; Daly 1982). Similarly, the accelerating relocation of industrial capital from the north-eastern region of the United States to the 'sun-belt cities' of the south-west was driven by the prospect of new, efficient infrastructure, low taxes and cheap, docile labour (Perry and Watkins 1978). More importantly, and for similar reasons, capital was switched away from the capitalist centre to the periphery, including Australia. Some of this capital outflow was aimed at securing control over raw materials in order to mitigate their rising cost, but a significant portion entailed the relocation of industrial production to selected Third World countries — Taiwan, South Korea, the Philippines and Singapore, to name the major recipients. Some Marxists, notably Warren (1973; 1978), see this as the natural outcome of capitalism's historic task — viz. to radically transform productive forces throughout the world as a prelude to generalised socialist revolution. However, it is clear that this pattern of development, strongly oriented to re-export to the capitalist centre, has been largely limited to particular Third World countries and particular manufacturing industries, with minimal 'trickle down' effects to the domestic sectors of the recipient countries (O'Leary and McEachern 1980).

The process of partial Third World industrialisation — and its reverse-side, partial de-industrialisation in the capitalist centre — is the main element in what has been called, 'the new international division of labour' (Wheelwright 1980). Dividing and relocating production to countries like South Korea allows large industrial capitalists to maintain and even enhance profit rates by reaping the benefits of 'growth ensembles' comprising low wages, long working hours, 'free' infrastructure and an absence of industrial unrest, all imposed by repressive, authoritarian regimes propped up by United

States aid and military support. Large TNCs are especially well placed to take advantage of these opportunities, having evolved the institutional means for moving capital and profits across national boundaries within the corporate group. Increasing internal capital mobility and an increasing proportion of international trade accounted for by commodity flows between companies in the same corporate group, has increased the bargaining power of TNCs *vis-a-vis* national governments and allows them to evade and subvert the latters' fiscal, monetary and exchange-rate policies (Muller 1979).

Intensifying economic crisis on a world scale has both reinforced Australian developments originating in the post-war boom and forced initial restructuring which may bring about substantial changes in Australia's position in the global capitalist system. In the former case it is clear that foreign, especially TNC, capital has further increased its ownership and control of Australian industry, especially in the mining and manufacturing sectors, and that Australian capital has become more dependent on, and less competitive with, large TNCs (Crough and Wheelwright 1982). However, this continuing pattern of foreign penetration is occurring in the context of the emergence of what Catley and McFarlane (1981) have termed, 'the Pacific-rim strategy'. Australia's role in this strategy appears to imply a large shift in economic specialisation away from import-competing manufacturing towards the export of minerals and other raw materials increasingly arising as internal flows within the TNCs.

There is some evidence to support this claim. It is clear that manufacturing industry has been shedding jobs—between 1974 and 1979, over 200 000 jobs were lost in this sector (Stilwell 1980:48), with losses being heaviest in textiles, clothing and footwear and 'other machinery and equipment', and moderate in fabricated metal products, transport equipment, 'miscellaneous manufacturing', chemicals and non-metallic mineral products (Robson 1979:62). The forces behind this trend relate to the increasingly successful competition of imports, especially from Asia, technological displacement due to the application of micro-processors, etc. to production (a change endemic to advanced capitalism), the global production and trade priorities of TNCs, and the largely defensive competitive reactions of Australian capitalists 'going offshore' to set up production in South-east Asia. What is not clear is the relative strength of each factor. However, some tentative conclusions are possible. Increasing import competition in the face of declining effective protection rates has been responsible for the decline of traditional industries like textiles, clothing and footwear. Transport and communications equipment, on the other hand, has experienced considerable technological change, although the motor vehicle industry is also clearly being restructured by two of the world's largest TNCs, General Motors and Ford, in the context of their new global strategies. Where a TNC controls a local firm it may well allow it to run down through competition with lower-priced imports produced by some other firm in the same corporate group, if that policy accords with the overall goals and priorities of the group. It is difficult to get reliable data on these developments—for obvious reasons—as it is for the movement offshore of Australian companies producing overseas, mainly in South-east Asia; their number and scale of operations have been growing quickly in the late 1970s (Wheelwright 1980:147).

Apart from the restructuring of manufacturing, the past decade has also witnessed capital-switching to other sectors. Throughout the 1970s individual capital cities underwent periodic property booms, reflected in central city office building, outer-suburban land development and 'gentrification'. However, in the late 1970s construction—as opposed to speculation—rose more slowly (in money terms), especially in the residential area. Some employment growth has occurred in the tertiary sector during the 1970s although this depended largely on public sector growth and not on private capital accumulation. With tightening public service staff limits as well as continuing technological displacement in tertiary industries like banking and retailing, the prospects for significant job creation in the tertiary sector appear slim. In fact, the switch of capital from manufacturing to the tertiary sector may well compound unemployment by funding further labour-displacing technological change in the latter.

Mining has been a major destination for capital-switching during this period, giving rise to the rhetoric of 'the resources boom'. Between October 1979 and June 1981, the total capital 'committed' to prospective major resource projects climbed from fourteen billion to thirty-one billion dollars, mainly in the oil and gas, coal and aluminium industries (Dick 1982). This was to be funded partly from new capital inflow, which experienced a quantum leap during this period, partly from retained profits generated since the last mining boom a decade earlier (and boosted by the generous taxation and subsidy policies of State and Federal governments) and partly by the mobilisation and redirection of local capital. The capacity of large mining TNCs to outbid other capitalists in Australian capital markets has serious implications for local employment prospects. Rising interest rates intensify pressures on manufacturers to rationalise production, leading to further de-skilling, displacement and offshore relocation. Given the highly capital-intensive nature of mining development, the extra jobs created by these projects are unlikely to compensate significantly for jobs lost elsewhere in the economy. Indeed, to the extent that resource projects are successful, similar and reinforcing effects may arise through balance-of-payments movements. The 'Gregory thesis' suggests, for example, that booming mineral exports will force exchange-rate changes which effectively cheapen (all) imports in relation to locally-produced goods (Gregory 1976). At the same time, in order to make many of these projects viable (and attract foreign investment in the first place), the state will have to engage in substantial infrastructural expenditure in advance of demand, especially in communications and electrification. Much of this expenditure will either be irrelevant to manufacturers—as in the case of railways extensions and ports servicing the new mining centres—or, like rising interest rates, positively harmful—as in the case of rising electricity charges or taxes to finance it. Public resources committed to mining projects obviously cannot be used to shore up manufacturing during restructuring or encourage job creation or compensate for falling real wages through the social wage—that is, through increased expenditure on housing, health, education and welfare. The fact that many of the proposed resource projects were shelved during 1982 and 1983, in the shadow of an increasingly severe global crisis, has delayed rather than averted these problems.

It is also worth stressing that capital can switch from manufacturing and other sectors into mining without either direct state intervention or a call on capital markets whenever capitalists reorient their existing operations. The prime example of this strategy arose when BHP diversified into oil and gas during the 1970s, resulting in declining employment levels in its steel-making and ship-building operations and the prospects of a continuing diversion of capital from these areas to mining (Larcombe 1980).

As might be expected, these developments have begun to be reflected at the level of spatial organisation. Much has been made of the drift of capital and population from New South Wales and Victoria to the resource-rich States of Queensland and Western Australia, though little firm data exists, especially on capital flows. Certainly there is a tendency for most of the capital recently sunk in and 'committed' to major resource projects to be concentrated in the latter States, since that is where the resources are to be found. Nevertheless, other conditions must be met before this tendency is realised. In particular, agreement must be reached between mining company and State government concerning mining leases, royalty levels, subsidies and the like. In the case of associated processing or manufacturing activities, agreement is also normally required on basic public infrastructural provision (supply and cost). Since large companies, especially TNCs, are relatively free to locate these associated activities interstate or overseas, they are well placed to play State governments off against each other, to extract maximum concessions in return for new investment and the extra jobs assumed to go with them. Nowhere is this more apparent than in the aluminium industry where the major TNCs have set up or planned refining and smelting operations in most States during the past decade in return for extensive transport and other subsidies and, most importantly, the guarantee of the considerable blocks of electricity required at prices well below other industrial and residential users. Victoria and New South Wales have been forced to match concessions with the smaller States in attracting aluminium smelters to Portland and the Hunter Valley, respectively.

Recent project delays and cancellations have placed State governments in a weak political position; having committed large sums to highly-specialised infrastructural supports they are poorly placed to withstand the tough bargaining stances of the aluminium companies, when and if they decide to re-activate their development plans.

Internal migration patterns have also begun to show a population drift to the north. Victoria, in particular, has suffered a net outflow of interstate movers, numbering 42 000 in the two years to March 1981, of whom half were between fifteen and thirty-four years of age (quoted in *The Age*, 25 March 1981). In other words, much of this outflow is over and above the normal movement of older, retired people in search of a warmer climate and an easier-paced lifestyle.

Migration north, especially to Queensland, is not just—or even primarily—due to natural-resource development, since the latter projects are generally capital-intensive with limited direct and indirect effects on employment. Thus, the fastest-growing region of Queensland, the Gold Coast to the south, and Sunshine Coast to the north of Brisbane, depends not on mining or manufacturing (directly) but on intensive urban development and speculation set off by the influx of permanent residents and the lucrative tourist trade. According to Mullins (1979*a*), Australia's 'sunbelt cities' (in comparison to America's) have grown and are growing rapidly on the basis of a (mass) consumption-oriented rather than manufacturing-oriented dynamic. Consumption of newly-constructed luxury housing and associated consumer durables, on the one hand, and tourist and recreational facilities, on the other hand, is providing the economic base, funded by the switch of capital from 'southern' manufacturing and, in the case of a small number of real-estate developments, Japanese property capital. What Mullins (or anyone else) has not done is to show the institutional mechanism by which this process is occurring; in what ways are financial institutions and state agencies mediating the flows of capital between and within the primary and secondary circuits (Harvey 1981) in the context of the historically-specific structural constraints outlined above? Nevertheless, at a general level, this is an important insight suggesting that as the crisis worsens and idle capital builds up in the Australian manufacturing and even mining sectors, capital is likely to switch into sunbelt-type development of an increasingly speculative nature in Queensland and elsewhere.

From the mid-1960s new mining towns have grown rapidly in Western Australia, Queensland and, to a lesser extent, the Northern Territory, reflecting the switch of capital into iron, nickel, bauxite, uranium and the glamour mineral of the post-OPEC period, coal (Burnley, Pryor and Rowland 1980). Most of these centres are 'closed' or company towns, administered by the company which also owns the houses and hostels that workers live in, as well as the shops, recreational facilities and other services. In-out migration tends to be very high, the population biased towards young single men, and wages significantly higher than elsewhere in the economy. In a very real sense these towns function like foreign enclaves or 'free trade zones' in some Third World countries; TNC capital controls indigenous labour using imported capital-intensive, high-technology methods producing primarily for export on the basis of generous government subsidies, with minimal (positive) impact on the domestic economy in general. The interests of the relatively well-paid but numerically insignificant workforce are increasingly separated from, and sometimes opposed to, the interests of indigenous workers in general. In Australia, the clearest example of opposed interests arose over uranium, with the miners and their union strongly in favour of uranium mining and export, against the declared opposition of other unions and the official stance of the Australian Council of Trade Unions. One group, however, has been quite directly and adversely affected by new mining development. With the active support of State governments, mining has extended into remote areas previously regarded as worthless and consequently reserved for Aborigines, encouraging the mobilisation of rural and urban blacks in the Land Rights Movement.

Where the new mining and processing developments are focused on existing centres, localised effects, both beneficial and otherwise, impinge on existing residents. Thus, in the case of Portland, and particularly in Sale, the Victorian town servicing the oil and gas drilling operations in Bass Strait, boom conditions have been created in the local environment, at least in the short term. However, in the long run, after the initial construction phase and with the reduction in the demand for local labour and goods, local multiplier effects are likely to fade, leaving the darker side of development—inflated housing and commodity prices, rising unemployment and increasing community conflict.

Other Australian towns have continued or started to decline, in line with the structural shifts noted earlier. Existing mining towns like Mt Isa (Queensland), Broken Hill (New South Wales) and Kalgoorlie (Western Australia) grew less quickly in the first half of the 1970s, as did resource-related towns in the Latrobe Valley (Victoria) and Lithgow (New South Wales). The most dramatic examples of decline have occurred more recently in the steel towns of Whyalla (South Australia) and Wollongong and Newcastle (New South Wales) where, as argued above, the investment strategy of BHP is resulting in a rundown of traditional operations in favour of oil and gas exploration and recovery (Aungles 1979; Larcombe 1980).

Capital city growth rates have slackened noticeably in the 1970s, although broadly in line with the national trend. Consequently, the capital cities just maintained their shares of State-wide population, except in the case of Perth which increased its share significantly. The general decline in population growth has followed from a substantial drop in overseas immigration and the general ageing of the population. Internal migration has begun to reverse the drift to the cities described earlier, with Sydney and Melbourne figuring as net losers by the end of the decade (ABS 1982*a*).

This pattern of metropolitan growth is largely explicable in the light of the developments noted earlier. Perth and Brisbane are growing more quickly than other capital cities, partly in line with the positive spillover effects of resource development within their States but, more importantly, due to the geographical switch of capital into urban development and the absence of a heavy dependence on manufacturing industries which are now in decline. Sydney, Melbourne and Adelaide, on the other hand, are experiencing employment decline and capital flight from precisely those industries—clothing, footwear, transport equipment, metal products, chemicals, printing, household appliances, etc.—which have historically been heavily concentrated in these cities. That metropolitan decline has not been more pronounced is due, in the first instance, to the continuing and relatively high growth and metropolitan concentration of industries in the tertiary sector, especially finance, government administration and public utilities. However, as noted earlier, the spectre of technological displacement and public austerity hangs over this avenue for future growth. In the case of Brisbane and Sydney the switch of capital into the built environment has reinforced growth in the former and helped stave off decline in the latter (ABS 1982*b*). More importantly, Sydney and Melbourne have maintained and extended their control over financial and administrative functions in the context of the increasing role of TNC penetration of the Australian economy and the emergence of what was earlier termed, 'the Pacific-rim strategy':

> What this means in the Australian context is that, though the nation as a whole may be relatively peripheral to world capitalism, the major cities such as Sydney and Melbourne remain important as intermediate steps in the hierarchy, serving important intra-corporation functions as regional centres for administration, marketing, research and development, etc. Far from being peripheralised, they become of growing importance, in the new intra-corporation division of labour (Stilwell 1980:74).

Melbourne and Sydney are still the major centres where the regional head offices of TNCs are located in order to co-ordinate their Australia-wide operations and penetration of South-east Asia (Edgington 1983). Similarly, the bulk of foreign capital inflow (and outflow), both direct and portfolio, is managed by associated financial institutions located there. This trend has been strongly reinforced recently with the influx of foreign banks in line with the Federal government's policy of deregulating the Australian banking system. Not surprisingly, the major share of new office building completed in the past decade was located in these two cities.

The CBDs of the capital cities have continued to shed retailing, warehousing, manufacturing and small-scale professional functions, increasingly replaced by managerial and administrative activities located in both the public and private sectors. This process has been mediated by the property transactions of state agencies and the major financial institutions. In spite of a brief period during the Whitlam administration, when policies for the decentralisation of public service employment to intra-urban sub-centres were proposed but not implemented, the public sector at the State and Federal levels remains tightly focused on the CBD where the dominant political institutions are located. In the private sector, the large insurance companies have significantly switched capital into landownership and development; between 1956 and 1976, the share of total assets held by the seven largest companies in the form of real property rose from less than 5 per cent to more than 20 per cent (Sandercock 1983*b*). Most of this investment is held in offices rather than residential housing, and, consequently, is concentrated in the CBDs. In the early 1970s this process resulted in a short-lived office building boom (Daly 1982 and Chapter 19 of this volume). With the resulting over-supply of office space construction slowed, but the move of financial institutions and large property developers into central city landownership has not. Thus, for example, by 1977, these interests controlled two-thirds of the rentable space in central Melbourne (Kilmartin and Thorns 1978:66–7). With the continuing profit squeeze on productive investment and the slow-down in the resources boom as mining TNCs readjust to falling sales in an increasingly gloomy world market, the economic basis for a new central city office building boom is fast emerging. Such a boom would feed off the inflated capital inflow of the early 1980s and the redirection of domestic savings out of the residential sector in the wake of inflating interest rates. This outcome would repeat history, to some extent, resembling the aftermath of the first mining boom in the late 1960s, but in a vastly different world characterised by an increasingly severe global crisis. The sharp upward swing of central city property development—especially in the areas of offices and hotels—in the early to mid-1980s is a clear indication of this tendency.

The process of suburbanisation, described above, continued into the 1970s, with the inner suburbs of each capital city experiencing a sustained population decline. For example, in the 1971–76 period, the inner areas of Melbourne, Sydney and Brisbane lost 16, 8 and 15 per cent of their residential populations at a time when the metropolitan populations grew by 4, 4 and 14 per cent respectively (Mullins 1982:48). In the case of Sydney, almost half of all new dwellings completed in 1976–77 fell into the western and south-western regions of the metropolitan area—that is, in suburbs on the outer fringe—while only 4 per cent were located in the central or inner area (Stilwell 1980:96).

This pattern of suburbanisation was associated, as in the previous post-war decades, with continuing employment decentralisation—in Sydney's case, half of all metropolitan jobs were located outside the city and inner suburbs by 1971 (Spearritt 1978*a*:134). Between 1968–69 and 1977–78, Melbourne's inner suburbs lost 54 000 jobs, while inner Sydney lost 39 000 jobs during the 1972–76 period (Stilwell 1980:102). About 30 per cent of Melbourne's loss was regained through the expansion of manufacturing in the middle and outer suburbs but, in Sydney, the only job gains were clustered in the Liverpool area on the south-western fringe. To the extent that new employment opportunities opened up in the cities during the 1970s, they were largely concentrated in other sectors, notably tertiary. The strong centralisation of the fastest-growing tertiary industries (finance, communications and public administration) in the central city has placed a brake on employment decentralisation. To the extent that new employment opportunities did not open up, urban unemployment rose and, as several commentators have stressed, was spread very unevenly over the metropolitan area (Stilwell 1980:Chapter 7).

The switch of capital away from urban residential construction in the late 1970s (excluding Sydney and Brisbane) also checked suburbanisation—far more than the uneven process of 'gentrification'. Indeed, gentrification may turn out to have been a limited, uneven and historically-unique instance of spatial reorganisation during the early phase of the current crisis. As that crisis intensifies and idle capital builds up in the primary circuit, including mining, it is (once again) likely to switch through to the built environment and into increasingly speculative ventures, in particular. Speculative property dealing may (as noted above) then focus on office development (as it did in the early 1970s) or long-standing 'high status' residential suburbs, rather than result in a new burst of gentrification. There were signs of this occurring in the 1980s, especially in Sydney, with the appearance of what might be called, 'the North Shore phenomenon'. Parts of Sydney's established lower North Shore (Mosman, Cammeray, Hunters Hill, Northbridge, etc.) experienced a rapid property boom in the late-1970s, pushing average housing prices in the metropolitan area to a level 50 per cent higher than in Melbourne. The basis of price rises here appeared to relate not just to the locational advantages or accessibility of these suburbs but also to a monopoly-rent element based on the inherently scarce supply of 'harbour-side' housing (see King, Chapter 18 in this volume). The North Shore boom has recently subsided, due in part to rising interest rates and the scarcity of mortgage finance. House prices in other capital cities, especially Melbourne, have begun to catch up with Sydney during the 1980s. However, as crisis tendencies worsen, the boom—not necessarily focused on Sydney's North Shore—may break out again, reinforced by the polarisation of class-based inequalities in the wake of falling real wages and regressive taxation and public-expenditure policies. With continuing capital inflow and domestic restructuring it may well be a case of—in the words of an Australian political cartoonist—'Inflation! Inflation! Man the real estate agencies!'

Whither the state?: prospects for urban policy

The turn-around in the Australian economy in the most recent period, 1983–85, has resulted in significant economic growth based, in particular, on a surge in new house construction for owner occupation which was based, in turn, on the generation of surplus domestic liquidity in the early phase of national recovery. The newly-elected Labor governments at the Federal and State levels were also moderately successful in expanding the construction of public housing from the very low base left by the Fraser government's cuts in the late 1970s and early 1980s. However, it is now apparent that these gains are likelv to be temporary. Even if the general economic recovery continues—and this is still doubtful and contingent on developments in the international economy—governments at all levels are increasingly unlikely to be able to guarantee adequate public or private housing provision or, indeed, to be able to impose their priorities in other urban policy areas.

The Hawke government is effectively subordinating urban policy to the perceived requirements of its current economic growth strategy. The blow-out in the Federal budget deficit experienced in the first year of Labor's rule has been followed by three budgets which have (successfully, to date) resulted in falling deficits. This general fiscal constraint has limited the degree to which the Federal government can intervene in urban service provision and, through the grants system and Loan Council, limits the degree to which State governments can do likewise, especially in the areas of public housing, public transport and infrastructural facilities.

Even more important are the indirect effects of the Federal government's monetary and financial policies. 'De-regulation' has arisen as a strategy for winding back direct government regulation of the Australian financial system and the system of international economic relations. The most visible signs of this process have been the decisions to allow foreign banks into the previously highly-protected domestic banking sector and the floating of the exchange rate. The result of these, and related decisions, has been to tie the Australian economy ever more firmly into the global economy which is increasingly dependent on the emergence of a highly-integrated and co-ordinated global financial system (Daly 1984; 1985). Money capital has become increasingly mobile, sensitive to interest-rate differentials between and within individual countries. Governments in Australia can no longer guarantee adequate finance to fund mass home-ownership, as they did in the halcyon days of high economic growth, low inflation and tightly-regulated banking during the 1950s and 1960s. In the new international financial system, a premium is placed on liquidity; capital sunk for long periods in housing or other forms of property investment cannot be readily shifted into more profitable avenues in the short to medium term, hence such outlets for investment are devalued. Indeed, government economic policies can worsen the situation for mortgage borrowers. By following tight monetary policies in order to check inflation, finance their budget deficits and attract sufficient capital inflow to reduce chronic balance-of-payments deficits, governments encourage high domestic interest rates, which either attract finance away from mortgage provision or impose rising repayment burdens on existing home-owners while pricing would-be home-owners out of the market. Rising interest rates in a period of rapid property-price inflation, such as that characterising the past twenty years in Australian cities, result in escalating deposit gaps and, eventually, in a reduction in the overall home-ownership rate. As an indication of the problems facing home buyers, especially first-timers, Daly (1985:35) has calculated the average 'deposit gap' in Melbourne and Sydney in 1985 at somewhere between $40 000 and $50 000.

At the same time, the demand for rental housing is increasing, partly as a result of the increasing difficulties in achieving home-ownership, partly as a result of demographic and life cycle factors which favour the rental alternative. However, the supply of rental housing is unlikely to keep pace with this new social demand. Governments are, as noted above, unlikely to be able to substantially boost their current modest public housing programmes. Corporate landlords are likely to disinvest in rental properties in order to invest in more readily realisable, short-term areas, in keeping with the general volatility of international money markets and the corresponding bias in favour of liquid investments. Even small or petty landlords are likely to disinvest as the taxation benefits historically associated with rental property—viz. absence of a capital gains tax and the possibility of 'negative gearing'—disappear. In summary, the prospects of an increasingly severe housing crisis are strong, since the continued financing of housing in all three dominant tenure forms—owner-occupation, public housing and private renting—is increasingly problematical. Moreover, the major cause of inadequate housing provision is the same in all three tenure categories; money capital is being increasingly attracted towards alternative investments which offer greater returns and greater liquidity, while governments in Australia directly and indirectly contribute to this state of affairs through their monetary and general economic growth policies, respectively. Daly and Paris (1985) trace the emergence of this housing crisis in New South Wales, the State where it is currently most evident and most serious.

As the domestic economic recovery continues, capitalists are faced with the problem of where to reinvest their growing profits, assuming, of course, that the international props to local prosperity are maintained. Where inadequately-profitable productive avenues of investment exist in Australia, idle capital will either be drawn into speculative ventures and government debt financing at home, or redirected to more productive investment elsewhere in the world through the institutional mechanisms of the international financial system and the organisational form of the TNC. Foreign capital inflow will likewise be directed into increasingly speculative ventures in the private sector of which large non-residential or mixed-use real-estate developments are likely to be prime targets.

Large Australian institutional investors, notably banks and insurance companies, moved heavily into commercial real estate during the 1970s (Kilmartin and Thorns 1978). By the early 1980s these major investors held around 25 per cent of their total assets in property, concentrated in the CBDs of the capital cities. Daly (1985: 30) has argued that they are unlikely to continue to expand their investment activities in this area, having already acquired the prime city sites; instead, he suggests, large Australian financial, manufacturing and property development companies will probably run down their local property interests in order to internationalise the scope and range of their corporate activities. Increasingly, central city development and redevelopment will depend on the intervention of specialist institutions—for example, property and unit trusts—set up to mobilise domestic savings and on the involvement of transnational construction and development corporations whose property interests are managed on a global scale.

Particularly important in this latter context, are the recent operations of large Japanese and Chinese developers. The proposed Victoria Project on the edge of Melbourne's CBD to be carried out by the giant Japanese construction firm Kumagai Gumi is a case in point (Berry and Huxley 1985). This is merely one, albeit the largest to date, of several Kumagai projects planned or in the process of construction in each of the States and the Northern Territory. These developers are perfectly placed to draw on the huge volume of loan capital circulating in the Euro and Asia dollar markets. Their size, financial strength and access to the international financial system, allow them to envisage projects the size and complexity of which were and are beyond the reach of Australian investors and financiers.

Their capacity to spatially concentrate substantial capital inflow in particular capital cities for the purposes of building large, spectacular and highly-visible projects has made them attractive to State governments, locked in competition with each other to attract new investment and employment growth. Indeed, in the volatile economic and electoral climate, each State government is under intense pressure to get 'cranes on the skyline' at almost any cost. In effect, this has meant both the offer of financial inducements like taxation relief and the strengthening temptation to modify, water-down and subvert their own regulatory controls on land use and environmental quality (Berry and Huxley 1985:41–2). In a situation of intense interstate competition for large, new and highly mobile project commitments, each State government will find it extremely difficult and, in electoral terms, suicidal to insist on a lengthy, onerous and expensive planning process or require strong environmental standards to be met.

More than that, each State government will be pushed into an entrepreneurial role, entailing the need to initiate, and partly finance, large developments, whether centred on the property sector or not. This entrepreneurial role can range from the provision of financial guarantees and commitment to take up a minimum proportion of rental space in the new project, to formal joint-venture arrangements as in the case of the Alcoa aluminium smelter at Portland in Victoria and the moves towards commercialising areas of public enterprise in Western Australia (E. Harman 1985). Daly (1985:33) has neatly summarised both the logic of this situation and the potential social costs attached:

> If finance (Australian and foreign) is footloose, governments perceive this (entrepreneurial) task as the attraction of investment funds to their own cities and for their own designated projects. Employment growth and visible change are seen as the rewards, and planning and environmental design are the victims in this change.

Conclusion

The prospects for strong and especially reformist urban policies in Australia (of the kind which characterised the Whitlam Federal government of the 1970s) are bleak. Neither the Federal nor State governments are strongly placed to counter the strategic power of large transnational property interests in an increasingly integrated global economy in which money and productive capital are highly mobile and the territorial powers of individual governments fixed. Nor, it must be stressed, can *all* State governments expect to succeed in attracting large, viable projects—there are simply not that many to go around and the smaller capitals, especially Adelaide and Hobart, are likely to lose to Sydney and Melbourne. Finally, there are reasons to think that even those States successful in capturing the majority of new projects are unlikely to reap all the hoped-for gains (Berry and Huxley 1985:48–54). The transnational-developers like Kumagai will recoup their investment and profits through construction in the short term, hurrying off to reinvest wherever in the world immediate profit prospects are greatest, leaving Australian investors and, possibly, governments to hold long-term equity in office blocks, hotels, shopping complexes, etc. which may never pay off. Whether or not the new offices fill up and remain full in the long run, hotels continue to operate at capacity and shopping centres thrive, will depend on exactly how the global economy develops over time and space, a process almost completely outside the control of governments in Australia.

This loss of political sovereignty is reminiscent of the situation in some Third World countries whose governments have sought to attract large foreign investors through the guarantee of cheap, docile labour, low taxes and lax regulations in the environmental, occupational health and related areas. The general benefits of promised industrial growth are certainly debatable in debt-ridden and repressively-governed countries like Brazil, Mexico and the Philippines. Is it fanciful, then, to suggest that cities like Melbourne and Sydney risk turning into 'zero-planning havens', increasingly integrated into and dependent on the international system, while becoming more and more insulated from the domestic economy and policy goals and controls of Australian governments?

Section II:
State, economy and urban issues

Chapter 4
State and capital in urban and regional development

Frank Stilwell

> The importance of town planning has long been appreciated (in Australia) and careful research, co-operation and ingenuity among land-owners, sub-dividers, finance institutions, shire councillors and MPs, has resulted in some incredible profiteering. The towns are hopeless.
> Bruce Petty, *Petty's Australia - and how it works!*

Introduction

Urban and regional development is an important aspect of the relationship between capital and the state. On the one hand, the historical form of development can be regarded as the outcome of a complex set of interacting decisions, by individuals, business interests, local governments, individual State governments and Federal governments. On the other hand, the spatial structure of the built environment and the associated distribution of employment and population sets important constraints on new decisions regarding government policy, public and private investment and so on. Thus, the study of urban and regional development provides a good case-study of the role of the state in the economic system.

The existing literature on Australian cities and regions unfortunately provides little insight into the nature of the capital/state relationship. There is a certain amount of descriptive historical material on the pattern of urban growth, particularly on the reasons for the high degree of metropolitan primacy within each of the individual Australian States (Neutze 1977; Stilwell 1974:Chapters 2–6). Much has also been written about the problems of the cities—congestion, pollution, housing and so on (Neutze 1965; Stilwell 1974:Chapters 7–11). Finally, there is a mass of literature on public policies, particularly decentralisation policy, which has long been seen by many as a panacea for both the problems of urban over-growth and rural underdevelopment (Neutze 1978; Stilwell 1974:Chapters 12–15). However, there are at least two problems with this conventional approach to urban and regional analysis.

Based on Head, B. (1983), Chapter 9 of *State and Economy in Australia* by kind permission of Oxford University Press.

First, there is the problem arising because of the failure to integrate the analysis of urban and regional development with the study of the total socio-economic system: thus, spatial phenomena (for example, congestion) are seen as having spatial causes (for example, metropolitan over-growth), and as being amenable to spatial solutions (for example, decentralisation). This diverts attention away from the roots of urban and regional problems in the general workings of the socio-economic system (property rights, class conflict, the quest for capital accumulation, and so on).

Second, there is the problem which arises from the failure to study the state/capital relationship in an analytical manner. The typical approach is normative: problems are seen to arise because of 'market imperfections' (for example, externalities, imperfect information, lack of foresight or co-ordination in location decisions), so therefore the government should introduce remedial policies (for example, decentralisation). This view implicitly sees the state as *deus ex machina*, as external to the socio-economic system, intervening so as to seek to implement policies on behalf of the community as a whole. This is very soothing but not very illuminating.

A more satisfactory approach needs to integrate the study of urban and regional development into a general analysis of the socio-economic system, and to develop an analysis of public policy which acknowledges that the state is an integral part of the working of the socio-economic system. That is the purpose of this chapter (though the former aspect is more fully developed elsewhere, see Stilwell 1980). The third section seeks to establish a framework for analysing the state, and subsequent sections look at particular aspects of policy. First, however, it is necessary to set out some initial propositions about the various dimensions of urban and regional development and the various levels of state intervention.

The state and urban and regional development: a taxonomic approach

In order to establish a framework for analysing the role of the state in relation to urban and regional development in Australia, certain preliminary issues need to be clarified. One concerns the various dimensions of urban and regional development. In one sense, all development occurs in a spatial continuum, but for analytical purposes, some sub-divisions are appropriate. The one adopted in this chapter distinguishes between three aspects.

Inter-regional development

In order to study the broad patterns of resource allocation in the nation as a whole it is useful to define regions in terms of the individual States which comprise Australia. Given the historical importance of these boundaries in shaping the form of development, and given the continuing importance of the individual Australian State governments, it seems appropriate to begin in this way. This is not to say that the regions thereby defined have particular significance as geographical entities or in terms of the conventional criteria for regional delineation; it is simply an initial categorisation which draws attention to certain historial and political forces shaping the process of economic development in the continent.

Intra-regional development

Within each of the individual States there is very considerable heterogeneity in terms of almost every conceivable criterion. Perhaps the most obvious aspect is the concentration of population and industry in Australian State capitals. In every State except Tasmania the capital has more than ten times the population of the next largest town or city, and in the cases of Victoria, South Australia and Western Australia this rises to a ratio of over twenty to one in each case. The causes and consequences of this high degree of metropolitan primacy within the boundaries of each of the individual States have been much discussed. There has also been much emphasis — in rhetoric if not in action — on policies of decentralisation aimed at securing a higher degree of 'intra-regional balance'. For our current purposes, it is clearly important to analyse how this distinctive feature of the Australian socio-economic system reflects particular aspects of the relationship between the state and economy.

Intra-urban development

The spatial form of the major Australian cities is also very distinctive. Most obviously, the overall density of population is very low by international standards; this is, of course, closely associated with the typical suburban form of detached dwellings on small blocks of land, and this in turn is linked with the dominant emphasis (particularly since the Second World War) on home ownership, rather than private rental or state-provided housing (Kilmartin and Thorns 1978:Chapter 7; also Kemeny, Chapter 16 of this volume). Related aspects involve the changing form of the central business district, the gentrification of the inner-city areas and the suburbanisation of manufacturing (Kendig 1979). Analysis of the ways in which these aspects of Australian cities have developed is also relevant to the current study.

Thus we have three levels of spatial disaggregation. Any given development affects them all: for example, if a business corporation establishes a new factory in an outer Sydney suburb, this bears directly on intra-urban development but also changes the balance of intra-regional development by further intensifying metropolitan primacy, and changes the balance of inter-regional development as between New South Wales and the other States. Of course, the selection of a particular location by the corporation is a decision that takes place within a political as well as an economic environment. It does, presumably, reflect the firm's estimates of costs and revenues in alternative locations but it also reflects the pattern of incentives and constraints determined by the state apparatus.

This raises the question of how to classify the various aspects or components of the state, a subject much debated in the literature. Miliband (1973) for example, defines the state as comprising the government, administration, judiciary, armed forces and police, political parties and parliamentary assemblies. For our purposes, we can concentrate primarily on the government. Other aspects of the state have had an important impact on the form of urban and regional development. For example, the judiciary has interpretated the Constitution in such a way as to restrict Federal government initiatives on the grounds that it cannot engage in location-specific expenditure and/or interfere with interstate trade through its regional policy. Second, the administration, and conservative Treasury public servants in particular, is regarded by some contemporary commentators as having been a major brake on innovative urban and regional policies in the early 1970s (Sandercock 1978; Lloyd and Troy 1981). However, our primary focus on government is not inappropriate, especially because it draws attention immediately to the important issue of the Federal structure of the Australian state: the division between *local governments, individual State governments* and the *Federal government*. Each of these bodies has had an influence on the spatial dimension of economic development; and the various forms this has taken can be usefully classified according to the three-fold distinction previously established. Thus, in Table 4.1 we have a three-by-three matrix of governmental bodies and the levels of spatial disaggregation at which their policies have operated.

This taxonomic approach indicates nine policy categories. In practice, some are much more important than others. Local government, for example, has nothing to do with the broad issues of inter-regional resource allocation and little to do with intra-regional questions such as decentralisation policy. State governments also have no formal role in relation to inter-regional resource allocation, though by competing with each other for capital investment (especially by transnational corporations) they do strongly influence the form of inter-regional development. The more important categories are indicated in Table 4.1 by giving examples of relevant policies. Subsequent sections of this chapter consider these in detail. However, a prerequisite for such analysis is a clear statement of competing views on the role of the state in the economic system. This matter has been more fully discussed but needs to be briefly considered in this context so as to establish a framework for the subsequent analysis of urban and regional policies.

Table 4.1 A general classification of regional and urban policies

Spatial level of policy	Level of government Federal	State	Local
Inter-regional	Commonwealth Grants Commission; Taxation and expenditure policies: the 'New Federalism'		
Intra-regional	Development of Canberra; Grants to the individual States for the development of growth centres	Decentralisation policies; Expenditure policies	
Intra-urban	DURD initiatives e.g., area improvement programme, land commissions, inner-city housing schemes	Metropolitan planning; transport policy	Zoning, planning permissions, etc.

The state: competing views

How can we interpret the role of the state? It has become a major co-ordinating mechanism in the contemporary capitalist economy. A historical approach provides some insights into the forces shaping this development. The last major economic depression of the 1930s gave rise to Keynesian economics which showed how management of aggregate demand could alleviate problems of demand deficiency. Coupled with the high level of military expenditure, this provided the rationale and foundation for increased state intervention in the economy during the 1950s and 1960s. Meanwhile, the growth of the 'welfare state' alleviated some of the problems of business by ensuring that the costs of such items as education, social security (and in some other capitalist countries, health), were borne by the state (Gough 1979). This helped to alleviate any major economic depression for the twenty years following. It was also an important element in the legitimation of the capitalist system (Habermas 1976; Theophanous 1980).

However, as with previous stages of capitalist development, one can now see in retrospect that one set of problems was solved only by the creation of the preconditions for others. The increased degree of state intervention created pressures leading to a rapid rate of inflation (Gamble and Walton 1976). Similarly, there has been a problem of financing the growing level of state expenditure—giving rise to the so-called 'fiscal crisis of the state' (J. O'Connor 1973). Since 1975, these forces have led to attempts to cut back (or at least restrain) the growth of state intervention. In Australia, this was the declared policy of the Federal government under the leadership of Fraser, although it was difficult to achieve in practice. (Indeed, one of the most spectacular areas of expenditure-cutting by the Fraser government was in respect of urban and regional development and the Labor government has done little in the 1980s to restore the priority given to this form of expenditure by the Whitlam government.)

However, while these general features of the development of the state are readily observable, there is no agreement about their implications for the analysis of it. Can it be said that the state is, in some sense, operating on behalf of the community as a whole, albeit in difficult economic circumstances partly beyond its own making? Or is the evidence more consistent with the orthodox Marxist view that the state primarily serves the interests of the dominant class? An intermediate possibility is the view that it is neither operating on behalf of the whole community nor continuously on behalf of one class, but operates differently in different periods, according to the strength of different groups or classes struggling for control of the state apparatus. If we are to avoid a purely descriptive account of urban and regional policies, it is useful to set our discussion in the context of these competing views. Let us consider each of the three possibilities in a little more detail.

The first view of the state is the *liberal pluralist* one which emphasises its role in relation to the implementation of public policies which serve—more or less efficiently—the interests of the whole community. In the extreme case, this interventionist role is considered to be extremely minor, because resource allocation, on the whole, is best left to the free operation of the market mechanism (Friedman 1962). At the other extreme, large-scale systematic government intervention is seen as justified because it corrects the various inefficiencies and injustices associated with a pure market system; Galbraith's (1974) view of the state as a source of countervailing power to monopoly capital is a variant of this approach. What these views have in common is that they see the state as not consistently aligned with one particular class within society; it operates on behalf of the whole community, though at any given point of time some groups may acquire more influence than others on its operations. Analysis of the state therefore begins by looking at how public policies come to reflect the competing interests—hence, the emphasis, on the one hand, on electoral and pressure-group politics and, on the other, on the way in which economic and social policies may contribute to serving the 'general interest' (for example, Keynesian economic measures serving the goal of full employment).

In stark contrast with this is the *orthodox Marxist* position which emphasises the role of the state as a body 'for managing the common affairs of the whole bourgeoisie'. In this view, the state can be expected systematically to serve the requirements of capital. The interests of the class *as a whole* are of paramount importance. Individual capitalists often do not perceive their common interests (or, if they do, they cannot co-ordinate their activities towards that end without 'external' assistance); hence the need for the state. Furthermore, since the interests of capital and labour are seen as fundamentally antagonistic, the role of the state inevitably involves the implementation of policies that work systematically against the interests of the working class. Of course, there are variants on this approach but they all share a fundamental economic determinism—the actions of the state follow more or less directly from the needs of capital. Analysis of the role of the state therefore begins with an analysis of the requirements of capital; Glyn and Sutcliffe's (1972) study of the United Kingdom provides an example, and a similar sort of reasoning is implicit in Catley and McFarlane's (1974) analysis of the way in which the Whitlam government in Australia was oriented towards the establishment of corporate capitalism in the interests of the capitalist class.

A third approach—which one may perhaps label *revisionist*—emphasises the role of the state in relation to the political struggle between capital and labour. In this view, the state becomes, in effect, an arena of class struggle, and therefore does not automatically serve the interests of only one class, and certainly not the interest of the community as a whole. The orthodox Marxist view is rejected because its reductionism ignores the possibility of the working class widening the struggle from the economic to the political sphere and exploiting internal conflicts within the capitalist class through the use of state power. The liberal pluralist view is discounted because of its denial that there are fundamental antagonisms between classes; in Parkin's words 'in a class stratified society the very notion of a national interest is highly problematic' (Parkin 1972:135). It is not necessary to view the class struggle as a political process independent of economic relations; rather, it is important to recognise the interdependence of the political and economic aspects. Thus, while the analysis of the state cannot proceed directly from the study of the logic of capital, the nature of the capital-accumulation process shapes the conditions in which the class struggle takes place. One particularly important aspect of this sort of approach is the recognition of fractions of capital whose interests frequently conflict, for example, high rents from urban land benefit the owners of urban property at the expense of industrial capital. Such intra-class conflicts, according to the orthodox Marxist view, strengthen the need for the state to act on behalf of the capital class as a whole. However, according to the revisionist view, they also open up the possibility of the working class exploiting such conflicts in its own interests and thereby strengthening the potential for gaining control over the state apparatus. Thus, there arises the possibility of the state being used for the transformation of a capitalist to a socialist system. This view has been forcefully developed by Holland (1975) in the United Kingdom and a variant of it is to be found in the book on Australia by Theophanous (1980).

These views are not, of course, fully comprehensive. Alternatively the state may be seen as a self-serving institution, as the private property of officials used for their personal advancement; there are elements of this in anarchist thought and in early Marxist writings on the state as a parasitic institution (C.Ward 1973). However, the above outline will suffice as a framework for interpreting the Australian experience regarding urban and regional development. It is to those specific matters that we now turn, using the classification of policies introduced in the second section of this chapter.

Inter-regional development

Looking at the broad pattern of economic development between the individual States and Territories of Australia, there are some fairly obvious interrelations between capital and the state. *Individual State governments* in Australia compete with each other for capital investment, especially from overseas; witness the various offices of the individual Australian State governments clustered in London along the Strand, each seeking to attract capital as well as labour. Witness, too, the State governments competing with each other, in terms of cheap electricity rates, to attract investment in aluminium smelting. The outcome is that electricity is provided to transnational corporations at a price well below that normally charged in the domestic market, thereby comprising a subsidy to capital financed from general State revenues (Hodgkinson 1980). Less obvious, but also important, are the capital/State linkages at a personal level such as the involvement of the business leaders in government bodies; the appointment of an ex-ICI executive to head the New South Wales Pollution and Environmental Control Commission was an obvious case in point. Such casual observations tend to support the general proposition that the role of individual State governments has tended to be very accommodating to the interests of capital. Given the mobility of capital and the interstate rivalry for investment which derives from the widespread commitment to the objective of maximising economic growth, this would seem to be a more-or-less inevitable outcome.

What is perhaps rather more interesting is the role of the *Federal government* in relation to the broad pattern of inter-regional development. The Federal government is in a unique position to affect this balance through its economic policies, and ever since Federation there has been a general commitment to using such measures in the pursuit of some degree of inter-regional equity. The need for such intervention reflected the tendency for private-sector investment to be concentrated in the more developed Australian States; this tendency is a general feature of capitalism and has given rise to the tendencies towards circular and cumulative causation so characteristic of regional economic performance (Myrdal 1963). The Federal system tended to accentuate the imbalances. As one writer put it,

> In Australia there were marked disparities in size, wealth and economic development between the colonies at Federation. In the process of national reorientation the small States suffered backwash effects from economic integration and their burden was increased by a national policy of developing manufacturing industry behind a protective tariff. In these circumstances, and having lost their major pre-Federation sources of revenue and facing a growing demand for national standards in taxation and the provision of social services, the governments of the smaller States began to find themselves in chronic financial difficulties. (May 1971:xii)

In order to deal with this situation, the Federal government adopted certain explicit inter-regional policies. Special grants paid to the smaller States were the most obvious measure of expenditure policy, though these have been of declining importance relative to general and specific-purpose grants. Certainly, this has led to a systematic variation between the interstate distribution of taxation and expenditures (Groenewegen 1979). However, it is difficult to derive an overall picture of these distributions, especially because many policies have no explicit regional allocation but nevertheless have an important impact on the inter-regional allocation of resources, for example, defence expenditure, tariff policy, etc. In the period 1972–75, the Federal government did initiate an experiment in regional-expenditure budgeting which might have gone some way to providing a data base for assessing the overall regional impact of Federal government policies, but this experiment was discontinued when the Liberals were returned to power (Australian Department of Urban and Regional Development 1972–75; Keating 1978).

The most significant change in policy during the late 1970s was the introduction of the system known as New Federalism. Ostensibly introduced to reverse the tendency towards the centralisation of fiscal powers, this policy gave fixed proportions of Federal revenues to the individual State governments (and to local governments) while empowering the State governments to levy additional tax surcharges if more revenue was required to finance expenditures (or to give rebates if there was more than sufficient revenue). One commentator interpreted this as a response to the fiscal crisis of the state, in that it seeks to slough off some of the growing expenditure commitments of the Federal government (Groenewegen 1976). Effectively it shifts the crisis from one part of the state apparatus to another, but, if combined with an ideological attack on public expenditure in general, and expenditures on the 'undeserving poor' in particular, it may temporarily serve to remove some of the problems of fiscal crisis.

What is important to stress is that these policy changes in Federal/State financial relations are taking place in the context of a wholesale re-structuring of the Australian regional economy, initiated not by the state but by capital. The international recession of the capitalist system in the 1970s led to an acceleration of the trend towards a 'new international division of labour' (Froebel et al. 1979) whereby the production process is divided by stages between a number of countries. Routine manufacturing operations are increasingly located in low-wage countries, particularly in free-trade zones, leading to what Alford (1978) has described as 'the rearrangement of the imperialist framework . . . from a centre-periphery system to an international production grid'. For Australia, the consequences are particularly striking, since the re-structuring involves the dismantling of significant parts of manufacturing industry; in effect a process of de-industrialisation. Some Australian-based manufacturing companies have moved offshore. Additionally, Australian-based companies have switched the nature of their investments, for example, BHP from steel manufacture into mineral and oil ventures (Larcombe 1980). The major thrust of investment came to be concentrated in large-scale mineral extraction and processing projects. These are extremely capital-intensive and hence generate relatively little employment; the proportion of the Australian workforce in mining, for example, is still under 2 per cent. Equally important, the spatial distribution of such investment is significantly different from manufacturing, being more oriented towards the less-industrialised States of Queensland and Western Australia, though by no means exclusively.

Although the initiative in this process of restructuring has clearly been in the hands of private capital — and transnational corporations in particular — the state has also been closely involved. Certainly the 25 per cent across-the-board cut in tariffs in 1973 accelerated the demise of many manufacturing enterprises, particularly in clothing and textiles. More generally, the Federal government has tended to accommodate itself to the process of structural change (albeit not as much as the Treasury and the Industries Assistance Commission, with their commitment to reduced protectionism, would have wished), seeing this as a prerequisite for an economic recovery based on the export-oriented minerals sector. As I have argued elsewhere, the Fraser government in particular initiated a range of changes in its economic and social policies designed to reduce the power of labour and thereby to make Australia more attractive for foreign capital (Stilwell 1980:Chapter 10). The Hawke government's 'accord' with the trade unions has sought to establish a less volatile industrial-relations climate, albeit through much more sophisticated means and with some benefits for the labour movement. Individual State governments have been more strident; Queensland in particular (and Western Australia in the late 1970s) initiated major oppression of trade union rights and civil liberties. The ruling classes in those States see (correctly) that their economic position is becoming more closely linked to other countries such as Japan and the United States than to the relatively-industrialised States in south-east Australia. Some see these developments leading to a 'fragmentation of the nation state' (Stevenson 1977), although other analysts do not share the view that the power of the mineral-based States has markedly increased (Harman and Head 1982).

We may appropriately conclude that the issue of inter-regional economic development in Australia is one that illustrates a wide range of complex interrelationships between capital and the state, on which we have only had space to touch very briefly here. The question remains, does the evidence on the capital/state relation in respect of inter-regional development lend support to any one of the general theories of the state? The activities of the individual State governments are apparently consistent in general terms with the orthodox Marxist position, in that interstate competition itself tends to lead each government, whatever the political complexion of the party in power, to be subservient to the needs of capital. However, the inter-regional policies of the Federal government are not obviously inconsistent with the liberal-pluralist view, in that there has been a general commitment to inter-regional equity. Finally, the recent policy changes may also be interpreted in the context of the revisionist view in that they suggest that the current economic crisis—manifested specifically in the fiscal crisis of the state—tends to open up the inter-regional policy issue as one in which the interests of capital and labour are in conflict. There are dramatic changes taking place in the inter-regional distribution of economic activity and these are initiated by capital in general and transnational capital in particular; to harness state power to counteract these tendencies has become one of the principal demands of the 1980s (Crough and Wheelwright 1982).

Intra-regional development

As noted in the second section of this chapter, the overwhelming feature of the distribution of economic activity within each Australian State is the high degree of *metropolitan primacy*. This can be interpreted fairly straightforwardly in terms of the mutually-reinforcing activities of capital and state. What is perhaps less easy to understand is the way in which the long-standing commitment to the objectives of decentralisation policy fits in to the same analysis. We deal with the former issue first. The pattern of metropolitan primacy has been a characteristic feature since the very origins of European settlement in the continent. The capital cities served as administrative centres, ports for the import of labour and various supplies and for the export of primary produce, particularly wool. Service industries and such manufacturing activity as developed to supply local needs were also heavily concentrated. Thus the administrative, commercial and industrial functions tended to be mutually reinforcing of metropolitan primacy. Unlike Europe, where a scattered population preceded the development of railways and other modern technology, the situation in Australia was not conducive to the development of village settlement, since large agricultural areas could be served by a modern transport system. Certainly, country towns did develop, but the radial focus of the transport networks (coupled with impediments such as variations in railways guages between some of the colonies) focused the commercial activities on the capital cities. In these circumstances the development of metropolitan primacy within each colony was inevitable (though the same forces simultaneously ensured that metropolitan primacy would *not* be a feature of the continent as a whole (Glynn 1970).

In more recent years, the consolidation of this uneven pattern of development has taken place as industrial enterprises seeking large pools of labour, access to the major markets and to ancillary services, have shown a marked preference for metropolitan locations (Stilwell 1974:Chapter 6). Moreover, the growth of the individual State bureaucracies has reinforced this process. These two forces led to a growing metropolitan dominance which was particularly marked during the first twenty-five years after the Second World War. The share of total State population in the State capital rose from 55 to 59 per cent between 1947 and 1971 in the case of New South Wales. Corresponding figures for other States were 63 to 68 per cent in Victoria, 36 to 45 per cent in Queensland, 55 to 62 per cent in Western Australia, 59 to 69 per cent in South Australia and 30 to 33 per cent in Tasmania.

This growing metropolitan dominance led to a growing concern with the question of *decentralisation*. Steering growth away from the major urban areas had long been seen as part of the general objective of 'populating the interior'. But after the Second World War, these concerns intensified, and there was a marked increase of interest in the decentralisation issue. This was encouraged by the Federal Labor government in the 1944–49 period and led to the establishment of Regional Development Committees. In New South Wales and Victoria the commitment to decentralisation was on-going, and various forms of financial assistance were given to local authorities for the provision of community and industrial services and to firms so as to reduce their costs of production and distribution. Additionally, attempts were made (albeit with less than startling success), to limit the peripheral growth of the metropolitan areas through the delineation of green belts.

The stated rationale for these policy commitments ranged from considerations of national security and defence, to the need to alleviate 'problems of urban over-growth'. Numerous individual State government reports reconfirmed the commitment to decentralisation (although the Victorian government in 1985 decided this was no longer appropriate); a committee of Federal and State government officials established in the 1960s endorsed it as an objective of national policy albeit very tentatively (Australian Committee on Decentralisation 1972) and the Labor government backed it with Federal funds in the period 1972–75, concentrating mainly on particular growth centres such as Albury-Wodonga and Bathurst-Orange.

However, the effectiveness of the policy has been limited. Numerous subsidies to individual business enterprises have been given, including rebates of payroll taxation for firms in non-metropolitan locations, but this has not prevented the metropolitan areas from increasing their share of total employment and population. Indeed, there has been no major development of cities outside the major metropolitan areas, with four exceptions: Canberra as a national capital; towns such as Broken Hill and Mt Isa based on resource extraction; towns such as Gladstone based on mineral processing; and areas such as the Gold Coast based on the tourist industry. These are important exceptions, but not attributable in general to decentralisation policy.

The principal lesson is that metropolitan primacy, established initially for a complex of historical, geographical, security and political reasons, came to be a cumulative phenomenon because individual capitalists sought to capture the economies of scale and other economic advantages associated with a metropolitan location. The nominal commitment by the state to decentralisation policy has been ineffective as a counter to these cumulative agglomeration pressures, and has not been vigorously pursued in practice; indeed its vigorous pursuit in any one individual State could run counter to the other objective of maximising the level of economic growth, since the more locational constraints are imposed by any one State, the more likely is capital to take flight elsewhere.

All in all, this suggests that the state as a whole, partly because of its Federal structure, does not now play the leading role in shaping the pattern of intra-regional development. The nominal commitment to decentralisation policy could be interpreted in the liberal-pluralist view as reflecting a concern with matters of general community welfare (the externalities associated with urban living, and so on). However, in practice the tentative nature of the policy suggests that the Marxist view of the state as serving the needs of capital—while seeking to legitimise itself through its apparent concern with community welfare—is more consistent with the evidence. When the needs of capital are consistent with the decentralisation objective, as in the case of resource-based towns, decentralisation has taken place. Moreover, when the needs of capital are such as to require less metropolitan labour, as in the context of the economic recession of the early 1980s, the state has responded by cutting back the immigration programme; this, together with the fall in birth rates (and not decentralisation policy *per se*) has slowed the tendency towards cumulative metropolitan dominance in the last decade (Daly 1985).

Intra-urban development

The relationship between capital and the state is perhaps most clearly illustrated at this most 'micro' level of spatial development processes.

In part this is because individual business and state institutions are more clearly identifiable at this level; the Victorian land scandals, usefully documented by Sandercock (1979), provide a prime example. Changes in zoning regulations, particularly in respect of land on the urban-rural interface, may create vast windfall gains to landowners. Hence, it is hardly surprising that speculative elements should seek to obtain advance information of any such zoning changes and/or seek to have influence on the changes through contacts with politicians and administrators of state instrumentalities. The capital/state relationship in these circumstances operates to undermine systematic urban planning as well as to intensify distributional inequalities and exacerbate the inflationary problem (Sandercock 1979:xii-xiv).

However, this is an extreme case which may be seen as indicating that it is corruption which leads to undesirable outcomes. What is more important to stress is that, even in the absence of explicit corruption, deals, and so on, the normal workings of the urban system (including urban planning) in Australian cities have operated in a class-biased manner. In part this arises simply because much urban development has been undertaken by capital in the direct pursuit of profits; the community as a whole has borne the external dis-economies associated with unplanned development. Additionally, where the state has been directly involved in shaping the form of urban expansion, it has tended to share the same pro-growth ideology and has accommodated itself to the forces generated by the capitalist system. For example, transport plans have extrapolated past trends in private-vehicle ownership and sought to plan for that anticipated demand, typically through the provision of intra-urban freeways which destroy low-income housing and communities so as to increase the accessibility of upper-income groups to the central business district. Similarly, it may be argued that metropolitan plans such as the Sydney Region Outline Plan of 1968, because they delineated the major areas for future development, have effectively served as 'speculators' guides' (Stretton 1970; Daly 1982; Chapters 10 and 19 of this volume).

A more systematic assessment of the interrelationship of capital and the state in the urban development process can be organised in terms of the different levels of government: local, State and Federal. This three-tier system, in the words of the Australian Institute of Urban Studies, 'blurs responsibilities for urban affairs', making for great problems of inter-governmental co-ordination (AIUS 1980:23). Nevertheless, it provides a convenient framework for analysing the role of the state in urban development.

The role of *local government* is relatively unimportant because of its limited jurisdiction, both territorially and in terms of its range of functions. With the exception of Brisbane, no local government is of sufficient magnititude to cope with metropolitan planning. Moreover, in comparison with local government in the United Kingdom,

Canada or the United States, local government in Australia handles a tiny share of total state expenditures. Though originally entrusted with a wide range of functions ranging from community health and welfare, to town and country planning, its role has shrunk in practice to the management of libraries, parks, swimming pools, secondary roads, garbage disposal and so on. In particular instances, where local government has a key strategic role in the urban development process—as in the case of the Councils of the Cities of Sydney and Melbourne—business interests have been active to ensure that policies are sympathetic to their requirements. There are other instances where local governments have come together to plan urban development, as in the case of the Cumberland County Council formed in 1945 to lay down guidelines for the orderly development of Sydney's suburbs (Sandercock 1977:179–86). There have also been attempts to revitalise local government, long seen as the Cinderella of the state apparatus, for example, the amalgamations proposed by the Barnett Committee, and the new policy initiated by the Federal government in 1973 enabling the Commonwealth Grants Commission to make payments to groups of local councils, as well as via the individual State governments. Nevertheless, local governments remain short of funds, particularly in areas characterised by low-income residents (Manning 1973); this intensifies their general tendency to be subservient to business interests, competing with each other for economic developments which add to rate revenues. Urban development tends to be modified by the structure of local zoning controls but local government typically has neither the scope nor the resources to operate as a strong countervailing force to business interests.

The role of Australian *State governments* is more important. These have long had a major role in shaping the form of urban development. This has been made explicit in recent decades through the publication of urban planning statements for the major cities but has been implicit in nearly all State government policies. The form of the public transport system provides an obvious example, since historically the form of the major metropolitan areas was shaped by radial expansion associated with the development of the railway system (and trams in some cases), and subsequently by a more scattered development, as both public and private expenditures were channelled into road transport. Housing provides another example, not only in respect of the location of public-authority housing, but also in relation to the legislation regulating private housing, such as minimum lot sizes. Policies towards the spatial distribution of expenditures on education, health and social services have also had a significant impact (Stimson 1982:222–78).

Leonie Sandercock (1977:1), in a comprehensive treatment of these issues, concludes that

> city planning in Australia this century has failed to improve the welfare of our city dwellers ... (and, moreover) to the extent that the

planning movement has been concerned with redistributive social justice, it has been frustrated by the established power structures and ideology of Australia's urban, industrial, bureaucratic society.

But to describe state intervention as a 'failure' is to implicitly accept the liberal view that urban planning is about social improvement of some general sort, rather than an expression of particular class interests and conflicts. Taking the latter view, Castells and others have sought to analyse the growth of state intervention in the city, and particularly its role in the provision of collective consumption, in terms of the needs of capital (Castells 1977; 1978; Kilmartin, Thorns and Burke 1985). Looked at in this way, the suburban form of urban development in Australia is very conducive to the maintenance of a high level of demand for goods and services (at least one television set, washing machine, car, and so on per average household) and to the dominance of individualistic ideologies which are conducive to social and political stability. Not that capital has been unified or conspiratorial in this respect; on the contrary, there appear to have been important conflicts between fractions of capital in the process of urban development. Moreover, capital and the state have met opposition to many features of the urban development process—urban protest groups have been an important countervailing force and the 'green bans' which held up millions of dollars of development projects in Sydney in the early 1970s were a particularly innovative form of urban social movement (Kilmartin and Thorns 1978:Chapter 8). On the whole, it seems appropriate to conclude that, while the role of individual State governments in the urban development process has been generally consistent with the needs of capital for accumulation and legitimation, state intervention has also been an arena of class conflict.

Finally, what of the *Federal government*? Historically, its direct intervention in the urban development process has been minimal, but an important change took place in 1972. The Labor government, coming to office at least partly because of its emphasis on urban reform and its consequent appeal to marginal urban electorates, was strongly committed to a more interventionist approach. Its principal vehicle for this, the Department of Urban and Regional Development (or DURD as it was affectionately known) initiated a whole range of policies dealing with intra-urban development. These included area-improvement programmes (designed to assist local governments improve facilities in relatively deprived suburbs), provision of expenditure to deal with backlogs in the provision of sewerage, the establishment of Land Commissions (seeking to stabilise the price of urban land) and direct purchase of housing in areas such as Glebe in Sydney (in order to maintain low-income housing in inner-city areas). A number of assessments of DURD's strategy have been made (T. Logan 1979; M. Logan 1978; Sandercock 1983*b*; Lloyd and Troy 1981).

Some see DURD as a challenging attempt to attack the problems of social inequality via urban policy. Others have argued that its policies effectively redefined inequality in terms of spatial issues, and thereby redirected attention away from the roots of inequality in the capitalist mode of production. Still others have pointed to the tendency for the main beneficiaries of some policies to be property developers, speculators and urban planning consultants (Wilmoth 1977). Perhaps the most balanced view is to see DURD as a reformist institution which brought into clearer focus the impediments to a more egalitarian society; economic, political, ideological, administrative (for example, the ongoing conflict with the Treasury). With the benefit of hindsight one must reject the argument that DURD was merely serving the interests of capital by providing the conditions for further capital accumulation in the cities.

Similarly, it would seem rather simplistic to regard DURD simply as an instrument of popular sovereignty, since it exposed fundamental class antagonisms, bureaucratic checks on progressive reform and so on. The evidence would seem most consistent with the view of the state as an arena of class struggle (while itself generating changes in the nature of the class structure through the development of the bureaucracy). Certainly, the changes in policy after the Liberals were returned to office in 1975 indicated a major shift in the balance of forces; DURD was disbanded and direct intervention in urban affairs was minimised (Patience and Head 1979), while the Federal government pursued a general economic strategy which intensified the problems of urban areas. As the report by the Australian Institute of Urban Studies points out, expenditure on the cities was being siphoned off into the major resource-based projects on which the strategy for economic recovery depended (AIUS 1980:15). In the 1980s, as it became clear that the 'resources boom' would not materialise, this tendency for the redirection of capital expenditure became less acute. But the ALP Federal government under the leadership of Bob Hawke did not seek to establish another actively interventionist department like DURD to shape the pattern of urban development.

Conclusion

Within the confines of this chapter it has only been possible to touch lightly on a range of interconnected issues concerned with the state and urban and regional development. Nevertheless, some tentative conclusions are possible.

First, it is difficult to disentangle the effects of the state from the activities of capital. This may appear a rather negative conclusion but it is nonetheless important. It suggests that the distinction which economists have typically drawn between the workings of the pure market economy and the effects of state intervention is untenable in practice. Indeed, the primary characteristic of contemporary capitalism is an integration of capital and the state. This is manifested in a network of personal and institutional links, and in terms of a shared ideology regarding the desirability of economic growth.

Second, given this general situation, our case-study of urban and regional development suggests that the needs of capital, while not always explicitly the key issues in policy formulation, have typically been decisive. A specific aspect of the Australian state which accentuates this tendency is the Federal structure which increases the potential for capital to play off elements in the state apparatus against one another. The more general reason is that capital holds the whip hand because the failure to provide the conditions for rapid capital accumulation generates economic crisis. Improved urban planning and decentralisation objectives have both been sacrificed in practice to the extent they have been seen as running counter to business interests. This is particularly apparent in the context of the late 1970s and early 1980s where the restructuring of capital coupled with the fiscal crisis of the state has made for particularly adverse impacts on the cities, and on working-class urban communities in particular (Stilwell 1980:Chapters 7 and 8; Schultz 1985).

Third, it should be stressed that, despite these interdependencies, there does exist some scope for the state to pursue urban and regional policies which serve non-capitalist interests. It is possible to interpret policies to improve the housing and health of urban citizens as serving the needs of capital, but it is difficult to place the same interpretation on all the policies of DURD with its strong commitment to redistributive measures. This suggests that the state is better viewed as an arena of class struggle than as automatically serving the needs of capital.

Chapter 5
The city, state and resource development in Western Australia

Elizabeth Harman

Introduction

There is a widespread piece of conventional wisdom which says that Perth is doing well from contemporary mining booms in Western Australia. This chapter is a critique of that assumption and can be read at two levels. First, it can be read for the empirical evidence provided on the impact of resource development on Perth. In writing the chapter however, I have been equally concerned with a problem of theory — namely, the uncritical application of a centre-periphery notion (whether orthodox or class-based) to explain the relationship between Perth and its regions. Since the richest of these ideas are those derived from world-system and dependency theories, the analysis can be read at a second level which primarily addresses the extent to which Perth can be understood as one link in a chain of dependency relations.

Among social scientists, the assumption that Perth is a 'winner' is quite probably derived from models which describe the metropolis as dominant in a regional system. Although the specific details vary, some version of the centre-periphery relationship in which cities enjoy advantages over their hinterlands are explicit in central place theory, urban base models, the notion of cumulative causation, Canadian staples theories and the dependency theories associated with explanations of Third World development. This dominance is assumed to be greatly strengthened where a city is cleary primate, as Perth is in Western Australia, the size ratio between Perth and Bunbury, the second largest centre, is now one to forty-three. It is equally well recognised, however, that while Perth may enjoy an obvious superiority at the State and regional level, it occupies a peripheral position in national and international economies. Nationally, Perth is subordinate to the financial and manufacturing bases of Melbourne and Sydney. The eastern metropolises are, in turn, seen as subordinate to Tokyo, London and New York in the international circuits of capital. The precise terms in which the international relations of dominance-

An earlier version of this chapter was presented to the Pacific Regional Science Association Conference at Surfer's Paradise, August 1981. In this present form, it is based on Williams, P. (ed.) (1983) Chapter 6 in *Social Process and the City*, by kind permission of George Allen & Unwin.

dependence are described depends on the historical period and theoretical perspective. Descriptions range from theories of colonisation which subordinate Australia to England to more recent notions such as the 'Pacific-rim' thesis which gives Japan a dominant role, while Mullins (1980), has combined the two in his discussion of 'old' and 'new' dependency relations.

Given this pattern, it is very tempting to assume that the impact of post-war mining developments in Western Australia can be analysed using the notion of a chain or hierarchy of power relations linking successively stronger classes within larger geographic regions. The notion of a hierarchy of dependency relations obviously has its origins in Frank's description of the patterns of Latin American development as a chain of metropolis-satellite relations in which *class* relations coincide with regional, national and international *geographies* (Frank 1969). On the surface, an analogous model seems to provide a simple and elegant expression of the observed patterns of urban and regional relationships in Western Australia and Australia. (For an extended discussion of these theories see the original chapter in Williams 1983.)

An interest in the urban and regional implications of Australian resource development has only emerged in recent years as it has become evident that the combined effects of mining and energy investment on the one hand, and de-industrialisation on the other, may be reshaping the economy and geography of this country.

It seems an opportune time, then, to consider the applicability of a model of urban and regional relations based on the centre-periphery notions which dominate so much of the literature. This chapter presents an examination of relationships which have evolved between Perth and its resource-rich hinterland in the Pilbara, Kimberley and Darling Ranges in the context of mineral development since the 1960s. The basic thesis is that the metropolitan-dominance relations which are depicted both in the centre-periphery notion and its elaboration as a chain or hierarchy are *not* appropriate for understanding the tendencies which are affecting Perth. The major problem is at the State level. There is no real dispute with the view that Perth is subordinate to the eastern metropolitan seaboard, although not all communications linking Western Australia with the rest of the world necessarily go via the east as the idea of a linked chain would suggest.

The central argument is that the term 'dominance' gives a misleading impression of the role played by Perth in resource development and the benefits enjoyed by metropolitan residents. When dominance is defined solely in demographic terms then Perth is certainly dominant. It is not only primate—it is still capturing the greatest share of the State's population growth and annually has increased its proportion of the total population. In 1977, 70.5 per cent of people lived in the city; 70.8 per cent in 1978; 71.1 per cent in 1979. But dominance is much more than number of people. It assumes a bias towards the metropolis in economic, social and political terms—for example, as the centre of innovation; technology and industry; in unequal exchange relations; in its ability to extract surplus from the regions; and as the focus of class and political power. Historically, Perth may have enjoyed such status in its role as port and service centre for the agricultural sector which dominated the economy prior to 1950. Even then, however, it more likely corresponded to some form of dependent urbanism acting as a channel for the export of surplus in the sense outlined by Harvey (1973:232). Indeed, Perth has never had a well-defined indigenous ruling class of sufficient import in this century to control its own development (Bolton 1972) and the locus of economic power has been elsewhere. Traditionally, the economy has been oriented to the export of raw materials (originally agricultural and now the export of minerals). The small secondary sector which existed prior to 1950 was primarily based on food processing. With the advent of the modern phase of mining in the 1960s, Perth's position as 'dominant' over other regions has not strengthened despite the impression given by the growth in metropolitan population; it has, on the contrary weakened.

The main argument is considered in two sections: one relating to the nature of state intervention in resource development in Western Australia; the other the logic of capitalist enterprise in mining and auxiliary activities in the State. The discussion of government policy serves to demonstrate how the activities of the state may interfere with any tendency for Perth to capture special advantages from regionally-based mining. The government has sought to attract investment by (among other things) financing infrastructure associated with major resource projects. There has been a consequent shift of public funds: first, from welfare to productive economic activity; second, from service-dependent populations to private capital; and third, from city to region.

Part of the government's rationale has been that resource-related expenditures will return economic activity, investment, jobs and income to the metropolitan area as a result of multipliers stimulated by the mining activity. The irony is that the operation of the major enterprises in the mining sector, in fact, impedes this process. The mining transnationals make their major decisions and relocate profits out of the State. More important, with respect to State policy, the major contractors and purchase suppliers are not local. As a result, the Perth-based manufacturing sector has not been growing as strongly as the government has suggested (E. Harman 1981*a*).

Perth has, nonetheless, had a significant role to play. In response to the needs of companies based in the east or overseas the metropolitan area has become a clearing house—a sort of commercial siphon or brokerage for business transactions which involve, on the one hand an inflow of investment, and on the other, an outflow of commodities, contracts, purchase orders and profits directly or indirectly derived from mining in the mineral-rich outer areas of Western Australia. Both private firms and public agencies are engaged in providing export-led services and together they account for a significant growth in tertiary, or more properly, quaternary employment over the last two decades.

In this service capacity, Perth has no special advantage over its hinterland. It simply fulfils a different function for mining capital. Nor are activities in the resource areas necessarily dependent on decisions taken in Perth. City and hinterland perform specialised functional roles, but are equally dependent on decisions taken outside the State and internationally by the brokers controlling activities associated with mining. In limited ways, the city does appear to be dominant (as in its hold on the population). In other ways, other regions have the upper hand (for example, in the balance of political power). An uncritical application of a centre-periphery model at the level of the State ignores these tendencies and countertendencies.

The role of the state in resource development in Western Australia: infrastructure policy

The contemporary boom in mining in Western Australia dates from the lifting of the Federal embargo on iron ore in 1960. The decade of the 1960s was an iron ore and nickel boom focused on the goldfields and Pilbara. In the 1970s, the focus shifted to gas from the North-West Shelf, bauxite in the south-west and potential diamond production in the Kimberleys. With the exception of a brief interregnum (1972–74) a Liberal-National Country Party coalition has ruled throughout the period with Sir Charles Court playing the major role in defining the government's development strategies, first as the responsible Minister and later as Premier.

There were two keystones to the Liberal policy, both of which have had important repercussions on Perth. The main instrument the government used to encourage mining and industrial investment in the State was an incentives package combining (a) limited royalties, (b) State control of labour and community opposition, and (c) State subsidies to production—notably in the form of energy pricing and provision of infrastructure. This section will focus specifically on the implications for Perth of the State's infrastructure policy. The other keystone to the policy has been the notion of multipliers, linkages or spin-offs from resource development. Western Australians have been persuaded that while the main mining projects may not produce many jobs and may initially be costly, ultimately there will be a payoff in the form of a highly-expanded job market, higher personal incomes and a strong manufacturing sector. These two keystones, the package of investment incentives and the ideological use of the multiplier, were the State's response to the competing and often contradictory pressures of accumulation and legitimation, or the need simultaneously to accommodate both the interests of companies and of voters (E. Harman 1981*b*).

Historically, the State has provided basic social infrastructure. Schemes which can be directly tied to the needs of a particular mining company, however, probably have their origins at Wittenoom in the 1940s when the State, under the initiative of a senior bureaucrat (Dumas), financed the construction of 150 houses for Australian Blue Asbestos (Layman 1981). Not all projects have had this type of support. In practice, projects which were more remote or which were judged to be marginal were given State support.

The infrastructure policy is costly and two tendencies derived from these costs have become increasingly evident in Perth:

- there has been a shift in the proportion of public funding for basic services out of the metropolitan area to the advantage of the resource regions;
- the price of major domestic services like gas, electricity and transport has risen sharply, coincident with the government taking on largely resource-related infrastructure commitments.

It should be noted at the outset that accurate information on the changing distribution of public expenditure in the State (by sector and region) is not easy to come by in Western Australia. The

Figure 5.1 Metropolitan share of public and private building, 1968–80

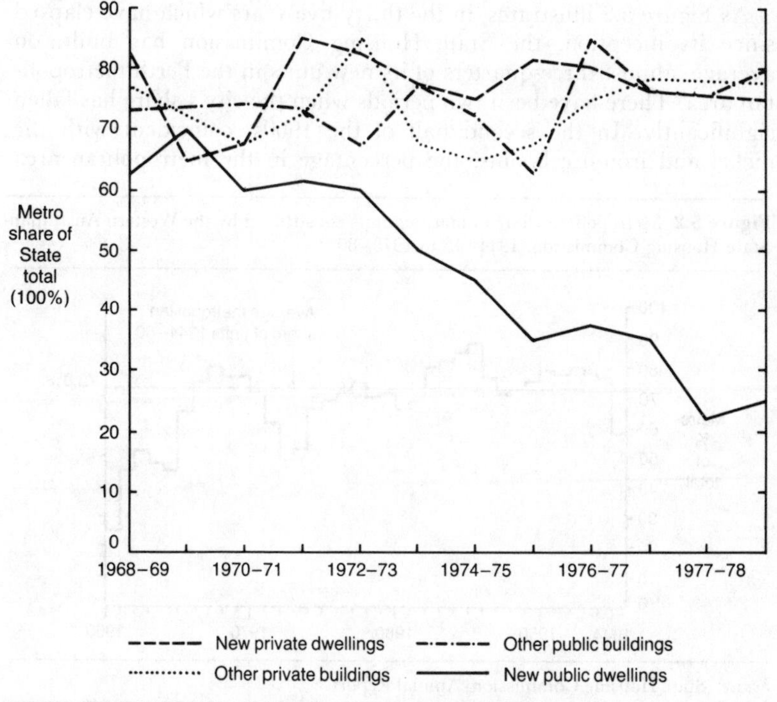

ambiguities surrounding the infrastructure programme and related expenditures were created in part by the structure of the Western Australian bureaucracy. The co-ordination of policy relating to major projects was handled by a non-statutory body, the Planning and Co-ordinating Authority chaired by the Department of Resources Development. Financial aspects were handled directly by Treasury. A sub-committee of the Planning and Co-ordinating Authority, the Townsites Development Committee, supervised (at least nominally) the greater part of State expenditure on social infrastructure in the towns. The activities of this group lay completely outside public scrutiny (see Bowman 1979, Chapter 4; Western Australia, Department of Town Planning 1982).

Figure 5.1 is based on buildings approvals and refers specifically to building programmes. It is clear that in the last decade public housing in the metropolitan area has received a declining share of public funds, capturing almost 70 per cent in 1969–70, but less than 25 per cent in 1979–80. This is clearly the outcome of deliberate policy decisions and not simply an aberration which has affected all construction. It might, for example, be argued that resource projects have buoyed up non-metropolitan economies and diverted the market as a whole. However, this is clearly not the case. Throughout the decade, the private sector has committed a constant 65 to 85 per cent of expenditures to Perth.

As Figure 5.2 illustrates, in the thirty-five years which have elapsed since its inception, the State Housing Commission has built, on average, almost three-quarters of its new units in the Perth metropolitan area. There have been two periods when the city's share has fallen significantly. In the second half of the 1960s, coincident with the nickel and iron-ore booms, the percentage in the metropolitan area

Figure 5.2 Metropolitan share of housing units constructed by the Western Australian State Housing Commission, 1944–45 to 1979–80

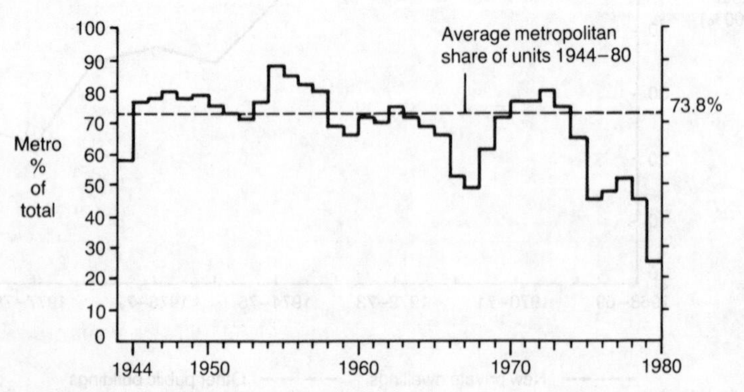

Source: State Housing Commission, Annual Reports

dropped to around 50 per cent. And again, since the mid-1970s, coincident with projects related to bauxite and gas, Perth's share has fallen to the point where, in 1979–80, it received just over a quarter of new State Housing Commission units. This contrasts strongly with the peak in the first half of the 1970s when the Whitlam government's commitment to urban development, and the rapid growth of the city itself, both had a positive effect on the metropolitan housing programme.

Alternative explanations such as the Commission's assumptions of responsibility for Aboriginal housing, Federal and State reduction of housing funds and the Commission claims of metropolitan 'oversupply' do not account for the magnitude of the metropolitan loss. Funds have been specifically earmarked for supporting resource developments. For example, in 1970, a major recipient of State Housing Commission funding in direct support of a major project, was Port Hedland. Eighty-six houses were built by the government and a new town (South Hedland) created to house workers associated with the

Figure 5.3 Metropolitan share of infrastructure expenditure by department, 1959–60 to 1980–81

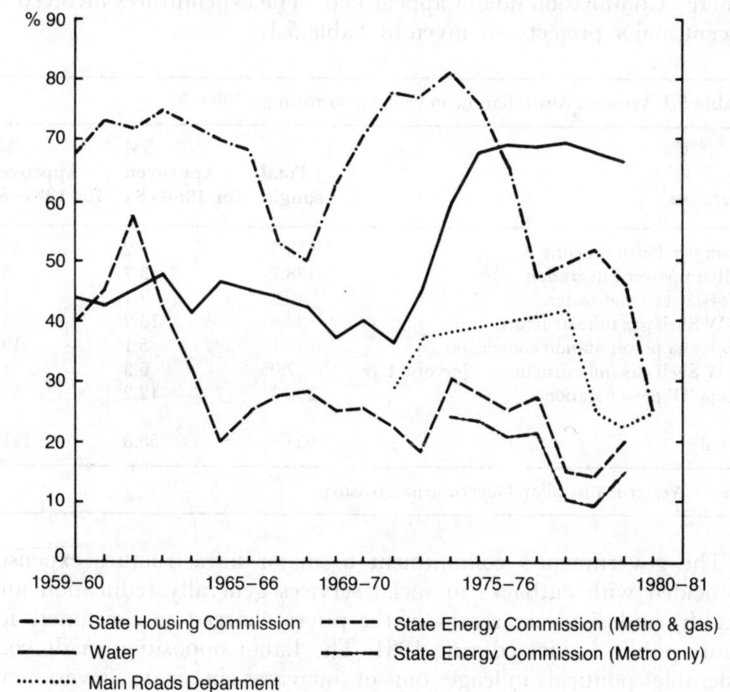

Source: Departments, Annual Reports

port operations of Mt Newman and Goldsworthy. On 1 April 1978, twenty million dollars was specially earmarked for a North-West housing programme to provide facilities in the Pilbara and the Kimberleys. This was described as part of the State's planning to cope with demands associated with major resource projects. Other resource-based communities in which the State has provided housing include Karratha, Wickham, Koolyanobbing and Capel. State housing is likely to play a greater rather than a lesser role in the future.

Figure 5.3 shows the trends in the metropolis' share of expenditure in other service areas. The city's share of expenditure on water and sewerage has shown a marked improvement over the period—a fact which may be accounted for both by urban priorities of the Whitlam government and by the increasing pressure on Perth's water supplies in the 1970s. A slight but discernable decline in the share of road, electricity and gas expenditure is apparent. It is useful to keep in mind that Figure 5.3 is a conservative estimate of the shift in expenditures out of Perth. The infrastructure programme was given its greatest impetus in the second half of the 1970s and major expenditures are not yet evident in Annual Reports. It is clear that the major resource-related commitments made, for example, by the State Energy Commission do not appear here. The expenditures involved in recent major projects are given in Table 5.1.

Table 5.1 Western Australian Loan Council borrowings, 1980–82

Purpose	Total sought	$M Approved for 1980–81	$M Approved for 1981–82
Dampier-Perth pipeline	553.3	9.2	35.5
Pilbara power integration	138.7	3.7	5.9
Worsley rail and water	46.2	7.1	1.6
N-W Shelf gas infrastructure	38.6	13.2	4.8
Kwinana power station conversion	39.1	5.1	19.0
N-W Shelf gas infrastructure—Jervoise Bay	7.05	6.3	1.6
Muja 'D' power station	236.3	12.2	52.8
Total	1055.6	56.8	121.2

Source: Western Australian Government Treasury

The government's commitment to major infrastructure expenses coincided with cutbacks in social services generally (education and health) and sharp increases in the prices charged to consumers for many public services during 1981. The Labor opposition made considerable political mileage out of increases in State government charges which they calculated as rising much faster than the rate of inflation. From 1980–81 to 1981–82 the average family faced an average weekly increase for State charges of $10, from $31.11 to $41.1 (M. Naylor, personal communication). Rising costs and cutbacks in services like education funding were interpreted as a product, in part, of the carrying costs associated with the infrastructure policy and unwillingness by the Liberals to levy significant mining royalties. However, the government itself charged that the rises must be laid at the feet of the Federal government's constraints on finance. The intricacies of State budgeting and Federal-State financing make it difficult to apportion the blame in any precise way. Nonetheless, it seemed clear that the public costs associated with the infrastructure policy were hitting consumers, notably metropolitan consumers, very hard.

This section has provided evidence (admittedly partial and limited) that seems to suggest there has been a shift in the distribution of public expenditures on infrastructure over the period of resource development. Prior to 1960 there was already a predilection to use State monies to provide supporting services and infrastructure for major development initiatives — the State's investment in Wittenoom in the 1940s and Kwinana in the early 1950s are cases in point, though the history of such intervention is earlier than this (Bolton 1981). This role was stepped up with the onset of the contemporary mineral projects. Brown (1981) has argued that increased public expenditures on resource areas are evident even in the 1960s when the major development agreements seemed to leave most infrastructure financing in the hands of the private sector. Certainly, by the 1970s the Liberal government was quite explicit in its pursuit of funding to support an active role in infrastructure provision.

As a result of this, there appears to have been a shift in the pattern of public expenditures away from services and facilities required to meet welfare needs in favour of those used to support the needs of labour and capital in the major mining areas. To use O'Connor's categories (J. O'Connor 1973) this has meant a shift out of social consumption (policies contributing mainly to the social and material support of the population) towards social investment (policies contributing mainly to private-sector profitably through provision of the necessary means of production).

There are at least three sets of factors which any explanation of this shift in the infrastructure programme must recognise and each level of explanation is embedded in the next. First, there is need to recognise the frontier nature of Western Australia's geography and history of development. It was until 1950 largely agrarian and until the 1960s was dependent on Federal revenue-sharing arrangements. Industrialisation at Kwinana from 1952 and the mineral boom since, have wrought a dramatic change in thinking in the State (Layman 1982; E. Harman 1981*b*). Mining is seen as the key to the State's industrial development, its economic viability, levels of public and private wealth, and to the opening up of relatively-uninhabited territory. The package of investment incentives including the infrastructure policy, is a concrete expression of the partnership now forged between the State government and large-scale mining interests in Western Australia (E. Harman 1981*b*). Galligan (1981) has called this the 'rentier' phase in resource policy and contrasts it with an 'entrepreneurial' phase in which governments are much more committed to the collection of resource revenues and the use of such revenues for public investment in productive activities.

The second point to note is that the mining developments in the State since the 1960s have been mega-projects involving major Australian and transnational companies. The capital controlled by such companies is highly mobile and the companies have become remarkably adept over the last quarter-century in creating the notion that there is an international capital shortage and forcing governments to compete with each other for investment. The infrastructure policy has evolved in Western Australia (as it has elsewhere in Australia and Canada) as a means of underbidding other jurisdictions.

The third and final point is that the priority given to the infrastructure policy has been greatly strengthened in the 1970s in the context of the international economic crisis and the belief that profit rates are falling. By the mid-1970s, the Western Australian government felt obliged to contribute to infrastructure costs to offset a decline in profit rates which threatened, in the words of Court, to 'prove Marx right' (Court 1978) and which brought the average return in the mining sector to a 'dangerously low' 12.6 per cent by 1980 (Court 1980). The increasing tendency for the state to provide basic infrastructure in advanced capitalist societies has been widely discussed in literature on the role of the state in general and in cities and settlements in particular (see, for example, J. O'Connor 1973; Saunders 1981: Chapter 8). This practice is seen as both a cause and a consequence of the crises of capitalism. Hence, what was originally conceived in Western Australia by Dumas and Court as a pragmatic policy designed to cope with conditions associated with specific projects, can now be seen in terms of international trends affecting advanced capitalist states.

The shifts in public expenditures from social consumption (welfare) to social investment (support of production) has an important geographical corollary. Since most of the supporting services are required in resource-rich regions, there has been diversion of funds out of the metropolitan area relative to the mineral-rich localities.

This would appear to contradict the logic of dependency models which view the state as promoting metropolitan dominance. The diversion of public funds out of social consumption and from Perth is evidence of the extent to which the position of most urban-based classes (welfare, working and middle-class groups) has weakened over time relative to capital-owning classes with interests in major mining ventures and auxiliary industries. That the majority of these are not located in Perth is evident from knowledge of the transnational ownership structures of most of the major companies and from evidence of income leakage out of the State (F. Harman 1981).

There is one conceivable way in which the diversion of public funds, loss of services and increased costs in Perth could still be seen as ultimately and indirectly contributing to metropolitan dominance. This is the situation where the outflow of public funds and rise in costs is more than compensated for in the form of return flows of economic activity in the secondary and tertiary sectors via the multiplier and spin-off. This is the prime benefit which Western Australians have been led to expect will flow to them from mineral development. To promote dominance, there must not only be a faster growth in the metropolitan economy *vis-a-vis* the regional economy — the growth must occur in key areas which will facilitate the extraction of mineral surplus by Perth-based interests (for example, the provision of expensive services to mining) or which promote the city's position as the centre of industry and innovation (for example, technologically-advanced local industries). Whether this compensation is, in fact, apparent in Perth is the question addressed in the next section.

Perth as a commercial clearing house

According to the State government, the benefits of mineral development would accure to the *present* generation (over 70 per cent of whom live in Perth) in the form of new job opportunities and higher incomes generated by multiplier effects. Benefits to *later* generations would exist in the form of a stable, diversified and relatively autonomous economy, including a strong manufacturing sector. Implicit in the arguments made by Sir Charles Court was an underlying theory of development which envisaged the economy moving through three stages: (a) an export-oriented staples economy dependent on foreign capital and skills; (b) a diversified second stage when multipliers and linkages and externalities encourage the growth of other sectors, and which transform the extractive base towards resource upgrading and manufacturing; and (c) the final stage of economic independence or autarky when the local economy has acquired its own indigenous capital and skills (E. Harman 1981*b*, Figure 4:185).

The health of the Western Australian manufacturing sector is a key to the whole discussion — not only because it is the pivot of the government development policy and an important means by which benefits should be returned to Perth, but because it has been seen as an important part of the definition of a dominant centre in most uses of the centre-periphery notion.

Manufacturing in Western Australia has been, and still is, overwhelmingly concentrated in Perth (84 per cent of employment), but the sector has always been very small, employing only 12.5 per cent of the labour force in the State compared to 19.7 per cent in Australia as a whole (1980 figures). It has largely focused on the processing of local resources (agricultural, forest and mineral products). Far from seeing the growth of a strong, diversified sector in Perth over the last two decades, manufacturing has: (a) declined in importance; (b) become even more specialised and dependent on the export sector; and (c) the regions, not Perth, have received the larger share of growth in the metals-related sectors.

The decline in the relative importance of the manufacturing sector is evident in employment figures. The 12.5 per cent of the Western Australian labour force working in manufacturing in 1980 represents a decline from 18.8 per cent in 1966 (see Figures 5.4 and 5.5). The decline is, of course, relative. There has not been an absolute loss in jobs as there has been in the eastern States, but in fact, a small increase. But this has been tiny; a mere 4000 jobs providing less than 2 per cent of the more than 200 000 new jobs created between 1966 and 1980.

Not all manufacturing groups have performed identically. A specialised metals-related sector has emerged encouraged by mining activity. This is not, however, necessarily a step towards diversifica-

Figure 5.4 Employment change by industry sector, Western Australia civilian employee series, 1971–80 by percentage

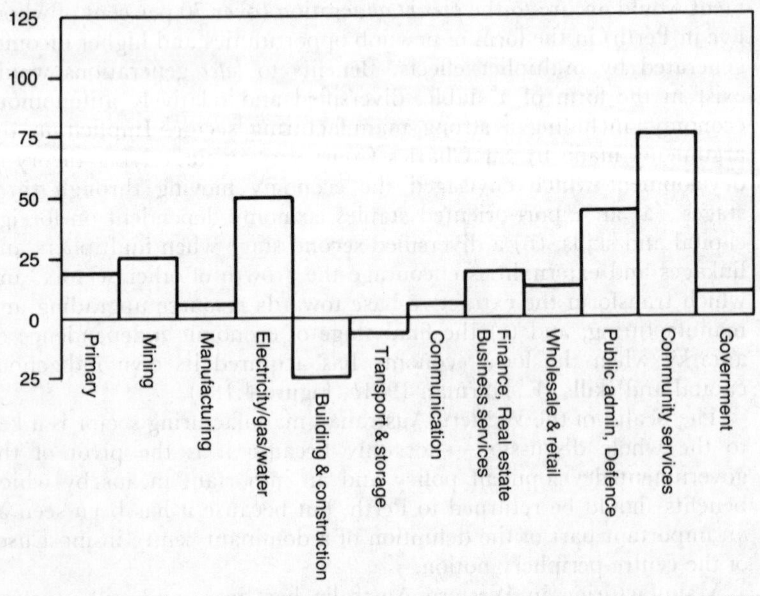

Source: ABS

Figure 5.5 Employment change by industry sector, Western Australia, census, 1961–76 by percentage

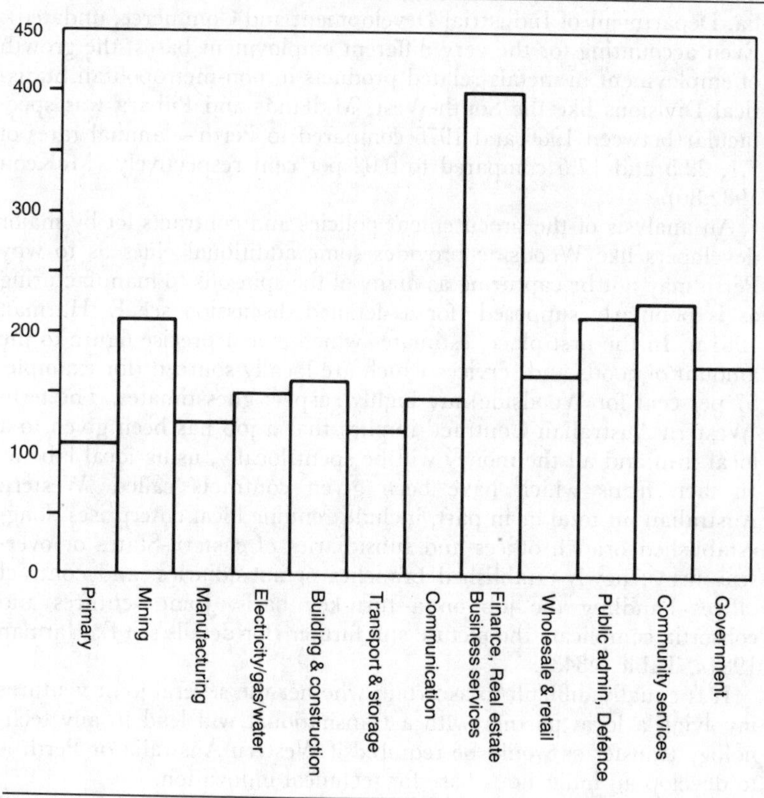

Source: Census

tion and economic dependence. The group is *more*, not less, dependent on the actions of the major transnationals controlling mining. The processing plants are owned by the same companies and are a part of their vertically-integrated structure. In addition, the metal-fabricating shops are very small in size.

Nor have the forces shaping the manufacturing sector encouraged metropolitan dominance. Perth has *not* been the major beneficiary of that growth in manufacturing which has been stimulated by the mining sector. Most of the resource up-grading is done in the regions and Perth's share of employment in most of the metals-related classes has fallen slightly over the last decade. While manufacturing accounted for 23 per cent of metropolitan employment at the 1961 census, by 1976 it had fallen to just over 16 per cent.

The South-West Statistical Division now has close to 10 per cent of the State's manufacturing employment, and important minerals-related activities such as mineral-sands processing and alumina production in the vicinity have helped make Bunbury a growth centre now surpassing Kalgoorlie as the State's second city (Western Australia, Department of Industrial Development and Commerce, undated). Even accounting for the very different employment bases, the growth of employment in metals-related products in non-metropolitan Statistical Divisions like the South-West, Midlands and Pilbara was spectacular between 1966 and 1976 compared to Perth—annual rates of 7.1, 22.5 and 17.5 compared to 0.02 per cent respectively (McKeon 1982:80).

An analysis of the procurement policies and contracts let by major developers like Woodside provides some additional clues as to why Perth may not be capturing as many of the spin-offs to manufacturing as is popularly supposed (for a detailed discussion see E. Harman 1981*a*). In the first place, estimates which give a precise figure to the amount of goods and services which are locally sourced (for example, 57 per cent for Woodside) are highly suspect guesstimates. The term 'Western Australian Contract' implies that a job has been given to a local firm and all the money will be spent locally, using local labour. In fact, firms which have been given contracts called 'Western Australian' in total or in part, include genuine local enterprises, long-established branch offices and subsidiaries of eastern-States or overseas firms; newly-established branches or subsidiaries; and contract offices handling the job on a turn-key basis. Joint ventures and consortia complicate the picture still further (for details see E. Harman 1981*a*, Table 5:343).

It is equally difficult to ascertain whether the several joint ventures involving a local partner with a transnational will lead to any technology transfer as would be required if Western Australia or Perth is to develop an indigenous base for technical innovation.

From Perth's perspective, most of the activity is concentrated outside the metropolitan area, notably in the Burrip Peninsula, although Karratha and Geraldton also feature. Some of the contradictions in this situation have been evident in the complaints by the Confederation of Western Australian Industry (representing local companies) that insufficient contracts have been let in the city. This has put local capitalists in alliance with the Trades and Labour Council also making representations to the government to get more local work from project contracts.

While the picture for manufacturing may be a little bleak, the same is not true for the tertiary sector in Perth. Over 80 per cent of new job creation in the State since 1966 has been in the tertiary sector with the private sector providing some 98 000 new positions (of a total of more than 200 000) while the public sector contributed a further 73 000. In fact, the *rate* of growth was fastest in public sector jobs and is evident in the strong increase in employment in public administration and defence, community services, electricity, gas and water (Figure 5.4). The rate of growth in privately-supplied services differs according to source and time-period. But it would appear that finance, real estate and business services have shown the strongest growth since the 1960s, outpacing even the growth in public sector classes according to Census changes (Figure 5.5). Over 70 per cent of tertiary employment exists in the metropolitan area and the expanding skyline has mirrored the unprecedented expansion of office space, notably from the late 1960s, and again in the early 1980s. The popular conception that this expansion is directly attributable to mining is reinforced by the prominence of Mt Newman House, Hamersley House and Allendale Square (Woodside) on St George's Terrace.

To what extent the growth in services can be explained as an outcome of mineral development is difficult to estimated precisely. The government's own input-output analysis of the alumina-bauxite industry concluded that the multiplier effect was much the greatest in services (Western Australia, Department of Resources Development 1980). It is also now recognised that an export-led service sector can provide the foundation for trade in newly-developed skills and services. The problem is that the tertiary sector has been taking an increasing proportion of Australian jobs throughout this century, with the real impetus coming from the expansion of quaternary or information-processing activities (Wilson 1980:278). The only evidence we have that contemporary mineral projects may now be giving this national trend an extra push in the resource-rich States, is by looking at comparative figures.

McKeon (1982:27) used Census figures (1966, 1971 and 1976) to demonstrate that while all other States declined in their share of Australian employment in the tertiary sector (or held even), Queensland increased its share from 14.1 per cent to 15.1, while Western Australia went up from 7.5 to 8.8 per cent. Likewise, Jarvie (1981) used the Census to show changes in tertiary employment by metropolitan area and also showed that while the percentage change in New South Wales and Victorian cities between 1971 and 1976, was 7.0 and 12.13 per cent respectively, it was a much stronger 19.8 and 20.9 per cent in Queensland and Western Australia. The problem with all these figures is that the increased share of tertiary employment taken by the peripheral resource-rich States parallels a similar increase in population shares. Both, of course, may be explained by expectations and needs associated with mining developments.

While the evidence is clearly circumstantial, it does suggest that Perth may be handling an increasing level of administrative population, directly and indirectly related to mineral development. For the major mining companies, the city is a commercial siphon or clearing house for the paperwork surrounding the inflow of investment destined for new projects and the outflow of commodities, purchase orders or profits. Major decisions may still be taken outside the State, orders ultimately sourced and profits relocated externally. But all of this still requires brokerage services in the local metropolis and hence the expansion of office space and employment. Property services are also likely to have increased to meet both the real and speculative demand for residential and commercial real estate. At least part of the growth in the public sector may be attributed to the greatly-expanded role of departments and agencies involved in supporting the major projects (for example, Treasury, Department of Resources Development, State Energy Commission, State Housing Commission). To ascertain the veracity of any of these speculations would require much more detailed historical analyses of local banking and other service activities and/or econometric analyses. Nonetheless, the suggestions paint a reasonable scenario.

Conclusions

If Perth does play the role of broker or commercial service centre, then it is functionally tied to mineral developments in the regions. And while city and region each have a specialised role to play, it is difficult to establish substantive grounds for calling Perth dominant or especially advantaged in this arrangement. Instead, the city qualifies for the description of some form of dependent urbanism. Perth plays a necessary role in *circulation* relating to mining in the regions, but a limited role in production. Perth-based firms, offices and agencies handle the movement of both money transactions and shipment of other commodities (that is, the inflow of private and public investment and the outflow of profits, and the inflow of purchase orders and outflow of minerals and mineral products). Firms engaged in other activities related to the resource sector are limited to some fabricating, engineering, design work and construction. In their role as siphons, city-based interests perform a relatively low-level function and have no real power to extract surplus. Union workers in the resource regions have more power to extract a share in the form of higher wage demands than city service workers, in both the private and public sector many of whom are women in low-paid non-managerial positions. (The power of Western Australian mining unions is still not sufficient however to prevent wage levels being lower than eastern-State equivalents.)

This interpretation of Perth's role helps to explain why so many Perth residents have difficulty in matching their personal reality with the statements that Western Australia is booming, is rich or is the 'State of Excitement'. It does explain why, despite the fact that economic activity is generating wealth in the State, residents are receiving relatively low incomes per capita compared to other Australians (F. Harman 1981). It explains why in this State (unlike others in the country) per capita incomes in metropolis and region are virtually equivalent (Table 5.2). In most States, urban incomes are much higher (a basic prediction of most centre-periphery models). It helps also to explain why the local social welfare agencies feel hard-pressed, as is evident in the startling increase in the demand for emergency relief services since 1975 and especially during 1981 (Western Australia Department of Community Welfare 1981).

Table 5.2 Metropolitan and non-metropolitan incomes by State

	Annual personal incomes 1976 (1)			**Mean income, 1973–74 (2)**		
	Metro $	**Non-metro $**	**Metro as % of non-metro**	**Capital city $**	**Rest of State $**	**Capital as % of rest of State**
NSW	4977	3567	139.5	4220	3410	123.7
Vic.	5144	3399	151.3	4230	3730	113.4
Qld	4496	3674	122.4	3670	3780	97.1
SA	4562	3777	120.8	3700	3780	97.9
Tas.	4395	3687	119.2	3730	3650	102.2
ACT	6475	4631	139.8	N.A.	N.A.	—
NT	6750	4656	145.0	N.A.	N.A.	—
WA	4534	4562	99.4	3800	4250	89.4

Sources: 1) Census 1976
2) ABS Catalogue No. 6504, 1973–74 (based on survey of consumer income and expenditure)

In 1982, there seemed little doubt that Perth was not a boom-town. Media headlines like 'Perth on a Tightrope after Resources Bust' (*Financial Review*, 24 March 1982:16) are a testimony to this. But even prior to this, in 1980–81 when it was apparent that a great deal of investment was occurring in the State and wealth was being generated, the evidence of any boom in Perth was conflicting and ambigious. On the one hand, there was an explosion in planned office construction and well-publicised sales of expensive prestige housing. On the other hand, the housing market overall seemed depressed in Western Australia, compared with the relative boom in building in Queensland (Indicative Planning Council 1981).

The contradictions in this description dissolve if we accept that population growth is as much a function of the expectation of boom conditions as of any actual increase in long-term job and income opportunities (a condition reminiscent of the notion of the boom as a self-fulfilling prophecy advanced by Copithorne 1980; see also, Daly Chapter 19 in this volume). The expansion in office space reflects both speculative expectations and the real increase in the demand for commercial services associated with Perth's role as a clearing house. The housing market is depressed especially at the middle and lower end of the price ranges by high interest rates and the fact that Perth residents have no special income advantage which would reduce this impediment.

The tendencies shaping this relationship between Perth and the rest of Western Australia since 1960, and the onset of the contemporary mining booms, do not appear to have given Perth much more than an expanded skyline and a larger population. It is difficult to find substantive evidence that the city has established the kind of metropolitan dominance and pattern of dependency theory. The lack of dominance appears to have come about as a result of both State policies which have directed public funds out of the metropolitan area, and the operations of mining capital which do not conform (except in superficial ways) to the logic assumed in the centre-periphery models.

Section III:
The conceptualisation of planning

Chapter 6
Urban planning, policy and management

Max Neutze

Introduction

Urban planning is a well established field of activity: it is incorporated in legislation and is the recognised activity of special purpose public authorities and a profession with its own training courses and professional organisations. In recent years people from other disciplines have taken an increasing interest in urban policy, and have included planning among the aspects of urban policy under discussion. Planning has also been criticised by those who believe that it has been ineffective in achieving government objectives. They see the need for more management of cities and less emphasis on long-term planning. The first section of this chapter distinguishes between planning, policy and management and shows how they are related.

The second, and larger section of the chapter attempts to focus the debate about urban policy by distinguishing the different levels of questions which different writers have been asking and by showing how they relate to one another. It seems useful to distinguish ideological, political, operational and technical questions. People arguing at different levels are unlikely to come to grips with one another and recognise, let alone resolve, their differences.

Planning, policy and management

Among the meanings of the verb 'to plan' given by the Oxford Dictionary, that which comes closest to its meaning in relation to urban policy is 'to arrange beforehand'. Planning is essentially an activity that is oriented to some future result. There is a sense, of course, in which all activities take a certain sequence: they are planned, carried out and then produce a result. But plans that are concerned with where urban facilities, services, housing and the like will be located are — or should be — always concerned, not only with

An earlier draft of this chapter was presented in the Architecture and Urban Planning section of ANZAAS, Adelaide, May 1980. I am grateful for comments and suggestions from Patrick Troy, Peter Harrison, Ian Alexander and Hal Kendig (M.N.). Originally published in *Australian Journal of Public Administration*, XLI(2) June 1982 and reproduced here by kind permission of the Editors.

the immediate future but also with the long-term future. Streets, houses, parks, schools, shops and factories last for a long time and cannot easily be moved, so it is very important to look well into the future in deciding where, and how large to build them, and what kind should be built.

Because urban buildings and infrastructure nearly always stay in the same place for a long time, and because the spatial relationships between them have a great influence on how a city functions, the term 'planning' has special significance for location—whether at an urban or regional scale. If someone is known simply as a 'planner' it is almost certain that he is a town planner—a 'planning authority' is concerned with urban or regional planning. Economic planners, corporate planners and service planners are seen to be special cases. Of course other kinds of planners, such as transport, water and other service planners are also concerned with location. The distinctive feature of 'planners' in the general sense, or land use planners, is that they are concerned with the location of everything—all land uses—and with the spatial relationships between them.

The need to plan future locations (land use) arises from interdependence—the best location for housing depends on where jobs are located and vice-versa—and from the fact that different facilities are installed at different times and by different people, firms and public authorities. The 'plan' provides for them all. If they are located as a result of separate and independent decisions taken at different times by different people the spatial arrangement is unlikely to be particularly efficient or equitable.

It is sometimes useful to distinguish between the making of plans and their implementation. From a semantic point of view the distinction is sensible. 'Arranging beforehand' is not the same thing as carrying out those arrangements. From the point of view of division of labour and making use of diverse skills also, this distinction has advantages. Planning requires vision, imagination, and an ability to grasp the relationships between different elements of the urban fabric. Implementation requires hard-nosed bureaucratic skills, an ability to design and implement controls, to negotiate with government departments and authorities and to cajole businessmen.

It is not surprising that many planners find the making of plans exciting and intellectually and aesthetically challenging, but find implementation a pedestrian and often disheartening chore. Bureaucrats are impatient with plan-making. They see it as woolly and idealistic and believe that it ignores market and political realities. Many worthwhile plans gather dust while decisions about urban development are made in response to current economic and political pressures, with only a cursory bow towards avoiding the worst excesses that can result from unbridled greed.

Many administrators who have become impatient about the visions of the planner can still see the need to maintain some minimum standards and to make allowance for efficient provision of public services. They have proposed that we give less attention to planning and more to urban management (Australian National Commission for UNESCO 1978). Management is primarily concerned with the day-to-day decisions that need to be made about location. It sees a need for collective (public) decisions and sees most of those decisions to be concerned with resource allocation. Hence the tendency of the advocates of urban management to redefine planning as resource allocation in cities.

There is a sense in which plan implementation *is* primarily management, and giving greater attention to urban management is a desirable shift in emphasis towards implementation. Urban management has, in one respect at least, a broader sphere of action than planning. Planning authorities have never been very successful in getting the co-operation of those public authorities responsible for provision of infrastructure services and social services such as education. But urban management regards land use and service location as part of the same problem and all grist to its mill.

In one sense, the advocates of urban management are more guilty of a lack of realism than the advocates of traditional planning. Except in small centres where the local authority is responsible for land use planning and for the provision of services, there are no authorities in Australia which could perform the functions of urban management, and therefore there can be no urban managers. There have been attempts in some State governments to exercise urban management but they have made little progress to date. These attempts are taken up again later in this chapter.

As long as urban management is primarily plan implementation it falls within the traditional planning framework. But if it became independent of planning, and pursued its own separate objectives such as efficiency in the provision of services, outside the land use planning framework, it would become a series of distinct policies rather than any part of urban planning. One of the strengths of urban planning is its holistic approach. It includes economy in the provision of services as one criterion among many in devising plans for the future shape of cities and regions. Without such comprehensive plans to provide criteria for their actions, operational authorities are likely to pursue partial, different and often conflicting objectives.

One of the advantages of urban management, at least in theory, is that it can include other policy instruments as well as land use controls — the main tool available in traditional plan implementation. On the other hand one of the absurdities of the recent discussions of urban management has been the concept of negotiated planning as an alternative to land use controls based on adopted land use plans. Negotiated planning means the use of the power to control land use in negotiating what development rights individual private land owners might be granted, as a means of achieving other policy objectives.

Presumably the outcome of the negotiations is always uncertain when they begin so that the result, in terms of land use, depends on the bargaining positions of the negotiators. While this procedure certainly uses land use controls to achieve public objectives, usually by requiring contributions in cash or kind towards the cost of public facilities, it is not part of planning in the sense of 'arranging beforehand'. Negotiated planning might be loosely described as unplanned planning, or controls without planning: 'wait and see what development is proposed and use the power to control land use to make the best deal you can'.

I would not want to argue in favour of completely rigid land use planning, so that once a plan is adopted it must be adhered to, come hell or high water. But I would argue that in the trade off between predictability and flexibility the long life and fixed location of urban development should push urban planning further towards predictability than most other kinds of planning. To simplify, planning without management is fruitless, but management without planning is pointless. Both statements are over-simplified but they do highlight the fact that each needs the other.

Policy is a much more general term than either planning or management. It encompasses both the objectives sought and the instruments used to achieve those objectives. Both planning and urban management are instruments used to achieve policy objectives. The term 'planning objective' is simply an abbreviation for 'policy objective pursued through planning'.

At the level of policy we need to be concerned both with those measures that are directed at influencing or controlling location and with those which, while mainly concerned with other objectives, still have an effect on location. We also need to ensure that, as far as possible, different measures do not have conflicting effects. Those who analyse spatial aspects of society and the economy, and those who make policy decisions, must concern themselves not only with possible conflicts between different parts of location policy, but also with the operations of the institutions involved in each and with the complementary and competitive relationships between them. The remainder of this chapter deals with aspects of urban (that is, location) policies, and concentrates on policies that have been implemented through planning measures.

The debate about urban policy

The debate about urban policy in general, and planning in particular, has suffered from the fact that the proponents are often arguing at different levels (Parkin 1979:291–4; Kilmartin and Thorns 1978). Some take as given the very aspects of policy which others question. Sometimes economic, social or political arrangements are taken as given because the author approves of them; on other occasions because he or she sees no likelihood that they can be changed. Few academic authors tell us the reason, even on those rare occasions when they spell out what they assume. I hope that this part of the chapter will help clarify this discussion by assisting readers to classify policy discussion into one of several levels. At each level there are two kinds of discussions. The first is analytical; an attempt to understand why policies have been adopted and what effect they have had. The second is prescriptive; recommendations about policy measures that should be adopted to achieve a desired objective.

These different levels form part of a hierarchy, in the order of ideology, politics, operations and techniques. The more general level of debate comes higher in the hierarchy. It is only if some agreement can be reached about the higher level questions that a useful analysis or discussion can be carried on at the lower level. To tackle questions about the operations of planning or other policy authorities, for example, it is necessary to take some ideological position and to make some assumptions about how political influences work. Those who believe that they are value-free technicians of urban policy may be unaware of the ideological or political positions they are taking but are none the less adopting particular positions.

Ideology

Views about urban policy differ most sharply at the ideological level. For the radical Right there should be no such thing as urban policy. Freedom, they would argue, cannot be maintained if governments interfere with the rights of the individuals, especially individual property owners (Denman 1978). Such libertarians believe that there should be very little government activity in cities. In particular, questions about distribution should be settled at the national level and redistribution should occur solely through cash payments. Governments should not enter into urban policy. Most, if not all, services could be provided by private firms, (Booth 1970), or by co-operation between small groups of families or property owners. Few urban scholars in Australia take this extreme view, though there are elements of it in some of John Paterson's writing (Paterson, Yencken and Gunn 1976). I find the views of the radical Right appealing in their consistency but lacking in humanity. They seem to take a view of the world which is far too individualistic to be useful in urban policy debates.

At the other extreme, the radical Left is more numerous and more articulate. They too are not primarily concerned with urban policy as such. In their view current urban problems are a symptom of inappropriate relationships between capital and labour in production. Without a radical change in those relationships there is little that can be achieved to improve cities, and little point in trying. People like

Manuel Castells have helped us to understand the implications of Marxist analysis for urban policy (Castells 1977). In particular they have shown more clearly that urban questions are almost always simply the manifestation in cities of broader social questions. They have also highlighted the importance of the distribution of power in determining the way issues are resolved. Although they aim to be explanatory, their theories are difficult to test. In the end one has either to accept their view of how society functions or to reject it, largely on faith or intuition. For myself I find some of their insights valuable but the implications of their analysis of society for urban policy difficult to understand and, as far as I understand it, difficult to accept.

Even if one accepts their analysis of society there are quite pragmatic reasons why one need not follow their view on policy. The fundamental changes in production relationships that they advocate seem most unlikely to occur in Australia. If that is true, they have little or nothing to say that is helpful. The question about how best to provide for collective consumption, of course, remains.

Between those two extremes are found the majority of policy analysts, including myself. There is still plenty of room for ideological disagreement even among those who claim the middle ground, between those who believe that solutions to urban problems must be sought mainly through government actions and those who believe that the main problems arise from inappropriate actions of governments and the general inefficiencies and insensitivities of bureaucracies.

There is some hope that empirical research can help to narrow the gap between these two ideological positions (for example, comparisons can be made between the experience of different countries). But it is unrealistic to expect too much. One group has an idealised view of the efficiency and discipline of the market and can see all the shortcomings of bureaucracies. The other is impressed with the monopolistic and exploitative aspects of private industry, the inefficiency of the market, shown for example in property speculation, and the inequity of the distribution of income and wealth the market produces. It sees government activities as a far better alternative and often turns a blind eye to their inefficiencies. One reason why it is difficult to reconcile these two views about the roles of governments and the market is that the ideal situations about which each group enthuses seldom occur. Even if they do occur in another country it is most likely that the results of adopting their policies would be different in Australia. For example, Australian business would probably behave differently from American business even if it were given the same freedom, and Australian authorities would be unlikely to perform in the same way as Swedish authorities even if they were given the same expanded powers and responsibilities. Indeed it can be argued persuasively, as Hugh Stretton (1978) has, that the particular roles played by the public and private sectors are much less important than how each behaves.

Ideological considerations affect the policies advocated even by those who accept the present broad distribution of responsibilities between government and the private sector. For example, one of the underlying problems in urban policy is that the demands of individuals for places to live, and of businesses for places to operate (and where they provide jobs and services) often change more rapidly than social and physical infrastructure (much of which is provided by governments) can be moved, or wears out and can be replaced. Passive or adaptive planning, which has been the main philosophy governing Melbourne's planning, for example, concentrates mainly on attempting to predict future private demands and then meeting the demands for infrastructure that result. More active planning puts more emphasis on trying to influence, or even direct the demands of private firms into locations where their demands will contribute to the efficient use of the available infrastructure. One approach takes the demands that arise in the market as given, the other tries to influence those demands. Which emphasis is adopted depends on how much a government wants to encourage growth in employment and how far it believes it can push firms around without losing them to another city or State.

The distinction between radical and conservative views seems to have fewer clear implications for urban policy than the distinction between those who want a more individualist and those who want a more collective society. Most people want to conserve some things and to change others. Physical conservation—of natural or man-made features of the environment—may be best achieved through radical changes in social relationships. That was the view of the Builders Labourers Federation. Those who want to change the social system, either to a more individualist or to a more collective one, may see marginal or gradual (rather than revolutionary) changes as the way to move towards their goal. For example, people on the radical Right argue for reduced government controls in particular areas and the radical Left for a more equal distribution of services in urban areas. Radicals of both kinds want to use policy measures not only to guide and restrict change, but also to stimulate and lead it.

Some people believe that the main objective of urban policies is to achieve a more equitable distribution of welfare by redistributing income, wealth and welfare from the rich and advantaged towards the poor and disadvantaged (Donnison and Soto 1980). For others the main objective is to improve the efficiency of resource allocation in both the short and the long term. Economists have long recognised equality and efficiency as two major social objectives (a third, stabilisation, has only indirect relevance for urban policy). Neoclassical economics holds that, at least over significant ranges of the achievable levels of efficiency and equality, more of one can only be obtained at the cost of having less of the other (Okun 1975). The reason is that they believe that differences in income are necessary to provide an incentive for owners of resources, including labour, to use them in the most productive way. Social Darwinists draw on biological analogies to support this view (Hardin 1977). That viewpoint is challenged by others who deny that the expectation of higher income is necessary as an incentive. One of the few empirical tests of this proposition is known as the New Jersey Income Maintenance Experiment (Watts and Rees 1977). It showed that placing a floor on incomes had little effect on work behaviour: people worked almost as much even when their incomes were guaranteed. Economists have tended to ignore the social and psychological satisfaction people gain from working and contributing to society. Although empirical studies, including some experiments (V. Smith 1980), can help to resolve these differences in belief about the need for financial incentives, such beliefs are firmly based on differences in views about the nature of society.

Whether or not equity and efficiency are competing objectives, the question of which should be the primary focus of urban policy remains. Those who are primarily concerned with efficiency give most of their attention to issues such as traffic congestion, efficient public transport, efficient provision of public services, land speculation and the resource allocation effects of taxes and charges. Those who are primarily concerned with distributive issues will place more emphasis on policies such as housing standards and housing costs at the lower end of the market, access to jobs and services, variations in levels of taxation, and differences in quality of services between locations.

Every policy measure both influences the efficiency of the allocation of resources and affects different groups of people in different ways, though often one of these effects is much more important. The relative importance to a policy analyst of the efficiency and equity objectives will affect not only the choice of policy issues that are analysed but also the policy measures that are considered and the relative weight that is given to their allocative and distributive effects in evaluating them.

An example may help to illustrate the conflict. It is easy to demonstrate that the present level of congestion on many city roads is inefficient and that some road users would be prepared to pay significantly more than their current costs of road use in the form of a road-user charge, while others would not. An optimal user-charge would allow those who value road use most to use them under less-congested conditions since others would be priced off them. However such a charge would change road use from being essentially a free service to being priced. It would allow those who can afford to pay more to use them and make things more difficult for those who cannot. The final effect on different groups depends on what is done with the revenue, but there is a strong likelihood that the poor would be worse off and the rich better off. Therefore our attitude to charging for the use of congested roads depends, in part, on the relative importance we place on efficiency and equity objectives.

Politics

Some people believe that governments make most of their decisions on the basis of a rational analysis of ways of achieving agreed objectives, and others believe that policy decisions are mainly the outcome of a struggle between different groups for power and influence. The differences between these views are seldom as clear as the ideological differences discussed above. Those who believe in the power of rational policy analysis generally accept that different groups have different objectives and that any policy measure has different effects on different groups. The fact that they give little attention to the process of policy formation presumably reflects a belief that governments are mainly swayed by rational analysis — which examines ways of achieving gains for particular groups — or at least that their behaviour can be analysed usefully in this way. This does not deny the importance and complexity of the political processes by which such group interests get translated into policy actions, but it does assume rationality in the long term.

The alternative view is that some groups have much greater power and influence in the political system than others, and that governments often act to preserve the power of such groups as well as to pursue specific policy objectives. The dominant group may be a racial group, capitalists, the ruling class, or even a regional group. Detailed analysis of political processes can help us to find out which groups have been successful in influencing policy, but it is much more difficult to test very general hypotheses about the influence of capitalists. People who hold this view are naturally pessimistic about achieving redistribution through government actions. If governments are under the thumbs of the rich or the capitalists they are unlikely to carry out more than a token amount of redistribution.

On a more prosaic level the study of the politics of urban policies can show how those policies influence the distribution of income, wealth and access to services between income, racial and ethnic groups and even age groups. Some policy decisions depend on which department or authority is more powerful. Other policies have been adopted because they benefit a particular minister's electorate. This has been particularly important in location policy since some services or facilities can readily be located in marginal electorates.

There is another important respect in which policy analysts differ in their approach to politics. It has become fashionable to stress that planning is a very political activity since planning actions and decisions always favour some groups at the expense of others. Those who regard planning as primarily a redistributive process see it as a way in which the relatively poor can use their political strength to lessen the economic disadvantages they suffer relative to the wealthy. Planning and other aspects of urban policy are among the items on the agenda in the struggle for shares of the product of society.

Some others, who also regard redistribution as an important part of planning, take a quite different approach. They see it more as a professional and less as a political activity. To them, the planner shares with the social worker and the housing manager a responsibility for assisting the weak and powerless. Their approach also is altruistic but, since they rarely ask the poor directly what they want, it tends also to be paternalistic. This approach seems especially suitable in relation to the very poor who are unlikely to be either numerous enough or skilled enough to exert much political muscle.

This somewhat old-fashioned approach has real limits since it does nothing to redistribute power to poor people so that they can determine their own future. Doing good by stealth can only last as long as the electorate can be misled, and appealing to the altruism of the powerful depends on their benevolence. At best it can be professional, compassionate and effective; at worst insensitive and degrading like some of the worst public housing. The election of a radical Right government, or cutting of funds in periods of economic stringency can spell the end of such policies.

Mobilising the poor politically involves alerting everyone, including the rich, to the distributional results of planning. Where the majority of voters have middle or higher incomes, as they do in Australia, forcing planning even further into the political arena may reduce rather than improve the ability of planning authorities to use planning to improve the conditions of the poor. Those on middle incomes may combine with the rich to force planning measures that disadvantage the poor. It is difficult to assess the likely results. How far have the failures of planning resulted from an incorrect analysis of the likely results of policy measures and how far from the actions of powerful groups whose well-being and wealth they threatened? If the former has been the main reason, then the professional paternalistic approach can be held responsible for much of the failure, but if it was the latter (opposition from the rich and powerful) this approach may be better than politicisation of planning issues. But it is only through the exercise of political power that any permanent redistribution can occur, and even minority groups, if they become active, can exercise a good deal of power.

Operation

If agreement can be reached about the ideological and political assumptions it is useful to begin to discuss operational questions about how to implement urban policies and what kinds of institutional arrangements are most appropriate for their formulation and implementation. There are a large number of questions here. I want to focus on one particular area that I have already introduced in discussing urban management: the distinction between operational and statutory planning.

The only way in which traditional land use planning can be implemented is by formulating and getting community and then government acceptance of statutory plans, which then provide the main criterion for the exercise of land use controls. If a change in land use is consistent with the land use plan it is permitted; otherwise it is not allowed. The procedure seems simple. The preparation of plans is, in theory at least, open and participatory since the plan is exhibited, can be objected to and is subject to public hearings. It is democratic in that the whole process is under the control of local governments or State government authorities. The rights of individual land owners are protected through rights of appeal at both the plan-approval and the development-application stages.

Statutory planning should not be idealised. Neither the preparation of draft schemes nor the administration of development controls allows for either openness or participation: on the contrary these procedures are secretive and open to manipulation by those with 'inside knowledge'. The appeals system tends to become legalistic, costly and time-consuming and the planning issues are often lost to sight.

Statutory planning has encountered endless difficulties in attempting to control land use and implement land use plans. Some of the reasons for its difficulties are easy to identify. Statutory planning decisions frequently oppose market forces. They often reduce the profits of individual landowners and developers compared with what they could make if the controls were relaxed. (It is arguable, of course, that their profits, as a group, would be even lower if there were no statutory planning, but this does not deter a particular developer, whose profits depend on a particular zoning decision, from trying to get it.)

There is one particular difficulty that might be overcome by a different, operational approach to planning. Land use plans include, at least implicitly, plans for future development of a wide range of urban services including transport, education, health services and open spaces. Since the appropriate location for these and other services depends on both the present and future location of housing, commercial and industrial areas, joint planning is obviously sensible. Unfortunately different services are provided by different departments or authorities that are responsible to ministers who are equal in rank to the minister for planning and more senior in the government hierarchy than local councils. Many were well established before land use planning became a serious activity of governments. They jealously guard their autonomy. Unlike private landowners, they are not required to get approval from the planning authority for their developments.

Operational planning is primarily oriented to planning, scheduling and installation of government services. It has so much potential for helping governments to achieve their location objectives that a number of attempts have been made to develop it into a coherent operation and to link it to statutory planning. While statutory planning works through controls that are essentially indicative and negative, operational planning acts through positive activities; urban investments of governments. It can include the whole public sector role in urban investments and servicing: public land development, public housing, provision of industrial estates and sites for shopping centres.

While such a step may seem rational and efficient it can only be taken if a high level of co-ordination can be achieved between the different responsible governments, authorities and departments. This is a formidable organisational problem in itself even without the jealousies among, and competition between, authorities. Nevertheless, some progress is being made and there is certainly now a greater awareness of the problems and the possibilities of operational planning.

Operational planning is mainly concerned with the implementation of a particular plan which contains its own ideological assumptions. It is not surprising that the whole issue seems beside the point to those who are primarily concerned with the redistribution of power, and seems downright dangerous to those who do not accept the ideological assumptions on which the plan is based.

Techniques

It is really only when most of the ideological, political and operational aspects of urban policy have been agreed that those technical questions that have preoccupied many academics and consultants should be considered. Many technical studies claim to be neutral with respect to ideological, political and operational issues. But in reality the 'technical' solutions they have proposed have ideological, political and operational implications that are hidden from view rather than exposed and defended. Most of the technical aspects of policy analysis revolve around two questions: first, what are the likely changes in the city in the future, especially as it grows; and second, how would it respond to various external changes and specific policy measures? Urban models are mostly designed to answer those questions. A few, especially in the transport field, are more ambitious and aim to sort out which policy measures will give the best results, judged by some simple criteria. These in particular have implications for each of the higher levels.

It is fairly fashionable now to say that most of these models, and especially those that aimed to model the whole city, have borne very little fruit. This includes the transportation models which cost millons of dollars to calibrate and had some general influence on the spending of many more millions of dollars. The reasons for their failures are fairly obvious. They are all based on a view of a city as a system. That in itself simply says that its various aspects are highly interdependent. But the models, like all models, are necessarily based on a grossly-simplified abstraction of the urban system. Urban model-building requires more knowledge than we have of which are the important relationships that need to be incorporated in the model. I would argue that general models of cities are impossible (Neutze 1978:Chapter 10). There are too many important relationships to be incorporated into a manageable model (Stretton 1978). They have, of course, taught us something about the complexity of cities and some simpler, partial models have proved more useful.

The comprehensive models were built on very shaky foundations in another respect as well. There has not been enough research for us to specify accurately all the relationships that form the building blocks for the models; for example, we do not understand adequately the factors that influence where people choose to live and where they choose to work. In the interest of technical virtuosity the 'experts' built models with strong internal logic that were based on an inadequate understanding of the real world they were trying to explore. The models reflected their authors' greater interest in techniques (for example, the intellectual fascination with entropy maximisation) than in real policy questions.

Disillusionment with the results of large model building is not limited to studies of location. In economics many of the econometric models that filled the pages of the best journals are seen now to have produced disappointing results (Lipsey 1979).

Even if they had worked in terms of their own objectives they would have contributed little to policy. First, they have seldom regarded the distributional results of policy measures as important enough to predict, though this is less true of some recently-developed simulation models of the housing market. Second, they could at most help with plan-making; they have little to contribute to the perhaps more important field of plan implementation, though they can be used to explore optimal sequences. Their final failure is that they have inevitably been based on experience in the recent past and, as historians will tell us, that is not necessarily a good guide to the future. Their predictions have seldom proved accurate. But they have not been alone in that; even those of us who rely on simpler kinds of policy analysis need to investigate some of the lessons of the recent past in urban policy in more detail.

Review

It may be useful to illustrate the different levels at which a policy issue can be discussed by reference to a particular example. Many of the earlier examples have related to fringe development but the case-study is policy towards the inner city.

At an ideological level the problems of the inner city can be seen as revealing the failure and the exploitative nature of capitalism in an acute form. The valuable social networks of inner suburbs are sacrificed when it becomes more profitable to provide jobs and services in the outer suburbs, and the low-cost housing of the poor is sacrificed when some inner areas become popular among the 'trendies'—in Paddington or North Adelaide.

From a different ideological standpoint inner city problems might be said to be mainly due to government interference in the market. For example, residential zoning has inhibited the expansion of industry and commerce in these areas and has therefore accelerated the flight of jobs and investment to the suburbs. Ideology, therefore, influences what is seen to be a problem and how the problem is defined, as well as where its causes are sought and what solutions are considered.

Different approaches at the political level also influence both analysis and prescription. Political power in the inner cities of Australia is held primarily by the owners and occupants of commercial properties. Most of the rate revenue also comes from these properties. The inner suburbs, which are mostly in different local government areas from the city centres, are dominated by residential voters but have only a limited rate base. In Sydney there is a long history of boundary changes by successive State governments which alternately give business and residents control over the City Council. State governments are also much involved in inner city policy-making. Depending on whether they are governments of the Right or the Left they will be more or less receptive to the views of the city business community.

Policy discussions that rely more on rational analysis point out the effects of zoning policies, of expansion of institutions, building of freeways and non-residential construction and conversion on the availability of low-cost housing (Kendig 1979). The problem that is considered at the political level depends on the ideological position taken.

At an operational level the relevant issues include the functions of local councils and of various State departments and authorities. For example, it has been mainly State authorities responsible for housing, education, transport and health, rather than the planning authority, that have been responsible for decisions affecting the inner city. Local councils have had some, but not very much, influence through zoning and controls over plot ratios. The non-planning role of local councils, for example, in the provision of social, cultural and recreational facilities has been more important. Broadly, it is only when the problems have been identified and analysed and the general political stance decided that operational suggestions can sensibly be made—what institutional arrangement will be most likely to provide the kinds of solutions that the ideological and political position of the observer leads him or her to regard as desirable and feasible.

Finally, some technical questions about the inner city. What effect have changes in transport costs and facilities had on the role and function of the inner city, and how would it change if, for example, more resources were put into public transport? Do their different property rating systems help to account for the differences between the central areas of Sydney and Melbourne? How much is the displacement of low income people likely to be affected by regulations restricting dual occupancy of housing? Which of these and many other questions are asked and which policies are considered depends to a large degree on the position taken with respect to the other levels.

Conclusions

Debates about location policy are often confused because the proponents are arguing at different levels, and never really meet. It would help if authors made clear, for example, what ideological position they take and whether they are arguing at the ideological, political, operational or technical level. This problem is illustrated by the confusion that results from the varying use of the terms planning, policy and management. It is unlikely that everyone will agree with the definitions of these terms and of the four levels of policy debate used in this chapter, but they should at least provide a starting point for some more fruitful discussions.

Chapter 7
Planning, urban crisis and urban management

Chris Paris and Peter Williams

Throughout the world, urban areas in general and large cities in particular pose fundamental problems of control and management. In poorer countries crises are immanent, if not ever present, as facilities related to water, power and sewerage, taken for granted elsewhere, are often non-existent or failing. In advanced capitalist countries, too, many large cities are in decline following the end of the long boom, shifts in technology and markets, the disintegration of national economies, energy problems and rapid industrial restructuring. Falling populations, diminishing city finances, growing unemployment and social problems are now common enough features of cities in Australia and elsewhere. It is in the context of this rapidly changing environment that we wish to consider the role of urban planning. Between the 1950s and 1970s planning was called upon to cope with the problems of growth and in particular to constrain and redirect the ever-expanding built environment and the economy which underpinned it. In the late 1970s and the 1980s the situation changed quite dramatically. While planning was still expected to tackle problems related to suburbanisation it is now being called upon to confront the substantially different problems of decline and economic restructuring. Ironically all this is happening at a time when there is an increasingly voluble debate about the link between planning and the vitality of capitalist economies.

The political Right is challenging the very existence of state intervention and within that process planning is an obvious target. Planning is believed to slow the process of adaptation, to increase cost and to favour the collective good over individual advantage. On the Left, the recognition that planning as a process can be strongly conservative and supportive of the *status quo* (and thus functional to capitalism) is tempered by the realisation that under present circumstances it is necessary to defend the principle of planning (if not the practice).

As the world changes, so our expectations of what planning can and should achieve are modified. Our aim in this chapter is to explore attempts to understand the nature of planning in the context of the changing social, political and economic context in which it takes place. In particular we are concerned to show how, in the face of

Originally published in *Journal of Australian Political Economy*, 16:67–73 and reproduced here by kind permission of the Editors.

shifting economic and political pressures, successive attempts to reinterpret and rejustify the role of planning, both practically and intellectually, have been doomed to fail because of the contradictory nature of the planning process in a market society such as Australia. By arguing in this way we are clearly accepting that an understanding of planning relates to the material context and to the conceptual viewpoint adopted. Furthermore, these two issues, context and concept, are, of course, interrelated. Part of our purpose, therefore, is to show how the changing realities of planning practice have both forced and been influenced by shifts in our theorisation of the social world.

The chapter proceeds by way of exploration of a number of approaches to planning and the reasons for their failure both in practice and in theory. In particular, attention is given to arguments related to planning either as technical and scientific management or as a co-ordinating management activity. Both approaches have been criticised by radicals for ignoring the realities of political and class power. Others, while recognising that planning is not a neutral exercise, suggest that it is essential to all modern societies. We argue that neither of these is sufficient for an understanding of planning. From an exploration of the positions described above we attempt to distil the essence of planning practice as the spatial management of class relations and from that position we argue the need for a total reconceptualisation of the planning process in theory. Furthermore, from that position we suggest that it is fruitless to blame planners for the failings of planning and also that the contradications of planning cannot somehow be resolved by further reorganisation. Instead there is a need to recognise the highly contradictory and contentious nature of the regulation of land use in market societies.

Planning and urban change

The role and content of urban planning has grown dramatically since the Second World War. Substantial claims for technical competence have been advanced by planners equipped with new 'scientific' approaches to studying and managing cities (for example, Eversley 1973). Cost-benefit analysis, impact analysis, local planning, structure planning and regional planning have waxed and waned, having been found wanting in the complex environment in which planning operates. Planners' claims to competence, however, have been challenged not only in terms of the techniques they have used. Other established professions and practitioners themselves have claimed central roles in ordering the built environment (for example, engineers, architects, valuers, estate agents, developers) and they have been reluctant to concede the central ground to the planning profession. Even so, the town planning profession has been relatively successful in gaining a position of some prominence. As noted already, however, such an achievement is increasingly questioned in the light of the ever-more complex problems being posed by cities and in cities and the growing appreciation that urban planning in itself has few powers for tackling these issues (Alexander 1982*a*; Neutze 1982; Chapter 6 of this volume).

Urban planners have responded to the changing environment and public perceptions of their role in two main ways. First, they have focused on a range of technical/scientific skills intended to promote planning to the status of a city 'science' (McLoughlin 1969; Chadwick 1971; Faludi 1973). As the problems increased and the success of solutions remained limited, the scientific approach lost much credibility. The second response has been to seek reorganisation, based upon the belief that planning was failing because it did not sit in the right place within the structure of government. In Australia, as the competence of the old main-line departments such as roads and construction was questioned, urban planners were able to advance their claims as having particular expertise as 'urban managers'. Conflicts between the old power blocks created the space for planners to establish themselves and the question was raised whether they should step forward and control. Planning has been constantly reorganised as a function itself and within the overall structure of government. Each attempt can be seen as a way of resolving the conflicts and problems posed by cities and urban areas in general. Yet all attempts at reorganisation so far have been destined to fail (see Lloyd and Troy 1981 for Federal attempts; Bowman 1978 and Power, et al. 1981 for change at a State level).

Planning's failures, however, have been seen in turn as a product of its weak organisational presence and its peripheral status alongside main-line departments, rather than of any inherent weaknesses. The arguments typically used to justify organisational reforms which have led to centralisation, concentration and intervention at a broader scale, is that they will provide the basis for better control of urban areas and thus a more successful contribution to production and prosperity. Such a view, however, rests on a number of dubious assumptions. First, it assumes that more planning leads to greater efficiency. Greater intervention by urban planners, however, does not in itself lead to greater efficiency: state agencies are not necessarily any better (they may be worse) than private organisations. Professional ideologies, for example, are very similar across the two sectors. Second, reform of the land market through explicit intervention may only streamline the conversion process of land rather than transform the market. Third, a focus on efficiency assumes consensus regarding equity issues and the need for public intervention. However, as Wilenski (1978:85) comments with regard to Sydney:

> ...it would be naive to assert that Sydney's present ills could have been avoided simply if politicians and bureaucrats had worked at the decision-making and coordinating mechanisms and got them right. Sydney's present inequalities are at least in part a result of

the inequalities of wealth and power in the city. The fact is that most of Sydney's disadvantages are disadvantages of its less affluent and less well organised citizens. For the affluent and the owners of capital, life in Sydney is fairly pleasant... If it is going too far to say that Sydney has developed in the way it has because it suited the interest of this minority of its citizens, then at the least one can argue that the development process was allowed to continue for so long in the way that it did because it did not much disadvantage them.

Urban management: content and contradiction

Given these arguments it is important to establish what are the specifically urban phenomena which urban planning might control and whether we can separate these from the environment (social, political and economic) in which cities are located and of which they are a part. Certainly it is possible to find content definitions of what planning or urban management is thought to be (for example, Paterson 1978). Usually these imply that it is simply concerned with the provision and regulation of a range of services (see also Neutze 1982 and Chapter 6 of this volume for a critical review of concepts of planning and urban management). Never, however, can planners satisfactorily define or resolve what is a specifically 'urban' problem (see also Jones and Stilwell 1983). Often 'urban' is effectively equated with 'built environment', particular administratively-defined areas, or even those things over which governments have most control, for example, public-sector investments. Despite the outward importance of public activity, however, cities are overwhelmingly private-market arenas (Katznelson 1981; A. Parkin 1982). They are sites for the production of goods and services and places where most people live out their daily lives. In that sense, while we may have difficulty defining 'urban' processes, there can be no doubting the significance of cities in advanced societies. Their functioning is central to the functioning of the economy and it is precisely this importance which both enhances the image of planning and at the same time undermines any claims that planners might have for comprehensiveness. In other words, the very breadth of the problem denies planners the possibility of dealing with it effectively, given their current powers and competence.

Recognising the contradictory position of planning constitutes a necessary step in re-interpreting and re-analysing its role. It is argued by many on the Left that urban planning is largely irrelevant to the major processes of change taking place within market economies. Hence Kilmartin and Thorns (1978:101) argue that 'the ability of the state to exercise control over the private sector through town planning is poor and probably restricted to rather minor matters such as planning standards'. Planning, however remains one factor operating in the space-economy, and indeed it may have a disproportionate impact upon certain sectors of the economy, for example, building and construction, small business and petty entrepreneurs. Regulative zoning also has a major impact on the kinds of dwellings which can be developed in an area and hence who can live there. Regulative roles may assist the popular image of planners as managers but they have relatively little to do with the control and management of accumulation at an aggregate level. More generally, it is clear that the regulation of land uses *does* affect both capital and labour since, in undertaking this function, planners influence the sites available for new factories, warehouses and homes, and this 'spatial management' affects rates of return, prices in different commodity markets, wages and costs of operation. As a consequence it influences the ways, and the rates at which, the built environment can change and thus aid or inhibit accumulation in general.

The precise function planning plays in any locality will in part depend upon particular local circumstances. In many situations planners may 'simply' administer laws about how cities should function. To a degree they regulate and control the way land is used but, despite the rhetoric of planners, planning is not an inherently 'creative' activity. Planners are frequently the legal guardians of a 'spatial *status quo*' and indeed, much land use planning derives its greatest influence precisely through powers prohibiting or modifying change. Planners rarely have the ability to initiate change, more often acting to preserve. In all cases, however, planners and the planning system itself do not create the situations to which they attempt to apply these laws, even though they may be asked to bear the responsibility for the health and vitality of metropolitan economies.

Moving urban planning to a central directive role within state bureaucracies without first recognising the strict limits on what urban planning may achieve, therefore, is little more than cosmetic. Reorganisation of planning by shifting departmental responsibilities cannot resolve real problems that exist with regard to the legal powers planners hold and the very complex social and economic systems operating in urban areas. Urban planning in practice almost invariably boils down to the implementation of a statutory land use planning system, whether it be in the centre of a government's structure or on its periphery, whether it be a local government or a State government. There is rarely anything in the training of planners, their operational milieux, their professional organisation or statutory responsibilities which equips them with any special competence for large-scale administration and policy formulation affecting other than land use issues. Sadly, attempts by planning educationalists to broaden the base and scope of planning education very often result in the loss of even traditional land use planning concerns, rendering young planners good critics of planning's shortcomings but ill-equipped to confront practical questions of land use policies.

Planners as managers

The identification of planning as 'urban management' clearly conflicts with the reality of urban planning's relatively weak capacity to manage and control cities. It was a recognition of this contradiction that provided a key component in the critique of Pahl's urban managerialist thesis (1970, 1975). Planners and planning were central to Pahl's attempt to define a series of 'gatekeeping' roles around which a new sociology of the city could develop. The concept was substantially refined by Pahl himself in response to critics who demonstrated the extreme difficulties of trying to identify any specific individuals or groups that could be 'held responsible' for what happened in cities. Urban managers came increasingly to be seen as 'mediators' rather than independent managers. But whatever the weaknesses of Pahl's formulations it promoted the study of planning to a central place in urban sociology (see, for instance, Norman 1975; Williams 1978).

Recent years have witnessed the widespread adoption of political economy approaches which stress the importance of the organisation and structuring of capitalist societies (see for example, Kilmartin and Thorns 1978; Sandercock 1977; and Stilwell 1980). This development has resulted in cities being viewed less as separate entities and rather more as arenas in which general social processes are played out. Within such perspectives planning has often been condemned as ideology and the very weakness of planning powers is seen as providing ample proof of the way the state has sought to maintain a pretence of regulation while at the same time actually allowing the market to operate freely (Paris 1982). While arguing against making too firm conclusions at this stage, Kilmartin and Thorns (1978: 101) suggested that urban planning in Australia exercised few positive powers and if anything 'favoured the priviledged and penalised the underprivileged'. Hence, radicals have viewed planning as something contributing to the reproduction of exploitative social relations.

More recently there has been a reaction to such views. While not returning to an uncritical acceptance of the role of planning, Sandercock has argued that planning cannot be dismissed as simplistically as some political economy approaches might suggest. 'Physical planning is not going to disappear. Both capitalist and socialist countries find too much value in the regulation of land use and development for that to happen' (Sandercock 1982:14).

This, however, tells us nothing about the particular nature of urban planning in different societies at different times. It is ahistoric and rests on a functionalist acceptance of the necessity and inevitability of physical planning. Crucially, it does not say anything about the relationship between state planning and capital accumulation, nor about its impact upon class relations or its contradictory role in specific societies. We are in sympathy both with positions which are critical of orthodox acceptance of the benefits of planning and also with those who dismiss it as state ideology. We argue, however, that a redefinition of urban planning is required but that it is quite inadequate simply to assert that it is difficult but necessary.

Towards a reformulation

Debates over the role of planning have become somewhat sterile and it is clearly necessary to change the basis for analysis. Recent work within Marxist and Weberian perspectives has opened up a number of debates around the role of the state, conflicts within and between government departments, class relations and the emergence of a new class of technical and professional workers. City planning stands as an activity and a profession at the centre of many of these relationships. It did not develop as some simple functional response to the needs of the state and the capitalist class. The emergence of a new professional activity was part of a complex process of social and economic change. The contradictions imposed by developments in production and reproduction, the inadequacies of existing technical competence, social conflicts and tensions all underlie the emergence of planning as an activity (Sutcliffe 1981). Its progressive advancement through the ranks of government departments has to be viewed in relation to changing relationship within government, contradictions and tensions within the state as well as surrounding it (Williams 1982). For example, we should stop seeing 'planning' and 'planners' in monolithic terms. Many planners are low-level bureaucrats with very little power or influence and their work is largely routine within existing bureaucratic State or local government organisations. Questions such as these have been largely ignored in attempts to establish planning's value to capitalism. In contrast to this we would maintain that urban planning often exists in a mediating relationship between fractions of capital as well as between capital and labour and that a class perspective on planning would provide a new and important focus to this area of work. For example, zoning should be seen as a way of resolving conflict over alternative forms of development, as it can affect which investments take place and who lives or works where.

Above all else it is essential to recognise planning's contradictory roles. Cities remain vital to advanced economies. Moreover, the reproduction of social relations, increasingly threatened by economic crisis and restructuring, becomes problematic without cities changing. For example, gentrification can involve substantial change in the class pattern of access to housing and location without involving any change of land use. The rapid loss of manufacturing employment from Australian cities and associated growth of unemployment have both occurred without land use change. Economic decline, quite simply, involves processes and relationships about which the control of land is, at best, marginally relevant. As constructive radical critics come to take wider political-economy perspectives on modern cities (McLoughlin 1983*a*) so, therefore, the reasons for supposing that town planners should be expected to understand or affect processes of change diminishes. Planning is charged with substantial responsibilities in these areas yet at the same time its powers favour stability rather than change. In Australia, as in most other western capitalist societies, land use planning systems are based on statutory powers affecting the capacity of private individuals and agencies to *change* land uses. Such planning often involves the preparation of maps and written documents indicating desired changes, but these rely on others to initiate development. The ability to affect major investment decisions of the state rarely lies with town planners. Other planners employed in state agencies, however, may be of greater importance, for example, highway officials and land commissioners. Town planning is neither simply an ideology (planning does exist and it does have effects) nor is it all-powerful (its powers are very limited). It is, instead, an activity which is historically and spatially specific, reflecting the constellation of conditions and relations present. It is not monolithic, neither is it inevitable in particular forms. It involves relationships and processes which must be analysed in action, rather than be discussed in a static and universal framework. It is highly desirable that our debates are shifted to this more fruitful ground.

Section IV:
Planning for metropolitan areas

Chapter 8
Land use and transport planning in Australian cities: capital takes all?

Ian Alexander

Introduction

Land use and transport planning in Australian cities is of relatively recent origin. Efforts were made to generate metropolitan planning from 1900 onwards, but it is only in the past forty years that any tangible progress has been made.

This chapter aims to provide an overview of the metropolitan land use and transport planning process in Australian State capital cities and to assess its effects. (Canberra has been deliberately excluded from this account, owing to its unique status as a city with a strong central planning agency and leasehold land tenure.) It argues that the results of metropolitan planning have been of mixed value from both a social and economic point of view; it appears that far stronger political commitment is required to solve metropolitan problems.

However, the chapter also questions the overall effectiveness of planning as an answer to 'urban' problems. This is at least partly because planning tends to attack the symptoms rather than the causes of those problems. As Mingione (1981:30) notes:

> It is neither convenient nor feasible to build a general theory of urban and regional questions, as these are only partial, non-autonomous aspects of a more general social process, *which cannot be broken down to isolated urban or regional problems.* [Emphasis added]

If this viewpoint is accepted it may mean that land use/transport planning can have no useful role in shaping the essence as opposed to the appearance of the urban system. But on a more positive note, it

Author's note: This chapter is a revised version of a paper presented to a conference on 'Urban Problems and Policies in Germany and Australia', (Alexander 1982) held at the ANU, Canberra in 1982. The author is indebted to Pat Troy and Chris Paris for the opportunity to participate in that 'talkfest', as it encouraged the development of ideas on the role of planning in capitalist society. The editors of this volume of readings are thanked for the chance to re-work these ideas. However, as it stands, the paper still undoubtedly begs many questions. This arises from strictures of space, the complexity of the topic and the belief (rationalisation?) that such a task should await further analysis and discussion. As McLoughlin points out in his introduction, our understanding of Australian cities and Australian planning is, as yet, only at an early stage.

may also mean that planning can be more effective by integrating with other arms of social and economic policy. Radical change and reform are required across the board before planning can have any decisive influence on the fundamental nature of the urban capitalist economy and society.

The planning system in Australian cities

State, capital and planning

Like planning systems in other capitalist societies, that in Australia appears to be operating under a number of powerful constraints. These constraints are seen to arise because Australian cities are developed 'mainly through private markets' (A. Parkin 1982:14), in particular the land and building development market. Many planning strategies, supposedly in the public interest, have been interpreted by the affected property owners as a threat to the viability of their investments. According to Sandercock (1977) this has been sufficient to see the demise of several attempts at development control and restraint, particularly in central city areas.

And yet, according to some of the recent spate of Marxist literature (for example, Castells 1977) planning is not framed in the public interest at all but rather in the interests of the dominant class, the capitalists. This interpretation coincides with a view that sees all state activities as basically supportive of capital. However, Stilwell (1983; Chapter 4 in this volume) argues that despite the fact that planning has often acted against the interests of the working class, it has the potential to be used in their favour.

This question is addressed although certainly not resolved here since it revolves around the wider debate on the role of the state in capitalist society, a debate which presents starkly opposing views and which is therefore far from over (see, for example, Jessop 1982; Saunders 1983; Clark and Dear 1984). This chapter does attempt to throw some light on the question, however, since as Kilmartin, Huxley and McLoughlin (1985) point out 'the process of planning essentially embodies the role of the state in a market economy'. Paris and Williams (1984; Chapter 7 in this volume) note that these processes 'must be analysed in action, rather than be discussed in a static and universal framework'; the following is an attempt to move in this direction.

Development of metropolitan planning

Whatever the ideological role of the state in capitalist society, there is little doubt that the power of the property-owning classes has been reinforced by the generally conservative nature of Australian government. The country has been governed by the Labor Party (the only party with any socialist pretensions) for less than one quarter of the years since Federation.

In any event, Australian urban planning has always been heavily restricted in scope by the Federal constitution itself. As Lloyd and Troy (1981:1) so accurately note: 'Those who framed the Australian constitution did not anticipate that the Commonwealth would participate directly in the development of Australia's cities and regions'. And participate the Commonwealth did not, except for brief attempts by Labor Party Federal governments in the 1940s and 1970s. Urban development and planning policies have been left in State government hands at all other times.

The history of land use and transport planning in Australian cities is therefore far from uniform in terms of legislation or policy. Early initiatives in land development and land use control were confined to local government level, even where the State governments initiated them. Legislation relating to such control, and to regulation over land subdivision was enacted in several States in the 1920s and 1930s, and was based heavily on British legislation of the same period (Fogg 1974:11–26).

But in the absence of metropolitan-wide government, there was no obvious framework for the initiation of metropolitan planning. This was one reason for moves to constitute metropolitan governments in the 1920s and 1930s (see, for example, Spearitt 1978*a*) which were successful only in Brisbane, where a metropolitan council was established in 1925. Such planning as there was at metropolitan level before 1940 took place on an *ad hoc* basis through the activities of individual government agencies responsible for the provision of public housing, infrastructure, including roads, sewerage and water, electricity, and services such as education and health (T. Logan 1984).

These activities were, of course, essential to the growth and development of urban Australia and its capitalist enterprise; this is the case in all capitalist states since their provision tends 'not to be profitable to supply and hence of little interest to commercial development companies' (Kirk 1980:187).

But the provision of infrastructure, important as it may be, is not equivalent to the conscious attempt to plan land use and transport patterns at metropolitan scale. Ironically, given the impediments within the Australian Constitution, the impetus for this type of planning came from the Commonwealth, through the activities of the Department of Post-war Reconstruction, which was part of a concerted reform effort of the Chifley Labor government (1944–49). The Commonwealth and State Housing Agreement Act of 1945 required the States to pass adequate legislation in the areas of 'rental housing, slum clearance and *town planning*' (Harrison 1974:203).

Following this, as illustrated in Table 8.1, each State set up a legal framework for metropolitan planning and an agency responsible for

Table 8.1 Summary of State government enabling legislation, major administrative arrangements and plans for metropolitan land use

State	Enabling legislation	Planning body	Generation & plan	Date of publication	Date of adoption
NSW	1945: Local Govt. Amendment Act	Cumberland County Council	1 Cumberland County Plan	1948	1951
	1963: State Planning Auth. Act	State Planning Authority	2 Sydney Region Outline Plan	1968	n.a.
	1974: Planning & Environment Commission Act	Planning & Environment Commission	3 Sydney Region Outline Plan Review	1980	n.a.
	1979: Environmental Planning and Assessment Act	Department of Environment and Planning			
Vic.	1949: Town and Country Planning Act	Melbourne and Metropolitan Board of works	1 Melbourne Metropolitan Scheme	1954	1968
		Town & Country Planning Board	2 Planning Policies for the Metro. Region	1971	n.a.
		Ministry of Planning and Environment	3 Metropolitan Strategy	1980	1982
SA	1955: Town Planning Act	Town Planning Committee	1 Metropolitan Development Plan	1963	1967
	1967: Planning & Development Act	State Planning Authority	2 Adelaide 2000	1980	n.a.
WA	1959: Metropolitan Region Scheme Act	Metropolitan Region Planning Authority	1 Metropolitan Region Scheme	1962	1963
			2 Perth Corridor Plan	1970	1973
			3 Corridor Plan Review (current)	1985	†n.a.
Qld	1959: City of Brisbane (Town Plan) Act	Council of the City of Brisbane	1 City of Brisbane Planning Scheme	1964	1965
	1977: City of Brisbane (TP Act)		2 City of Brisbane T Plan	1976	1977
Tas.	1944: Town & Country Planning Act	Southern Metropolitan Major Planning Authority (1958 since lapsed).	1 Metropolitan Planning Scheme	1962	n.a.
	1982: Local Government Act				

* n.a.: not adopted by government † expected completion 1987

Sources: Fogg 1974; Harrison 1974; Bowman 1979

plan preparation and implementation. The functions of these agencies has varied both between States and over time; the details need not concern us here, but a key point to note is that few of these authorities have both planning powers and responsibility for public service or facility provision. Hence the single-purpose authorities referred to above retained a crucial role in the urban development process, and one which has often not been well co-ordinated with the policies and activities of the planning authorities. The planning authorities have been responsible for the drawing up and administering of plans for the future development of their respective metropolitan areas. These plans have focused on land use, but they have also included recommendations on, for example, the provision of transport routes; however, the task of providing those routes remained with the transport authorities, namely State roads departments and public transport operators.

In addition, the transport systems in each city were the subject of separate studies and policy recommendations from 1965 onwards, as shown in Table 8.2. While such studies usually took the metropolitan land use plans as their starting points, they often produced recommendations which ran counter to the spirit of those plans — this point is pursued below.

Table 8.2 Summary of major transport studies, Australian State capital cities, 1964

City	Study	Date
Sydney	Sydney Area Transportation Study	1974
	Urban Transport Advisory Committee Report	1976
Melbourne	Melbourne Transportation Study	1969
	Victorian Transport Study	1980
Adelaide	Metropolitan Adelaide Transport Study	1968
Perth	Perth Transportation Study	1970
	Perth, Transport 2000	1982
Brisbane	Brisbane Area Transport Study	1965
Hobart	Hobart Area Transportation Study	1964

Source: Black 1976

But as far as land use is concerned, the 'first generation' of Australian metropolitan plans (as Bunker (1971) termed them) were very much in the development-control mode of earlier legislation; only the scale was different. In all cities a Statutory Plan or Planning Scheme broadly defining the land uses allowable was produced to cover the entire existing and envisaged future metropolitan areas. An example, the Cumberland County Council (1948) Planning Scheme for Sydney is shown in Figure 8.1. The point here is not to discuss the details, but to emphasise the essentially traditional nature of the approach which relied on the negative zoning mechanism. These zonings provided a relatively rigid framework within which local authorities drew up their own land use plans, but as we shall see one which was not robust enough to control development trends which were contrary to the intent of the plans.

Figure 8.1 Example of a 'first generation' metropolitan plan: the Cumberland Plan for Sydney, 1948; as depicted by Bunker (1971)

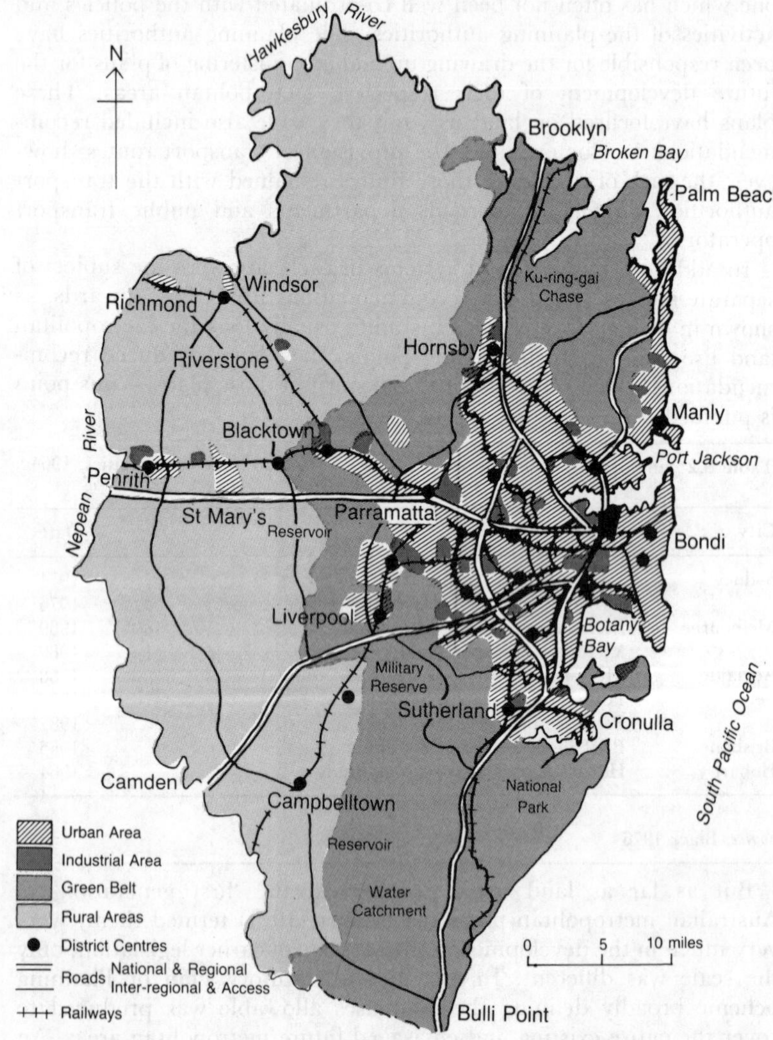

The second generation of plans, drawn up from the late-1960s onwards, were much less concerned with land use detail, and more with the overall form or structure of the metropolitan areas. This is illustrated by the example of the Perth Corridor Plan (1970) as shown in Figure 8.2. It should be noted, however, that the plans were still backed by the planning scheme provisions and their subsequent revisions.

Figure 8.2 Example of a 'second generation' metropolitan plan, the Corridor plan for Perth, 1970

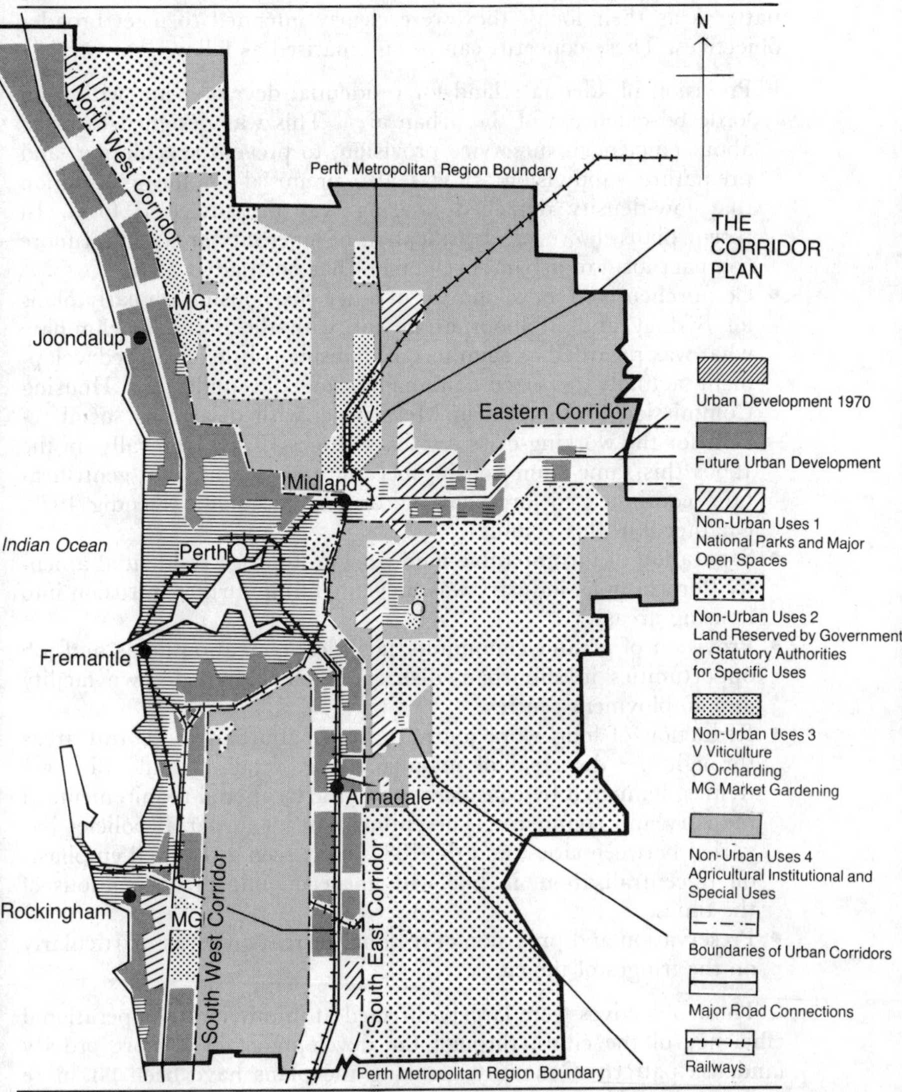

A third generation of plans has been identified by T. Logan (1981). Starting with the Sydney Region Outline Plan Review in 1980 (Table 8.2), and then extending to Melbourne and Perth, this round of plans appears to be focused more on means of implementation than on new spatial strategies. However, urban consolidation is a common theme, reflecting the resource constraints of the 1980s. Indeed as T. Logan (1984:1047) argues, the concern of each generation of plans can be linked to the economic climate of the time at which they were produced.

Major concerns

While the plans may have had the cities' development and land use patterns as their focus, they were clearly intended to meet broader objectives. These concerns can be summarised as follows:

- Provision of adequate land for residential development, within an 'orderly' extension of the urban area. This was designed to bring about efficiencies in service provision, to prevent speculation, and premature subdivision. It was also premised on the assumption that low-density detached housing was the preferred form. In recent plans, however, densification of inner city areas and a more compact form of urban development has been advocated.
- Comprehensive redevelopment of inner city housing (in early plans for Sydney and Melbourne) in line with the desire to eliminate what was regarded as slum terrace housing. Little of this redevelopment actually occurred, although some did under the Housing Commission of Victoria in Melbourne, with disastrous social results for the working-class residents (Jones 1972). Ironically, in the 1960s this same slum housing became fashionable and 'gentrification' continued to force out the original residents (Kendig 1979; Chapter 9 in this volume).
- Separation of incompatible land uses to improve residential amenity (for example, industry was prevented from further intrusion into housing areas).
- Provision of greater community facilities, recreation areas and job opportunities in suburban 'districts' each with their own facility and employment centres.
- Reduction of long work journeys from suburban to central areas through the dispersal of manufacturing, retailing and office activities, tempered by consideration of the locational requirements of industry and commerce. The enthusiasm for dispersal policies has varied between cities, and the 1980s have seen a renewed emphasis on re-centralisation, in line with the economic preoccupations of the times.
- Preservation and provision of regional recreation areas, particularly on the fringes of the cities.

These objectives were largely directed at improving the operational efficiency of the cities, through the development of a more orderly land use pattern. Generally speaking the plans have been far more concerned with these matters than with those of social justice or equity, although the equity element was strongly emphasised in certain plans such as the Cumberland Plan for Sydney (Figure 8.1; Alexander 1981*a*). Australian metropolitan planning can, therefore, be viewed primarily as a means to facilitate the accumulation of capital and its more productive valorisation.

Efficiency considerations were also paramount in the transport studies of the 1960s and 1970s, which recommended strategies to overcome growing problems of traffic congestion in the cities; however, these strategies emphasised private rather than public transport.

Specific aspects of land use and transport planning

Urban land conversion

Because of the focus of the Australian planning system on land use regulation on the one hand, and on the form and direction of urban expansion on the other, it plays a significant role in the processes of land use change. Planning has the ability, through zoning and building form and bulk codes, to control the extent of development and the conversion of land from one use to another; for example, the redevelopment of single-unit residential development to higher densities, or the spread of commercial and industrial uses into residential areas. On the fringe of the city, as Neutze (1978:172) observes 'urban planning since World War II has been preoccupied with the conversion of land from rural to urban use'.

It was hoped that these controls would bring visual order to scattered subdivisions and lower the costly provision of fragmented services which were common problems in Australian city fringe areas up to the 1950s. It was also hoped that speculation associated with the land-conversion process would be reduced by preventing premature subdivision.

Coupled with the gradual introduction of means whereby land had to be serviced before subdivision, it seems that these controls have succeeded in achieving their goals (Neutze 1978:175). Ironically, however, they have helped to fuel land-price increases rather than dampening them. This has resulted because planning controls have generally reduced the supply of land available for development in the face of continuing heavy demand for housing land.

Furthermore, the controls may well have encouraged speculation by directing attention to areas certain to be designated for development in future years. This is particularly true of the second generation of plans where clear indications of the future extent and direction of urban development were given. In a country where land speculation has been dubbed a 'national hobby' it is not surprising that investors have used metropolitan plans as a 'punters guide to successful land speculation' (Harrison 1974:216). Here we have a prime example of the system of private land development bending public-sector planning to its own purposes; Australian planning history is replete with examples of this process (Sandercock 1977; Logan and Ogilvy 1981). Troy (1978:6) however, suggests that planners must share some of the blame since 'they fail to recognise that their activities increase the scarcity of urban land'. In any event, this situation was exploited by astute developers.

It is instructive to note however, that during the period of rapid land-price inflation — the 1950s and 1960s — the problem was significantly reduced in one Australian city, Adelaide. Here, the government had chosen to intervene in the land-conversion process in a much more active way than through zoning and subdivision control. For many years the South Australian Housing Trust, a government housing authority, purchased large tracts of land on the urban fringe for future development. The motive for such intervention was by no means altruistic; as Stretton (1975) notes, it was initiated by a conservative State government anxious to attract industry to Adelaide, and using cheap housing in an effort to dampen wage demands and hence provide employers with a lower cost of variable capital (labour). But whatever the motive, the intervention discouraged speculation and helped to stabilise land prices (Neutze 1978:295). It was also successful in bringing a greater provision of facilities for new housing areas at an early stage of development, such as at Elizabeth to the north of Adelaide. In other cities, the lack of facilities in new housing areas has been a chronic problem of post-war suburban development.

A high degree of intervention in the land market was advocated by the Federal Labor government between 1972 and 1975, for slightly different reasons. It moved to set up joint Commonwealth/State Land Commissions to acquire, subdivide and service land for housing to make it available at a 'fair price'. As shown by Troy (1978), this programme met with resistance from conservatively-inclined State governments in New South Wales, Victoria, Western Australia and Queensland. But in the State where a full-scale Commission was established with a significant share of the land development process (again South Australia), the programme did reduce land-price inflation. Elsewhere, smaller-scale Land Councils had little impact on land prices.

The implication is clear: *conventional land use planning alone is insufficient to achieve an equitable system of land conversion from rural to urban use.*

Public facility provision

As noted above, metropolitan planning in Australia has had a continuing concern with the greater provision of community facilities — including shops, hospitals and educational establishments — in suburban areas. Some limited successes have been achieved in this direction, particularly in Sydney.

However, glaring deficiencies remain in the supply of hospital, educational and cultural facilities in outer-suburban areas developed since the 1950s (Stretton 1975; Black 1977; Donald 1981). This situation is attributable to two facts, that:

- Planning has not possessed direct control over the provision and location of publicly-provided facilities; the job has been given to special-purpose government agencies and authorities;

- These agencies do not necessarily regard territorial justice in facility provision as an important goal, but rather tend to locate facilities according to traditional efficiency criteria.

This reflects the fragmented nature of control over public-sector facility location and provision; entrenched and powerful bureaucracies have been able to ignore planning provisions where it has suited them. Even within these bureaucracies, however, there has not always been the ability or willingness to control effectively the location and expansion of centralised government services, as Donald (1981:78) points out in a case study of hospital location in Sydney.

Only where the land use planning authorities have been able to exert a direct control over facility provision, such as in the case of Elizabeth cited above, has the supply of facilities reached satisfactory levels in suburban areas. In the other States, planning agencies have generally only had direct control over open space and recreation-area provision. In Sydney, for example, the Cumberland County Council took an active role in providing regional and local open space in the 1950s, and this helped to reduce inequalities between districts over this period (Alexander 1981*a*:164). In Perth, the Metropolitan Region Planning Authority has played an active part in the acquisition of Regional Open Space and this has improved the standard of provision in that city (City of Perth Town Planning Department 1982).

In New South Wales, the State Planning Authority took responsibility in the 1960s for the land assembly and planning of the Mt Druitt town centre in the western suburbs; while the Macarthur Development Board, a governmental authority, has had some success in attracting jobs and facilities to the south-western sector of Sydney in recent years through land acquisition, service and subdivision activity (Harrison 1978). Again, therefore, the implication is clear: *direct control over facility location and provision is the only sure way in which to achieve planning objectives.*

Planning and employment

Metropolitan planners have also attempted to steer employment to the most 'appropriate' locations within the cities. Just what have been regarded as appropriate locations has varied from plan to plan and with the philosophies behind the plans. The emphasis in the first generation of plans was on the need to disperse manufacturing jobs from central to suburban areas; such jobs were the single most important source of employment at the time.

We have here an interesting example of a planning policy which in broad terms appears to be in the interests of both capital and labour. Industrial capital has increasingly sought suburban locations in order to improve productivity by installation of less labour-intensive machinery which happens to be more space-extensive. A suburban location is also sought by many employers to gain better access to an increasingly suburbanised and possibly cheaper resident workforce which may contain segments of non-unionised, and hence cheaper (more exploitable), labour. It should also be noted that suburbanisation is in line with the overall necessity for the capitalist system to expand in order to survive. As Harvey (1973) has pointed out, suburbanisation necessitates increases in the consumption of household goods and services, including the motor car. It acts, therefore, as an instrument to increase the value of labour, by increasing the necessary level of subsistence of the working class. In itself, this process highlights a fundamental contradiction within the system; the necessity to increase consumption on the one hand, and reduce labour costs on the other.

In terms of physical access to jobs, as opposed to wage rates, comparative analysis shows that manufacturing job dispersal led to some significant improvements in the *overall* balance of jobs and resident workers during the 1950s. The improvement was greatest in Sydney, which is a reflection of the high priority placed on equitable job distribution in the Cumberland Plan (for further details see Alexander 1981*a*). However, as Allport (1983; Chapter 15 in this volume) emphasises, the newly-created suburban jobs were not equally accessible to all sections of the workforce, particularly women. Many suburban women, particularly those with children, seeking to re-enter the workforce were restricted in job choice despite the dispersal. These women often did not have access to a car and given the paucity of cross-suburban public transport (Manning 1978; Black 1978) were forced to look for jobs within walking or cycling distance of home, in order to balance the demands of work on the one hand and home duties on the other. If such jobs were not available within this restricted radius, they were often forced to go without. The spatial benefits of job suburbanisation encouraged by the metropolitan plans, therefore, need to be measured in terms of gender and accessibility as much as in terms of the balance of jobs and residents. As Maher, O'Connor and Logan (1981) point out, these factors are critical to job availability and job choice in suburban areas.

In this regard, dispersal plans which sought to steer activity and jobs to suburban centres accessible by both private and public transport were of most benefit. Thus the metropolitan planners in both Sydney and Adelaide were largely successful in locating new *retail* developments at established district centres; compared to the situation in Melbourne and Perth, this afforded suburban retail workers and consumers with more equitable access to the new facilities (Alexander 1981*a*:163).

But what effect did such dispersal have on the job choice of inner-city residents? It has been claimed that the process, coupled with the recent rapid decline of the manufacturing job sector (especially in Sydney, Melbourne and Adelaide), has further disadvantaged low-income inner-city residents by reducing job opportunities. In some cases inner-city workers, thrown out of jobs by closure of manufacturing firms, have been unable to find alternative local employment; this may be partly as a result of reduced job choice in the inner city resulting from continuing dispersal. These workers are left with the prospect either of searching in the suburban areas for a new job and reverse-commuting in the event of finding one, or moving house to the suburbs to be closer to the shrinking pool of industrial jobs. Such a move may not always be possible, because of cost or family constraints (Beed 1981:227).

Little and Carter (1979) argue that job centralisation and population consolidation in inner areas will generate a higher overall level of job availability than continued suburbanisation. However, the evidence for this assertion is tenuous (K. O'Connor 1979; Beed 1981). It appears that the unemployment problems of inner-city residents, acute as they may be, have less to do with spatial trends or land use planning than with overall macro-economic developments and the changing structure of the Australian economy.

A final point to be made in relation to job location is that planning has largely failed in its aims (apparent in second-generation plans in Sydney and Perth) to disperse the growing office sector. Centralisation of office development has occurred in all cities in recent decades, and although this has started to break down in the last few years, it has not yet done so sufficiently to ease severe job access and work-journey problems for suburban residents seeking office jobs (Alexander 1982*b*). Strong efforts were made by the Federal Department of Urban and Regional Development between 1972 and 1975 to initiate government and private-sector office relocation from central to suburban areas; but, like other urban initiatives, these were scotched on the re-election of a conservative Federal government in 1975.

In any event it has to be recognised that in seeking to disperse office development, planning has pitted itself against very powerful and entrenched financial interests. Often these go beyond national, let alone State, boundaries; foreign capital has been extensively involved in office development in Australian city CBD areas in recent years (see, for example, Daly 1984). Despite some tentative government support for office dispersal in the 1970s, third-generation plans are much less concerned with office dispersal, in some instances (for example, Melbourne) advocating centralisation. All States are now making renewed efforts to attract international capital to central-city office development projects in order to revive flagging economies. The partnership of State and capital seems to be particularly strong in the office development sector (Berry and Huxley 1985).

Transportation planning

Given the continued suburban expansion of Australian cities and the accompanying rises in car ownership, it is not surprising that there has been a dramatic swing from public to private transport since 1950 (as illustrated in Figure 8.3). Car travel now accounts for over 85 per cent of all vehicle mileage in Australian cities (Newman and Kenworthy 1981). The scatter and low density of suburban activity and areas makes them ideally suited to car travel; the public transport systems remain focused on the central areas, which have become less significant as job and activity concentrations (Neutze 1981:101). In any event, public transport is particularly ill-suited to the new scattered pattern of land use in suburban Australia, a pattern which —as noted above—is of fundamental importance to the continuing expansion of capitalist enterprise. On an international comparison, Australian cities are second only to those in the United States in terms of car ownership and car usage; when combined with their low densities, this gives Australian cities particularly high levels of energy consumption (Newman and Kenworthy 1979).

Figure 8.3 The growing dominance of the car: work journey modal split, Sydney and Melbourne 1900–80

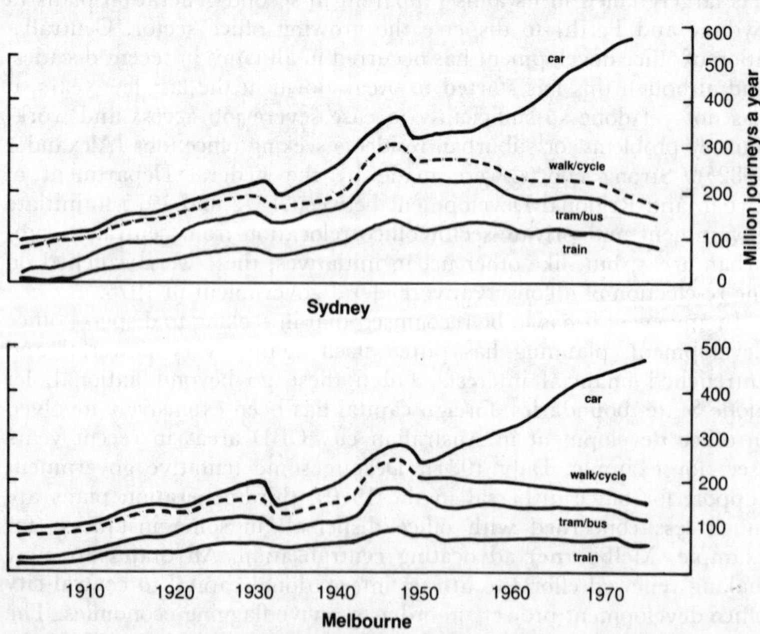

It is not surprising, therefore, that urban planning has recently—and arguably rather belatedly—turned its attention to ways of conserving energy usage in urban areas. As yet, however, few original proposals have surfaced and the main emphasis is on revival of ideas such as urban consolidation and multi-centred cities (Bunker 1985; Chapter 10 in this volume). Some claim that such measures are likely to save considerable amounts in liquid fuel usage (for example,

Newman 1981; White et al. 1978). But it appears that the savings are likely to be marginal given the prediliction of capitalist enterprise for scattered locations and Australians' particularly strong attachment to car usage. While recent years have seen a mild upswing in the use of public transport the trend is as yet limited, and has probably had little impact on urban energy consumption.

In any event, it is somewhat ironic that planners are now apparently concerned about the high level of car usage and petrol consumption in cities since, to a large extent, this level of car usage has been encouraged and facilitated by land use/transport planning. As noted above, land use planning has succeeded in accelarating the dispersal of industrial and retail activity, and has sought to initiate office dispersal; yet activity dispersal has been one of the more important causes of the increasing swing to car travel.

The transportation studies of the 1960s and 1970s (Table 8.2) further encouraged car travel by their use of demand-modelling techniques which assumed a continuation of increased car usage and 'sought to provide road space to cater for that demand' (Maher 1982*a*:100). As Beed (1981:79) points out, this type of 'trend planning' is 'forced to make the assumption that currently expressed transport preferences represent a satisfactory or unavoidable situation that must apply in the future'.

The inevitable outcome of this approach were recommendations squarely in the 'big-build' mould; they emphasised roads to a far greater extent than public transport. The road expenditure programmes involved comprehensive freeway networks along the lines of those in United States cities, while the public transport proposals were largely directed to reinforcing the radially-oriented and increasingly financially-troubled rail and bus networks.

But even without these studies, the capital-works programmes of State government transport authorities in the 1950–80 period focused strongly on road building; few new public transport systems have been provided. In fact the 1950s and 1960s saw a gradual rundown of public transport services, epitomised by the removal of tram networks in all mainland capitals except Melbourne (Spearritt 1984). The removal was largely justified in terms of the trams' role in impeding 'free traffic flow'—the constant preoccupation of the traffic engineer.

However, it became clear in the 1970s that the freeway-network programmes were too ambitious, even for the powerful road-construction authorities to proceed with in toto, because of increased financial constraints on road building due to government expenditure restraints, and steeply rising costs and rising community opposition to freeway construction and its associated social impacts, particularly in inner-city areas.

There has therefore been something of a re-orientation of transport planning priorities in the last decade. Road-building programmes, such as that put forward by the Urban Transport Advisory Committee (1976) in Sydney, are now of a much more modest scale

(Dobinson 1982). Freeway networks have been scaled down by State governments in Sydney, Melbourne and Adelaide and in Perth to a lesser extent. This action followed the precedent set by the stance of the Whitlam government (1972–75) against the funding of inner-city freeways, in itself a response to rising community concern.

In addition, current Labor State governments, particularly those in New South Wales and Victoria, have further reordered transport expenditure priorities in favour of public transport (Spearritt 1984). A new light-rail system has started development in Adelaide, and a decision to electrify the scant suburban rail network has been made in Perth. While the road authorities are still keen on pushing ahead with planned networks in those cities, they are having to recognise the new priorities, and the reduced level of Federal funding to roads which is now evident.

However, the extent to which this new transport environment will bring passengers back to public transport is unclear, even though some modest increases in patronage have been recorded in recent years. The public transport systems remain oriented to the CBD, and even with some metropolitan plans now firmly advocating job centralisation, the system needs to be reoriented to serve the more diffuse journey patterns that now prevail. Otherwise, no matter how much investment is made in new facilities, deficits seem likely to become even more chronic and the systems even more marginal in terms of the overall urban transport task.

Summary and conclusions

It is evident that land use/transport planning has had a chequered history in Australian cities, and one which is at best a mixed success story. While opinion on the effectiveness of planning may vary, there is little that has occurred in recent years to alter the conclusion of Peter Harrison (1974:218) that 'the controls and restraints imposed on metropolitan development by statutory land use controls have been of limited influence'.

Within this limited influence, however, metropolitan planning has made the following major gains:

- produced a more orderly pattern of extension of urban areas; brought about a better balance of jobs and resident workers, (but not necessarily for female workers) particularly in the industrial-job market, and in cities where equity has been an important goal;
- provided some outer-suburban residents with a greater degree of access to retail and social facilities than would otherwise have occurred.

On the other hand, planners have often failed to meet their goals, particularly where they have aimed against prevailing market trends or against the plans of government agencies. This is illustrated by:

- the gradual demise of the public transport system and the failure, until recently, to enact public-transport improvements; and the general encouragement of car dependence through the planning process;
- the continuation of land-price inflation on developing urban fringes and the lack of adequate public facilities in many new suburban areas.

Only where steps have been taken for government to initiate and participate directly in the land-development process has significant success been achieved, as in the case of South Australia. This implies that planning needs a far greater degree of political commitment in order to succeed in its aims.

Given earlier questions raised on the role of the state, it may be suggested that such state participation in the urban land economy will only serve to reinforce the operation of capitalist enterprise with all its associated inequalities. Yet examples cited in this chapter, such as that of the South Australian Housing Trust's operations in Adelaide, suggest that co-ordinated state planning action *can* lead to tangible benefits to the working class such as improved housing and facility provision. It may well be that the motivation for this action was the expansion of industrial capital; the state has acted in a role similar to the Owens and Cadburys of the nineteenth century. Even so, benefits have flowed both in terms of improved living conditions, and in the control of the land-development and property-speculation activities of finance capital with its inequitable side-effects. Paris and Williams (1984:72; Chapter 7 in this volume) maintain that planning 'most often exists in a mediating relationship between fractions of capital as well as between capital and labour'.

From evidence in this chapter it would seem that the first of these roles is far more common than the second. Yet the point remains that in fulfilling this role the state can still generate worthwhile additional benefits for labour. And beyond that—perhaps as in the case of public versus private transport—the state can be seen to have acted occasionally in a mediating role on behalf of labour. Thus there does seem some ground for supporting Stilwell's argument that the state should be seen as 'an arena of class struggle rather than automatically serving the needs of capital' (1983:215; Chapter 4 in this volume).

This debate however may seem rather academic in the 1980s, when the focus of public policy attention has shifted from cities to the national economy. Funding available for urban infrastructure and housing, thanks to the demands of the so-called resources boom and the expenditure restraints of government, has been drastically curtailed. Unemployment in the cities is high, and there seems little that planning can do to address the underlying economic problems thrown up by the restructuring of the Australian economy, notably the 'decline of manufacturing industry and its urban-based employment in favour of the mining and energy industries, which are both capital intensive and rural based' (Sandercock 1983*d*:42).

This suggests a rather bleak urban future, with increasing levels of unemployment, particularly in the cities of south-eastern Australia where manufacturing industry is concentrated. Acute problems have already emerged in cities such as Newcastle, Wollongong, Whyalla, Melbourne and Adelaide where the declining steel, textile, white-goods and car-building industries are based (Stilwell 1980; Sandercock and Melser 1985). The squeeze on urban capital expenditure is likely to result in increasing deficiencies in public service provision which will exacerbate problems of public transport and housing provision, and increase inequalities within the cities (Australian Institute of Urban Studies 1980). The extent to which land use and transport planning can correct these trends is probably limited, due to its focus on land use regulation and transport-route location rather than more positive intervention in the urban economy. However, planning can be viewed as but one arm of a social and economic policy aimed at reviving the economic base of the cities, and at providing a more equitable access — both economic and physical — to urban resources.

This aim can only be achieved if the state plays a larger role in the land development process, in the production of goods and services within the cities and in the expropriation of surplus value created by the production process. Radical changes in the processes of production and in the nature of an economic system which clearly depends on the expansion of the necessary level of subsistence of the working class, cannot be expected in the short term. Such a system is, in the case of urban Australia, heavily dependent for its survival on the encouragement of suburbanisation and the high level of consumer-goods demand that accompanies it.

In the light of this chapter's arguments, however, it seems fair to suggest that the role of the state *can* gradually be transformed from one where it is acting largely on behalf of private capital to one where it plays a major part in redirecting capital from private to public purposes. Co-ordinated enterprises operating in the land-development, public-facility provision and manufacturing spheres would be one step in this direction. If this occurs, we may yet live to see the day when planning plays a decisive role in shaping the urban economy less in the interests of the capitalist class and more in the interests of those whose labour is vital to the survival of that class.

Chapter 9
The shape of Melbourne: a political geography of Melbourne's planning in the 1970s and 1980s

Bill Logan

During the early 1970s two major plans were drawn up with the aim of controlling the shape of metropolitan Melbourne for the remainder of the century. These were the 1971 'Master Plan' and the 1974 'Strategy Plan'. They were formulated by separate planning authorities, although both received the official blessing of the Victorian State government. The first plan was carried out by the Melbourne and Metropolitan Board of Works (MMBW); the second was the work of the Melbourne City Council (MCC), the municipal government of the innermost and, because it contains the central business district (CBD), the most important of the metropolis's local government areas. The plans covered different geographical areas and their objectives conflicted fundamentally: the 1971 Master Plan was primarily concerned with channelling peripheral expansion and bolstering the traditional mono-nuclear structure of the metropolis, whereas the Strategy Plan was aimed at achieving 'specialised growth' in a contained CBD and the protection of the remainder of the inner city and suburbs against the growth pressures of commercial and industrial redevelopment.

Before either of these plans had time to make a real impact on Melbourne's urban form (or, indeed, for planners to sort out the inconsistencies between them), a third plan was unveiled which cut across the objectives of both and represented a complete volte-face in terms of government planning intentions. This 'Metropolitan Strategy Plan' was released by the MMBW in 1979 and received State government endorsement in 1980. It was a new regional plan based essentially on the notions of metropolitan containment, inner-city redevelopment, and the establishment of suburban 'activity centres'.

In attempting to understand the decision-making processes which led to this confused succession of plans for Melbourne, two basic points need to be made at the outset. First, the way that the processes operate is to a large extent the result of the extreme fragmentation of Melbourne's urban management. A 'divide and rule' situation exists which enables the State government and its leading officials to maintain their supremacy in Melbourne's planning but which means that

Based on Cox K.R. and Johnston R.J. (eds.) (1982), Chapter 8 in *Conflict, Politics and the Urban Scene* and published here by kind permission of Longmans, London.

all of the authorities with statutory responsibilities in the planning field are weakened and made more vulnerable to pressure-group activities. Melbourne's planning therefore represents the outcome of an elaborate power play with the actors constantly moving into the limelight and out again, regrouping and enjoying varying degrees of success in influencing the direction of planning policy formulation. The power play is not only between classes (the 'capitalists versus the rest' conflict of the over-simplified Cockburn (1977) thesis on the operation of the local state); in Melbourne's case at least, the conflicts are just as much between competing fractions of the same class, between various levels of government and competing sections of the bureaucracy, and between individual politicians, bureaucrats, planners and property-owners. In my view, study of the interactions between individuals is most significant because it is at this scale that decisions are made and conflicts experienced. That is, while the capitalist economic structure might provide an impersonal backdrop to the performance, an understanding of the detailed plot and of the actors requires finer analysis using humanistic approaches emphasising human agency and the study of the perceptions and motivations behind decision-making and planning action.

The second point is that the roles which each of the actors takes in this power play are only in part a direct response to the issues at hand—the so-called 'objective reality' of the Melbourne situation; they are often very much more the result of the way the actors' previous life-histories have led them to perceive that situation. Thus it may be argued that interpretations are more important than the 'facts'—for it is on the basis of interpretations that people act, that politicians formulate policies, planners intervene in the community, and social scientists 'explain' the processes of urban change that remodel our cities.

In the late 1970s the Melbourne planning power play was manifested publicly in an urban-form debate in which the main participants were social scientists (especially geographers and economists) as well as politicians, bureaucrats and planners. Opinions about the most desirable future shape for Melbourne and the most appropriate policies governments might introduce to achieve the desired morphology fell into a number of broad camps. Each of these was based on a distinctive set of value judgements about the city—and, beyond it, about society in general. The final government decision flows from an appraisal of the relative merits of these value judgements as well as the government's consideration of its own survival needs in this context of pluralistic pressure-group activity.

Figure 9.1 attempts to summarise this model of the political process of policy decision-making. Founded on the concepts of power and political conflict, it seeks to emphasise the fact that decision-makers and the planners responsible for the implementation of their decisions perceive issues differently, and that their perception of the problem

Figure 9.1 The political process of policy formulation and implementation – a conflict perspective

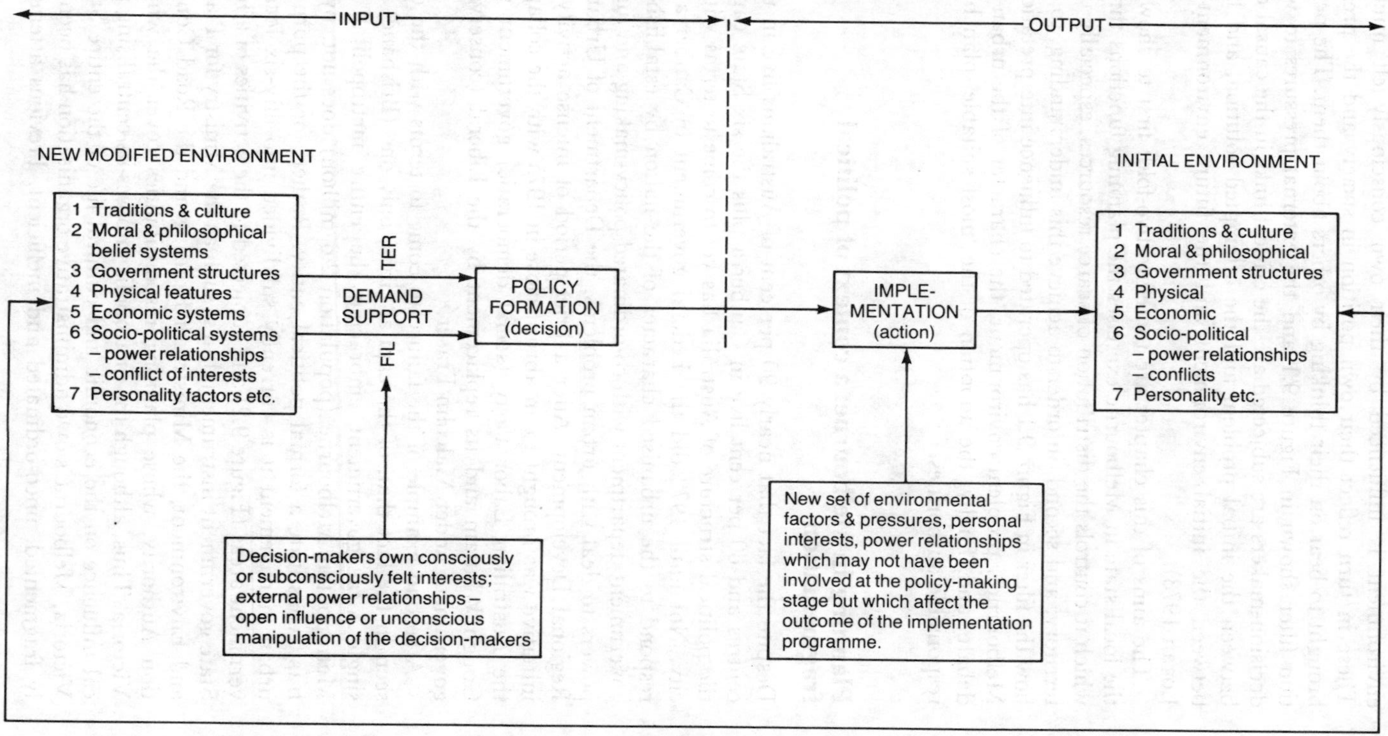

INPUT

OUTPUT

NEW MODIFIED ENVIRONMENT

1 Traditions & culture
2 Moral & philosophical belief systems
3 Government structures
4 Physical features
5 Economic systems
6 Socio-political systems
– power relationships
– conflict of interests
7 Personality factors etc.

FILTER

DEMAND
SUPPORT

POLICY FORMATION (decision)

IMPLE-MENTATION (action)

INITIAL ENVIRONMENT

1 Traditions & culture
2 Moral & philosophical
3 Government structures
4 Physical
5 Economic
6 Socio-political
– power relationships
– conflicts
7 Personality etc.

Decision-makers own consciously or subconsciously felt interests; external power relationships – open influence or unconscious manipulation of the decision-makers

New set of environmental factors & pressures, personal interests, power relationships which may not have been involved at the policy-making stage but which affect the outcome of the implementation programme.

environment is influenced by their own consciously-felt interests. These in turn reflect their own position in society and the pressure brought to bear on their thinking by others about them. The perception filter shown in Figure 9.1 and the external pressures to which decision-makers are subjected are the critical links in the causal chain between the initial problem and the attempted solution, and hence between the initial environment and the future environment (W. Logan 1978).

The aims of this chapter are therefore two-fold: first to show how the local state in Melbourne exercises the planning functions through which it controls the distribution of scarce resources, especially urban territory; and second, in order to achieve this understanding, to show how the filter in Figure 9.1 has operated to influence interpretations of Melbourne's problem environment, the character of the urban form debate, and, finally, the adoption of the 'most suitable' plan by the responsible authorities.

Planning in Melbourne: a context of political fragmentation

Despite the fact that nearly 90 per cent of Australians live in urban centres and 60 per cent live in Canberra plus the six State capitals, the political structure of Australia has yet to come to terms with the city. Not until 1972 did the Federal government in Canberra fully respond to the urbanised character of the nation by establishing a government department with co-ordinated policy-making and funding powers to deal with urban problems, the Department of Urban and Regional Development. After a brief period of intense activity, this initiative was brought to an abrupt close in 1975 with the collapse of the Australian Labor Party (social democratic) government under Gough Whitlam and its replacement by the Liberal (conservative) government under Malcolm Fraser.

A second example of the failure to come to terms with the city is seen in the fact that, of the capital cities, only one (Brisbane) has a single local government embracing the entire metropolitan area. Metropolitan Melbourne (population 2.6 million) does not, by contrast, constitute a formal political entity. Rather, for the purpose of urban management it is currently subdivided into fifty-six local government areas (Figure 9.2) and subjected to the activities of a host of State government instrumentalities, such as the Ministry for Planning and Environment, the Ministry of Housing and the Road Construction Authority, whose planning responsibilities cover the whole of Victoria. Thus, although the metropolis imposes its centralising political influence on the economic and cultural life of the entire State of Victoria, Melbourne's own administrative organisation has been highly fragmented, unco-ordinated and inefficient. Previous attempts to

Figure 9.2 The Melbourne metropolitan area: regions and local government areas

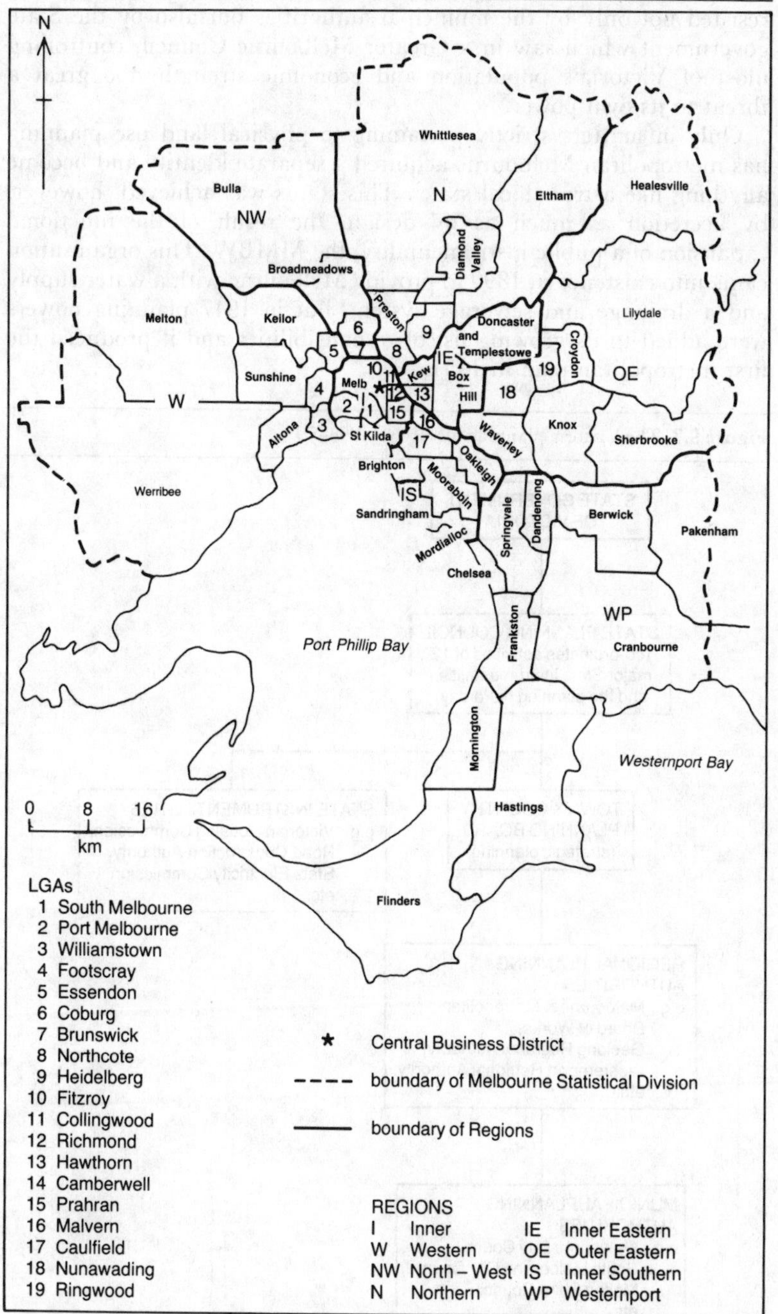

overcome these problems by creating a Greater Melbourne Council (in 1913, 1915, 1936 and 1951) invariably met with failure, being resisted not only by the municipal authorities but also by the State government which saw in a Greater Melbourne Council, controlling most of Victoria's population and economic strength, too great a threat to its own power.

Only in matters strictly pertaining to physical land use planning has metropolitan Melbourne acquired a separate identity and become anything like a true 'local state'. This status was achieved, however, by accretion as much as by design, the result of the functional expansion of a public instrumentality, the MMBW. This organisation came into existence in 1890 to provide Melbourne with a water supply and a drainage and sewerage system, but in 1947 planning powers were added to its growing list of responsibilities and it produced the first metropolitan plan in 1954.

Figure 9.3 The Victoria planning hierarchy, 1968–79

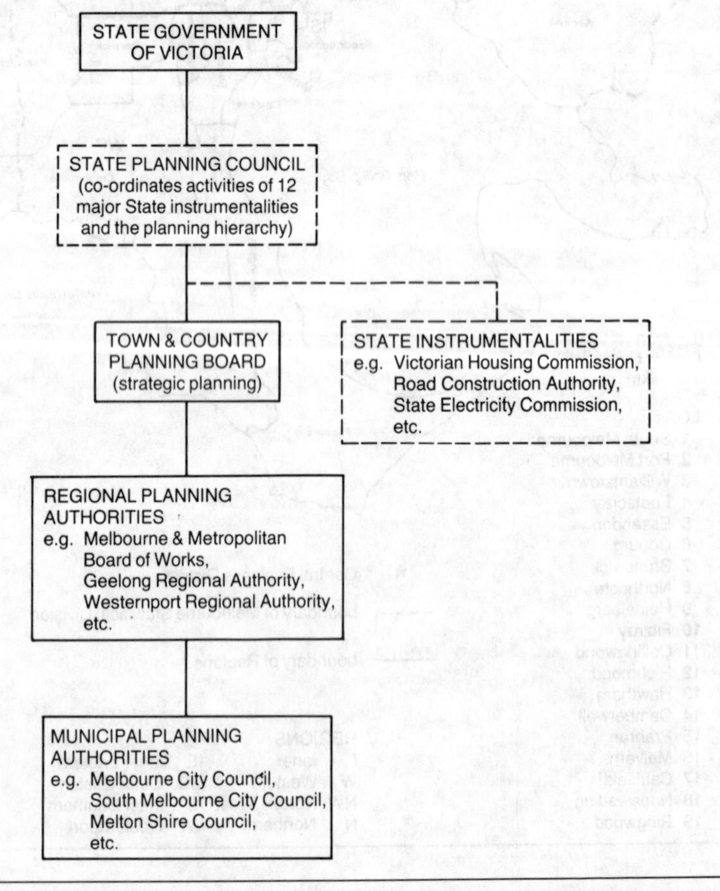

In a planning hierarchy (Figure 9.3) formalised in 1968 under the aegis of Rupert Hamer, Victoria's Liberal Party Premier (1972–81) who was then the Minister for Local Government, limits were set to the MMBW's further expansion into the planning sphere. It became one of a middle layer of regional planning authorities whose task was defined as drawing up regional schemes in conformity with the general statements of planning policy promulgated by the superior State Town and Country Planning Board. The responsibility for detailed local-area planning was defined as belonging to the municipal authorities. Moreover the regional planning scheme would be controlled on a day-to-day basis through a planning-permit scheme administered by the municipal councils on the regional authority's behalf.

While this arrangement secured the MMBW's power to influence the shape of metropolitan Melbourne in theory, its effectiveness was restricted in practical terms. Just as jealousy has characterised the relations between Federal, State and municipal governments in the Australian political hierarchy, so too does it mark the interactions between the various levels of the Victorian planning hierarchy. The local governments have never totally accepted the overriding powers regarding land use planning of the regional authorities and frequent disagreements have occurred, especially over the issue of planning permits. Meanwhile the State instrumentalities, particularly those responsible for housing and roads, have strenuously defended their own fields from encroachment. The emergence in the late 1970s of a Department of Planning, now the Ministry for Planning and Environment, further complicated the power play.

Planning initiatives in the early 1970s

The effects of this fragmentation on Melbourne's planning were first dramatically seen in the early 1970s in the conflict between and the failures of the Master Plan and the Strategy Plan.

The MMBW's Master Plan, 1971

The broad configuration of the 1971 plan was determined by the conditions of the 1960s—rapid population growth based on strong rates of both natural increase and overseas immigration, together with suburban sprawl based on cheap petrol, the desire for low-density living and the ideology of private home-ownership. Few raised the possibility that these conditions might change, especially that population mobility via the motor car might be suddenly and rapidly reduced. Thus, in 1966, when the Minister for Local Government called upon the Town and Country Planning Board, the MMBW and a citizens' lobby, the Town and Country Planning Association of Victoria, to reassess metropolitan growth goals, all three put forward proposals for further outward expansion although in different arrangements of growth corridors and satellite towns. The citizen's group advocated a single ten-kilometre wide corridor stretching to the south-east into Gippsland and based on a new rapid-transport spine; the Town and Country Planning Board proposed linear growth in three radial corridors of metro-towns; and the MMBW recommended a plan for seven radial corridors and a satellite town at Sunbury (Figure 9.4).

Figure 9.4 The MMBW 'Master Plan', 1971

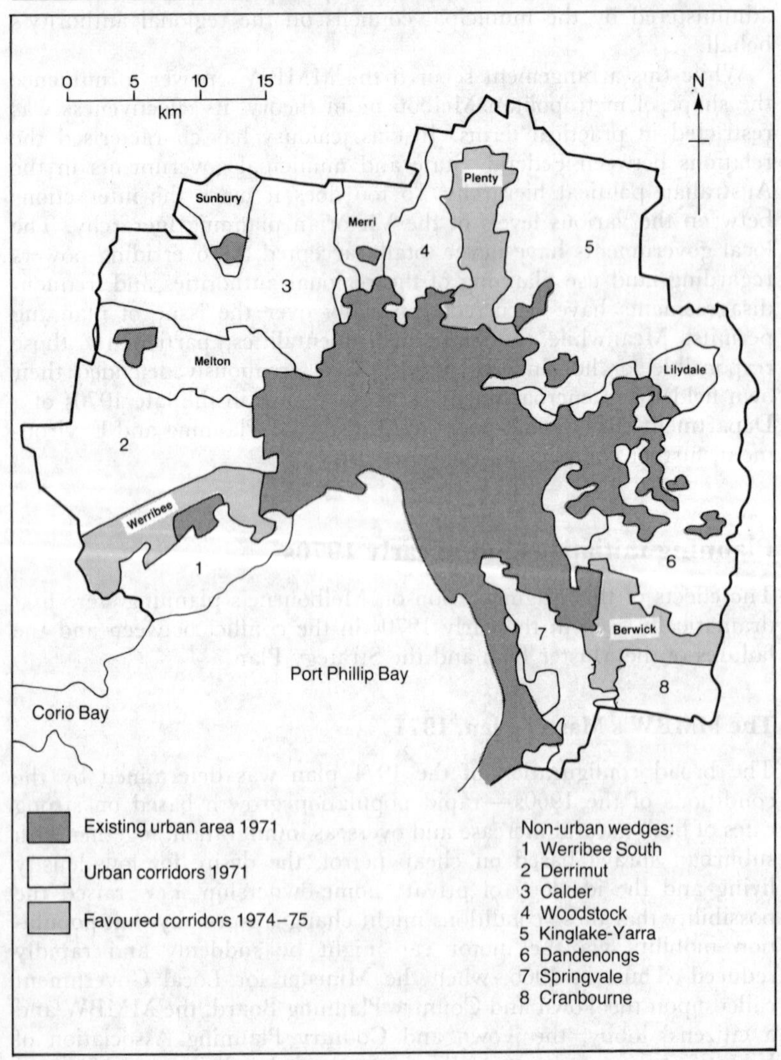

The MMBW's plan was selected as government policy and, after the hearing of objections in 1972, its implementation began. The plan had two main advantages from the Liberal government's point of view. First, the recommended corridor design would strengthen the traditional CBD which was becoming increasingly eccentric in location within the built-up area as suburban growth favoured the east and south-east and shunned the drier basalt plains to the west and north-west. In this way the electoral and financial support of important inner-city interests—especially the CBD retailers and property owners, including banks, insurance companies and other finance institutions—was maintained for the government. Second, the alternative plans, by concentrating growth into too few directions, would have created enormous problems of green-acre speculation. The MMBW plan, on the other hand, would have spread the pressures more thinly and made them more easily managed. The government's intention was not to eliminate speculation—only public ownership of the reservoir of fringe land could achieve that. In its view some degree of speculation was preferable to such a 'socialist' measure.

Several commentators, notably Sandercock (1977, 1979), have argued that in fact the State government, MMBW and the large land-speculating companies, especially the finance institutions, conspired together to determine the specific design features of the plan, particularly the boundaries of the growth corridors. Neutze (1977), on the other hand, has argued that finance institutions have had little positive influence on the way Australian cities in general have developed, seeing their role as supplying (or refusing) funds for the initiatives of others rather than being large-scale developers in their own right. In any case, there is an increasingly historical quality about this controversy concerning the forces behind fringe development. During the implementation stage several significant modifications were made to the plan, including a reduction in the number of corridors for initial development from seven to three and the creation of the Melton satellite town; such policy changes caught many speculators by surprise. These changes were made in 1974–75 and partly reflected the enthusiasm for decentralisation then flourishing in Australia. But they also represented the first step towards the fundamental policy revision which culminated in the 1980 'Metropolitan Strategy Plan'. The urban debate no longer focuses on the outer suburbs and sprawl, but on the inner city and containment.

The MCC's Strategy Plan, 1974

The State government, MMBW, inner metropolitan local governments and centrally-located business enterprises had become increasingly worried during the 1960s that Melbourne's heart was failing. The population of the eight municipalities comprising the Inner Region (Figure 9.2) had fallen by 18 per cent between the Censuses of

1947 and 1971; that of the City of Melbourne had plummeted by 24 per cent. Throughout the 1960s attempts had been made to reverse the downward trend by implementing the public housing authority's redevelopment policies in the inner suburbs. But the authority's method—drastic block clearance using compulsory acquisition powers—and the bleak high-rise flats with which the nineteenth century terrace houses were replaced—had failed to win public acceptance and were eventually abandoned by the government in the early 1970s.

Again the Minister for Local Government (Hamer) stepped in, evidently this time at the instigation of the Melbourne Chamber of Commerce, an influential lobby comprising leading CBD retailing and commercial companies. Normally espousing a free-enterprise philosophy, the Chamber now advocated government intervention in the interest of maintaining the profitability of the city centre in general and the enterprises it represented in particular. Arguing the need for a revitalised CBD to fit the MMBW's policy of balanced growth between the eastern and western corridors, Hamer was able to persuade the MCC in 1971 that it should, as responsible planning authority for the central area under his three-tiered planning hierarchy, embark upon an intensive study to identify the most appropriate growth strategy for the city of Melbourne.

Once the Strategy Plan was released its overwhelming conservation bias was immediately obvious. Hailed by the press, planning profession and public alike as 'flexible and sensitive', a 'new greening of old Melbourne', it had broken with Australian tradition by placing the environment before growth. It had opted for a 'specialised growth' strategy under which the CBD was not only to become narrower in functional range but was to be prevented from further outward expansion by the introduction of tight 'plot ratio' restrictions. That is, by controlling the ratio between the total floor space permitted in a new building and the site area, the plan would prevent future high-rise commercial and office developments in the CBD fringe. It would thus concentrate CBD functions in the highly accessible 'Golden Mile' of the traditional CBD and would protect both the investments in CBD land and buildings already made by members of the Chamber, and the character of the inner residential suburbs which were beginning to regain popularity with the middle-class professionals working either in the CBD or in educational and medical institutions nearby. In addition, the plan sought specifically to preserve historical precincts and to up-grade community facilities in all residential neighbourhoods.

In a burst of initial enthusiasm, the MCC approved the main policies and the City Planning Department has been implementing some aspects of the plan since 1975. However, it quickly became evident that a head-on collision between the regional and municipal levels of the planning hierarchy was inevitable. The MMBW's forward planning was based on retaining maximum growth at the centre, whereas the MCC's strategy was aimed at containing commercial growth to the CBD proper and maintaining the existing physical and social character of the rest of the inner city.

How had such widely differing solutions to the same problem environment arisen? The MCC at the time was a club-like body dominated by a faction of conservative councillors representing the CBD businessmen known as the Civic Group—generally regarded as a front for the Liberal Party—and kept in power by a weighted electoral system. How had it arrived at a position of approving a plan that seemed to oppose its own interests? In the case of the MMBW's Master Plan, at least the proposed urban form was consistent with the interests of big business; very clearly a different set of pressures had been exerted on the policy formulated behind the MCC's Strategy Plan.

The inner Melbourne power play, 1974

The Strategy Plan reflected the ambitions of an alliance of three sets of actors (Figure 9.5). The first set comprised a small but highly vocal group of new middle-income professional and managerial residents—the 'gentry'—who had begun moving back into the inner suburbs in the late-1960s and who, by the mid-1970s, had firmly established their territorial hold (W. Logan 1982, 1985). They had been attracted initially by the inner-suburban residential environment which seemed to them to offer a relief from the monotony of the suburbs and the chance to create what Relph (1976) calls 'authentic places'—socially-heterogeneous village-like communities set in the nineteenth century streetscapes at the heart of a twentieth century metropolis. Banding together into resident-action groups to create a new force in Melbourne's urban politics, and supported by such middle-class single-issue pressure groups as the National Trust, they fought fiercely and successfully against the efforts of the public housing and freeway construction authorities in the early 1970s to modernise their adopted neighbourhoods.

The gentry have frequently been seen as involved in a conspiracy with the Town Hall and CBD businessmen (Fisher 1974; Colenutt 1976; CURA 1977) aimed at raising property values and, hence, municipal rates. Certainly the gentry in inner Melbourne were able to dominate the public-participation planning exercises which were conducted by Interplan, the planning consultants hired by the MCC to draw up the Strategy Plan, and they were able to win many environmental improvements from the MCC which had an impact on property values. The gentry's requests seemed to strike a chord with the middle-class professional backgrounds of the Interplan team. One of the most basic points put by the gentry was for the plan to arrest the outward expansion of CBD land uses, and it was on this point

Figure 9.5 The power context of environmental planning, 1974

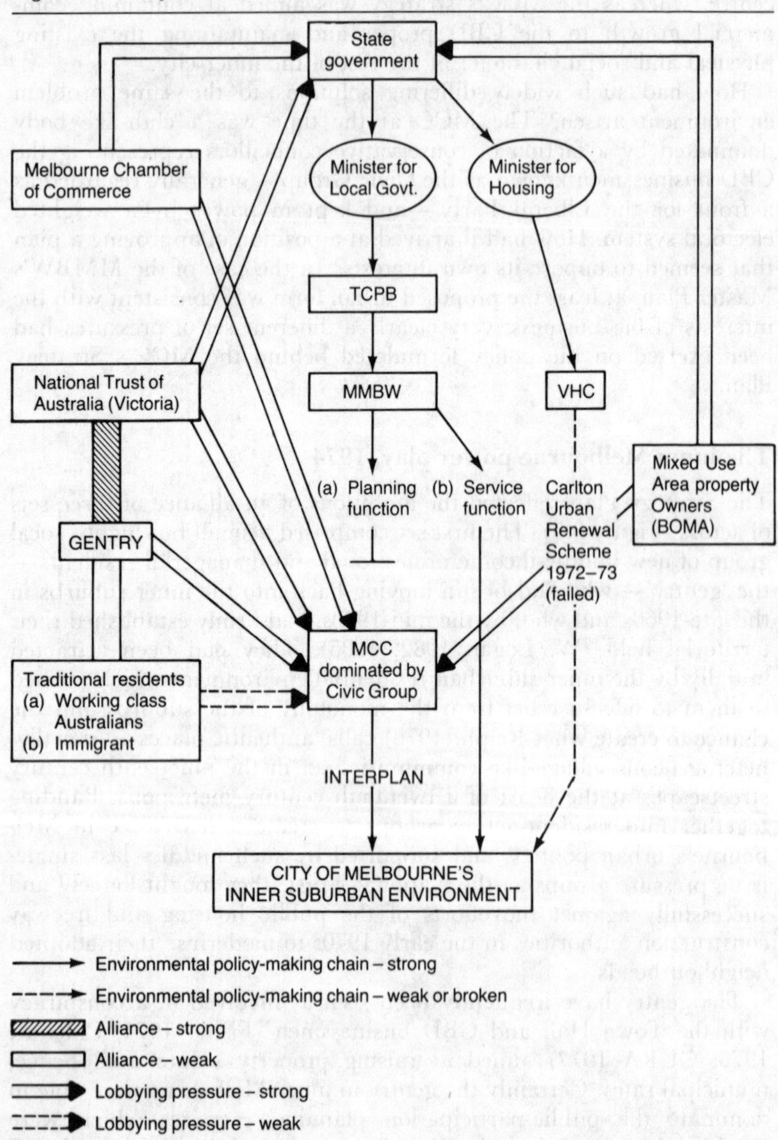

that the second group of actors — the CBD businessmen, especially as represented by the Melbourne Chamber of Commerce — had been prompted to join forces with the gentry. Normally the residents and the businessmen have opposed each other in municipal affairs, but in the early 1970s both groups had a common ambition to contain the CBD. The gentry wanted to protect its investments, both financial and, above all, emotional, in inner-suburban housing by the creation of a medium-rise mixed commercial residential buffer zone between the CBD and the residential suburbs. The Chamber, on the other hand, sought to protect its members' investments in real estate in the traditional 'Golden Mile'.

Consideration of the part played by the third set of actors supporting the Strategy Plan — the senior bureaucrats at the Town Hall — dispels the prima facie appearance of a totally class-bound and economically-motivated alliance. For its part, the MCC was involved in a desperate campaign to push itself forward as the major planning authority for the central area — a campaign which, as we shall see, is having a repeat performance in the mid-1980s. Its bureaucrats, especially the Town Clerk, City Planner and City Engineer, and to a certain extent, the elected councillors — their personal ambitions fused with the public status of the Council — were anxious to ward off the planning interests of competing authorities. Against a backdrop of a poor planning record and the fear that it would be reduced to being 'merely the garbage collectors and pot-hole menders', the MCC sought support from whatever source it could find in order to force through its Strategy Plan.

I have dealt in detail elsewhere with the nature of these bureaucrats' ambitions (W. Logan, 1985). While there is no doubt that they saw increased rate revenues coming from the gentrification process, the dominant motivation appears to have been the desire to exert their personal control over the political machine beneath them and to see their own ideas and pet projects forced through the decision-making apparatus. Rather than demonstrating the interpretation of the urban managers conspiring together to 'reinforce a particular distributional form or recompense' (Williams 1976:76), the Melbourne case study, in so far as it relates to the Town Hall actors, shows a quest for personal power rather than economic rewards. If the MCC bureaucrats espoused a philosophy of planning intervention, it was to promote a society based on the work ethic and a belief in free enterprise which would lead to economic growth and prosperity for society as a whole. Gentrification was therefore perceived as worth encouraging because it helped renew the inner city without the need for government intervention. They upheld a technocratic approach of planning based, like that of Davies' (1972) 'evangelistic bureaucrats' on the assumption that a planning elite could bring the public to a consensus on planning issues. Thus the Town Clerk could write (quoted in Cowen 1966)

> A first essential (for sound planning) is the right attitude...Just as the individual by energy and thought cultivates his mind and develops discernment and the appreciation of superior values, so it is with the community at large. But this needs energy and thought, it requires someone to evangelise, to take the gospel and the hope of salvation to the masses... We must produce in the community an

outlook and a conviction of mind which must in the end influence decision-making at all levels.

Figure 9.5 shows two other sets of actors whose interests were not well served by the Strategy Plan: the first set comprised the working-class residents who became only marginally involved in the planning process, their interests being represented (where they were represented at all) by the gentry or by external social caretakers; the second set were the owners of property in the CBD fringe who wanted a continuation of high-rise development in this area which became known after the Strategy Plan term 'Mixed Use Area'. At the implementation stage (Figure 9.1), this latter group was able to mount fresh opposition. It operated chiefly through the Building Owners' and Managers' Association (BOMA), a small secretariat which acted mainly behind the scenes rather than in public debate. Established in 1970 to act as a watch-dog against any municipal decision which might affect the value of its members' investments, it was able in this case to exert pressure on the State government and the MMBW to revise the CBD containment policy. In 1976–77 the State government happened to be passing through its own ideological crisis over the planning intervention issue, and Premier Hamer and his supporters were faced with hostile anti-planning tactics. The MMBW saw its own planning status under attack and welcomed the chance to undermine the MCC's plan.

Officially the Strategy Plan became bogged down in legislative difficulties. The MCC was not able to adopt the plan *in toto*, a planning stalemate was created in the inner city which continued into the 1980s, and market forces were left relatively free to determine the direction of inner-city change. The fragile alliance of gentry, Town Hall and CBD, always more of a marriage of convenience than a natural group of mutually-supporting elements, had failed in its central bid and did not survive the first year of the plan's implementation. By this time, in any case, the scenario for urban planning had been transformed by the advent of the Fraser government and cutbacks in Federal funding as well as by major demographic and economic factors affecting the entire country.

The changing context of the 1970s

During the 1970s metropolitan Melbourne's population and economic growth rates began to falter. The Inner Region (see Figure 9.2) lost a further 16 per cent of its residents between 1971 and 1976, the sharpest decline recorded, and by the 1981 Census had its lowest population (245 400) since the 1930s. This decline continued to be the result of the out-migration of young working-class families, particularly those of immigrant background. Previously these shifts had been counter-balanced by the inflow of new overseas arrivals, but this flow dried up as the official immigration programme responded to economic recession and rising unemployment after 1974. The two groups still increasing in the inner area — the gentry and the young adults attached to tertiary education and medical institutions — came in small family units and, although they might fully occupy the existing dwelling stock, they did little to stabilise the total population numbers.

In the 1960s it was conventional to attribute inner Melbourne's decline to the increasing space needs of factories and to the suburbanisation of retailing. By the late-1970s, however, suburban sprawl was itself being checked by the growing fuel crisis. Petrol prices doubled in the second half of the 1970s in Australia and, although still low by European standards, they began to make suburban residents re-think their residential and workplace priorities. Signs began to appear in the property market that many outer-suburban families were looking for accommodation closer to the metropolitan centre, adding to the impetus of the gentrification process in the inner suburbs. Judging by CBD retail figures, which showed a fall of 17.5 per cent between 1972 and 1977, another consequence of the increased congestion and costs of travel was that suburban residents were shunning the CBD for shopping and recreational purposes. Employment in retailing and associated services had also fallen back in the CBD, generating a continuing stream of complaints from leading retailers and property owners, Melbourne City councillors and town planners.

In addition to economic recession, structural changes in the national economy began to compound the problems, especially for the inner city. The most optimistic forecasts predicted that depressed economic growth-rates would continue until the late 1980s at least and that some occupational categories would experience long-term decline and be marked by high levels of chronic unemployment (Little 1977); these predictions have proved to be correct. The most vulnerable have been blue-collar jobs in manufacturing although routine clerical and administrative jobs, especially for women, also seem threatened. Traditionally these types of work have been most heavily concentrated in Melbourne's inner areas.

In short, by the end of the 1970s, it was clear that metropolitan Melbourne faced a critical period of readjustment. Instead of unlimited growth, it was confronted by a static suburban frontier, the closure of factories, the decline of the traditional metropolitan core, and the development of quite new patterns of social and spatial differentiation. But these 'facts' of economic and social change did not speak for themselves; rather there was ample scope for interpretation, and planners, politicians and social-scientist observers reacted to this new problem environment in a variety of ways. Different values were ascribed to the various elements involved in the change process;

indeed, different meanings were attached to the change process itself. This attribution of meaning depended to a large extent on how the individual participant or observer viewed society and the city as a whole; his/her socio-political attitude acted as a filter affecting the way the changes taking place were perceived and interpreted.

The urban form debate, circa 1980

These interpretations and the consequent policy recommendations for Melbourne's planning fell into three broad camps, which may be roughly labelled as conservative, social democratic and 'radical'.

First, the conservative camp comprised those who saw the city essentially as an economic system to be kept in order by strong government based on efficient business principles, with some intervention (as in job retraining). The provision of a climate of economic stability and planning certainty were the main (if not the only) justification for government intervention. Gradually, in Melbourne, this body of opinion came down on the side of metropolitan containment and inner-area redevelopment as the most cost-effective way of managing the metropolis.

These views were very clearly expressed in the late 1970s reports of the MMBW (1977, 1979*a*, 1980) and of its economic consultant, F.M Little (1977; Little and Carter 1979). Each of the reports was heavily dependent upon physical-determinist assumptions, seeking to draw causal links between the shape of the city and the emergence and solution of current economic and social problems.

> The land use policies which we adopt to mould the size and shape of Melbourne are going to have a marked effect upon the way that the economic process unfolds here. Indeed . . . the way Australians manage their cities is likely to have much more effect than the traditional economic instruments (such as tariff policies) upon our ability to adjust to economic changes (Little, 1977:19)

One of the major underlying themes of these reports was the fate of unemployed city factory and other unskilled workers. The reports argued that government should assist these workers to retrain for jobs in the expanding service sector of the revitalised CBD; the policies were presented as favouring employers, not employees. This would be most effectively achieved by increasing the density of the inner suburbs because, it was argued, it would lay the basis for an enlarged number and range of service jobs, particularly in public transport, personal services and entertainment. In brief, the thrust of this policy advice was towards the redevelopment of the inner city at considerably higher population densities along European lines, with greater social and land use mix than had been conventionally advocated in Australian urban planning.

The second interpretation placed greater weight on the social elements in the problem environment, was opposed to further centralised investment, and demonstrated deeper empathy with middle and outer suburban residents.

The historian and planning theorist, Hugh Stretton (1970), was the first major Australian social scientist to reassert the advantages of low-density suburban living for households in the young family stage of their life cycle. During the 1970s this pro-suburbanisation stance was taken up by the influential Monash University geographers M. Logan (1977), Maher (1976) and K. O'Connor (1978). Although they no doubt recognised that the fuel situation must bring an end to continuing sprawl, their emphasis remained on the deconcentration of central city functions and the encouragement of a more loosely-knit metropolitan structure of multi-nodal forms.

There was a clear socio-political position behind this mode of interpretation: for M. Logan and his fellow social democrats, the deconcentration strategy had important equity implications. It was seen as what most Australian city-dwellers want, and they maintained that it would be more desirable socially, as well as more efficient in terms of work-residence relationships, to encourage the rapid dispersal of economic and cultural functions, notably from the CBD. Drawing connections between the social condition and the shape of the city, M. Logan (1977:10) argued that 'a single-centred expansive metropolis is the most unequal urban form' and concluded that:

> The alternative, a multiple-centred city is far more equal and I suspect far more efficient. It encourages the cultural, commercial and administrative activities to move to the people; it gives the suburbs a focus and a sense of identity.

While attention was drawn to the conflict between CBD interests and those of the suburban residents — capitalism versus the people — it was in many ways no more than reinforcing the existing popular preferences with unexceptionable political arguments. On the question of the gentrification of the inner suburbs, this mode of interpretation remained ambiguous, although there was an implied support for government to adopt residential relocation policies to fit the changing spatial patterns of job availability.

A third mode of interpretation saw a paradoxical union of participants in the debate — Left-wing observers acting as working-class caretakers and certain conservation-oriented elements of the gentry, coming together to put forward a 'radical' anti-growth argument focusing on the inner suburbs. Both groups insisted that much of the hardship already suffered in the inner suburbs was due to misguided government planning policy which had sought to solve social and environmental problems by encouraging greater capital investment, both public and private. Both rejected the dominant ideology of the city as a 'growth machine' (Molotch 1976) and the political power structure based on a system of vested economic interests.

The planning objectives of the gentry have been referred to above and are well demonstrated in the many documents produced by the gentry's resident action groups (for example, Carlton Association 1969, 1972*a*, 1972*b*, 1972*c*). By contrast, the views of the working-class supporters were both less well-documented and less politically realistic. Their approach was essentially directed towards social conservation (as distinct from the gentry's main emphasis on physical conservation) through the maintenance and moderate expansion of manufacturing and commercial enterprises in the inner area and the curbing of the gentrification pressures. Here the two groups obviously parted company, for both were really competing for the same housing and territory. However, this conflict remained latent, with few of either the gentry or the working class being aware of their involvement in it. Even in the mid-1980s, when increasing inflation of house prices alongside rising unemployment among the lower-income residents make the inequities more striking, this conflict has still to surface.

How such inequities can be eradicated in the Melbourne situation remains to be explained. The Australian social democratic experiment in the years 1972–75 proved too radical for this affluent and basically conservative nation. Marxist analysts are few on the ground and, although one might agree in theoretical terms that the final solution to the urban housing problem and other resource allocation inequities must await the passing of capitalism, this looks like being a long wait in the Australian case. Radicals may confidently interpret the current economic changes affecting Australian CBDs as the start of the collapse of the capitalist city—but for the time being they are forced into supporting the band-aid measures, such as the establishment of tenant unions, low-cost housing co-operatives, rate rebates and income supplements, advocated by critics to their Right.

The new Metropolitan Strategy Plan, 1980

Melbourne's politicians did not wait until this largely academic debate had run its course. While they were no doubt forced to take these opposing arguments into account, and may perhaps have had their own perceptions and attitudes widened as a result, these were merely the overt pressures influencing the planning decision-making process. It remains to consider the covert pressures referred to in Figure 9.1. The adoption of this latest of 'most suitable' plans for Melbourne—the 1980 Metropolitan Strategy Plan—appears to have been mainly determined by a combination of the decision-makers' already-entrenched socio-political attitudes, and their desire to further their own personal ambitions (not necessarily economic) in the face of external pressures exerted by the various lobby groups.

The Chairman of the MMBW since 1966, Alan Croxford, was a case in point. He had already, in a sense, pre-empted the public debate by a series of media statements dating from the early 1970s which clearly revealed his own position — a position to which he had evidently been able to convert not only his own organisation but also, subsequently, the State government. His opinion that inner Melbourne was becoming the 'hole in the middle of a swelling doughnut' and that a costly new infrastructure was being unnecessarily built at the metropolitan fringe while established infrastructure was underutilised in the inner areas, appealed to those who, like him, perceived urban management in conservative terms — the maintenance of an efficient economic system.

But other motives are revealed by analysing the groups and individuals who stood to benefit most by the revised metropolitan policy. Once again the collusion theory falls short; while the capitalists (in this instance, the large property-owners and speculators) may have worked to dominate urban politics in pursuit of their own ends, they were not alone in this. Moreover, while the new strategy emphasising inner-city redevelopment offered great potential for profit-making in the 1980s, those speculators involved in green-acre activities in the 1960s and 1970s were not major investors in inner-suburban property. Indeed, it is misleading to regard speculators and developers as a monolithic group; many of them had their fingers badly burnt by the policy reversal which they very clearly were not in a position to influence.

It seemed evident in the early 1980s that among the main beneficiaries of the policy change were the MMBW itself and its powerful bureaucrats. They had seen the development of the 1974 Strategy Plan by a municipal authority as undercutting their own planning status, and, with the reduction in Federal funding to the cities after 1975 and an end to suburban growth in sight, they were anxious to redefine their role and thereby maintain their prestige. Inner-city redevelopment seemed the best answer. But their ambitions did not cease there; the MMBW again began jockeying for supreme planning powers in metropolitan Melbourne. The Darvall Report on the MMBW in April 1977 (Victoria, 1978) streamlined the organisation by reducing municipal representation on its committees, and Croxford emerged as potentially the most powerful individual in the planning scene. Later, the Bains Report on local government in Victoria (Victoria 1979) renewed the call for a Greater Melbourne Council. The MMBW again seemed eager to assume this function, with Croxford in the principal role. Had this come about, the MMBW would have become the manager of a unified 'local state', not merely in physical planning matters but over the whole range of local government services. Once more the ambitions of the bureaucratic institutions and of the leading bureaucrats had become fused, with the managerialist thesis as described by Pahl (1975) and focusing on the role of individual decision-makers, seeming to be particularly applicable to this Melbourne situation.

The politics of Melbourne's planning in the 1980s

Most of the major planning conflicts in Melbourne in the 1980s have been concentrated in the inner areas. Figure 9.6 attempts to summarise the deployment of actors who were gathering at the start of the decade to support or oppose the new metropolitan plan. At that stage

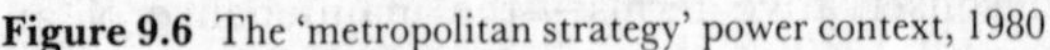

Figure 9.6 The 'metropolitan strategy' power context, 1980

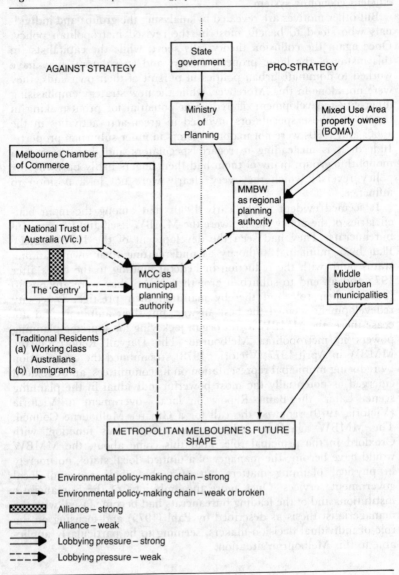

the protagonists seemed likely to be the MMBW backed by BOMA and the middle-suburban municipalities, while the antagonists would be the MCC supported (probably) by the Melbourne Chamber of Commerce and the gentry.

In the late-1970s an uneasy truce had existed between the CBD interests represented by the Chamber and the CBD-fringe interests represented by BOMA. Both seemed dissatisfied with the planning stalemate and economic stagnation of the previous five years. Not only the retailers but also the finance institutions, with either property holdings in the CBD or mortgage capital to lend, had become concerned about the dearth of new building, a situation which they attributed to a surfeit of planning delays and restrictions imposed by the municipal council. The property owners in the Mixed Use Area had long made the same points. Development capital, along with population, were seen to be heading north to the sunshine State of Queensland. Thus Joy (1977:25), the Victorian manager of the major Melbourne-based National Bank of Australasia, indicated that a new wave of mixed public and private investment would be more than welcome; urging a large-scale demolition and rebuilding programme for the inner suburbs, he asserted that

> We cannot wait until the residents burn down the existing buildings, as seems to be happening in the south Bronx or other parts of New York, or for enemy bombers to start an urban renewal process as happened in parts of London.

So disgruntled were they with the existing planning situation that they appeared prepared to abandon the MCC in favour of a management-oriented MMBW, a move that was only headed off when a new Chamber-instigated Conservative Party was formed and was able to seize control of the MCC political machinery during 1978–79.

But the Chamber and BOMA parted ways again once it was realised that the new metropolitan plan proposed merely the maintenance of activity levels in the CBD rather than any real growth, and that it failed to envisage containing the CBD functions to the CBD proper. In addition, the objective of focusing new growth on twenty suburban 'activity centres', which had won the middle-suburban councils' enthusiasm, was seen as further undermining the CBD focus.

For their part, the gentry reacted quickly to what they saw as a new stage in an old battle with over-bearing bureaucracy. But there was some indication that their hold on the inner suburbs was going to be seriously challenged, that the MMBW was preparing to fight the residents. Croxford had long asserted that political conflict in the inner areas had diverted development to the outer suburbs and must be stopped. To his voice was added that of the MMBW's chief planner, Dennis Simsion, who, as reported in *The Age* (7 March 1979), argued before an Urban Development Industries Association audience that:

> The past has seen an era where the political bargaining process has been used as a tool of the articulate, albeit strongly motivated minorities with sectional interests...
>
> The State must bear the responsibility and accept the credit and take the odium for creating zones where higher density development can take place as of right.

A clash between the MMBW and the gentry appeared likely, a clash that may perhaps have put to rest the gentry-government conspiracy thesis—unless, of course, the gentry had been able to find new means of influencing the decision-making process so that the new threat to their well-being was deflected into low-status neighbourhoods in which they had no interest. Alternative low-status jobs generated in the inner area by the new plan would have been of small comfort to working-class residents if they were to be finally displaced by high-rise redevelopments.

Perhaps the main loser would have been the MCC, whose planning responsibilities were under question and seemed bound to be severely curtailed. Indeed, in December 1980, the State Liberal government, increasingly embarrassed by the MCC's performance and under mounting pressure from major CBD retailers, sacked the MCC and three Commissioners were installed in its place in April 1981. It was intended that the Commissioners would run the city until legislation was passed restructuring the MCC. The residential areas were to be severed from the city, so that the new MCC would have been responsibile for the CBD and adjacent areas only, placing it potentially in the control of commercial and property interests.

Premier Hamer had been forced into these extraordinary measures to win back prestige as leading player in a free-enterprise party and regain votes in the State election scheduled for early 1982. But at this point the plot got out of hand. Hamer's measures were largely counter-productive. The developers were not convinced that Melbourne was on the move again; Hamer's party support collapsed and he was forced into an early retirement in June 1981. The State elections duly came in April 1982 and the Liberals lost office. The new Labor government under Premier John Cain promised to reinstate an elected MCC and to implement the 1974 Strategy Plan for inner Melbourne.

Planning under Cain: Melbourne in the mid-1980s

John Cain came on to the scene as something of a *deus ex machina*, his election completely upsetting the plot that had been building to a head since the late 1960s and providing a cast of new leading actors. The policy changes wrought by the Cain government have often been surprising, even to close ALP supporters. It was always clear that

Figure 9.7 Major development projects under the Cain government, 1982 onwards

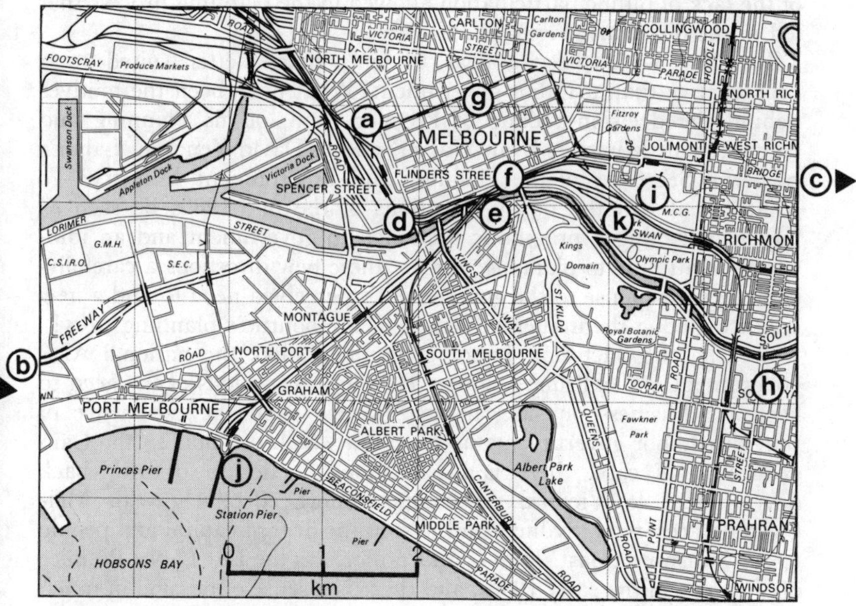

a West Melbourne Remand Centre
b Lara Prison & Correctional Training Centre
c Box Hill Orana Housing Development
d World Trade Centre Hotel
e South Bank Redevelopment
f Flinders St Station Renewal
g Victoria Central
h South Yarra Chia Development
i MCG Lights
j Port Melbourne Station Pier
k National Tennis Centre

Cain and his faction in the Labor Party were but mildly socialist, although with a commitment to greater social justice and social planning. So, while taking some important initiatives to improve the quality of life for residents in Melbourne's unattractive western suburbs, much of the Cain government's planning effort has in fact been directed towards encouraging more intensive development in and around Melbourne's CBD. And to do this, the State government has had to take CBD planning powers away from the elected MCC which it had just reinstated — an elected council which, from 1982 to 1985, was in fact controlled by Labor councillors! Some of the decisions, such as the determination to construct a National Tennis

Centre on valuable inner-city parkland, have been controversial, not only because of the nature of the projects themselves but also because of the lack of public participation allowed in the planning process that led to the decisions (Figure 9.7).

In some ways these appear to be policies better suited to a conservative than a Labor government. What have been the motives behind the decision-making of Premier Cain, of his Planning and Environment Minister, Evan Walker, and of David Yencken, Labor's powerful Secretary of the Planning and Environment Ministry? To what extent can the policy directions of the mid-1980s be seen as merely reflecting a pragmatic approach to government and an idiosyncratic attitude to planning? Or are these new directions a carefully-considered response to the government's perceived need to find a new balance among the influential actors in Melbourne's planning story?

Clearly, the Victorian Labor government, like the national ALP government under Prime Minister Hawke, is conscious of the need to keep big business on side, having learned from the experience of previous Labor governments in Australia which did not. In the Cain government's case, there is in addition the desire to draw back development to Victoria, to compete more effectively with Melbourne's arch-rival, Sydney, and to stop the drift of capital and people to the Sunshine Coast. John Cain's father was the last Labor Premier of Victoria, in the early 1950s, and there is a sense of mission in much of what Cain junior does: he seems set on ensuring that his government breaks previous Labor records for holding office; and he seems determined to sweep through Victoria's administrative structures with a new broom.

Thus one of the government's most notable achievements in the planning field to date has been to strip the MMBW of its planning powers and to put the restructured Ministry for Planning and Environment in charge of metropolitan planning. Since the MCC has also lost its powers to plan for the CBD, this gives the State government almost complete control, eliminates potential rivals for planning power, and totally destroys Hamer's conception of a three-layered planning hierarchy. At the same time, the government has charged the Local Government Commission with the restructuring of Victoria's municipal geography, reducing the number and increasing the size of local government areas so that they can cope more satisfactorily with the growing services they are being asked to provide, especially in the planning and social-service areas. Once again, the amalgamation of the innermost municipalities of Melbourne is being considered along with the merger of numerous small rural municipalities. This issue has the potential to generate considerable resentment towards the Cain government but, if a damaging backlash at the next State election does not prevent the restructuring from being carried out, it will lead to a much less fragmented framework for planning in Melbourne and Victoria.

At the local level the government has sought to achieve a new coalition of support for its planning decisions. The developers, BOMA and the Melbourne Chamber of Commerce have been appeased by attempts to reduce bureaucratic delays in the planning and development process and by the signs of new capital, including much from Asia and the Middle East, flowing towards Melbourne. Property-owners and developers in the Mixed Use Area around the CBD have been pleased by the minister's determination to upgrade the Yarra River as one of the city's key environmental features and to allow extensive redevelopment of the South Bank and lower Yarra. The government's assembling of land around the Museum underground station in the north of the CBD and sponsoring of a monumental hotel-office complex on the site will inevitably generate widespread redevelopment and satisfy property-owners in the northern section of the Mixed Use Area.

Both the minister and the Secretary for Planning and Environment are architects by training and this has been reflected in the site-specific and aesthetic approach they have taken in much recent decision-making. It might be argued that this is better attuned to the way the developer approaches his work. At the same time, the architectural background of these leading decision-makers has helped to keep the inner-suburban gentry onside; one of the first actions of the Cain government in planning was to amend the legislation to make clear that local governments would not be liable for compensation where they proclaimed urban conservation areas, and the result has been the almost total coverage of the City of Melbourne's and surrounding nineteenth century residential suburbs by conservation zoning. Ironically, the advent of a Labor government has encouraged the further 'gentrification' of inner Melbourne and done little to protect low-income residents and other groups with little clout in the political and planning processes (see Chapter 18 in this volume).

If current planning policies concentrating on the redevelopment of the inner city are carried through, the Melbourne we know will be transformed. With its revitalised CBD, beautified Yarra Banks, monumental cultural and sporting facilities and conserved terrace-house neighbourhoods, Melbourne's ability to compete with Sydney as a commercial and tourist focus will be strengthened. In this process, as always, there will be winners and losers. What the recent events show is that under a Labor government the winners and losers are virtually the same as under previous Liberal governments. The late 1980s may see a revival of concern, probably led by middle-class residents and environmental groups, about the impact of the government's pro-development and anti-participation approach to planning. Thus the story of physical and social change in the metropolis will continue to demand investigation by political geographers who will analyse its causes and consequences. This new analysis will again profit by concentrating on the role of the actors involved in the governmental policy-making and plan implementation, and on the interplay between the decision-makers' own perceptions, attitudes and ambitions and the attempts by individuals and groups in society to manipulate the planning process in their own favour. In this way, geographers will correctly put the political element back into their explanations of city-forming processes.

Chapter 10

Heroic measures: urban consolidation in Australia

Ray Bunker

A new phrase has been coined in recent years to describe the old precept of metropolitan planning in Australia—compactness without congestion and spaciousness without sprawl (Winston 1961:26). It is urban consolidation. According to a recent publication by the New South Wales Department of Environment and Planning this 'means increasing the density of dwellings or population or both'. However the emphasis has been placed, in effect, on the distribution of residential population. Growing intensity of activity and of use of land through the displacement of residential uses by business enterprises is not seen as consolidation. Similary the most effective form of consolidation is where population numbers and densities are raised: increased density of dwellings accompanied by population loss is viewed somewhat grudgingly in 'it could have been worse' terms.

Pyramids into plateaus

The population densities of Australian cities are more like those of North America than those of Europe or the United Kingdom. The 1981 Census provided data about these residential densities. The figures relate population to areas of broad residential land use in each city, using uniform criteria and definitions so that the statistics are comparable. Table 10.1 shows the residential densities and population of the largest Australian cities in 1981. Despite the fact that most Australians live in a low-density suburban setting, the continuing spread of the largest cities is seen generally to have some undesirable

Table 10.1 Population numbers and densities of selected Australian cities, 1981

City	Population	Residential density (people per sq. km)
Sydney	2 876 508	3160
Melbourne	2 578 759	2537
Brisbane	942 836	2186
Adelaide	882 520	2178
Perth	809 035	1702

Source: Australian Bureau of Statistics publications.

features and efforts have been made in recent years to make them more compact, to consolidate them and make urban development more dense. The issue has been around for a long time (Paterson 1980) but changing conditions in the last ten years have reopened the debate and brought new considerations to bear. At the same time research has uncovered more of the dynamics and dimensions of urban Australia (for example, Neutze 1977, 1978; Burnley 1980; Stimson 1982; Kilmartin and Thorns 1978; Huxley and McLoughlin 1985). The outcome has been the advocacy of heroic measures to achieve diverse ends and satisfy differing perceptions of metropolitan needs. The measures are heroic in that they are bold and only partly informed.

Population trends

Table 10.2 Family types, Sydney, Melbourne and Adelaide, 1976 and 1981

	Sydney		Melbourne		Adelaide	
Family type	**1976**	**1981**	**1976**	**1981**	**1976**	**1981**
			% of families			
Head only	22.4	25.7	20.3	23.9	19.8	23.6
Head and dependants*	3.7	5.1	3.3	4.6	3.7	5.4
Head and spouse only	21.9	20.9	21.6	21.1	23.8	23.8
Head, spouse and dependants*	26.5	26.6	28.6	29.0	27.3	26.4
Head and other adults	5.4	5.3	4.9	4.7	4.5	4.5
Head, other adults and dependants*	1.4	1.3	1.3	1.3	1.4	1.4
Head, spouse and other adults	9.5	8.0	9.7	7.7	9.5	8.2
Head, spouse, other adults and dependants*	9.1	7.1	10.3	7.8	9.9	6.9
	100%	100%	100%	100%	100%	100%

* 'children' in 1976

Source: Bunker 1983:65

Table 10.3 Occupancy rate of private dwellings Sydney, Melbourne and Adelaide, 1971, 1976 and 1981

	Sydney			Melbourne			Adelaide		
	1971	**1976**	**1981**	**1971**	**1976**	**1981**	**1971**	**1976**	**1981**
Average number of people per occupied private dwelling	3.19	3.01	2.92	3.31	3.11	2.97	3.24	3.01	2.82

Source: Bunker 1983:64

Table 10.4 Population changes in the different parts of Sydney, Melbourne and Adelaide, 1971–76 and 1976–81

	Percentage change on base population				
	Core	**Inner**	**Middle**	**Outer**	**Fringe**
Sydney					
1971–76	−9.6	−2.7	3.1	4.0	25.1
1976–81	−3.1	−1.3	−1.3	6.0	28.5
Melbourne					
1971–76	−16.2	−11.0	−6.3	16.8	40.7
1976–81	−5.2	−3.6	−3.8	7.4	29.2
Adelaide					
1971–76		−4.0	−2.0	35.6	
1976–81		−7.5	−2.6	19.1	

Source: Bunker 1983:70, 79, 89

At the heart of the revival of interest in low-density metropolitan suburbs are changing population characteristics. A falling birth rate has contributed to the increased ageing of the population. With other

Figure 10.1 Classification of neighbourhoods in Sydney

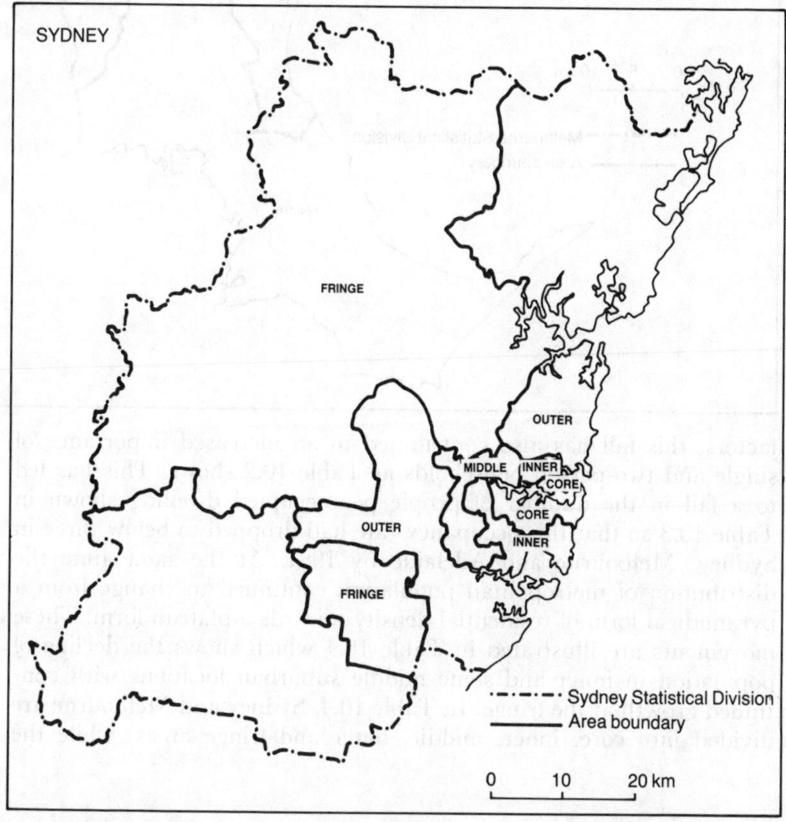

Figure 10.2 Classification of neighbourhoods in Melbourne

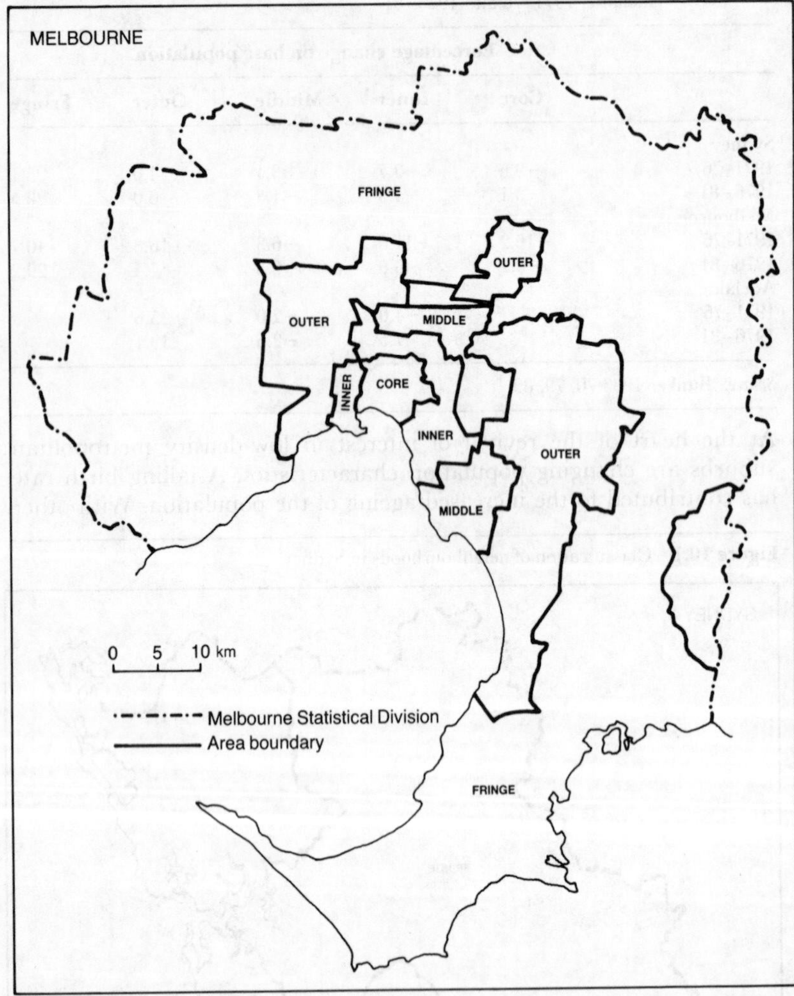

factors, this fall has also contributed to an increased importance of single and two-person households as Table 10.2 shows. This has led to a fall in the number of people per occupied dwelling shown in Table 10.3 so that this occupancy rate had dropped to below three in Sydney, Melbourne and Adelaide by 1981. At the same time the distribution of metropolitan population continued to change from a pyramidical form of residential density towards a plateau form. These movements are illustrated in Table 10.4 which shows the decline of population in inner and some middle suburban locations with continued growth at the fringe. In Table 10.4, Sydney and Melbourne are divided into core, inner, middle, outer and fringe areas, while the

Figure 10.3 Classification of neighbourhoods in Adelaide

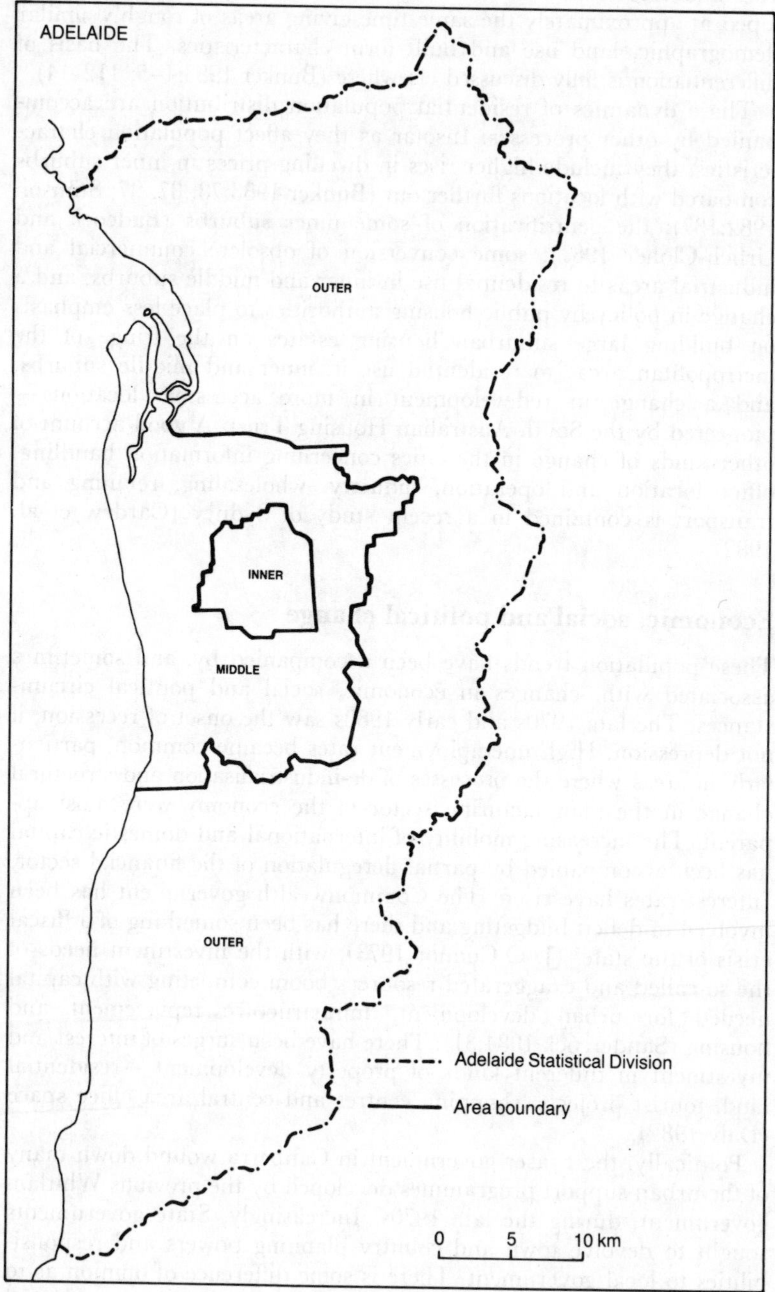

smaller city of Adelaide is separated into three parts (see Figures 10.1, 10.2 and 10.3 respectively). These sub-regions represent areas developed at approximately the same time giving areas of roughly similar demographic, land use and built form characteristics. The basis of differentiation is fully discussed elsewhere (Bunker 1983:4–5; 112–14).

These dynamics of residential population distribution are accompanied by other processes. Insofar as they affect population characteristics, they include higher rises in dwelling prices in inner suburbs compared with locations further out (Bunker 1983:78, 87, 97; Stimson 1982:137); the gentrification of some inner suburbs (Badcock and Urlich-Cloher 1981); some conversion of obsolete commercial and industrial areas to residential use in inner and middle suburbs; and a change in policy by public housing authorities to place less emphasis on building large suburban housing estates on the fringe of the metropolitan areas to residential use in inner and middle suburbs; and a change in redevelopment in more accessible locations—pioneered by the South Australian Housing Trust. A good account of other kinds of change in the cities concerning information handling, office location and operation, industry, wholesaling, retailing and transport is contained in a recent study of Sydney (Cardew et al. 1982).

Economic, social and political change

These population trends have been accompanied by, and sometimes associated with, changes in economic, social and political circumstances. The late 1970s and early 1980s saw the onset of recession, if not depression. High unemployment rates became common, particularly in areas where the processes of de-industrialisation and structural change in the manufacturing sector of the economy were most apparent. The increasing mobility of international and domestic capital has been accompanied by partial deregulation of the financial sector. Interest rates have risen. The Commonwealth government has been involved in deficit budgeting and there has been something of a 'fiscal crisis of the state' (J. O'Connor 1973), with the investment needs of the so-called and exaggerated resources boom competing with capital needed for urban development, infrastructure replacement and housing (Sandercock 1984:31). There have been surges of interest and investment in different kinds of property development—residential land, tourist projects, shopping centres and central area office space (Daly 1982).

Politically, the Fraser government in Canberra wound down many of the urban support programmes developed by the previous Whitlam government, during the late 1970s. Increasingly, State governments sought to devolve town and country planning powers and responsibilities to local government. There is some difference of opinion as to whether this went very far, but undoubtedly there has been a general strengthening in the capability and expertise of local councils.

Ideologies, images and imperatives

Such fundamental and comprehensive changes meant that the whole character of metropolitan development and change has been progressively reassessed and reinterpreted. This has been accompanied by an increasing body of research and writing about Australian urbanisation. It also meant a redirection of planning effort away from merely organising and shaping the suburban fringe, so apparent in the Sydney Region Outline Plan (NSW State Planning Authority 1968), to a renewed concern with, and reinterpretation of, the role and character of the inner and middle suburbs (NSW Planning and Environment Commission 1980; MMBW 1977).

Urban consolidation could not be looked at in isolation. It represented issues concerning the whole character and perception of metropolitan areas. Academics, professionals, real estate experts, journalists and politicians all offered explanations and prescriptions about the changing metropolitan scene. One journalist wrote about the way 'the ample facilities of our inner suburbs are ignored in favour of soul-destroying potential slums out west'. He was incensed by the heavy cost of fringe development and stated that 'the opportunity cost of these indifferent (inner) suburbs is the highly tax-intensive slums on the perimeters of our great cities' (Keegan 1985). An article in the *National Times* seven years earlier, emphasised that this kind of comment should only be made within an overall metropolitan context, so that

> given that land on the urban fringe is likely to be cheaper than in inner and middle suburbs, maintaining the supply of serviced allotments on the urban fringe is necessary to contain housing costs. This is why the *National Times* article advocated 'satellite cities' on the urban fringe. This would partly ensure more equitable urban expansion because it would involve the location of employment and social facilities as well as residential suburbs in these areas. (Bunker and Orchard 1982:11)

Other perspectives on urban consolidation can be developed in terms of the political economy of Australian cities. If the role of the state in urban development is interpreted, for example, as helping the fastest possible accumulation of capital in the private sector, allied with the 'state grant economy' existing in Australia then there will be 'relative underdevelopment of the "collective means of consumption", of the collectively used non-productive infrastructure' (Szelenyi 1981:587) and the need to maximise the use of that infrastructure. This statement then needs to be amplified in the light of increasing complexity and volatility affecting investment of different kinds given the needs of national economic management and competing demands for highly mobile and expensive capital. Within public capital spending there are clear choices between public housing, urban infrastructure and services, and the development of 'productive' works such as coal-mines, railways, power stations to promote a resources boom or tourist facilities to spread surplus wealth around. Owners and managers of private capital funds have different interests depending on whether they invest in property, industrial, commercial or financial ventures (Badcock 1984:66–7). This leads them to respond differently to changing economic conditions and financial circumstances. Inner suburbs are particularly vulnerable in these changing conditions; some become refurbished and upgraded (Badcock 1984:162–8), others become concentrations of the disadvantaged and unemployed.

Recent arguments for urban consolidation

More prosaically, the recent arguments for containment and consolidation of urban spread have tended to fall into four categories.

The first of these arose from the rise in liquid fuel prices brought about by the OPEC countries. These price increases, and fears of fuel shortage, led to the contention that a more compact city form, minimisation of travel by car and intensification of use of land would be an appropriate response (Jay 1978). In the event, Australia's own oil production has helped the rise in real cost of oil to be contained to moderate proportions; the recession has slowed down the rate of growth of trip-making by car; and adjustments other than to land use have been made in response to rising oil prices such as the use of more fuel-efficient cars and more judicious trip-making (SA Department of Urban and Regional Affairs 1980). The increasing attraction of inner and middle suburbs for living, as shown in the pattern of property price increases in recent years, reflects both a recognition that their locational advantages had been under-valued previously and an increased interest in Victorian and early twentieth century housing stock. Perceptions about future oil shortages and higher prices may however, have also played a part in this.

The second reason for increasing interest in urban consolidation is the need for efficiency in spending of scarce capital funds on urban infrastructure by State governments. Physical and social infrastructure has been developed for significantly larger populations than those now living in inner and some middle suburbs. In Adelaide, for example, funds had been directed to the rebuilding of inner-area schools and the enlargement of their grounds in the 1970s (Bunker and Orchard 1982). A few years later, enrolments in these schools had dropped substantially, while expensive new schools were still being built in outer areas. By encouraging urban consolidation, it is argued, some of this spare capacity could be utilised, and outer suburban growth slowed.

Again, this contention is disarmingly simplistic. In many cases facilities, services and standards in the inner and middle suburbs are inferior to those now being provided in new residential areas. Much of the physical infrastructure requires major renovation and upgrading.

Any increase in residential population could require substantial expenditure and use of land for schools, open space, health and welfare services, and transport. Given the strong case made for saving public costs in urban development by consolidation, it is surprising that so little work has been done to identify the nature of these supposed savings. Little consideration has been given, either, to the running costs of public services after facilities have been established or upgraded.

A third reason for renewed interest in urban consolidation is some mismatch between the needs of households for shelter and the dwelling stock. The latter is fixed in the short term. There has been an increasing demand for rental accommodation, whether provided by the public or private sector. There is more need for aged person's accommodation and the increasing number of single or two-person households could justify the building of more multi-unit dwellings. It was these considerations that led a study of urban consolidation potential in Adelaide to conclude 'that the building of smaller and more densely arranged dwellings, a high proportion of them for public and private rental, in the inner and middle suburbs of metropolitan Adelaide (should) be accelerated over the next decade' (Bunker and Orchard 1982:67).

A final reason advanced to support urban consolidation is the cost of housing. Multi-unit housing is seen as cheaper than detached cottages because it is less costly to build per dwelling and uses less land. Unfortunately, these arguments lose most of their force in practice.

Land costs in areas suitable for, and zoned for, multi-unit housing are high. Poor-quality flat developments in the late 1960s and early 1970s led to more restrictive height and density limits on multi-unit dwellings, and also led to extensive 'down-zoning' or the changing of residential zones so that the areas available for multi-unit dwellings were effectively reduced. A 1980 report commented that 'the fact that land is generally valued at its potential rather than its current use, combined with a system which severely restricts the supply of land, places a premium on the land which is zoned for higher density development' (Indicative Planning Council 1980:45).

Costs of building multi-unit housing are also high. There has been an over-reaction against the poor development standards of earlier times which caused much local protest. Higher and more restrictive standards operate, clearly supported by most local councils and residents. The New South Wales Department of Environment and Planning commissioned a study to examine the effects of these standards on housing costs. It found that these were higher in regard to multi-unit housing. Table 10.5 shows the *additional* costs to build to modal or highest local government standards in the Sydney area in the late-1970s. The cost penalties for town houses and flats are much more severe in this regard than for detached cottages.

Table 10.5 Added cost to develop or build at modal and highest standards—Sydney area, late 1970s

Dwelling type	Added cost due to standards at modal value	Added cost due to standards at highest value
Suburban allotment	$3 440	$8 830
Allotment and detached house	$6 240	$11 630
Town house	$13 400	$30 100
Flat	$5 520	$22 400

Source: NSW Department of Environment and Planning 1982:10

Much policy concerning multi-unit housing and medium-density development has been formed without consideration of feasibility, and a recent study in this regard came to the conclusion that it was unlikely that extensive redevelopment with multi-unit dwellings would lower the cost of housing significantly (Cardew, 1982).

This kind of debate about the cost of housing threw up a demand for 'deregulation', or the relaxation of stringent residential development standards. Much of the rationale in this regard was presented in a book appropriately titled *A Mansion or No House*, (Paterson et al. 1976). There was much appeal in this argument for many investors, developers, architects, macro-economists and those with a concern for the provision of lower-cost housing. But this simple argument was clouded by other factors. With regard to the perceptions of developers the *Report on Multi-Unit Dwelling Development in Australia* commented:

> Any attempt to draw a casual relationship between costs imposed by local governments and the level of commencements is clouded by the other significant changes in the entire climate of the housing market. Demographic changes, increased interest rates, periods of tight finance availability and a decline in the expectation of making substantial capital gains have meant that the production of multi-unit dwellings for large-scale investors has become uneconomic and has virtually ceased. (Indicative Planning Council 1980:47)

Policies attempting consolidation

The actions taken by State governments to promote urban consolidation in the late-1970s and early-1980s fell into two categories. The first was concerned with attempts to increase the density of built form and encourage multi-unit dwelling construction. This was achieved by stopping down-zoning, by seeking to increase the areas where medium and high density development and redevelopment could take place, and by trying to relax local planning standards and provisions which inhibited or limited the building of multi-unit dwellings. Such measures included 'dual occupancy' provisions by which additional dwellings could be added to the detached cottage or its curtilage. This could take a variety of forms including the conversion, adaptation or extension of existing dwellings, or the building of an additional dwelling as exemplified and popularised in the 'granny flat' (MMBW 1982). Other proposals included a move in New South Wales to allow medium-density housing up to two storeys in height in all residential zones subject to certain standards regarding landscaping, floor area and private open space being satisfied; this measure was later withdrawn.

Two policies were also introduced in New South Wales to help the building of non-private dwellings in residential areas. State Environmental Planning Policy 5 enabled housing for aged and disabled persons to be built in any residential area, while Policy 9 authorised the establishment of group houses of a non-institutional nature for special groups or disadvantaged people (NSW Department of Environment and Planning, 1984:26).

These kinds of measures imposed considerable pressure on local councils by metropolitan or State planning authorities. Ideologically, they were part of the 'deregulation' thrust of the early 1980s; the freeing of the market so that the pent-up demand for medium density housing could take place. The impact of these kinds of policies is best exemplified in New South Wales.

In the late 1970s, the rate of population growth in Sydney increased. Considerable capital was committed by the State government in New South Wales to the development of coal-mines, railways, power stations, ports, coal loaders and other infrastructure hoping to promote coal exports and attract industries such as aluminium smelting to sources of relatively cheap power. A fiscal crisis became apparent when the demands for urban infrastructure, and rising expectations of people for adequate social and physical services, conflicted with the need for the capitalist state to provide the necessary conditions for the accumulation and reproduction of capital (Sandercock 1984:31). In this climate some alarming estimates of the capital costs of providing infrastructure for fringe metropolitan development were generated. It was estimated in the early 1980s that the equivalent of $13 500 was needed to provide each new household with seven types of public enterprise—schools, technical and further education, child care, community health, hospitals, main roads and water sewerage and drainage. In addition local government services were estimated to cost well over $5 000 for each household (Wilmoth 1982:31). A Housing Balance Sheet was developed to estimate the demand for housing in Sydney over the next five years. To meet this demand the government identified a number of instruments it could use, including an Urban Consolidation Program, Urban Development Program and the provision of some medium density housing through the Housing and Land Commissions (Reed and Wilmoth 1983).

Faced with these formidable estimates the State government decided to establish a target of 12 000 commencements of 'other' dwellings a year for the Sydney Region for the next five years — about 40 to 50 per cent of the total new residential construction needed from year to year. 'Other dwellings' include not only private multi-unit dwellings but also dual occupancies, housing for aged persons and boarding houses. The total for 'other dwellings' was split up among local government areas and issued as targets to be met, in January, 1983.

These targets are fairly formidable. The level of construction of 'other dwellings' in recent years has been about one-third of total dwelling commencements. While there were 10 259 commencements of 'other dwellings' in 1980–81, this was a ten-year record and the figure fell to 5 081 in 1982–83. Nevertheless, the Department of Environment and Planning considered the level of 12 000 represented an appropriate target figure given the right market conditions and adequate suitable zoned land. Many councils have carried out reviews of their zoning provisions and identified changes to zoning and development standards to encourage multi-unit dwelling construction, but some targets seem contentious and arbitrary.

The second kind of action taken to further urban consolidation was to use public housing authorities in programmes of infill, purchase and rehabilitation of existing dwellings, conversion of cottages to dual occupancy etc., particularly in inner and middle suburbs. As an extension of this, vacant or under-utilised land owned by government authorities was made available for residential development where this was suitable. The most prominent and dramatic example of this action was the decision by the South Australian government in 1983 to delete a provision for a north-south transport corridor in Adelaide which had existed for twelve years. During this period, land and property had been steadily acquired for the transport facility and the change of policy made much of this land available for public housing. While first refusal for surplus land was usually given to public housing authorities in this kind of situation, sometimes the land was sold to private enterprise for housing. These kinds of actions, though more limited in scope than those in the first category which were intended to influence the total residential development process over the whole urban area, did demonstrate that residential population could be increased more effectively by infill housing or the conversion of non-residential buildings to residential use than by redeveloping existing housing stock to medium density configurations. In Sydney, Melbourne and Adelaide, processes have been established to sell off or lease land surplus to government requirements, but again, a number of other factors often inhibit the apparent potential of such land for housing such as poor location, unattractive surroundings, difficult site conditions or the need to use land for public purposes such as open space and community uses.

With a degree of de-industrialisation affecting some kinds of manufacturing industry, industrial premises and areas have occasionally become redundant or no longer represent the highest and best use of land. Some rezoning of these areas and their rehabilitation or redevelopment for residential purposes has taken place.

So . . . What?

So urban consolidation is a complex issue, with many interdependencies and unknowns attending it; what has been learned about it?

The first outcome is the obvious need for a balanced metropolitan policy of development, including urban consolidation and fringe expansion with due consideration to the efficiency and equity aspects of both. In particular, the urban-consolidation focus on inner and middle suburbs could inflate land values and overtax existing facilities, thereby making access more difficult to low-income earners. Further, it can be demonstrated that a reasonable range of housing types and densities needs to be provided in outer and fringe locations. Ironically, more scope exists to do this in planning and progressive development of these newer areas than in existing suburbs. Substantial investment, both in land and infrastructure has already been made in many fringe areas and a high rate of development to recoup this is desirable where this has occurred. One researcher concluded that Sydney's inner suburbs are already largely developed for medium-density housing and that there is little capacity for denser residential development (Archer 1980:9).

Clearly this approach means that different policies are needed in different kinds of locations. And these policies need to be developed with local authorities taking a prominent part in their formulation as they will be responsible for implementation. More generally, to develop, implement, monitor and adjust policies about the distribution of residential population, housing types and densities, an effective information system is needed. It needs to be paralleled by and interwoven with a decision-making system about urban development. These structures would ensure the blending of information concerning trends and policy imperatives in the planning process in the style suggested by Breheny and Roberts (1978; 1980) and Bracken (1982). A range of forecasts could be generated regarding population characteristics. It would include a 'projection' or best estimate of trends under existing policy influences. It would also show alternative 'predictions' of population distribution given the injection of policy thrusts and actions to encourage urban consolidation. The characteristics of such a mixed information and decision-making system are discussed elsewhere (Bunker 1983:46–7). The out puts are linked and integrated estimates of future population, dwellings and land development needs for sub-areas of the metropolitan region for varying time-periods.

In generating these different predictions and evaluating their public cost, it is necessary to prepare expenditure estimates for parts of the existing urban area and its fringes. Ideally, these calculations should include spending on both physical and social infrastructure and services. Importantly, they should include estimates of the costs of running and operating these public services as well as establishing them. For example, fringe development could take much of the expansion of metropolitan community and social services to the detriment of needs-based assessments of what is required in inner areas (Sandercock 1984:34).

In Australia, these information and policy-generating systems are unevenly developed. In Adelaide, there is a very effective forecasting system with annual revisions of forecasts of population distribution, dwelling demand and distribution of serviced lots. It takes account of demolition of dwellings, vacancy rates, occupancy rates, migration, land availability, household headship-rates by age groups etc. (Bell 1983). But apart from a brief attempt in the late 1970s to illustrate and examine more compact and less-compact forms of metropolitan development, the forecasts have taken the form of a best-estimate trend projection. There is little examination of different assumptions regarding, for example, the scale and location of public-housing construction or the timing and magnitude of releases of major areas for development. On the other hand, Sydney has provided examples of policy pronouncements without adequate information about their feasibility.

An illustration of how a forecasting system of the kind outlined might work in the construction, monitoring and modification of urban development policy is contained in a study of urban consolidation in Adelaide (Bunker and Orchard 1982). In that excerise four predictions were constructed to represent different degrees of urban consolidation over the decade 1981–91 and compared with the best-estimate trend forecast provided by the State government's excellent population-forecasting and land-monitoring unit. The predictions involved the inner and middle suburbs of Adelaide where it was estimated 16 900 allotments represented the potential for future residential development. After taking into account the likely effect of demolitions and changing occupancy rates together with different assumptions about the rate of take-up of this land, four sets of figures were generated representing different predictions about possible population and dwelling totals in 1990. These predictions are shown in Table 10.6 together with a best-estimate projection based on existing trends with no policy inputs to stimulate urban consolidation. The predictions assume policy initiatives to encourage urban consolidation, particularly in accelerating the rate of development of vacant land. The best-estimate projection is used as a yardstick in the manner used in structure planning in Gloucestershire (Breheny and Roberts 1980). As the 1981 population of the area covered in Table 10.6 was almost

602 000, it will be seen that the more optimistic predictions of the effect of consolidation policies need to be achieved merely to retain existing levels of population.

Table 10.6 Projection and predictions of population and dwelling stock in inner and middle suburbs of Adelaide, 1991

	Dwelling Stock	Population
Best estimate projection	250 400	593 600
Prediction 1	253 450	599 200
Prediction 2	254 800	600 400
Prediction 3	258 850	612 150
Prediction 4	260 200	613 350

Source: Bunker and Orchard 1982:57

An important methodological point emerges here; the planning process frequently generates alternative futures, selects one, or a combination of those originally formulated, and then implements that chosen strategy. In the case of the Adelaide study it was pointed out that a large number of influences affect the distribution of population in the metropolitan area. Only some of these are under the control of government rating systems for land, charging policies for the connection of water supply and sewerage and their operation, transport pricing, zoning, residential development standards etc. (US Department of Housing and Urban Development 1980). Of these, some are exercised in a way that is at best neutral in their contribution to urban consolidation and some are quite unhelpful. The Adelaide study resisted the conclusion that urban consolidation was so important an objective in metropolitan development that the State government would co-ordinate and align policy influences of all kinds to ensure this. Instead, it assumed that the government would make some attempts to encourage consolidation and that the impact of these initiatives could be monitored and related to the predictions established in the study, which in turn were generated within explicit statements of the capacity of the urban mosaic to absorb consolidation. If the State government desired a higher rate or degree of consolidation it could pull more of its policy levers to achieve that. This approach has the advantage that it recognises the lack of understanding surrounding the impact of each policy instrument in achieving consolidation and that even more uncertainty surrounds their combined effect. These impacts are also likely to change over time. The planning process thus becomes one of the selection of desirable population targets, adjustment of policy measures to influence consolidation as appropriate and adjustment of the desired outcome as events unfold and side-effects emerge. This approach has something of a black-box flavour in that causes and effects in terms of population distribution are not precisely quantified and articulated.

But, given the large number of influences on population distribution and densities, and the fact that some of the most important are not under the control of government, this approach can be defended. It places reasonable bounds around alternative futures in terms of population distribution and develops information-providing and policy-adjustment processes to achieve one of those states.

Summary

Given the concern with population trends which did so much to recycle the issue of urban consolidation, it is ironic that urban-consolidation policies are likely to have little significant influence on that distribution, particularly in the short term.

In Sydney, an examination of the scope for urban consolidation concluded that less than 3 per cent of the population at the end of the century would be affected by changes to built form designed to encourage urban consolidation. The most extreme prediction favouring consolidation in Adelaide, requiring fairly heroic policy thrusts 'represents a redistribution of population to the Central Sector of the order of three and one-half per cent of the 1991 forecast population' (Bunker and Orchard 1982:51).

But the issue is an important one, because it is about all aspects of metropolitan development and all its dimensions. These include the political economy of cities, decision and policy-making processes, inter-government relations and design and development standards. Urban consolidation exemplifies a general process of re-examination of Australian cities in new conditions and with added insights. Does this re-examination reveal a trend towards more complex and less equal cities? (Forster 1984:ix) This may well be the most significant aspect of urban consolidation. Heroic measures are indeed needed.

Chapter 11
Local planning: practice and potential in metropolitan Melbourne

Toni Logan

Since the 1950s land use plans have been developed for most Australian cities. Usually the plans have been formulated by regional or State agencies but their implementation largely has been delegated to local government authorities. While a substantial body of literature exists analysing the preparation, content and adequacy of the metropolitan planning policies (for example, Stretton 1970; Sandercock 1977; Harrison 1978; Alexander 1981*a* and Chapter 8 of this volume), there is a dearth of research about local planning. Most Australian cities are fragmented into a large number of municipalities so it is not surprising that researchers have been hesitant to explore the issue. As well, State agencies appear to have been little concerned with evaluating local planning so there has been a lack a guidance in the establishment of information systems and many local planning authorities have established their own, widely varying systems, making comparative studies difficult. However, recent theoretical debates about the nature of planning and of local government emphasise the need to bridge the information gap. This chapter examines the role of local planners operating within the ambit of a single regional plan for metropolitan Melbourne. The study focuses on the inner and middle-ring suburbs that have experienced population decline and the way local planning responds to changing economic and social circumstances in existing, older built-up areas.

Changing theoretical context

During the 1970s a major shift occurred in the debate about the nature of urban planning. At the beginning of the decade the focus was on procedures: theories relating to how planning agencies should operate. The prevailing view (Davidoff and Reiner 1962; McLoughlin 1969; Faludi 1973) was that planning should be a rational approach to the ordering of land uses within cities. Community goals were to be formulated and the means available for achieving those goals systematically evaluated to identify the most socially-desirable option. This was then translated into a land use plan implemented by government

Based on Williams, P. (ed.) (1984) Chapter 5 in *Conflict and Development*, and reproduced here by kind permission of George Allen & Unwin.

agencies with powers to regulate the location, density and quality of private development. The model was an iterative one, recognising the need for periodic review of goals, plans and control mechanisms to adapt to changing circumstances. Closely linked to this view of planning as a rational process was an emphasis on quantitative techniques for analysing urban trends, simulating policy outcomes and aiding decision-making. Planners were envisaged as value-neutral, technical experts making reasoned choices in the public interest.

By the end of the decade the theoretical debate had moved from these essentially introspective and apolitical concerns with procedure, to focus on the wider social and economic context of planning; a change reflecting the influence of political economy perspectives. Early work by Rex and Moore (1967), Pahl (1970) and Harvey (1973), for example, drew attention to the substantial inequalities among urban residents in their access to public goods. So a central issue became the extent to which planners contribute to, or are able to ameliorate, the social and economic inequalities in cities. Within the political-economy perspectives there are at least two separate strands, linked to the intellectual traditions of Marx and of Weber. Broadly, the contemporary Marxists see the prime role of the public sector as maintenance of the dominant mode of capitalist production, although there are variations in the degree of economic determinism incorporated in this view. In its more rigid forms (Miliband 1973; Lojkine 1976) the public sector and monopoly capital are fused into a single repressive mechanism. Thus, Cockburn (1977) maintains that local government is simply an extension of national government whose function is to serve the interests of capital; and Castells (quoted in Pahl 1977:53) argues that 'town planning cannot be an instrument of social change, but only one of domination, integration and regulation of conflicts'.

A less deterministic view is held by other Marxists, such as Poulantzas (1973) and in the later writing of Castells (1978), encompassing the possibility of some autonomy of the public sector from the economic class struggle. They believe that, through political structures, organised labour can win concessions in conflict with the short-term interests of specific fractions of capital, although only if the long-term interests of the dominant classes are not threatened. This is a more comfortable position for urban planners in that it offers hope that they 'can create alternative solutions which address systemic problems, but, do so with minimal harm to the lower classes' (Fainstein and Fainstein 1979:399). Increasingly it is being argued that explanations of the role of the public sector in general, and of urban and regional planning in particular, need to go beyond the mode of production type of analysis (Szelenyi 1977; Harloe 1978).

This conclusion moves toward the contemporary Weberian position which holds that the political operation of the public sector is not necessarily subservient to economic class relations and that allocational processes are increasingly affected by bureaucrats. So Pahl (1970:215) suggests that local planners are among a group of 'social gatekeepers who help to distribute and control urban resources' with a high degree of autonomy. In a later revision of this concept of urban managerialism, Pahl (1977:51) admits that he may have attributed 'too much power and influence to the middle-dogs' but affirms his belief in the growing autonomy of the public sector as a whole in corporatist economies. Saunders (1979;1983) further refines the discussion on the relative weight of economic and political functions of government. He suggests that the public sector is more likely to be an instrument of capital at national and regional levels than at local level, where political struggles hinge on social consumption issues in which specific class interests are usually difficult to identify.

Within these political-economy perspectives there is a growing realisation that theoretical stereotypes of government need to be examined empirically in order to explain their varied roles in different countries, cities and neighbourhoods. This point is articulated well by Williams (1982:95) who stresses 'the need to explain the high degree of variation which exists within institutions operating within the urban realm'; that is the direction in which this chapter moves.

Local government in Melbourne

Much of the recent discussion on the role of local government and planning originated in England (Cockburn 1977; Saunders 1979; Kirk 1980; Dunleavy 1980) where municipal bodies have a longer history and wider range of functions. In Australia, local authorities are very much creatures of the State governments who have delegated little power, provided few resources and imposed highly-centralised administrative controls. Although a comprehensive system of local government was established in Victoria by the late nineteenth century its range of activities and areal boundaries have been slower to change than in several other States with more recent systems (Victoria 1979).

Within metropolitan Melbourne there are fifty-four local government authorities. In 1976–77 their functional distribution of expenditure was: roads (29 per cent), general administration (22 per cent), cultural and recreational (20 per cent), environment (12 per cent), health and welfare (9 per cent) (Victoria 1979:18). This allocation contrasts sharply with English local authorities whose dominant expenditures relate to education, social welfare and housing, which are mainly functions of State governments in Australia. Under existing statutes, local councils can expand their responsibilities, but resource constraints are severe. Approximately 60 per cent of municipal revenues in Melbourne derive from property rates, 15 per cent from State grants and the remainder from licences, fees and fines (A. Parkin

1982:62). This dependence on rates as the major source of revenue appears likely to entrench inequalities within the metropolitan area but although the generally regressive nature of rates is widely acknowledged (Mowbray 1982), the differences by local government area have received little attention. However, a New South Wales study (Groenewegen 1976*b*:47) does indicate that 'local government areas with low per capita rateable values tended to utilize their tax bases heavily, while those with high values tended to a low utilization of tax base…'

The Board of Review (Victoria 1979) also provides insight into the management procedures and internal organisation of councils. It contends that the majority have no special mechanism for formulating objectives and policies, determining priorities and allocating resources. These functions tend to occur as a result of, rather than prior to, annual budget estimates. Also, there tends to be a traditional dual management system in which the Municipal Clerk and Engineer are equal in status; town planning is frequently an adjunct to the work of the Engineer.

The framework for local planning in Melbourne

When the State of Victoria accepted town and country planning as a legitimate function of government, the delivery system was structured so that local councils were to play the key role. Guided and coordinated by the Town and Country Planning Board, local governments could, if they wished, prepare and administer a planning scheme by which the location of new development was to be controlled (Town and Country Planning Act 1944). Essentially a planning scheme consists of maps showing land use zones and an ordinance which indicates for each zone the land uses that (a) do not require a permit, (b) are allowed under specific conditions, (c) may be permitted at the discretion of the responsible planning authority or (d) are prohibited. This system was based on pre-war English legislation which had already been subjected to a severe critique because of its negative, permissive and parochial outcomes (Uthwatt 1942). The most that such a regulatory system of land use planning can do is to exclude particular land uses from certain locations and to ensure that when development does occur it conforms to defined standards relating to such matters as site-coverage, building form, parking provision and landscaping. What it cannot do is to ensure that particular kinds of development occur at certain locations.

The Town and Country Planning Act is largely concerned with specifying procedures for scheme preparation and implementation rather than with assistance on policy issues. The Third Schedule to the Act identifies matters which may be included in schemes and the emphasis is clearly on physical matters; vehicular and pedestrian thoroughfares, utilities, public reservations, the regulation of private use of land and, since the early 1970s, advertising signs and the conservation of sites, buildings or areas. Only in 1979 was the Act amended to allow a statement of objectives to be included in a planning scheme. Once schemes are gazetted, applications for a planning permit must be made for all development rights not conferred on a specific plot by the zoning ordinance.

In metropolitan Melbourne weaknesses in the new planning system soon became apparent. Very few local councils had the resources to tackle the preparation of a planning scheme so in 1949 the task was consolidated to metropolitan scale and transferred to the Melbourne and Metropolitan Board of Works (MMBW), a statutory authority responsible for water, sewerage and drainage services. Since then the MMBW has produced three 'plans'. The first (MMBW 1954) was strongly influenced by the low rates of population and economic growth of the preceding decades. It attempted to set limits to the outward sprawl of urban development, but allowed greater capacity for growth in the more pleasant eastern half of the city and encouraged the decentralisation of retailing and manufacturing to suburban locations. By the late 1960s unexpectedly high rates of population and economic growth, as well as the desire to link land use and transport planning, brought a major change in policy. The second plan (MMBW 1971) was based on the assumption of continuing high rates of urban growth which were to be accommodated in 'balanced' radial corridors. But by the late 1970s growth rates had declined markedly and the regional planning authority revised its policy to place more emphasis on redevelopment of the existing urban area, arguing that this would enable the city to cope with 'issues of energy management, capital shortage, structural unemployment and concern for the environment' (MMBW 1979*a*:19). This third plan (Amendment 150) has yet to be formally approved by State government.

During the post-war period the metropolitan area doubled in population size. Much of the new physical development required decisions on planning-permit applications. Increasingly the MMBW delegated development-control powers back to local councils, who by the 1980s, had been empowered to decide on the discretionary uses for most zones, handling approximately 80 per cent of permit applications (Burr 1982). In the late 1970s many councils wanted to formulate policies to meet specific local problems for which the broad-brush metropolitan scheme was considered inadequate. So the statutory framework was altered to allow councils to prepare local development schemes within general objectives laid down by the MMBW. No local development schemes have been approved yet although several are in preparation; (in 1985 the provision for local development schemes was removed).

Thus there emerged a planning system for metropolitan Melbourne in which there is a major division of responsibility between policy formulation, mainly by the MMBW, and policy implementation, mainly by local councils. But despite the extensive delegation of development-control powers to municipalities and their briefly-acquired right to prepare local development schemes, the regional authority retained certain key powers. The MMBW administers development control over zone boundaries and for all land use change within strategically important fringe areas such as rural, conservation, reserved living and reserved industrial zones. It also formally proposes changes to the Metropolitan Planning Scheme which frequently affect inner and middle ring suburbs; for example, Amendment 150, which is to encourage increased residential diversity and a district centre policy.

At State level, the Ministry for Planning and Environment (MPE) is responsible for the general administration of the Town and Country Planning Act. More specifically, it advises the minister on whether to approve planning schemes or their amendment, and all rezonings. In 1985, the planning powers of the MMBW were transferred to the ministry. Thus the MPE has the potential to exert substantial influence over local planning in Melbourne. Also, the Act endows the minister with overriding powers to initiate and amend planning instruments; for example, a Ministerial Interim Development Order has recently been introduced to provide greater control over land use changes in the central area of the city.

Planning activities at local level

To document the work of local planners in some detail, during 1981 the author interviewed officers in charge of planning in twenty-eight of the fifty-four suburban municipalities of Melbourne. Those selected had experienced population decline over the 1971–76 intercensal period and were inner and middle-ring suburbs. Over much of the post-war period the key concern for the regional planning authority has focused on the transition from rural to urban land uses at the metropolitan fringe. Now, in a period of meagre population and economic growth, the potential for planners to influence redevelopment of the existing built-up area has become a more important issue.

The group of municipalities surveyed was typical of inner areas in Australian cities (Stimson 1982) in which the elderly, the poor and migrants are concentrated. There was also variation in the number of full-time professional staff working in planning (see Table 11.1). The information suggests that the uneven distribution of staff relates particularly to income levels of the resident population and, to a lesser degree, to the proportion of residents born overseas, the size of the municipality and the number of planning-permit applications. Sometimes full-time staff were augmented by consultants and part-time staff, but in all cases these sources made a minor contribution (see T. Logan 1984:105).

Table 11.1 Planning staff and permit applications, 1980

Municipality	Number of full-time planning staff	% time allocated to forward planning	Number of planning applications	% applications for new development
Altona	1	very low	70	n.a.*
Box Hill	3	10	200	38
Brighton	1	20	140	43
Brunswick	1	40	118	n.a.
Camberwell	8	50	253	25
Caulfield	4	30	163	23
Chelsea	1	10	96	24
Coburg	1	very low	140	n.a.
Collingwood	1	very low	174	n.a.
Essendon	1.5	very low	219	29
Fitzroy	3	33	233	n.a.
Footscray	2	very low	264	13
Hawthorn	1	very low	142	18
Heidelberg	5	40	151	38
Kew	3	25	108	18
Malvern	3	25	235	16
Moorabbin	3	very low	172	30
Mordialloc	1	very low	164	27
Northcote	3	30	201	n.a.
Oakleigh	1	very low	270	24
Port Melbourne	0.5	very low	80	n.a.
Prahran	3	30	324	12
Preston	2	very low	248	n.a.
Richmond	1.25	very low	240	n.a.
St Kilda	2	40	225	n.a.
Sandringham	2	30	130	n.a.
South Melbourne	3	20	215	n.a.
Williamstown	1	very low	120	n.a.

* Data not comparable

Source: Survey interviews by the author

The planners drew a sharp distinction between 'statutory' and 'forward' tasks, and the division of responsibilities among their staff frequently reflected this split. Statutory work largely revolves around development control—reporting to council on applications for planning permits. Forward planning loosely means the survey and analysis leading to the formulation of local policies or strategies. Of the eighteen municipalities that employed more than one planner, thirteen had a clear functional division between staff involved in statutory work and those in forward planning. The major weakness of this arrangement was recognised by some interviewees who commented on the growing dichotomy between short-term decisions on permit applications and longer-term policy development. There was a lack of feedback from development control into policy work; a perceived need to bring greater realism into policy formulation. Overall, statutory tasks clearly dominated.

Staffing levels were an issue of concern. The recent expansion of local planning work—both in the handling of permit applications and in policy making—has not been matched by a sufficient increase in staff resources. What happens in this situation, especially where councils employ few planners, is that development-control work receives priority. This conforms to analyses of the English planning system (McLoughlin 1973*a*; Underwood 1981).

The development control function

As indicated previously, for most of the zones in the Melbourne Metropolitan Planning Scheme, the MMBW has delegated authority to local councils to decide on the discretionary uses. Applications for planning permission are made not only in regard to new development, but also for extensions or renovations to existing development and for changes of use within existing buildings. This involves planning staff in answering telephone and over-the-counter inquiries about possible permit applications; in visits to the relevant sites; in reporting to council on whether formal applications should be granted; in preparing and presenting cases to the Town Planning Appeals Tribunal (now the Planning Appeals Board) to support council's refusal, allowance or conditional allowance of a permit; and enforcement work requiring inspections to ensure compliance with the permit conditions. Since most councils meet on a three-week cycle there is a continuing flow of permit applications to be dealt with and regular deadlines to be met. It is little wonder that in councils employing a small number of planners, dealing with planning-permit applications occupies most staff time.

The number of permit applications handled by each municipality varied considerably (see Table 11.1) but not in a clear relationship with size, population characteristics or distance from the central business district. The fact that applications for new development account for a relatively small proportion of the total could be a reflection of the current depressed economy, but the number of permit applications can be a misleading indicator of the amount of development because some uses are allowed as-of-right in particular zones; for example, detached houses in most residential zones, factories in industrial zones and shops in business zones.

Appeals work comprises another aspect of statutory planning. An applicant can challenge a decision by council to refuse planning permission, to impose conditions on permit approval or to request further information, as well as when it has failed to make a decision within two months. 'Third parties' too can challenge a council decision if it has overruled objections opposing the granting of a permit;

during 1980 all such challenges were heard by the Town Planning Appeals Tribunal. The survey showed a large variation in the number of appeals cases in which councils were involved, from just one to more than thirty per year. Some planners viewed appeals as costly and time-consuming and were trying to reduce their frequency. The most common technique was to arrange for some kind of negotiation between the various parties, such as a round-table discussion or an objectors meeting. Many planners stressed that better information from councils and more carefully-prepared recommendations were helpful in this regard but these measures are largely contingent upon adequate levels of staffing. The problem is a cumulative one; if staff have insufficient time to prepare sensible policies to assist in handling permit applications, appeals are likely to be more numerous, leaving even less time for policy formulation.

Ad hoc policies

In their study of planning work in the London boroughs, Healey and Underwood (1977) drew a useful distinction between two broad types of policy. The first type evolves largely in response to problems of development control, so it usually relates to a particular class of land uses and, essentially, results from an *ad hoc* policy-formulation process. The second type of policy attempts to anticipate future problems rather than to respond to them. It frequently involves a longer-term, integrated approach; the definition of goals for the municipality as a whole and the evaluation of alternative means for achieving those goals. Thus, this second policy type resembles the rational model of planning discussed above. The survey of Melbourne planners found an ovewhelming predominance of the first type of policy.

All twenty-eight councils had some form of policy for *residential* land uses. Usually this took the form of a code specifying standards for the development of multi-unit dwellings. Councils first felt the need for such codes in the early 1970s when flats became a discretionary use in some residential zones, largely because of councils' concern at the rapid increase in poor-quality flat construction that had been possible under the Metropolitan Scheme. Two broad kinds of guidelines were introduced: on-site controls, covering such matters as height-limits, site-coverage, privacy from overlooking, car parking provisions and landscaping; and location controls, usually some form of density 'zoning'. In 1979 the MMBW standardised minimum on-site controls over flat development yet many councils believe the standards to be insufficiently stringent, so have retained their own flat codes, some of which reflect an exclusionary motive as they specify minimum standards so high that it becomes uneconomic for multi-unit dwellings to be developed (Paterson et al. 1976). Here there is clearly potential for regional-local conflict because the MMBW (1981) policy is to encourage greater residential diversity by an increase in the number of multi-unit dwellings.

Most councils had more general residential policies although these were rarely available in public documents and many planners simply worked within guidelines gleaned from previous council decisions. Councillors were particularly concerned at the recent population decline because of the possibility of reduced funding from higher levels of government where allocations are usually based on population numbers. Also, some planners argued, councillors feared that reduced population levels would pave the way for amalgamations of local authorities.

In several inner municipalities with relatively high concentrations of low-income groups, housing policies reflected a recognition of the way processes of gentrification and institutional expansion were reducing the supply of low-cost accommodation for these groups, especially in boarding and apartment houses. Planning regulations as such can do little to affect this trend, although it was realised that the imposition of high standards for new flat construction might be restricting the housing opportunities of low-income groups. Most of these councils were working with State agencies on large-scale projects or 'spot purchase' programmes to increase the supply of public housing. Two were receiving State funding to support emergency housing projects and a co-operative rental housing association. At a more modest scale, the planners were exploring the possibilities of converting vacant shop premises to residential uses and of rezoning industrial land or public reservations for this purpose.

Several municipalities characterised by a predominance of middle-income groups were approaching the problem of population loss differently. Two had increased the minimum size standards and environmental requirements for multi-unit dwellings hoping to attract families rather than one or two-person households. Two other councils were encouraging the construction of two houses on a single block, at high levels of environmental standards, while several others were exploring the possibilities of a variety of dual-occupancy types.

Spreading across areas of different income levels was that recognition of the lack of suitable accommodation for the elderly. The current housing stock of predominantly detached, three-bedroom dwellings is not appropriate to the specialised needs of this growing age group. Public and private bodies have responded with proposals for 'granny flats', suburban retirement villages, hostels and nursing homes. Because of their age and the scarcity of suitable accommodation, many elderly people are vulnerable to commercial exploitation, so planners were attempting to ensure adequate facilities and space standards in such developments although they realised that this would probably lead to higher accommodation costs for a group with generally restricted financial resources. This kind of dilemma emphasises the broad economic and social constraints that mould local planning into a reactive rather than a creative role.

Policies for *commercial* land uses were also common but again, few were documented. The increasing gains to scale in the retail industry have caused substantial locational change; the large supermarkets, discount houses, department stores and take-away food outlets have been developed primarily at the major older suburban centres on public-transport routes or at the new 'free-standing' regional centres. So the smaller shopping centres have less business, with growing numbers of vacant shops and buildings of derelict appearance. Some councils have adapted to this trend by allowing service and light industries to locate more freely in small centres, while others are exploring the possibility of conversion to residential uses.

In many larger, older centres a similar impact was apparent; an over-supply of shop premises relative to demand. There was wide-spread consensus among the planners on the need to consolidate such centres by encouraging offices, consulting rooms and service industries to locate on the fringes or above ground floor, and by facilitating a thickening-up of many of these linear centres, through the development of arcades leading to off-street parking. In some municipalities extensive shopping-centre surveys have been undertaken, frequently resulting in the formulation of retailing strategies that favour the promotion of only a few centres. Some of the planners commented that this kind of strategy was difficult to implement in the face of strong parochial pressures within council.

Municipal planners sometimes contributed to the design of shopping centres. This involvement has varied from relatively small-scale measures like the design of paving and seating or concern with the preservation of streetscapes, to small-centre layout and the development of pedestrian malls. Other planners were trying to revitalise existing centres by suggestions for a new kind of zoning to permit extended weekend trading. Again, all that local planners can do is to respond to big problems in small ways.

In relation to policies for *industrial* land, the planners from these inner and middle-ring suburbs noted a reduced demand for space by heavier industries and an increased demand by lighter industries, small in scale. Some councils had responded to this trend by proposing more mixed zonings to accommodate factories and other uses, allowing multiple uses on a single site, encouraging the subdivision of large industrial sites and facilitating the provision of 'factory-ettes' for rental. In terms of development quality, some councils had industrial codes which attempted to improve the aesthetic appearance of factory areas by imposing extra set-back and landscaping requirements. A few had framed codes or by-laws to set maximum noise levels from industrial establishments or to deal with the increased heavy traffic generated by transport depots locating in industrial zones.

Conservation policy is a relatively new addition to the range of planning responsibilities and the approaches of local councils varied considerably. Some, from both relatively low and high-income areas, were conducting comprehensive studies to identify historic buildings or streetscapes worthy of preservation. Many of the studies were the direct result of planners' advocacy, while in other cases they were a response to requests from local residents. Generally the surveys were carried out by specialist consultants, sometimes with co-operation of the local historical society and occasionally, with a Federal subsidy. Although effective historic-building preservation policies depend on increased funding from State or Federal sources, some planners had adapted the development-control system to achieve a degree of conservation; for example, to grant dispensation on car-parking provisions for historic-building preservation in commercial areas or more flexible use of discretionary powers to encourage the recycling of old buildings.

Some planners had moved well beyond the traditional boundaries of town planning to participate with other council departments in the development of policy. One such area is *recreation*, where the planners' involvement varies from detailed design of playgrounds and bicycle paths to comprehensive studies assessing changing leisure needs within their municipalities. Another common venture is in *traffic management* where town planners co-operate in evaluating techniques aimed at reducing the flow of traffic in residential zones.

Comprehensive integrated policy

In the Victorian planning system a comprehensive approach to policy-making is characteristic of metropolitan and regional levels but rarely of the local scale. In the survey of twenty-eight Melbourne councils only three were making a conscious attempt to develop policies as part of a comprehensive strategy for their municipality.

Dissatisfaction with the appropriateness of the Metropolitan Planning Scheme led one council in a low-income suburb to set out its value base in the form of a 'forward planning strategy', adopted by council and distributed for public comment. The strategy identified community goals for a period of three to five years which included: retaining the existing level and diversity of population, especially through the provision of low and medium income housing; improving residential amenity by encouraging rehabilitation and sympathetic infill development; encouraging industrial and commercial development appropriate to the area and its labour skills; promoting continued use of public transport; upgrading of local recreation and shopping opportunities; and improving social, health and welfare programmes.

The strategy was organised into three broad groups — administration, physical planning and social planning — each having detailed objectives, policies and recommendations for action. For example, in the physical planning section, the objectives for residential development focused on the preservation of the scale and character of residential areas and the provision of housing for the existing income groups. Policies included: retention and expansion of low-income housing; preservation of significant buildings; sensitive infill development and encouragement of new housing on under-used sites; industrial and commercial zones. The actions recommended to implement these policies covered the use of conservation guidelines in development-control decisions in residential areas and the formulation of guidelines in relation to height, set-back and scale of new buildings in mixed-use and residential areas.

Concurrently with this process the planning department proposed a series of zoning changes which divided the municipality into precincts for which objectives were stated, as well as 'preferred' and 'discouraged' uses. These were seen as necessary to guide private developers and council in its decisions on discretionary uses. It was intended that those guidelines would be incorporated into a series of local development schemes when the relevant legislative provisions came into operation but, in the meantime, the efforts of the planning department were concentrated on 'problem areas', notably the major retail precincts. The overall process, then, was a progression from comprehensive strategy, through definition of precincts, to a focus on problematic areas; that is, from the broad to the particular.

A second council in another low-income suburb, had adopted a similar approach but was not as far advanced in the process. It had outlined goals for a grouping of council functions into several categories: the general community; finance and organisation; conservation and environment; leisure and recreation; land use; physical services; personal services. Physical services were given first priority and, with the help of a consultant, objectives, policies and 'guides to action' have been prepared for these services, primarily relating to transport and roads.

The third council, again in a low-income suburb, had explicitly rejected the previous kind of approach, arguing the need to avoid the imposition of an overall 'master plan'. Instead, it was working towards a comprehensive strategy from the particular to the broad scale. The municipality had been subdivided into twelve neighbourhoods and the planning staff were investigating the problems and needs of each, using formal and informal surveys of residents and traders. This work was supplemented by Federally-funded neighbourhood traffic studies, carried out by consultants. Initially the neighbourhoods chosen for study were those centering on shopping areas, two of which had been completed by 1980. Those studies culminated in detailed recommendations relating to traffic management, pedestrian safety, car parking, neighbourhood parks, residential densities and landscaping.

A few planners from other councils indicated that they wished to develop comprehensive, integrated policy for their municipalities but maintained that they were constrained by the conservative attitudes or short-term political motives of councillors. Others believed the major constraint on such an approach was lack of staff. In this regard it is relevant to note that the three individual councils described above each have at least three planning staff.

Conclusions

The Victorian planning system is limited by statute to imposing regulatory controls over physical development initiated by the private sector. In a period of rapid economic and population growth, as in the 1950s and 1960s, such a planning system *may* be effective in redirecting urban expansion, in redistributing residential and employment opportunities and in conserving historic or natural landscapes. But in a period of economic decline, as we are now experiencing, far less scope exists for planners to influence private development because there is so little of it. In the current recession, State governments have been anxious to promote development, but it is the regional and State planning agencies that retain the major policy-making functions and key control powers so they are the bodies negotiating with large development companies. At a general level it can be argued that regional and State bodies are assisting fractions of capital, but a major reason is to increase employment opportunities. A positive system of planning, with more direct government involvement in development might change this relationship but the public purse is limited at all levels so a major change in this direction is unlikely in the near future, despite the fact that in 1985 most States and the nation have Labor governments.

What emerges clearly from this study of local planners in Melbourne is their powerlessness to grapple with current economic and social trends affecting land uses. Local planners can only respond to such trends in minor ways, providing 'a neighbourhood protection service' (Underwood 1981:146) to make peoples' residential environments slightly better. Nevertheless, the study demonstrates that there is considerable variation in the extent to which local planners respond to this limited scope of activity.

All council planning departments perform statutory functions associated with development control, administering the discretionary uses for particular zones of the Metropolitan Planning Scheme. This often involves the formulation of control codes for specific uses, universally for multi-unit dwellings and, to a lesser extent, for commercial centres, amusement parlours, industrial uses and car parking. Beyond this statutory function the next stage is the emergence of an *ad hoc* land-management role. Some planning departments have prepared detailed and comprehensive policies for individual land uses; most frequently for housing, but also for retailing, leisure and conservation. The formulation process usually involves extensive surveys, consultation with discussion groups or advisory committees, and the definition of a strategy. A few planning departments have moved to a third stage, one of co-ordinated land management. Here the critical variable was an integrated approach to policy formulation. Sometimes the process was from the 'top' down, in that the council or planners devised municipality-wide policies which were then refined at neighbourhood level; in another instance the process was from the 'bottom' up, beginning at the neighbourhoods and stressing citizen participation at this level, before developing detailed policies for the whole municipality.

Overlaying these distinctions in the type of policy-development process were a number of discernible policy emphases. In some middle-income suburbs there was an obvious urban-design approach to planning, a concern for aesthetics evident in conservation policies or detailed involvement in designs for particular projects. In some less-affluent suburbs a social-welfare approach was evident with land use policies strongly influenced by concern for low-income groups, migrants or the elderly. In another case, a low-income suburb, the emphasis was on efficiency in corporate management for the entire range of local government functions.

The second major finding relates to inequalities among local government areas. The study showed that it is predominantly the low-income suburbs where planning departments are understaffed and therefore could be expected to have fewer resources for policy development and public consultation. Clearly, in the more affluent suburbs, there are large numbers of residents, with an advanced understanding of the way the planning system works, who are able to exert pressures to exclude land uses they regard as detrimental to their neighbourhood.

Local planning has been a neglected area of research in Australia. The variation in planning tasks, their emphases and approaches needs to be explored further. This kind of research might be handled best by a series of in-depth case studies, probably requiring interviews with all planning staff in a particular municipality, in addition to councillors and active pressure groups in the resident and business communities. Ideally, it would involve participant-observation methods of inquiry (Paterson 1974) with researchers becoming involved in the day-to-day work of the planning department, as well as attending meetings of council committees, management teams and council itself, over an extended period. Such a research project is heavily demanding in time and labour and very dependent on the goodwill of councillors and council officers, so probably is likely to proceed incrementally.

Another area of needed research highlighted by the survey relates to evaluating the effectiveness of outcomes of planning. There has been a widespread assumption that once planning policies are formally adopted they will be implemented almost automatically, via the process of development control. But one recent research finding at the metropolitan scale of planning casts doubt on this assumption. Kelleher (1981) has shown that parts of a conservation zone in the Metropolitan Planning Scheme, defined because of rare natural features, have been severely eroded by development permitted as a result of the MMBW's exercise of discretion in the consideration of permit applications and also by the decisions of the Town Planning Appeals Tribunal. There is an obvious need then to explore the relationship between planning objectives and outcomes at both metropolitan and local levels. For example, the aggregate result of delegating to local councils the discretionary power to approve multi-unit dwellings in residential zones might mean that an overwhelmingly restrictive policy has emerged, as the sum of the fifty-odd parts. This is a particularly important issue currently, as Amendment 150 to the Metropolitan Planning Scheme to encourage greater residential diversity is being introduced.

The study underlines the need for empirical research into Australian planning practice to evaluate the relevance of current theoretical arguments. We have seen that the rational model of the planning process bears little resemblance to the way most local planners operate in Melbourne. And while the Marxist interpretation of the planner's role as one of support for capitalist interests appears valid, it is only partially so. It is of little assistance in fully explaining bureaucratic responses at regional and State levels or why and how some local planners can improve residential environments in suburbs ranging across a variety of income levels. At the same time, it is difficult to support strongly Pahl's notion of local planners as urban managers; certainly in Melbourne they have very few resources to allocate. Nevertheless, the political economy emphasis on the way broad social and economic forces limit the scope of local planning and generate inequalities within cities, *is* validated by this study.

Finally, the effectiveness of planning should be explored at an even wider level. What are the tangible or intangible results from planning work? Is it possible to develop a methodology for assessing the value of planning? How would conditions differ if there had been a different planning system, or none at all? These are important issues which need to be confronted if the planning function is to gain greater credibility.

Section V:

Spatial equity, social equity and planning

Chapter 12
Socio-spatial inequality in Sydney

Ron Horvath and David Tait

According to its media-produced image, Sydney is a 'city given over to the good life', 'bent on conspicuous consumption', a place seen as a 'fitting cathedral for the worship of wealth' (*Sydney Morning Herald*). But Sydney also has an underside where poverty and unemployment are everyday realities. Within two kilometres of the finest streets in Sydney such as Wolseley Cresent in Point Piper or Lindsay Avenue in Darling Point can be found one of the major concentrations of poverty in metropolitan Sydney—Kings Cross and Woolloomooloo. If poverty is defined in terms of households earning $6000 per year or less, then Sydney had about 14 per cent of its households under the poverty line in 1981.

How are wealth and poverty distributed in Sydney? One of the major sources of information about the question is the population Census. This chapter describes the patterns of socio-spatial inequality in Sydney using the 1981 Census, extending an analysis presented in *Sydney: a Social Atlas* (Horvath and Tait 1984). Data on seventy-seven census variables were used for the 4613 Collection Districts in the Sydney Major Urban Area, and a correlation matrix formed for the variables. The focus is therefore on neighbourhoods rather than individuals. It is neighbourhoods and municipalities which frequently form the basis units of urban planning, and attract stigma. In order to understand the current patterns of inequality in Sydney, it is necessary to examine the underlying processes which shaped them. The chapter will describe the forms of economic restructuring the city has recently experienced and discusses the impact of this on inequality between classes, ethnic groups and families.

The restructuring of Sydney

The development of a city's social landscape is closely associated with changes in its economic life. The form of Sydney's urban restructuring over the last decade has been related to the character of the economic restructuring the city has recently experienced, in ways which this chapter will outline (Soja et al. 1983; Cardew et al. 1982).

The late 1960s and early 1970s was the period when the Australian economy began to feel the effects of a wider international restructuring crisis. Manufacturing, largely organised by monopoly capital, started to go into decline while the mineral sector organised by global capital grew (Gibson 1984). One effect of these changes was to alter significantly the economic functions performed by Sydney. Sydney's stature as a manufacturing centre declined while its stature as a control centre within the newly-emerging hierarchy of global capitalist cities grew. The advent of global capitalism had as one of its effects the concentration of industrial and financial control in a number of major cities like London, New York, Tokyo, and Los Angeles. Sydney has, during the past decade, become increasingly the major control centre articulating the Australian economy with the international economy (Daly (forthcoming)); we will briefly examine the impact of these changes especially in employment in Sydney between 1971 and 1981.

Given the widespread pattern of job loss in metropolitan regions in advanced capitalist countries, the addition of over 100 000 jobs between 1971 and 1981 to Sydney's economy, an increase of almost 10 per cent, suggests a moderately successful adaption to the newly-emerging global capitalist order. However, the benefits of this 'success' were not distributed equally between industrial sectors or neighbourhoods. Manufacturing underwent substantial restructuring over the decade, which can be interpreted as a consequence of the decline of monopoly capitalism and the emergence of global capitalism (Gibson and Horvath 1983). This type of capitalism brings with it a new international division of labour, involving the spread of manufacturing to newly-industrialising and Third World countries and a decline of manufacturing in most advanced capitalist nations. Metropolitan Sydney lost about 60 000 jobs in manufacturing between 1971 and 1981, a decline of 18 per cent. Construction was the only other industry sector to experience employment loss, with jobs some 4 per cent lower over the decade. The only major occupational category to register decline was that of trades, process workers, and labourers which lost over 20 000 jobs, a decline of over 5 per cent; this points to the decline of Sydney as a manufacturing city.

By contrast, there has been substantial growth in employment in the finance (40 per cent) and community services (57 per cent) industries which together added some 110 000 jobs between 1971 and 1981. The growth in these two industrial sectors largely accounts for the most rapidly growing occupation group, professional and technical workers (51 per cent). Over 65 000 professional and technical jobs were added to Sydney's employment stock between 1971 and 1981. Administrative and clerical jobs also increased by over 33 000 during that period. As factory jobs disappeared office employment became more plentiful.

When we examine the spatial distribution of changes in population, labour force (where the employed live) and jobs (where people work) between 1971 and 1981, we obtain a general view of the spatial effects

Figure 12.1 Population, labour force, and employment changes, 1971–81

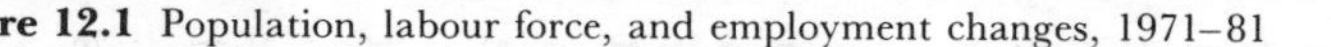

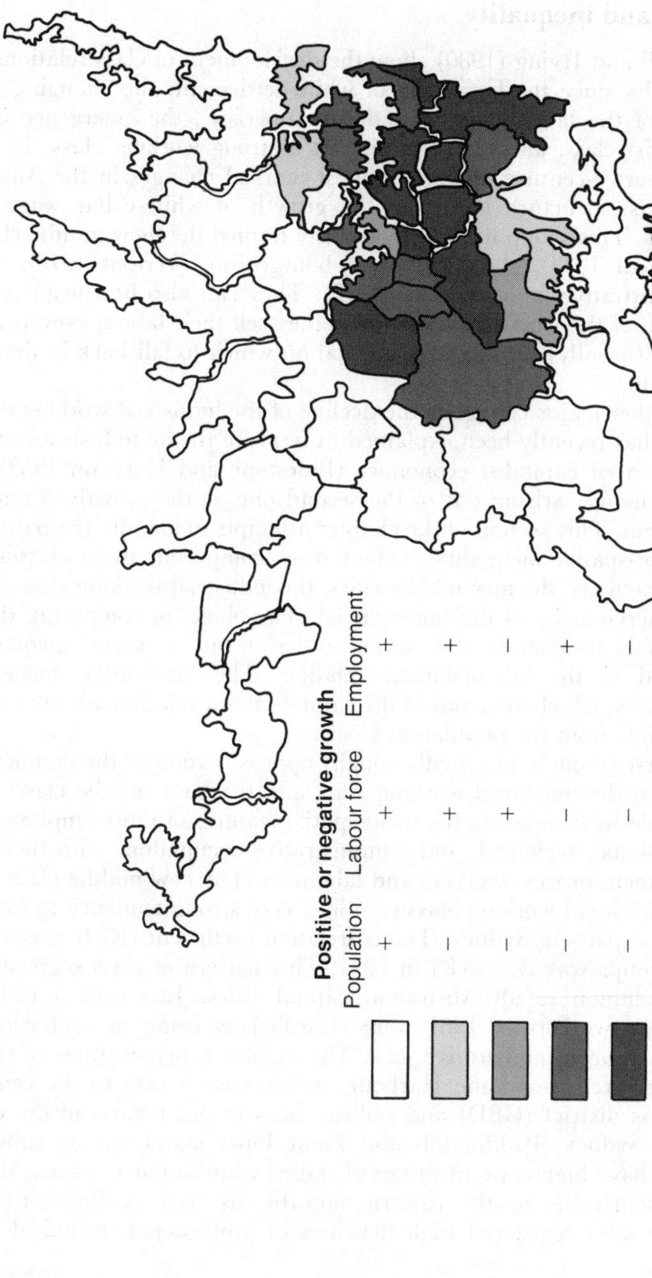

Source: ABS 1971, 1981. Census

of restructuring (Figure 12.1). A general zonal pattern is evident with decline in population, labour force and jobs confined to the inner city and inner suburbs and growth taking place in the outer suburbs.

Class and inequality

Connell and Irving (1980) show the development of class relations in Australia since the beginning of white settlement, the changing fortunes of the landed gentry and 'squattocracy', the emergence of a capitalist class, and the formation of a strong working class. In the last quarter-century one of the most marked changes in the Australian class structure has been the growth of white-collar wage labourers. This group has been variously termed the 'new middle class' (Carchedi 1977), the 'new petty bourgeoisie' (Wright 1976), and 'administrative labor' (Becker 1977). They can also be considered a fraction of the working class in that they sell their labour power, and do not (usually) have land or capital on which to fall back in time of hardship.

Another major change is the decline of the industrial working class which has recently been explained in terms of the de-industrialisation of advanced capitalist economies (Bluestone and Harrison 1982). A third change, arising out of the second one, is the growth of unemployment. This section of the chapter attempts to identify the patterns of socio-spatial inequality evident from comparing three classes or class fractions: the new middle class, the industrial working class, and the reserve army of the unemployed. The object of comparing these groups is to identify the 'second-order' forms of social inequality internal to the labour-labour relation. The 'first-order' forms of inequality, which arise out of the capital-labour relation are not easily accessible from the population Census.

A first (though admittedly rough) approximation of the distinction between the industrial working class and the 'new middle class' can be made by comparing the socio-spatial features of those employed in professional, technical, and administrative occupations with those of tradesmen, process workers and labourers. The new middle class and the traditional working class exhibit a very strong tendency to live in different parts of Sydney. The correlation coefficient (R) between the two groups was R = 0.83 in 1981. This pattern of class segregation was common to all Australian capital cities. Just over a fifth of Sydney's workers in 1981 were classified as being in professional, technical or administrative jobs. The highest concentrations of these workers are around the Harbour, within easy access to the central business district (CBD) and railway lines to other parts of the city. North Sydney, Paddington and Point Piper stand out as suburbs which have high concentrations of skilled white-collar workers. Many neighbourhoods in the eastern suburbs, as well as Balmain and Manly, also registered high densities of professional, technical and administrative workers. Affluence may purchase proximity to work and views of the Harbour Bridge, but it may also buy space in the suburbs; so professionals, technical workers and managers form a relatively high proportion of the population in lower-density suburbs in the north, such as Baulkham Hills and Ku-ring-gai, or in the south, such as Sutherland. In 1981 the distribution of the industrial working class in Sydney was almost the mirror image of that of professional, technical and administrative workers. The major concentration of working-class people in Sydney is in a belt on the southern side of the Harbour, extending from Waverley and Randwick in the east to Fairfield in the west and branching north-west to the Blue Mountains. Not only do these groups live in different neighbourhoods, they work in different parts of the city. There is a tendency for the new middle class to work in the CBD (R = 0.50) whereas the industrial working class do not (R = minus 0.60), reflects the fact that office work is still highly centralised despite the recent suburbanisation of offices (Alexander 1982*b*), whereas manufacturing jobs are more decentralised.

In addition to living and working in different parts of Sydney, the two groups display significant differences in their income and educational characteristics. Of the seventy-seven variables analysed by Horvath and Tait (1984), many of the highest correlation coefficients are found in Table 12.1. Professional, technical and administrative workers tend to be better paid, have more educational qualifications and live in less-crowded housing than blue-collar workers. These variables point to significant inequalities arising in the sphere of production (income) that are reflected in patterns of consumption (education and housing). Moreover, unemployment is a much more serious problem in industrial working-class neighbourhoods than new middle-class ones. Economic restructuring has decimated manufac-

Table 12.1 Correlation between certain occupational and socio-economic variables

	Variables	**Professional, technical and administrative workers**	**Trades, process, labourers**
Income	Persons earning ($15 000 per year	0.83	–0.73
Education	Tertiary qualifications	0.90	–0.82
	No qualifications	–0.80	0.75
Housing	Overcrowding (occupancy ratio)	0.53	–0.31
Unemployment	Unemployed persons	–0.53	0.38
	Unemployed persons 15–24 years	–0.47	0.34

Source: ABS, 1981 Census

turing jobs (and trades, process, labouring jobs) while at the same time creating more finance and community-sector jobs in professional and technical occupations. So it is residents of the traditional working-class neighbourhoods who tend to experience job loss, while residents of middle-class neighbourhoods are more likely to experience job gains.

Neighbourhoods with high rates of unemployment, where Marx's 'reserve army of the unemployed' live, represent a third class group which the data in the *Social Atlas of Sydney* allow us to examine. The unemployed live in very distinctive neighbourhoods in social and spatial terms. Unemployed persons tend to live in industrial working-class neighbourhoods where education attainment, as well as income, is low. Consequently there is a tendency for accommodation to be smaller and rented, and for car ownership to be lower. Neighbourhoods where unemployment is greater are more likely to have Aborigines or migrants living there, as well as more separated and divorced people and single-parent families.

Table 12.2 High unemployment versus low unemployment neighbourhoods

Social categories	Low unemployment variables	R	High unemployment variables	R
Class fraction occupation	Professional, technical, and administrative	–0.53	Trades, process work, labour	0.38
	Clerical	–0.68		
	Sales	–0.56		
Education and income	Trade qualification	–0.68	No qualification	0.54
	Persons with income >$15 000	–0.65	Household income <$6000	0.52
Sphere of consumption (housing and cars)	Owner occupation	–0.51	Renting	0.71
			Public housing	0.42
	Dwelling being purchased	–0.47		
	Dwellings > 6 rooms	–0.62		
	2 cars	–0.67	No car	0.67
Ethnic or migration status	Australian born parents	–0.50	Aborigines	0.53
			Overseas born	0.55
Family status	Nuclear family	–0.25	Separated, divorced	0.58
			Single parent families	0.42

Source: ABS, 1981 Census

Unemployment is also unevenly distributed spatially. Unemployment is low in the prosperous North Shore and southern parts of Sydney. The high-unemployment neighbourhoods are concentrated in two areas, the inner city and the outer western suburbs. The first of

Figure 12.2 Growth in unemployment 1976–81

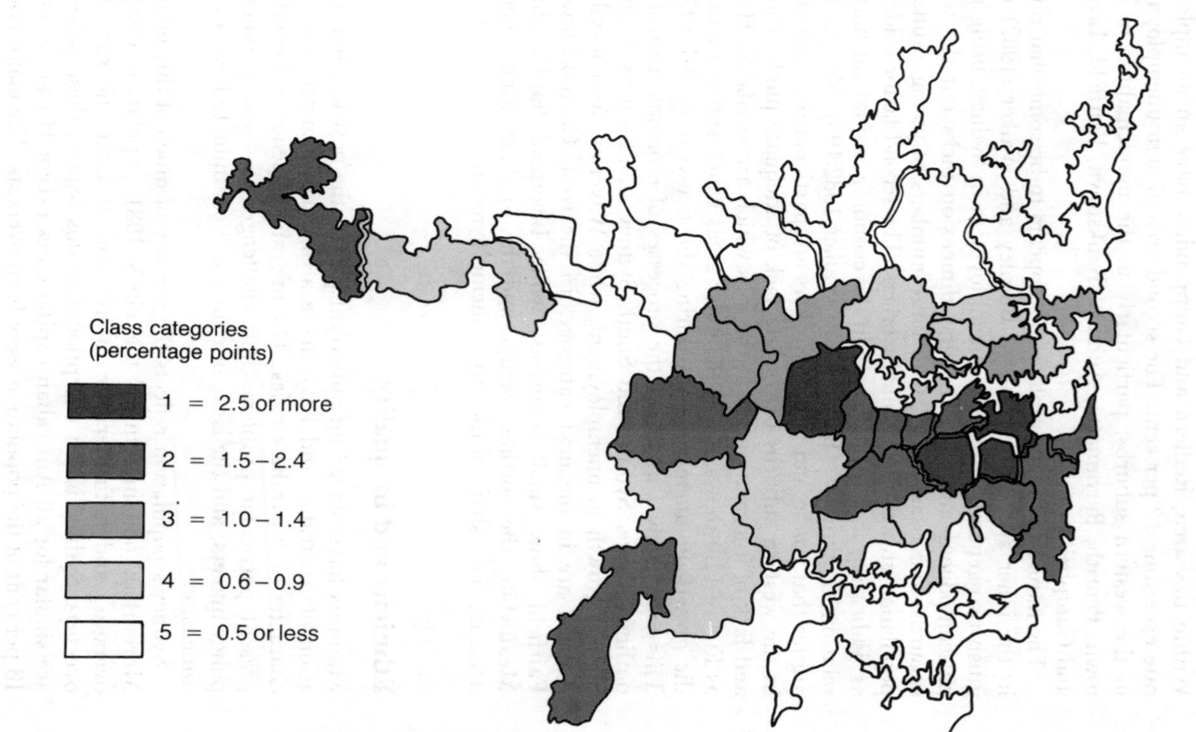

these begins on the edges of Potts Point and Elizabeth Bay near Kings Cross and extends south-west to include Woolloomooloo, Darlinghurst, East Sydney, Surry Hills, Redfern, Chippendale, Newtown, Macdonaldtown, Erskineville, Enmore, Marrickville and St Peters. Within this area, Redfern and Chippendale have an unemployment rate exceeding 12 per cent. The second area of high unemployment is in the western suburbs, particularly in the municipalities of Blacktown, Penrith, Parramatta, Auburn, Bankstown, Fairfield, Liverpool and Campbelltown.

The nature of the unemployment appears to be somewhat different in the inner and outer suburbs. Burnley and Walker (1982) distinguish two general patterns of unemployment in Sydney, using principal-component analysis. The first dimension picks out the western suburbs, and is associated with large numbers of young adults, high population growth and manual workers. The second factor is identified as 'indicating structural change in the economy and labour market in relation to ethnicity' (Burnley and Walker 1982:193). Vipond (1982) argues that young and female workers are particularly disadvantaged in the western suburbs because of lack of adequate public transport and lack of information about the jobs which are available. However as Figure 12.2 shows, it was the inner areas which suffered most from the growth in unemployment during the five-year period 1976–81. This was partly a result of the processes of economic restructuring outlined above. Sydney and South Sydney stand out as having the highest growth in unemployment, while Waverley, Marrickville and Auburn are in the next category. In the west, Campbelltown and Fairfield show small increases, while Liverpool hardly changed. Meanwhile, the northern wedge and the southern fringe tended to decrease their share of the city's unemployment.

Ethnicity and inequality

Migrants have played an important part in the post-war industrialisation of Australia, and have made a distinctive contribution to the character of Australia's cities. The migrant presence will continue to present particular problems and challenges to social planners and policy makers, and the issue of equity will continue to have an ethnic dimension.

Sydney's population reflects the recency of much of this migration. More than one in four of the city's 1981 population were born overseas, and a further one in five had at least one parent born overseas. Sydney is not exceptional in this regard; these proportions are similar for all Australian capital cities except Hobart where only 13 per cent of the population were born overseas. The major countries of origin of Sydney's migrants include the British Isles (221 000), Italy (59 000), New Zealand (49 000), Greece (43 000), Yugoslavia (43 000) and Lebanon (36 000).

Who are the recent overseas-born migrants? Among migrants of less than five years residence, persons from Asia (particularly Vietnam and the Middle East) outnumber Europeans by five to four. The flow of migrants from Southern Europe, which reshaped the southern-central suburbs of Sydney after the Second World War, has essentially ceased. Persons born in Britain or Ireland continue to move into Sydney, but at a slower rate than previously. They have been partly replaced by New Zealanders, who formed the largest single group of overseas-born living in Sydney less than five years.

Table 12.3 Country of birth of overseas migrants, Sydney 1981

Country of birth	**Total** %	**< 5 years** %
Europe	63.7	29.2
UK and Ireland	28.2	16.5
Italy	7.6	1.2
Yugoslavia	5.5	1.4
Greece	5.5	0.9
Germany	2.8	1.1
Other	14.1	8.1
Asia/Middle East	19.5	38.5
Lebanon	4.6	5.1
Vietnam	2.0	9.8
Other	12.9	23.6
English speaking countries outside Europe	7.9	20.6
New Zealand	6.3	17.7
Canada/USA	1.6	2.9
Other	8.9	20.6
Total	100.0	100.0

Source: ABS, 1981 Census

The spatial impact of migration on Sydney can be seen by comparing the distribution of the migrants born in non-English-speaking countries with the distribution of those born in Australia of Australian parents. These two groups tend to live in different parts of Sydney as the correlation coefficient of minus 0.88 clearly shows. The overseas-born tend to inhabit a discontinuous east-west belt running through the middle of Sydney from Waverley in the east to Parramatta and Liverpool in the west. In sharp contrast, the Australian-born, of Australian parents, live predominantly in the northern and southern suburbs of the city (Figure 12.3).

Migrants to Sydney are a heterogenous group. Selective migration policies based on job skills, combined with refugee-resettlement and family-reunion schemes have meant that migrants have occupied slots at all levels of the occupational hierarchy. The 1981 census recorded some 1300 doctors and dentists who were Asian-born, compared to

Figure 12.3 Ethnicity

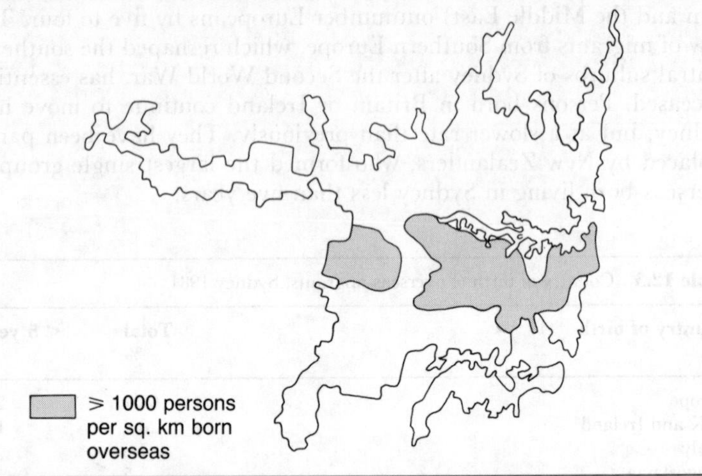

only 700 from the British Isles. Greeks were twice as likely as the Australian-born to be employers or self-employed.

Nevertheless, migrants from non-English-speaking countries are in general disadvantaged compared to other groups in Sydney society. At an individual level this is reflected in unemployment rates for Vietnamese and Lebanese running at twice the rate of that for the Australian-born. This inequality has a very clear spatial dimension, which becomes evident when migrant neighbourhoods are compared with neighbourhoods with higher concentrations of Australian-born people with Australian parents (Table 12.4).

Regardless of whether one looks at indicators of income, occupation or consumption, migrant areas are worse off. Fewer higher-income individuals (earning more than $15 000 per year) live in migrant neighbourhoods than in second-generation Australian neighbourhoods. Migrant neighbourhoods tend to have relatively more blue-collar workers, and fewer white-collar workers. Unemployment rates (as well as youth-unemployment rates) are higher in migrant neighbourhoods; few people have trade qualifications, fewer households have cars (so residents are more dependent on public transport), houses tend to be smaller and fewer people are homeowners.

This pattern of differentiation between migrant and second-generation Australian neigbourhoods extends beyond production and consumption relationships (of which all the variables in Table 12.4 are measures) into the sphere of culture. Second-generation Australians tend to live in Church of England (R = 0.80) and mainstream Protestant (R = 0.59) neighbourhoods, while migrants tend to live in Catholic (R = 0.32) ones. The religious diversity of recent migrants was reflected in the sharp increase in the size of Sydney's Muslim community from less than 9000 in 1971 to about 35 000 in 1981.

Table 12.4 Migrant versus second generation Australian neighbourhoods

	Variables	Persons born in non-English-speaking countries	Both parents Australian-born
Income	Persons with >$15 000	–0.49	0.38
Occupation	Professional, technical, and administrative	–0.39	0.26
	Trade, process workers, labourers	0.43	–0.23
	Clerical	–0.35	0.31
Unemployment	Unemployed persons	0.48	–0.50
	Unemployed persons aged 15–24 years	0.32	0.35
Housing and automobile	Dwellings with 2 cars	–0.46	0.54
	Dwellings with no cars	0.36	–0.44
	Commuters travelling by private motor vehicle	–0.31	0.42
	Occupied private dwellings > 6 rooms	–0.32	0.36
	Purchasing dwellings	–0.38	0.46
Education	Trade qualifications	–0.47	0.49

Source: ABS, 1981 Census

One of the key aspects of culture is of course language, and Sydney had some 400 000 of its overseas-born residents who spoke a language other than English at home. About a quarter of them said they did not speak English at all, or not well. These people are even more concentrated geographically than migrants from non-English-speaking countries in general, perhaps reflecting the tendency for recent migrants to settle initially in core migrant areas, while more established migrants tend to disperse.

To the extent that economic and social disadvantage follows ethnic lines, it stresses the need for social programmes to take account of the ethnic diversity of these groups, and emphasises the need for multicultural goals to be related to attempts to address economic inequalities through employment and housing policies.

Another major policy question is concerned with the extent to which different migrant groups are being assimilated into the wider society, and to what extent they are retaining their cultural identities. One way of examining the geographical dimension of this process is by using the index of residential segregation. This index measures the degree to which the spatial distribution of a given subpopulation, for example, a migrant group, differs from that of the entire populations. The index ranges from zero, indicating no difference to 100 indicating complete spatial (and, by inference, social) segregation. It is assumed that where assimilation is occurring, migrant groups should exhibit falling index values over time.

The index of residential segregation generally varies according to how long a particular birthplace-group has lived in Australia, that is, the Vietnamese and Lebanese are the most recent migrants and have the highest indices; the Greeks, Yugoslavs and Italians, largely post-Second World War migrants, have intermediate scores; and the traditional migrants from the United Kingdom and Ireland have the lowest scores. These patterns of residential segregation may also reflect the ease with which different groups are integrated into a predominantly English-speaking society. The index of residential segregation for Aborigines is 67.1, midway between those for the Vietnamese and the Lebanese. Residential segregation, in the case of the Aborigines is over-determined by a variety of factors, including racism.

Table 12.5 Index of residential segregation by birthplace

All overseas-born	20.9
Overseas-born resident for less than 5 years	37.4
English-speaking countries	
UK/Irish	17.6
New Zealand	35.8
Non-English-speaking countries/regions	31.0
Italy	44.6
Yugoslavia	47.1
SE-Asia	47.1
Vietnam	79.0
Greece	55.1
Lebanon	62.4
Australian-born of Australian-born parents	19.4
Aborigines/Torres Strait Islanders	67.1

Source: ABS, 1981 Census

Family and inequality

If 'industry' and 'occupation' are the units for describing economic activity, the 'family' is one of the central categories for describing consumption. The family is the unit which transmits class inequalities in the sphere of production to the sphere of consumption. It is the institution which, in a capitalist society, turns parental unemployment into child poverty. This section outlines where families of different sorts and in different life cycle stages live in Sydney and how this spatial pattern interacts with the processes of economic restructuring discussed above. Finally it describes the distribution of family poverty in Sydney.

Two-parent families with dependant children are disproportionately concentrated in the outer fringes of the metropolitan area, from Avalon on the north coast, right along the northern perimeter of the city (with heavy concentrations in French's Forest, Baulkham Hills and Penrith), along the western suburbs (Fairfield, Liverpool, Campbelltown) and down the southern perimeter in Sutherland. This zonal pattern is quite common, and tends to reflect the generally lower cost and greater availability of land in the outer areas for newly-forming households. Meanwhile group households, separated or divorced people, and older persons tend to live in the inner suburbs.

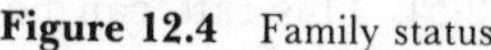

Figure 12.4 Family status

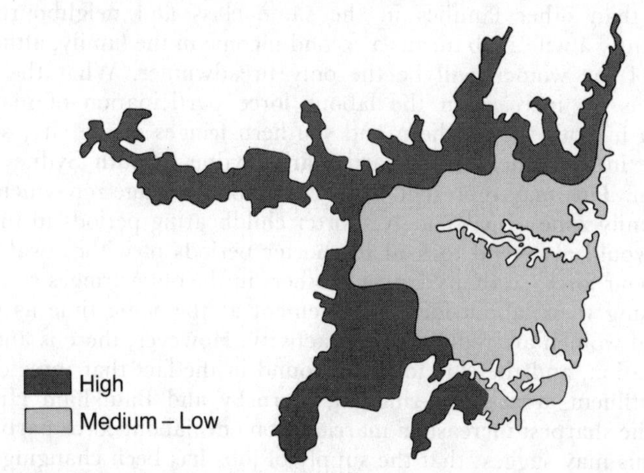

The family zones indicate life cycle mobility, as people tend to grow up in the outer suburbs, move further in for study or work (and perhaps share a flat with others), and move out again into owner-occupation. This life cycle mobility does not apply to the same extent to various migrant groups (Burnley 1981). Perhaps for this reason, the family zones are more evident on the north shore than across the migrant belt; 'gentrification' may be an alternative to moving to the outer suburbs for young professionals setting up home. However, the zonal pattern is still sufficiently dominant for the presence of nuclear family pockets in the inner suburbs to demand an explanation. There are only three Census Districts in the inner suburbs in which more than half the families comprise two parents and dependant children. They are Randwick (a naval base), the northern tip of Woollahra (another naval base), and part of Manly (an army base).

Two life cycle groups which have been particularly affected by changes in the labour market, brought about by economic restructuring, have been young people and mothers. The economic changes affecting these groups have had marked geographical implications for the distribution of inequality in Sydney.

The youth unemployment rates in the nuclear family areas of Penrith, Blacktown and Campbelltown are high, in 1981 frequently about 12 per cent (Matwijiw 1985), which are matched in the inner city in Darlinghurst and Redfern ('non-family' areas). This problem also has migrant and gender dimensions. Unemployment is most acute for young women born in non-English-speaking countries: almost half of the Census subdivision Matwijiw (1985) maps show unemployment rates of over 15.4 per cent.

The distribution of married women in the labour force has been changing quite noticeably since 1976 (Figure 12.5). This rate can be seen as an indicator of families with greater access to consumption goods than other families in the same class and neighbourhood. Frequently a wife's job means a second income in the family, although some of the women will be the only breadwinner. What the map shows is an increase in the labour force participation of married women in both the northern and southern fringes of the city, and a decline in the inner areas, particularly Sydney, South Sydney and Auburn. This may represent the pressure of mortgage repayments in the 'family zone'. Increasingly shorter childbearing periods in the life cycle would also tend to lead to shorter periods of withdrawal from the labour force, so that younger mothers in the outer fringes could be increasing their labour-force involvement at the same time as older married women are reducing their activity. However, there is another explanation, and the clue to this is found in the fact that three of the most affluent areas—Ku-ring-gai, Hornsby and Baulkham Hills—show the sharpest increase in married women's labour-force participation; this may suggest that the supply of jobs has been changing.

Women living in traditional working-class areas, particularly in the inner suburbs, are those most likely to have been hit by the decline of manufacturing jobs; the second family income becomes less attainable, with consequences for family standards of living. Meanwhile, the women who live in the more affluent parts of Sydney are more likely to have the educational qualifications or job skills required by the expanding sectors of the economy. Married women in these areas are in a better position to supplement the family income. This provides a clear example of the way economic changes result in increasing inequalities between families. So how is family poverty distributed geographically? While nuclear families tend to be common on the outer fringes of the city, poor families are disproportionately con-

Figure 12.5 Labour force participation of married women: change 1976–81

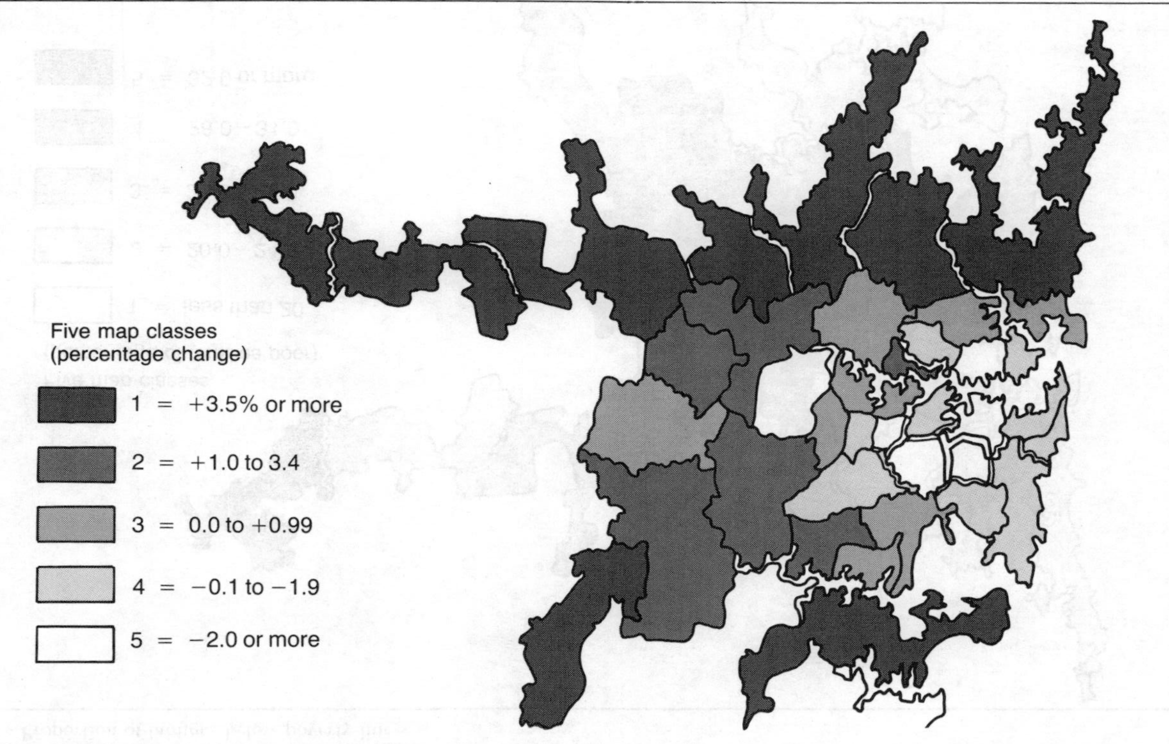

Figure 12.6 Proportion of families below poverty line

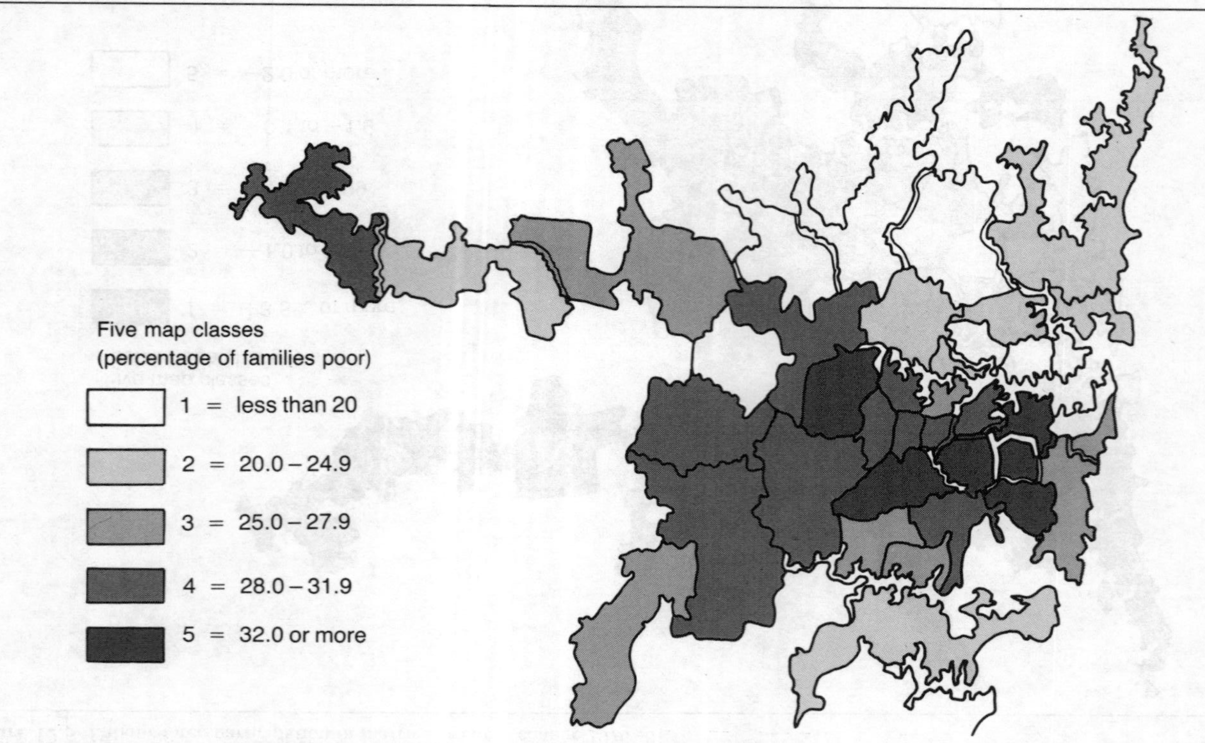

centrated in the inner and inner-western suburbs (Figure 12.6); many of these will be one-parent families or older couples. The map presents the proportion of families in the lowest quarter of the family income distribution, after adjusting for family size. The familiar socio-economic pattern emerges, with Baulkham Hills and Ku-ring-gai experiencing the least family poverty, and South Sydney the worst. Poverty extends right across the migrant belt to Fairfield, but the highest proportions of families in poverty extend from Sydney and Botany westwards to Canterbury.

Conclusions

This chapter has argued that Sydney is an 'unfairly structured city' (Badcock 1984), fragmented along class, ethnic and family lines. These social divisions are reflected in corresponding patterns of spatial inequality, as differences in class-based income (from the sphere of production) largely shape differences in access to consumption goods like housing, cars and views of the Harbour, and thus affect the family. The patterns of inequality are changing in response to processes of economic restructuring, as Sydney undergoes a rapid and sometimes painful transition from a manufacturing centre organised by monopoly capital to an industrial and financial control node within emerging global capitalism. The class system translates these changes into changes in family welfare. Families of professionals and other workers in the growing sectors of the economy tend to be improving their standards of living, particularly where families have more than one income. Meanwhile families of those in the declining sectors tend to be losing. Working-class women and migrants are among those for whom poverty and unemployment are becoming increasingly common.

The restructuring crisis of capitalism is thus writ large on the social landscape of Sydney.

Chapter 13
Basic inequalities of land use planning

Bob Graham

Planners, and town planners in particular, claim for themselves a commitment to social justice and a concern for the general welfare of society. These aspirations are frequently made quite explicit by planners: 'the direction of the development of land use to serve the economic and social welfare of the community' (Brown and Sherrard 1951:3).

Such assertions and claims form much of the justification for actions and recommendations by planners. There is a belief that because such statements are included in planning documents, then those documents will achieve the stated aims when implemented.

Structure plans, planning schemes, planning studies, land use plans and other planning documents frequently use such statements as justification for their existence and operations. That such a view holds wide credence in the planning profession stems in part from the belief that planning is based on value-free analysis and rational decision-making. This decision-making is seen to occur in situations where the problems of power and welfare distribution are largely ignored.

Based on this view the planner becomes, 'an allocator of scarce resources' with the particular intention of 'altering the distribution of real incomes' (Eversley 1973).

The 'scare resource' with which planners are concerned is land. The scarcity of land is created artificially through pricing mechanisms and land use controls, which commodify land as a finite material resource and its absolute or relative immobility.

By looking at the attempts of planners to affect the distribution of wealth, and controls associated with the 'scarce resource' we can gain some insight into the real results of land use planning. Planners are part of the system used to allocate land and the wealth and power associated with its ownership and control. If planners are committed to better levels of distributional equity, then by inference, they must hold the view that the system which they support and help to function will achieve better levels of distributional equity. Planning does affect the distribution of resources by its influence (or lack of it) over the location of jobs, housing, facilities, access to these things, the value of property rights, and the price of resources to consumers.

To suggest that planners and planning do not 'alter the distribution of real incomes' or in some way assist the economically and socially disadvantaged would probably be an uncomfortable suggestion for most planners. To suggest that they actively work against a more equitable distribution of wealth would probably be hotly denied.

For example, a major cause of inequality stems from the differences between owner-occupiers and those dependent upon rental accommodation. Owner-occupiers pay only the market value of their accommodation at the time of purchase and their continuing payments are based on this fixed price which declines as a proportion of total income over time, whereas rental payments are adjusted upwards according to market conditions. The average monthly mortgage payment in Hobart in 1981 was $75, as compared to average monthly rental levels of $140 (ABS, 1981 Census). Owner-occupiers also receive capital gains, tax rebates for rates and land taxes paid and other indirect benefits. Inequalities also arise through relative location, access to facilities, environmental quality and the relative cost and availability of services. Planning has a substantial influence over the location of housing, the distribution of housing types, the environmental quality of different areas and the transport infrastructure that is developed to serve these areas.

How, then, does land use planning relate to these matters and what have been the results in terms of distributional equity? These questions have been looked at in Hobart to gain some insight into the relationship between planning and distributional equity (Graham 1981*a*).

In Hobart

In common with the rest of Australia, resources in terms of wealth and property are unevenly distributed in Hobart. The people on the lowest incomes live in the areas with the lowest property values. Also there is a distinct pattern of social segregation by income and economic status.

The sub-markets created by the uneven distribution of wealth operate to ensure spatial segregation of residents in terms of social and economic status. Table 13.1 identifies some characteristics for each of the sub-markets in Hobart. Although these data relate to 1976, checking of the 1981 Census and 1983–84 valuations reveals little change in these relationships, apart from some upward movement in social and economic status of two small inner-suburban areas.

These sub-markets contain groups with similar levels of available economic resources, which occupy similar positions in space. Their existence appears to be essential for the operation of the overall land market because of the need:

- for an ordered hierarchy of small market areas within which stability can be established so that investments can be made and returns on investment realised;

Table 13.1 Residential sub-markets, Hobart 1976

Annual household income $	% with tertiary qualifications	% who rent	% purchasing	% owners	Median rental/ mth $	Median mortgage payment/ mth $
<8 000	3.1	87	—	13	108	—
8–9 000	6	50	24	26	117	100
9–10 000	9	37	33	30	136	78
10–11 000	10	34	34	32	135	87
11–12 000	12	22	48	30	163	57
12–13 000	13	19	52	29	167	73
13–14 000	15	17	58	25	157	67
>14 000	20	11	64	25	211	80

Source: ABS, 1976 Census

- for the creation and maintenance of situations of artificial scarcity so that rents and prices can be maintained;
- to ensure orderly relationships between construction, economic growth and new development.

The geographical structure associated with these sub-markets forms a decision environment within which consumers make choices. These choices tend to conform to, and re-enforce the structure.

It is also possible to identify a series of amenity attributes that vary considerably between sub-markets, and which provide some of the outward signs of inequity in our society. These are summarised in Table 13.2

Table 13.2 Physical attributes of residential areas in land use sub-markets

Low social and economic status	High social and economic status
Smaller and older dwellings	Larger and/or newer dwellings
Small areas of open space	More open space (public and private)
Low environmental quality	High environmental quality
Poor visual amenity and outlook	High standards of visual amenity—views, etc.
Low level of public facilities	Good public facilities
Mixed land uses	Purely residential land uses
Land use instability	Land use stability

Source: Hobart City Council, Land Use, Recreation and Housing Condition Surveys 1977, 1978, 1979

The observed inequalities have arisen as a result of the operation of the land market over time. The land market provides the mechanism whereby groups are sorted out according to their power and influence in that market.

Because the aggregate of land transactions, developments and redevelopments are the main elements of land use change, the main means by which the 'scarce resource' of land in cities is distributed is the land market. It is the allocation mechanism for this 'scarce resource'. It is intrinsically inequitable because of the inequitable distribution of wealth in society.

It follows that in order for planners to achieve the social and welfare aims they set for themselves, they must influence both the land market and the distribution of land and the resources associated with the ownership of land. The next section analyses the role of planners in this area, using Hobart as an example.

Planning and equity

If planning and planners have as an overall aim the welfare of the population, then there should be some evidence that planning works to redress the inequities observed above. This proposition was tested in Hobart by first looking at a number of planning actions and second at the end result of those actions. The matters investigated were zoning, infrastructure, roads, transport and the provision of open space.

Hobart has had a number of zoning schemes covering different parts of the city since 1948 (City of Hobart 1968; 1972; 1976; 1977). By setting aside specific areas for specified land uses, these zoning schemes tend to reflect the patterns of the land use distribution that have arisen through the market. The zoning schemes define rules which set the limits within which landowners may operate. These rules have a significant influence on the level of stability in the land market in any particular area. This is to the advantage of those who hold wealth and power through the ownership of property as they have the most to gain from a stable market situation in which development rights are clearly defined.

Zoning schemes also seek to protect residential amenities which can be affected by loss of privacy, noise and environmental pollution, overshadowing, loss of open areas, loss of sunlight and increase in traffic.

These things can happen when residential areas are invaded by non-residential uses, when development density increases and when new and inappropriate forms of development occur. In Hobart, zoning schemes have tended to provide the greatest protection in terms of amenity to those areas with the highest social and economic status. For example, Hobart was, until recently, covered by a planning scheme, the provisions of which are shown in Table 13.3 for two residential areas.

Sandy Bay is a high-income suburb, whereas North Hobart is a low-income suburb. The wholly residential nature of North Hobart

Table 13.3 Provisions of planning scheme, Sandy Bay and North Hobart

	Sandy Bay	**North Hobart**
Permitted uses	Home occupation 1 & 2 Family dwelling	Home occupation 1 & 2 Family dwelling Group House
Discretional (minor uses in both zones have been omitted)	Bank, restaurant, club, education, hospital, place of assembly	Bank, restaurant, club, education, hospital, place of assembly, apartment building, motel, guest house, hostel, service station, shop, show room, liquid fuel depot
Density factor (Open Space Ratio: open space/floor area of development)	2.5	1.9
Boundary setbacks	5 m	3 m
Height	6.5 m	8 m (no limit in part)

has been under attack for forty years, an attack that has been encouraged by planners. The Cook Plan (Cook 1945:27) which became the basis for by-law zoning says that 'old insanitary dwellings will be replaced by modern factories' and identifies North Hobart as one of the main areas where this process is to occur. North Hobart was described as 'old and decadent'. Because dwellings in the area were old, assumed to be insanitary and *had lower land values*, the solution was to replace them with 'modern factories' (Cook 1945:31). Surveys in 1978 and 1980 revealed that most of this housing stock is still sound and habitable.

Zoning plans have allowed and encouraged a reduction in low-income areas while protecting high-income areas. In addition, by promoting land use changes in older, low-income suburbs the following consequences have arisen: loss of use value of residential property for remaining residents (the majority of whom are tenants—87 per cent in 1981); poor levels of social and local economic facilities due to falling demand and the weak political position of residents; loss of housing stock for those most in need of low cost accommodation close to facilities; a decline in the levels of social cohesion through population loss and the break-up of established social networks. All of these things have happened in the areas housing those people with the least resources to cope with change and disruption.

It has long been recognised that land use zoning provides an important support mechanism for the land market. By introducing stability and some degree of certainty in to the market, zoning provides an environment in which the market can successfully operate (see, for example, New York Supreme Court decision on the Zoning Ordinance; Harvey 1974). Zoning schemes are seen as legal documents affecting property rights. The only group who have property rights are those who own property. The zoning schemes set the limits within which those rights are exercised. Those who own more property have more rights.

Market processes depend upon and exacerbate existing inequalities and the land market contributes to the unequal distribution of power and wealth deriving from the control and ownership of land. Zoning plans are an integral part of that process and planners who devise and administer them are contributing to inequality in society.

Investment by public authorities in infrastructure, particularly roads, water and sewerage, has been a major factor influencing the nature, rate and direction of development in Australian urban areas. Town planners are involved in preparing plans and programmes for infrastructure provision. An analysis of programmes of infrastructure provision in Hobart provides a basis for assessing the contribution of these programmes to equity (Graham 1981*b*).

This analysis reveals that the programmes provide support for land-development processes which allow exchange value to be realised through the property market. This has been done by means of the extension of infrastructure at the urban fringe, the provision of arterial roads and urban circulation and parking spaces, and the provision of certain facilities.

The extension of road, water and sewerage services at the urban periphery is usually associated with re-zoning from rural to urban uses, a dramatic rise in land value and public subsidies to support the infrastructure provision. The benefits accruing to landowners are realised upon sale of the land (in some cases as much as 2000 per cent), and these benefits are assisted by planners who provide for re-zoning and assist with infrastructure planning.

In common with other Australian cities, Hobart has, over the last twenty-five years, carried out substantial traffic works in the inner city to assist the motor car. Planners have been involved in the planning and implementation of these programmes.

Private transport has benefitted at the expense of public transport. In 1960, Hobart had suburban railways, ferries, trams, trolley buses and motor buses. Today, only motor buses and one ferry remain, carrying less than half the volume of passengers, despite a trebling of the city-centre workforce. Planners have recommended and supported the construction of five multi-storey car parks and numerous ground-level parking facilities to cater for the motor car.

The land use impacts are two-fold: first, they aid the process of peripheral expansion and the process of land use change at the urban fringe; second, they have led to the loss of inner-city residential property through both central area expansion and road construction and road widening. Between 1966 and 1980, 250 residences were lost to road widening and parking schemes.

The process has supported a system of transport that favours the rich. For example, in Hobart's richest suburb in 1981, only 2 per cent of households had no motor vehicle whereas 24 per cent of households in the poorest suburb had no motor vehicle.

In addition, the development of roads in the inner city, (the area where the poorest live), has adversely affected these areas by increased noise, dust and fumes, loss of residential amenity, forced relocation of families and the promotion of land use change. It has reduced the value of housing stock for residents (predominantly tenants) while increasing the value of land. This has contributed to speculation and land use change, and the subsequent realisation of profits through re-zoning and re-development.

Planning for parks and recreation facilities, green belts and so on, is often seen as a major contribution by planners to assisting the public good. If there was any commitment to social equity it might be in this area that the planners efforts are evident. Evidence from Hobart suggests the contrary. Table 13.4 shows the distribution of this facility whereby the rich, particularly those who live in the three most affluent areas, get a much better deal than the poor.

Table 13.4

Suburb	Rank-average income	Open space as percentage of total area
Sandy Bay	1	28
Lenah Valley	2	21
Mt Nelson	3	12
Dynnyrne	4	3
West Hobart	5	7
Glebe	6	3
Battery Point	7	10
South Hobart	8	7
New Town	9	9
North Hobart	10	0

Source: Graham 1981*a*

Planning has failed to deliver, to the less affluent, a basic facility of urban life — local, usable open space. This evidence provides little support for the view that planning has aims to promote the social and economic welfare of the community.

Planning and development

The above discussion demonstrates how planners are actively involved in supporting a system in which 'property and property relations play the key part in forming the contours of inequality...' (Westergaard and Resler 1975). In reaching this conclusion it is necessary to identify the reasons why. From the analysis carried out in Hobart, reasons can be identified in a number of areas.

First, in a number of cases, planners were found to have a direct interest in property development by being property-owners and developers in their own right. Their views consistently supported those who made gains out of the development process. Planners, particularly those in senior positions, were found to have a conservative, development-oriented outlook, because they frequently received their basic education and experience in the development-oriented disciplines of architecture, engineering or surveying. Moreover, planning frameworks are frequently a sub-section of an engineering or building department and planning practice emphasises statutory planning and development control which relates directly to the development process. Most planners have direct day-to-day contact with developers, architects, builders and surveyors. Planners are pressing to become accepted as professionals and are under pressure to conform to the apolitical conservative norms of other professional groups. Furthermore, they are under pressure to conform to the wishes of employers, many of whom are development-oriented. Planners generally hold middle-class values which are oriented toward maintaining the *status quo* rather than identifying with other classes with different value systems. There is still a continuing and deep-seated belief that the creation of reasonable physical conditions will lead to social improvement; there is little recognition of the fact that the prime motivation of development is profit and not social improvement.

Finally, planners generally subscribe to the view that there is a broad consensus of community opinion and that compromise solutions can be found to social and economic problems. For example, zoning schemes assume that all individuals have equal power in the market; thus, anything but marginal interference with the market is not warranted as the market will distribute resources equitably. Consequently, planners avoid questioning the role of developers and the wealthy and powerful. For all of these reasons, planners working in a situation where service to property is the basic function find it difficult to develop and implement an alternative view based on social justice. The way in which planning schemes are operated works against the achievement of social aims by planners.

First, they are drawn up so as to provide a basis for well-off, articulate residents to prevent incursion into their areas by unwanted developments. At the same time, in residential areas occupied by lower-income residents, the schemes are more permissive, allowing a greater range of non-residential uses, denser development and lower standards. If the residents are poor and their living areas less physically attractive, it is assumed that they require less protection under planning schemes. This double standard is common and widespread in Australian urban planning schemes. The *Journal of the Royal Australian Planning Institute* covering the period 1975–85, contains not one adverse comment on this feature of planning schemes.

Second, planning schemes have come to be regarded as 'flexible' documents—that is, the deciding authority can bend the rules to suit the demands of developers. In fact, flexibility has come to be seen as a positive aspect in planning schemes. This situation benefits speculator-developers, and those with the power, wealth and influence to protect their own areas, while developing other areas of the city, in that control in certain areas of the city is loosened without alternatives for control and management being available. As a result planning is seen as bringing about order and efficiency in physical development and providing for the requirements of commerce and industry.

Third, planners and the plans they produce tend to support the bureaucratic ideals of the organisations that finance planning. In particular, at local government level, planning schemes provide a land use framework for the infrastructure operation that forms the public support side to the property-development market.

In summary, planning often provides support to a development process based on individual preferences of those who have control over property and wealth and their desire to make money out of the land market. This form of planning is essentially conservative and tends to support the *status quo* merely by its stance (or lack of it) on social issues. It is closely allied to the view that the individual is the best judge of his own welfare and that the market system is an adequate means of allocating resources. It does not question whether a reliance on the land market produces a situation which is consistent with social justice.

As Sandercock (1977:51) suggests in discussing the early days of planning in Victoria, 'Planners only eventually won the acceptance of the power holders when they demonstrated that they were compliant and docile—estate managers of capitalism'.

Conclusion

As long as planning and planners give support to a system of land development and change whose very basis is inequality, then their ability to achieve the social goals which they frequently profess will be severely limited. If planners are to be effective in these areas, then it is likely that the role of capital in urban development and change will have to be challenged.

While planners themselves clearly are not in a position to do this on their own, there are a number of measures that could be taken within the profession to achieve some movement away from the present situation. This include:

- removing assumptions from planning schemes about land use change proceeding in accordance with market forces;
- the introduction of 'positive discrimination' in planning practice towards those with limited wealth and power;

- acceptance of the political nature of planning and its use by those in positions of power for their own benefit, and a strong public stance against this position;
- the use of planning techniques to discourage speculator-developers, particularly where their operations have adverse social impacts;
- a broadening of the base for planning education to include such matters as the political economy of urban development, and to give it more independence from the development professions;
- a reduction of direct links between planners and the development industry;
- developing alternative professional associations that are committed to educating and informing the public about the processes of urban growth and change, and providing direct assistance to groups and individuals disadvantaged by these processes;
- actively working to reduce the impact of the land market as the dominant force in land use change.

These proposals are only partial and would have only a marginal effect. They do not represent an answer to the difficult question of access to wealth and power, but at least they may provide some basis for planners working towards better levels of social justice.

Chapter 14

Spatial organisation and local unemployment rates in metropolitan Adelaide: significant issue or spatial fetish?

Clive Forster

The catastrophic increase in unemployment in Australia during the past decade has drawn fresh attention to the long-recognised fact that residential unemployment rates tend to vary considerably from place to place within our large cities. In examining the similar phenomenon in British cities Metcalf and Richardson (1976), Cheshire (1979), Thrift (1979) and others argue that spatial concentrations of unemployment are largely the inevitable consequence of an overall deficiency in the demand for labour acting upon a residentially-differentiated population. Particularly following the publication of the Inner Area Studies (UK, Department of the Environment 1977), it has been argued that the analysis of intra-urban spatial variations in unemployment is of little relevance. Attempts to relate such variations to elements of urban spatial organisation have been criticised even more strongly as downright counter-productive and symptomatic of 'spatial fetishism'—a deviant practice strongly to be discouraged:

> The mode of analysis of employment and unemployment described by studies of inner areas of all kinds and frozen in the urban land-use models of Alonso, Muth, and others is part of the continuing highly ideological tradition of spatial fetishism whereby problems of society become problems of space, somehow embedded in the qualities of space itself. (Thrift, 1979: 177)

It is conceded that spatial concentrations exist, and, though less readily, that they may exacerbate the plight of the unemployed. But the clear implication is that to undertake spatial analysis, and especially to seek explanations related even partially to spatial organisation is to miss the point:

> A concentration on area-based explanations of deprivation is likely to obscure the fundamentally structural rather than spatial or pathological origins of deprivation... Area effects may intensify or compound such deprivations but they should not blind us to their origins. (Hamnett 1979: 257)

Yet several recent studies of unemployment in Australian cities have focused specifically upon spatial variation in local unemploy-

Based on the original publication in *Australian Geographical Studies*, 21 (April 1983) are reproduced here by kind permission of the Editors.

ment rates and, though concurring with the British writers in stressing the fundamental importance of the overall deficiency in demand for labour, have also suggested area-based explanations. In Melbourne, Maher argues that:

> ...inequities in employment that are reflected in high unemployment rates stem from forces that generate specialised local employment structures on the one hand, and segregate occupational groups via the housing market on the other. In short, this view assumes that equity in employment on the metropolitan scale has the important dimension of location as it constrains accessibility to employment. (Maher et al., 1981: 130)

Stilwell (1980:222 et. seq.) and Vipond (1980*a*; 1980*b*; 1981*a*; 1981*b*) also argue that relationships sufficiently strong to have policy implications exist between local unemployment rates and urban spatial structure in Sydney.

This chapter examines spatial variation in local unemployment rates in Adelaide. The question of whether or not significant relationships exist here between patterns of unemployment and metropolitan spatial organisation is of relevance to the general debate concerning the utility of area-based analyses of unemployment and other dimensions of inequality that manifest themselves in western cities. It also has particular local significance, for Adelaide has suffered in recent years from the highest overall unemployment rate of any large Australian city, and has a long history, by Australian standards, of government intervention in the spatial organisation of housing and employment (Stretton 1975; Forster 1974, 1977, 1978).

The analysis is based mainly upon the 1976 Census, using the 142 Local Government Area (LGA) subdivisions within the Adelaide Statistical Division as a convenient level of spatial disaggregation. Commonwealth Employment Service office data are used in a subsidiary role to provide an impression of trends since 1976 and to throw some light on contrasts in unemployment patterns between adults and juniors. (For a more detailed discussion of data sources see Forster 1983*a*:34–5.)

Patterns

In the Adelaide Statistical Division as a whole at the 1976 Census 3.1 per cent of the male workforce and 4.4 per cent of the female workforce described themselves as unemployed, but rates varied considerably between LGA subdivisions. In the case of males the lowest rate was 0.7 per cent and the highest 10.7 per cent with a mean of 3.3 per cent. Female rates varied from 1.7 to 9.7 with a mean of 4.4. The Pearson's correlation coefficient between the male and female rates for the 142 subdivisions was 0.48, but as Figure 14.1 shows there were clear contrasts between the spatial distributions of the higher values.

Figure 14.1 Male and female unemployment, metropolitan Adelaide, 1976

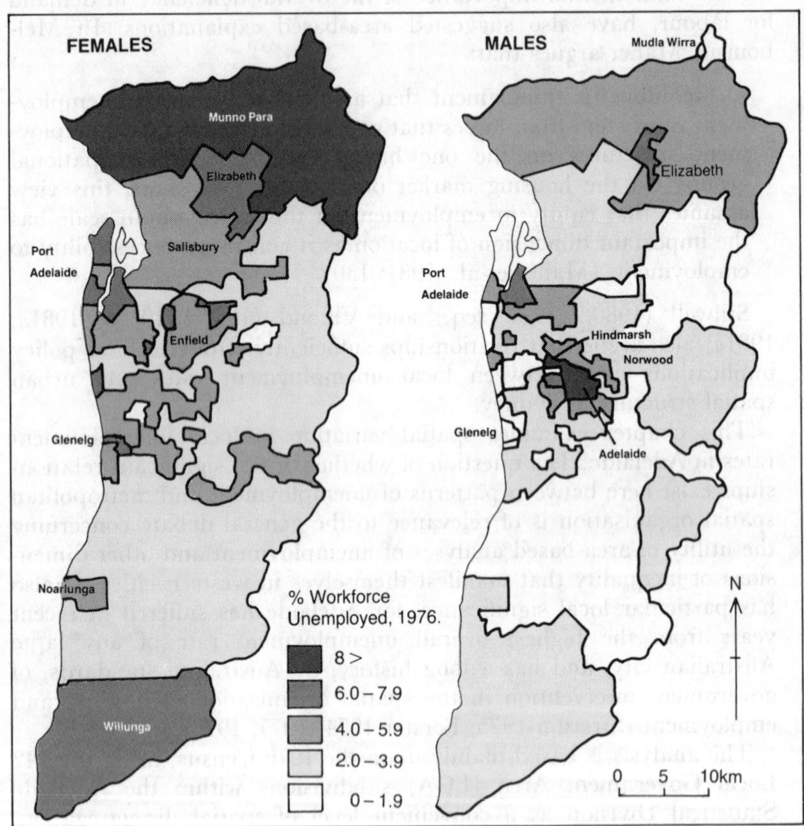

Source: Forster 1983

Male unemployment was highest in and around the city centre, where a contiguous group of subdivisions had rates of over 8 per cent. The old-established subsidiary centres of Glenelg and Port Adelaide also had rates of between 6 and 8 per cent. The only areas of post-1945 residential development with male unemployment rates of over 6 per cent were Elizabeth and Mudla Wirra on the northern fringe of the metropolitan area. Female unemployment rates on the other hand were relatively low in the city centre and the older suburbs, with the exception of a pocket of high employment in Glenelg. The highest female rates occurred in the outer northern suburbs of Elizabeth, Salisbury and Munno Para, with pockets of moderately high rates scattered throughout the western and northern suburbs in Port Adelaide, Woodville and Enfield. With the exception of female unemployment in the largely rural LGA of Willunga in the extreme south, rates for both sexes were below average throughout the eastern and southern suburbs.

Table 14.1 Total unemployment, Adelaide Statistical Division 1976–81

	Population Census June 1976	%	CES registrations June 1976	%	CES registrations March 1981	%	% increase CES registrations 1976–81
Adult males			5 320	41.2	18 886	47.1	255.0
Junior males			2 718	21.1	7 941	19.8	192.2
Total males	7 986	54.5	8 038	62.3	26 827	66.9	233.8
% male workforce	3.1						
Adult females			2 005	15.5	5 645	14.1	181.5
Junior females			2 864	22.2	7 621	19.0	166.1
Total females	6 668	45.5	4 869	37.7	13.266	33.1	172.5
% female workforce	4.4						
Total unemployed	14 653	100.0	12 907	100.0	40 093	100.0	210.6

After 1976, however, total unemployment in Adelaide increased markedly, (Table 14.1). In June 1976 almost 13 000 persons were registered as unemployed at CES offices within the Adelaide Statistical Division. The number of registered male unemployed was almost the same as the number recorded in the 1976 Census. But the number of registered females was only 73.2 per cent of the Census figure, largely as the result of the non-registration of unemployed married females ineligible for benefits because their husbands were in work. By March 1981 total registrations with the CES had risen to over 40 000. The overall rate of increase between 1976 and 1981 therefore exceeded 200 per cent, though part of this apparent increase may have been seasonal in nature, as in most recent years unemployment has been greater in March than in June (Australian Department of Employment and Youth Affairs 1981).

The number of CES offices within the Adelaide Statistical Division increased from ten in 1976 to eighteen in 1981 and the attendant changes in catchment-area boundaries, plus the spillover of registrations between areas, prevent changes in the spatial distribution of unemployment from being identified with precision. But as Figure 14.2 shows, there was a striking increase in registrations in the northern and western suburbs.

Unlike the 1976 Census data, the CES figures allow some comparisons to be made between the spatial distributions of adult and junior (aged below twenty-one) unemployment. Adult males made up only 41 per cent of the Statistical Division's registered unemployed in 1976 (Table 14.1). Junior males comprised 21 per cent, junior females 22 per cent and adult females the remaining 16 per cent. By 1981 the adult male share of registrations had risen to 47 per cent and the percentages in the other categories had all declined. The share of unemployment made up by junior females showed the greatest fall, from 22 per cent to 19 per cent.

Figure 14.2 shows that the demographic composition of registered unemployment varied quite considerably between offices. In outer-suburban, largely working-class areas like Elizabeth, Salisbury and

Figure 14.2 Registered unemployed persons, metropolitan Adelaide, 1976–81

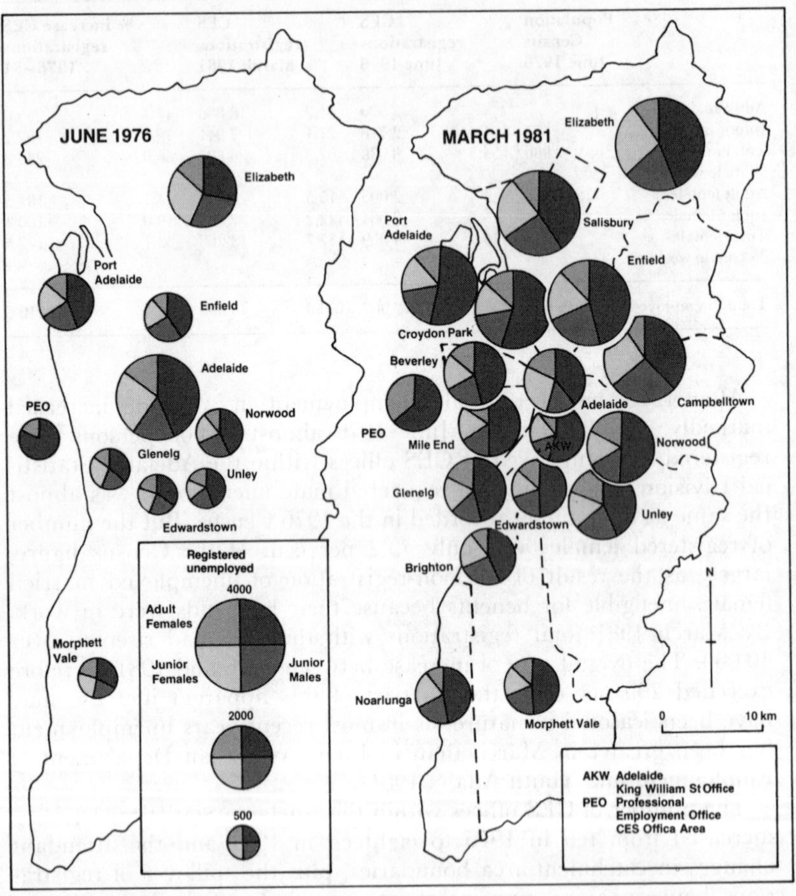

Source: Forster 1983

Campbelltown, approximately half the registrations in 1981 were juniors and only 10 per cent were adult females. Offices serving the older-established western working-class areas (Croydon, Port Adelaide, Beverley, Mile End) exhibited a rather different pattern with adult males making up half the registrations, juniors approximately 35 per cent and adult females up to 15 per cent. In the inner suburbs of Norwood and Unley over 18 per cent of the registrations were adult females, possibly reflecting the large numbers of young, unmarried adults moving into the inner parts of these catchment areas in recent years. In the city-centre office of Adelaide 27 per cent of the registrations were junior females but many of these lived elsewhere and chose to register at the central office because of the importance of the central business district (CBD) as a source of job opportunities for women (Forster 1978).

The patterns of spatial variation in unemployment within Adelaide in some respects resemble very closely those noted in Sydney by Stilwell (1980) and Vipond (1980*a*) where adult male unemployment rates were also highest in the city centre and inner suburbs and junior and female adult rates were highest in outer working-class areas such as Liverpool, Blacktown and Mount Druitt. However the changes that Vipond argues have occurred in Sydney since 1976, with female rates increasing in the inner suburbs and an increasing contrast between the spatial distributions of adult and junior unemployment, are not apparent in the Adelaide CES data. This may be due at least partly to the less satisfactory nature of Adelaide CES office areas as areal units for longitudinal analysis, but it also points to significant differences in the unemployment histories of the two cities. Between 1976 and 1979 registered unemployment in Sydney rose from 61 983 to 76 539, an increase of 23.5 per cent (Vipond, 1980*a*: 327). During the same period registrations in Adelaide rose by 167.9 per cent, from 12 907 to 34 574. The trends in registered adult male unemployment contrast even more sharply, with a 193.1 per cent increase in Adelaide compared with only 18.1 per cent in Sydney. As a result the share of registered unemployment made up of adult males in outer-Adelaide suburbs such as Elizabeth has increased since 1976. (Data from the 1981 Census which became available after the original paper was first published confirm that a marked convergence occurred between patterns of recorded male and female unemployment since 1976. However, variations in age-adjusted workforce participation rates (Forster 1983*b*) suggest that levels of female *hidden* unemployment in 1981 were significantly higher than elsewhere in Elizabeth and neighbouring suburbs.)

Explanation

Any attempt to suggest reasons for intra-urban variation in residential unemployment rates faces the problem of disentangling a complex web of casual relationships. In his analysis of unemployment in Sydney, Stilwell (1980: 111 et seq.) works sequentially through a list of factors under the three headings of *age, sex and ethnicity, industry and occupation*, and *location*. Vipond (1980*a*; 1980*b*; 1981*a*; 1981*b*) refers to a similar range of variables while conveying a greater sense of interrelatedness. In attempting to explore the relationship in Adelaide between variation in unemployment rates and urban spatial organisation a rather different approach has been adopted, focusing upon what are seen as two key themes: the phenomenon of residential segregation and the concept of accessibility. However, like the other Australian studies, the analysis relies upon aggregate areal data and as Burnley (1980: 240–5) points out the complex links between, for example, age, ethnicity, occupation, residential location and unemployment are difficult enough to identify even at the level of the individual. Casual inferences can only be made with great caution.

Residential segregation

Critics of area-based explanations in urban geography have argued that patterns of spatial variation in unemployment, and other types of deprivation, are merely the spatially-manifest symptoms of a phenomenon that varies spatially as—and because—it varies in its impact on different ages, social classes, ethnic groups and so on (Hamnett 1979). According to this view, residential unemployment rates in Adelaide, or in any other city, vary largely as a result of spatial variations in populations characteristics. Thus it is only to be expected that male and female rates are below average throughout the belt of affluent suburbs in the east and south-east of the metropolitan area (Figure 14.1), and higher on the western and northern, working-class, side of the city. Because unemployment rates among juniors are particularly high (ABS 1981) it is similarly only to be expected that recently-developed outer suburbs with large percentages of their workforces in the fifteen-to-nineteen-year age-group will have high overall unemployment rates. In outer suburban working-class areas like Elizabeth, rates show the combined effect of age-structure and social class. Stilwell, Burnley and Horvath and Tait (Chapter 12 in this volume) also point out that in Sydney, suburbs with high percentages of residents who are migrants from non-English-speaking countries have inflated unemployment rates. In Adelaide too, high rates occur in Norwood, Campbelltown and Thebarton, where a large percentage of residents are of Greek or Italian origin, but it is not clear from aggregate data that unemployment in these areas is linked with ethnicity rather than with age or social class.

The relationship between residential segregation and patterns of unemployment has tended to be dismissed as a passive association of phenomena in urban space; what Thrift (1979:177) terms a spatial 'reflect'. Yet residential segregation does not occur at random. As so much of the empirical research carried out in recent years has been at pains to demonstrate, it is largely the result of the processes that operate to produce and allocate a heterogenous and spatially-differentiated housing stock. Important links can be detected between the operation of housing markets in Adelaide and the geography of unemployment, links that are particularly apparent in the areas of greatest concentration of residential unemployment. As in most western cities the highest rates of male unemployment occur close to the city centre and in the equally old-established suburbs of Glenelg and Port Adelaide (Figure 14.1). As Figure 14.3 shows, these suburbs also comprise the largest reservoirs of privately-rented accommodation in the metropolitan area, including almost all the available boarding and lodging premises (Badcock and Urlich-Cloher 1978:22–5). They tend to house a population highly vulnerable to a general fall in the demand for labour and could therefore be regarded as an extreme case of the 'passive' spatial relationship already discussed between social class and unemployment. But in addition, even during periods of 'full' employment these inner, older, suburbs actively collect people, particularly single transient males, who are unemployed or susceptible to regular bouts of unemployment. Adelaide LGA for example, had a male unemployment rate of 5 per cent at the 1971 Census when the overall rate for the Adelaide Statistical Division was only 1.6 per cent. A similar situation existed in Sydney (Vipond 1980*b*). A range of factors contribute to high male unemployment rates in the innermost suburbs. Proximity to welfare agencies, shelters and the main public hospitals as well as to opportunities for casual unskilled work makes the inner city positively attractive to

Figure 14.3 Private and SAHT rented tenure, metropolitan Adelaide, 1976

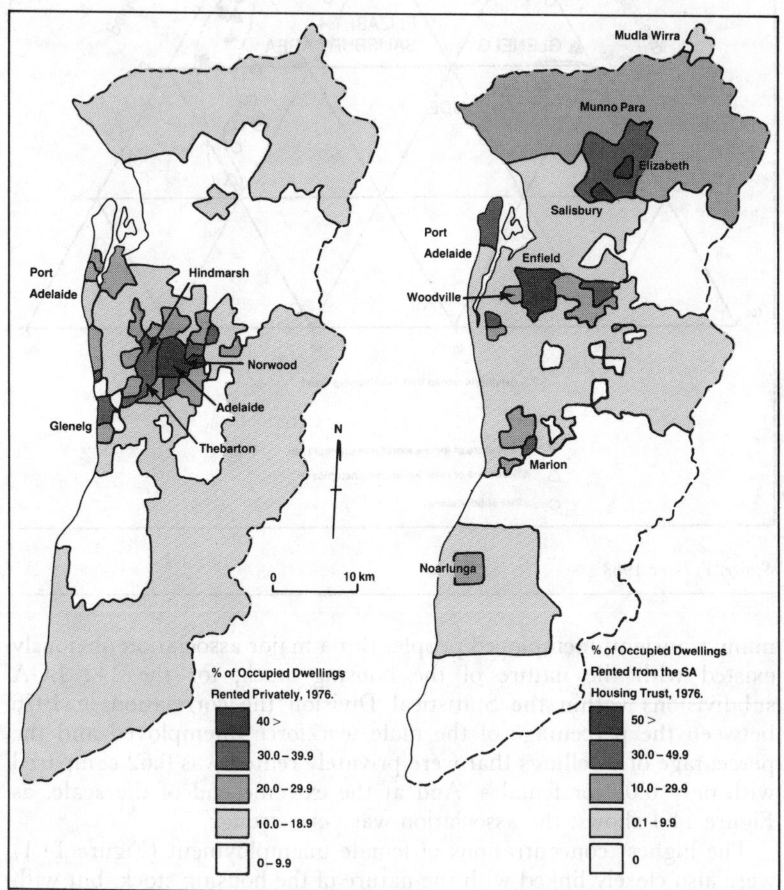

Source: Forster 1983

Figure 14.4 Housing tenure mix and unemployment rates, metropolitan Adelaide, 1976

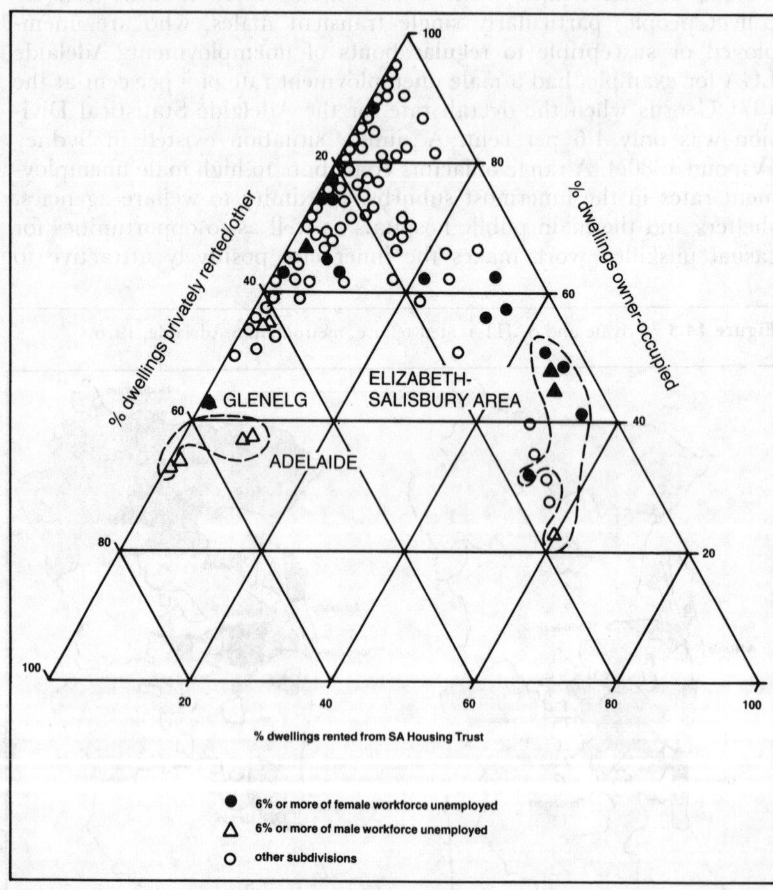

Source: Forster 1983

many transient unemployed people. But a major association obviously existed with the nature of the housing stock; for the 142 LGA subdivisions within the Statistical Division the correlation in 1976 between the percentage of the male workforce unemployed and the percentage of dwellings that were privately rented was 0.62 compared with only 0.09 for females. And at the extreme end of the scale, as Figure 14.4 shows, the association was very strong.

The highest concentrations of female unemployment (Figure 14.1) were also closely linked with the nature of the housing stock, but with the public rather than the privately-rented sector (Figure 14.3). Of the fifteen LGA subdivisions where over 30 per cent of dwellings were rented from the South Australian Housing Trust at the 1976 Census, ten had female unemployment rates of 6 per cent or over (Figure 14.4). The correlation for all 142 LGA subdivisions between female unemployment rates and the percentage of dwellings that were rented from the Housing Trust was not high (R = 0.36), partly because many of the older-established Housing Trust estates in Marion, Enfield and Woodville had ageing populations with few school-leavers and high percentages of pensioner residents. But in newer, outer-suburban areas in Elizabeth, Salisbury and Munno Para, and to a lesser extent Noarlunga, the association was strong. (The 1981 Census has subsequently revealed that female unemployment rates had in fact risen most steeply in the inner suburbs since 1976. But as noted earlier, Housing Trust areas in the middle and outer suburbs were associated with the very low age-adjusted female workforce-participation rates (Forster 1983*b*; Morgan 1983), suggesting continued higher levels of hidden unemployment than in the inner suburbs.)

Female unemployment in outer-suburban Housing Trust areas is clearly the result in part of population characteristics that are particularly vulnerable to falls in the general demand for labour such as occurred in Adelaide during the 1970s. The areas are heavily dependent upon semi-skilled or unskilled work in manufacturing, and a household survey carried out in Elizabeth in 1972 showed that many families were also reaching the stage in the life cycle when children were entering the workforce and married women, freed of some home duties, increasingly wished to do so if jobs were available. But in addition, the selection and allocation processes of the Housing Trust Act, however unintentionally or reluctantly, to increase the concentration in these areas of households with members who are unemployed or face a high risk of unemployment. A recent study of allocation processes (Coates 1979) showed that whereas it is stated Housing Trust policy to attempt to meet applicants' locational preferences when making offers of rental accommodation, forces of supply and demand make it difficult to do so in practice. The large outer-suburban estates in Elizabeth, Salisbury, Munno Para and, to a lesser extent, Noarlunga are much less popular than estates closer to the city. As a result the turnover of tenants is higher, vacancy rates are twice to three times as high, and waiting-times are half as long or less (Kendig 1981: Chapter 4).

Families in urgent need of public-sector accommodation because of financial crisis resulting from unemployment or intermittent employment are therefore likely to be channelled towards the outer suburbs. As families with unemployed household heads, single-parent families, benefit card-holders and other 'welfare' categories have made up an increasing proportion of applicants for housing in recent years (South Australian Housing Trust 1981:8), the consequences are all too predictable.

Accessibility

Residential areas in Adelaide vary, not only in their housing stock and population composition, but also in their location relative to employment opportunities of various types, and in the quality of their transport and communications linkages with centres of employment. Several writers have argued that such variations in accessibility have had a significant influence upon local unemployment rates in other Australian cities:

> ...proximity to major employment opportunities is an important determinant of unemployment rates. The metropolitan area may be considered as a single labour market in that people do traverse it for employment purposes. However it is a far from perfect market. One's knowledge of employment opportunities, one's ability to get job interviews, one's ability to get to the workplace itself, all vary systematically between suburbs. (Stilwell 1980: 120)

Stiwell argues that high male unemployment rates in inner Sydney are partly the result of reduced accessibility to suitable jobs following the decline of traditional manufacturing industries through a combination of suburbanisation and structural change in the economy, producing a mismatch between job opportunities and the skills of local residents similar to that postulated in Britain by the Inner Area Studies (Thrift 1979:176–9). But, with the possible exception of Port Adelaide, there is little sign in Adelaide that such a mismatch contributes significantly to the spatial concentration of male unemployment, perhaps because Adelaide has a much less important heritage of nineteenth century manufacturing than Sydney or Melbourne. Because Adelaide is much smaller than Sydney or Melbourne it may also be argued that, at least for people with cars, it forms a single spatial labour market with all jobs spatially accessible to all residents, though obviously to varying degrees (Robins 1981:205–10). Most adult males do have the use of a car for the journey to work if necessary and, despite the suburbanisation of blue-collar employment, the inner suburbs where the highest rates of male unemployment are found are very accessible to the main concentrations of job opportunities, even for those without cars (Forster 1978).

For females, and for juniors of both sexes, the situation is different. These sections of the workforce are much less likely to have access to a car for the journey to work (Manning, 1976; Black 1977), and are therefore more reliant upon jobs near home or those easily reached by public transport. Women with families face particular difficulties, for constraints of duration and timing, as well as cost, affect their range of travel (Howe and O'Connor 1977; Chapter 15 in this volume). Jobs held by women in metropolitan Adelaide are still strongly centralised (Forster 1978) and outer suburbs such as Elizabeth and Noarlunga therefore possess poor accessibility to employment, other than having quite good rail links with the city centre. Surveys have shown that adult females in Elizabeth rely upon an inadequate range of local job opportunities (Forster 1974: 22; Australian Department of Labour, 1975:543). Vipond (1981*b*) argues that heavy unemployment among juniors and females in the outer-western suburbs of Sydney is partly the result of a lack of local job opportunities and also of the poor dissemination to these remote areas of information about job opportunities elsewhere. Stilwell (1980:121) also suggests that people living in outer-suburban working-class areas may be discriminated against by employers, though it is not clear whether the discrimination is based on the remoteness of the suburbs or their poor 'social image', or both. There is no shortage of similar anecdotes concerning Elizabeth and other Housing Trust suburbs in outer Adelaide. On the demand side, it is also the experience of CES officers (pers. comm.) that metropolitan employers of blue-collar or unskilled white-collar labour prefer to recruit people who live near to the place of work, thus reducing the pool of vacancies for which unemployed people living in peripheral suburbs have a realistic chance of competing.

Implications for urban policy

It is clear that various categories of unemployment are spatially concentrated in certain locales within metropolitan Adelaide. In assessing the significance of this fact for urban policy, three questions can be asked. First, do the spatial concentrations significantly exacerbate the plight of unemployed people? Second, how are they related to the spatial organisation of housing, employment, transportation and communications? Finally, can policies relating to spatial organisation do anything worthwhile about them?

In the case of the primarily adult male unemployment concentrations in Adelaide's inner, older, suburbs the answer to the first question is possibly 'no'. These areas are accessible to the main concentrations of job opportunities. They are well served by public transport. They are close to the main public and private welfare institutions. To the second question one could answer that the concentrations are related to spatial organisation mainly to the extent that they reflect the restricted availability of cheap privately-rented accommodation, including boarding and lodging places. As for policies, the main concern may increasingly be to maintain the supply of low-cost accommodation in central accessible locations for people, including the unemployed, who need it. The City of Adelaide Plan (Urban Systems Corporation 1974:117) made the policy recommendation that 'The assistance of the national Government should be sought in all aspects of providing a fair share of City housing for low income and disadvantaged groups,' and the Housing Trust has subsequently acquired a significant stock of rental property, including boarding houses, in the city of Adelaide itself and in the surrounding inner suburbs.

In the outer suburbs of Adelaide, particularly to the north, where large concentrations of junior and female adult unemployment have been added to in recent years by increasing numbers of unemployed adult males, the answers to the questions are rather different. To take the second question first, the processes that produce residential segregation have caused Elizabeth, Munno Para, Salisbury and Noarlunga to have resident workforces with age and social-class characteristics that were vulnerable to the decline in the demand for labour that developed during the 1970s in Adelaide as a whole. Selection and allocation processes within the public housing stock have acted to channel additional unemployed people into these areas. Poor accessibility to job opportunities has had a compounding effect. It reduced the chances of unemployed people getting new jobs, and by contributing to the continued unpopularity of the areas among people seeking housing it perpetuated or even intensified the forces producing residential segregation.

Does the spatial concentration of unemployment in outer-suburban Housing Trust areas matter? By 1981 over 8 per cent of the whole metropolitan workforce was officially unemployed, and one can expect there to be many more hidden unemployed (Stricker and Sheehan 1981). With forty registered unemployed to each registered job vacancy (Australian Department of Employment and Youth Affairs 1981:10) it could be argued with some justification that residential location does little more than affect one's position in the dole queue by a few places. To put it another way, in the absence of any sign of unmet demand for labour within the metropolitan economy, attempts to reduce high local levels of unemployment by spatial measures such as changing housing-allocation policies or relocating jobs or improving transport and communications networks can only succeed at the expense of somewhere—or someone—else (Feldman 1977). But even accepting Feldman's point of view, it seems to the author that it *does* matter if a given level of unemployment is shared less equitably and borne with more hardship because a significant proportion of it is spatially concentrated in outer-suburban public-authority housing estates that have few facilities for people with low mobility and little money, and offer a poor chance to compete for the jobs that do become available in the metropolitan area. It should also be remembered that an overall improvement in the level of demand for labour does not necessarily solve the unemployment problems of areas like Elizabeth. In 1969, a time of 'full' employment, female unemployment in Elizabeth was estimated from CES figures as representing 7.1 per cent of the workforce, and by far the most common principal reason given for being unemployed was the lack of suitable work within reasonable travelling distance (Australian Department of Labour 1975:539–40).

If one believes that the spatial concentration of unemployment in outer, working-class suburbs *does* matter, can policies relating to spatial organisation do anything worthwhile about it? It might be said, with the benefit of hindsight, that large public-authority housing estates should not have been located in peripheral areas with a high level of dependence on the private car for transportation, and with inadequate local job opportunities, especially for school-leavers and adult females. It is equally easy to say that such housing, now and in the future, should not be allocated to households vulnerable to unemployment. But the housing is there, and cannot be moved. Despite recent Housing Trust policies that emphasise building or acquiring property in the inner and middle suburbs, housing areas like Elizabeth will continue to provide a significant proportion of the vacancies available for allocation to people in urgent housing need. Stilwell (1980:169–72) and Vipond (1981*b*) have advocated a range of ameliorative policies for similar outer-suburban areas in Sydney, including direct job-creation schemes, improvements in public transport and in the dissemination of information about job vacancies, and incentives for employees to locate in the areas concerned. However, industrial-location schemes are difficult to implement in times of economic recession, and funds for public transport and job-creation are scarce.

What can be done? Spatial policies certainly cannot 'solve' metropolitan Adelaide's unemployment crisis. But for the sake of employed and unemployed people alike, public authorities should seize any chances that arise to widen the range of job opportunities located in Adelaide's outer northern and southern suburbs, to improve public transport and information channels, and to reduce the spatial concentration of unemployed people in Housing Trust estates. At the local-government level a balance should also be sought in the application of building and zoning regulations, between the need to separate incompatible land uses and the desirability of allowing a range of housing types and employment-generating activities to exist in reasonable proximity to one another. Higher levels of government also need to recognise the burdens of service provision that fall upon councils with high levels of unemployment. At the very least, policy-makers should attempt to ensure that spatial policies do not exacerbate the hardship caused by high levels of unemployment in the metropolitan economy.

Conclusions: Significant issue or spatial fetish?

The rapid increase in unemployment since the mid-1970s has been one of the most significant trends in Australian society. Discussion of the nature, causes and consequences of various aspects of unemployment has been prominent in the writings of economists, sociologists, psychologists, political theorists and other social scientists, not to mention its impact on the theatre, literature and popular music. Yet in spite of the fact that marked spatial disparities in unemployment rates clearly exist within our cities, geographers have largely ignored the topic (though Burnley (1980) and Maher et al. (1981) deal with it briefly), and the main detailed published analyses have been by economists. Exploration of the British and North American literature leads one to the conclusion that the main contribution by geographers to the study of unemployment in western cities since the mid-1970s has been to argue that the spatial dimension of the topic is irrelevant and its study counter-productive.

The lack of analysis by geographers of intra-urban variations in unemployment rates, in Australia or elsewhere, may simply reflect the discipline's renunciation of its former fetishes and perversions. But it may also represent an unfortunate over-reaction to criticism, resulting in a significant, though not fundamental, aspect of the unemployment crisis receiving less attention than it deserves. This simple analysis of patterns of unemployment in Adelaide was carried out with the aim of gaining a better understanding of the spatial consequences of structural economic processes, of the exacerbating effects such spatial consequences may have, and of whether appropriate, albeit ameliorative, policies could be adopted in response. And perhaps in the end any assessment of the contribution the spatial perspective can make to understanding and dealing with the unemployment crisis in Adelaide or elsewhere depends upon one's attitude towards reformist, ameliorative policies. As Boddy concludes in a review of the British inner-cities debate:

> The gulf therefore remains between analyses of policies and processes... which can offer marginal reform but no solution and more radical structural analyses which can offer no social policy recommendations. The difference is one of political commitment, whether to the existing system on the one hand or to fundamental structural change on the other, though in practice the gulf is frequently bridged by a rather ragged radical reformism. (Boddy 1981: 603–4)

It is obviously important to accept that the spatial dimension of unemployment and similar phenomena is of subsidiary importance. This does not mean that spatial analysis is irrelevant or, as seems often to be suggested (Hamnett 1979:257), leads inevitably to more fundamental structural processes and solutions being ignored. More detailed analyses of local unemployment and workforce-participation rates and of journey-to-work patterns can provide further insights into the nature of spatial labour sub-markets in Australian cities, their relationship to housing-market processes, and the spatial dimension of urban unemployment. It will be unfortunate if accusations of spatial fetishism and obfuscation discourage the pursuit of these and related questions.

Chapter 15

Women and suburban housing: post-war planning in Sydney, 1943–61

Carolyn Allport

The war-time background

The commitment to reconstruction planning, begun during the early 1940s in Australia, came from four distinct sources: the legacy of the depression, an experience that many groups in the community, but particularly the labour movement were determined would not be repeated; social reform movements of the late 1930s, usually middle-class led, which had seen the growth in New South Wales and Victoria of slum-abolition groups and the mammoth investigatory work of the Federal government's Joint Committee on Social Security; the military need for morale on the home front and the practicabilities of planning for demobilisation after the war which was intimately tied to the reassertion of women's traditional role as unpaid housekeepers and baby-minders. The reconstruction debate, spearheaded by the Commonwealth government's Department of Post-War Reconstruction and paralleled by State government departments and a plethora of community groups, did review almost all aspects of economic and social life within the context of the growing acceptance of central government planning. The canvas was indeed wide. Yet the planning of national policies was complicated by the international negotiations concerning full employment, tariff reductions and international monetary stabilisation, and the assertions of economic superiority by the United States. Not the least troublesome was the thorny question of Commonwealth-State functions and relations.

The establishment of the Commonwealth Housing Commission (CHC), and the publication of its Report in 1944, was crucial since it brought the focus of city reform, town planning and slum clearance within the parameters of financial commitment by both State and Federal governments. Its major policy recommendations—the funding, by the Commonwealth, of low-cost housing to be built and administered by the States with the proviso that such funding be co-ordinated with town planning policies—transformed the structure and design of post-war housing in Australia. Although the commission's Final Report said that all poor people should be helped with housing, the State Housing Commissions' programmes have been

Based on Williams P. (ed.) (1983) Chapter 4 in *Social Process and the City*, and reproduced here by kind permission of George Allen & Unwin.

shown to have 'helped only a small proportion of these people' (Neutze 1981:108).

The Commonwealth's aim was to reduce inequalities by intervening at the lower end of the housing market in harness with town planning policies aimed at slum clearance, the relief of traffic congestion, decentralisation and a decent urban environment. Orderly decentralisation to new suburban nodes (an example of physical determinism) was an idea borrowed from the United Kingdom, especially Abercrombie's Greater London Plan of 1944, and embodied in the Scheme produced by the Cumberland County Council (1948), the Sydney metropolitan planning authority at that time. But both housing and town-planning policies embraced assumptions about the continuation of traditional gender roles—that men would go out to work and that women would stay at home, bearing and raising children. This was not only supported by the political Right; there were many on the Left who saw that planned decentralisation could save working-class families from exploitation by inner-city landlords.

One of the most radicalising influences was the appointment of a woman, Mary Margaret Ryan, to the CHC during the war. Interest and enthusiasm culminated in the Australian Women's Charter Conference in November 1943 which declared in favour of town planning, slum clearance, decentralisation and community centres and the release of women from household drudgery in order to bear and raise children in better conditions (see Ryan 1944; Book IV, 11). Much emphasis was placed on the desirability of modern 'streamlined' kitchens, laundries and bathrooms (see *Australian Women's Weekly* 8 May 1943:31; and Commonwealth Housing Commission 1944:90 and 124).

The widespread belief that technology reduces the time spent on housework has been strongly challenged by the available evidence. Indeed one survey (Cowan 1974) comparing urban and rural housewives in 1930 and 1947 showed that by the latter date, the average time spent on housework had actually *increased* (from about sixty to seventy-eight hours per week) suggesting higher standards of household care (see also Vanek 1974:117; Game and Pringle 1979).

While technology was to be the saviour of the housewife in the kitchen, improved physical support services were judged to be necessary to help women to become more integrated with the community. Mona Ravenscroft (1943:48), an active anthropologist member of the Union of Australian Women (UAW), warned that new housing schemes would need to take into consideration the different work environment associated with peace-time conditions. If suburban sprawl were to continue, it must be balanced by adequate cultural outlets. Thus the enthusiasm for community centres grew within the CHC and the SHCs and these centres fitted in well with the neighbourhood-district-region scheme of the Cumberland County Council (1948:115–16). These community centres were intended to have a wide range of educational, cultural, recreational and child-care facilities. Child-care provision was supported by many groups such as the Kindergarten Union, the Women's Services Guild and the UAW all of whom lobbied the Federal government (Australian Department of the Treasury 1945). However, there was substantial opposition from the churches and other conservative groups on the grounds that such provisions 'undermined the family, the basis and unity of society' (Spearritt 1984:594). The Community Facilities Committee (1944:4) bowed to such pressures and Federal financial support was withdrawn. This dealt severe blows to low-income municipalities such as Redfern in Sydney, which had then to bear the main burden of child-care and community centre provisions.

In the final analysis, the position of women, whether in the workforce or in the home, was not considered important enough to outweigh other exigencies or the views of vested interest groups as to the appropriate role women should play in the new post-war society. It is important to recognise that part of the movement for improved domestic conditions was inextricably linked to the propaganda for a reaffirmation of the family as a cornerstone of society. A sparkling new home with American features and a kitchen equipped with all the latest gadgets were considered to be the most effective way of encouraging women to breed more.

Post-war reality

While reconstruction planning publicly raised the question of the situation of housewives and had been particularly critical of their working environments, it offered only dreams in answer to women's needs. The ensuing reality was very different. In order to examine whether these early planning ideas, and the operation of the later Cumberland Plan, made an impact on the working lives of women in post-war Sydney, one needs to adopt vastly different perspectives from those previously used in urban studies. Recent issues of the *International Journal of Urban and Regional Research* (1978) and *Signs: Journal of Women in Culture and Society* (1980) devoted to 'Women and the City' reinforce the methodological and research necessity of viewing women in the urban environment in a more specialised context. Even where women articulate the same urban needs as men, such as in the journey to work, the sexual division of labour within the home has often made the expression of their journey-to-work needs very different in form and structure from that of men.

At the general level, women's place in the urban system is clearly derived from the sexual division of labour which places the house/home as the essential locus of the domestic relations of production. Since the major proportion of women's domestic labour is structured through the system of marriage and the payment for such labour is indirect, Gamarnikow (1978:395–6) asserts that women's relation to capital in the urban system is one of double dependence—on the husband as controller and appropriator of labour power and on the male wage as the material conditions of capitalist domestic labour. Such dependence is then reflected and reinforced by the sexual dichotomies in the labour market and the low wages and status accorded to women's employment. Even though the Australian Women's Charter Conference, representing over ninety women's organisations, made the call in 1943 for a wage for the wife/housekeeper/mother and for equal pay for women, the patriarchal state in Australia has been loath to enter into the field of the domestic relations of production. Quite the contrary, the state in Australia has acted, with few recent exceptions, to reinforce such economic dependence and power relationships.

Central to the definition of such domestic relations of production, and of vital relevance to urban planning is the equation of 'house' with 'home' and the placing of home as the pivot of an idealised domestic community sharply separated from work. In their seminal essay, *Landscape with Figures: Home and Community in English Society*, Davidoff, L'Esperance and Newby (1976:139–75) correctly argue that the 'beau-ideal', the twin exultation of the rural village community and the home, gained special importance as a reaction to nineteenth century industrialisation and reached its most defined level in the ideology of middle-class suburbanisation. Such suburban ideology is seen as 'the quest for an organic community; small, self-sufficient and sharply differentiated from the outside world while the house and garden became both the setting and symbol of the domestic community' (Dresser 1978:559).

Such separation of home and workplace has formed a central tenet of town planning ideology since its modern beginnings with Howard (1902) and others, and is mirrored in the Cumberland County Council Plan for post-war Sydney. Further, such geographic segregation intensifies the privatised nature of many women's lives and their exclusion from the public world. Saegert (1980) argues that such long-standing beliefs have meant that the city and the suburb have symbolic gender associations. The city and urban life is equated with men—aggressive, assertive, definers of important world events, intellectual, powerful, active and sometimes dangerous, while suburban life is akin to women—domesticity, repose, closeness to nature, lack of seriousness, mindlessness and safety. That some present-day Sydney suburbs are very different from the 'domestic retreat' mentality so dominant in the suburbs of the 1920s and again in the 1950s and 1960s, owes much to the changing economic and social roles of women and the expression of their changing urban demands as it does to any effective town planning. This is most particularly seen in the provision of localised child-care schemes.

The powerful longevity of the domestic ideology not only sharply defined a division between the public nature of the city and the private nature of the suburb but also clearly restricted and delineated women's role within the privatised sector. It had immediate relevance to the middle-class woman of the nineteenth century—the 'angel of the house'. However, the pattern of working-class women's lives in the inner suburbs close to the city of Sydney and usually employed in the paid workforce, meant that such women remained largely divorced from the domestic suburban ideology, at least until the 1920s in Australia. With the opening up of suburban estates in the 1920s it was possible for more affluent sections of the working class to join in the suburban home-ownership dream. However, home-ownership rates remained below 50 per cent and little real incursion was made into the pattern of inner-city rental housing characteristic of working-class housing in Australia (Spearritt 1978*a*:27–56). A decade and a half of depression and war pulled the 'house and garden' dream further away from such people. Yet the experience of evictions, homelessness and family dislocation during the Depression did harden the conviction for the dream of home ownership. Such feelings were intensified by the experience of war-time housing difficulties. Much of the housing stock had decayed through neglect, material shortages and war-time building restriction. New building in particular was severely controlled, service personnel were given priority in rental accommodation and young marrieds usually lived with parents or relatives in the family home. Such policies produced conditions of gross overcrowding in many cases and privacy was rare. The dislocation produced by these housing restrictions further exacerbated the dislocations caused by the absence of family men on service duties.

By the time the CHC presented its report, the housing shortage in Australia was acute—some 300 000 dwellings (CHC 1944:19). In Sydney alone, the shortage was estimated at 69 000 homes (Housing Commission of New South Wales 1943:4). It is quite understandable then that in the post-war period with low interest rates, easy borrowing through War Service Loans, accumulated savings, lump-sum cash payments for ex-service personnel, expansions in the lending policies of co-operative building societies and savings banks, the provision of low-cost rental, and after 1956, low-cost owner-occupied housing by the State Housing Commissions, many more members of the working class could share in the suburban dream. Home-ownership rates for Australia rose from 52.6 per cent (1947) to 63 per cent (1954) and to 70 per cent by 1961 (Kemeny 1978:92; Chapter 16 in this volume).

Such developments had an important spatial consequence, as large areas on the fringe of inter-war development jumped in population. Table 15.1 shows clearly the large decrease in residential population of the inner city of Sydney and the corresponding growth of outer municipalities such as Ryde, Bankstown and Sutherland which, although subdivided in the twenties, had remained mixed-residential and market-gardening areas throughout the 1930s and early 1940s.

Table 15.1 Suburban population in Sydney 1933–54

	1933	Total %	1947	Total %	1954	Total %
Inner city	385,571	29.0	400,323	24.3	365,612	19.6
Eastern suburbs	176,791	13.3	229,991	14.0	215,338	11.6
Illawara	126,496	9.5	176,573	10.7	235,482	12.7
Canterbury-Bankstown	104,434	7.9	142,042	8.6	211,935	11.4
Inner western	141,275	10.6	165,364	10.0	156,033	8.3
Outer western	114,634	8.6	145,038	8.8	199,446	10.7
Fairfield-Liverpool	21,931	1.7	40,640	2.5	71,652	3.9
Northern harbourside	97,544	7.3	119,255	7.2	117,087	6.3
Manly-Warringah	39,313	3.0	66,631	4.1	92,487	5.0
Ku-ring-gai-Willoughby	70,442	5.3	91,819	5.6	104,660	5.6
Ryde-Hornsby	50,971	3.3	68,196	4.2	91,953	4.9
Total	1,329,402	100.0	1,645,872	100.0	1,861,685	100.0

Source: New South Wales, Government of, 1957:63–4

While it is easy to understand people's desire for a home of their own, given the importance of the Depression and war experiences, it is more difficult to explain their preference for 'new' homes as opposed to the purchase of older homes in the city. There seem to be two important factors which, taken with the rundown of the building stock since the 1930s, provide at least a partial answer. These are the psychological retreatism seen in many guises during the 1950s and the financial policies of the lending bodies.

It is often argued that the character of suburbanisation, with its focus on domestic life, produces insularity, particularly a retreat from more international, or even national issues in preference to a concentration on purely selfish parochial issues. It may well be the case that in the immediate post-war years, many young people were weary with the restrictions of war and with the dominance of the international situation caused by the war. Their return to normalcy may well have been articulated as an escape from the pressures, the horrors and the experiences of war-time—particularly for the men. As such a new start in an outer suburb with access to much country space, building a home in peace and serenity and being together for the first time in many years, often seemed the perfect way to put the war behind them. While such desires for domestic security were no doubt prevalent, one must also remember that divorce reached an all-time high rate of 11.6 per cent per 10 000 of mean population in 1947, largely as a response to hasty war-time marriages and the psychological problems of returning soliders (Coughlan 1957:116).

For most working-class households moving out to these suburban areas, it was the financial factor which most operated to induce their location choices and their preferences for new buildings. Most lending institutions were prepared to lend between 75 and 90 per cent of the cost of a new home with the land as security, while a much larger deposit was required to purchase existing housing (Hill 1959:141).

Given that many working-class households had some capital, their only real alternative was to purchase cheap land in the outer suburbs and build their own home. Existing in an economic climate of shortages and efficient black markets, the owner-builder became a common feature of these suburban developments. Books, correspondence courses, various exhibitions and the proliferation of ready-cut building forms, all assisted the amateurs to build their own castles. By 1953, it was estimated that half of the new houses in New South Wales were being built by their owners (New South Wales, Government of, 1957:680).

Suburban women and urban access

To complete this assessment of the relationship of women to the suburban environment and urban planning a further series of issues must be considered. Focus must fall initially on women's access to housing. If such access is determined by marriage, then the question arises as to the degree of implicit discrimination which may apply to single, divorced or widowed women. Research conducted in the United States indicates that female-headed households, while being over-represented in welfare housing, are discriminated against by lending institutions (Wekerle 1980:207). Certainly, changes in headship rates among flat-dwellers in Sydney indicate that women, whether single or married, are able to exercise access to this sector of the housing market, although the growth in headships rates is less for women than for men (Cardew 1980:81). Nonetheless, in the immediate post-war period the institutional approach to housing assumed that women exercised their access through marriage. The rating system developed by the CHC for the allocation of post-war dwellings identified female access through marriage and the family (including service widowhood). However, if an ex-service woman had combat-zone experience or the equivalent then priority points were awarded, although less than for a man with equivalent experience. There is no mention of single women at all, even if those single women had dependants (CHC 1944:267). Similarly, suitability for a war-service loan, although more liberal, necessitated that the applicant, whether serviceman or servicewoman, should satisfy the director 'that he is married or is about to marry, or has dependants for whom it is necessary for him to maintain a home' (Hill 1959:43). Both the CHC and State Housing Commission systems favoured large families, yet of the 35 000 applicants to the New South Wales Housing Commission in 1946, only 30 per cent expressed demand for three or four-bedroom houses, while 69 per cent demanded either small family units (39 per cent) or two-bedroom housing (30 per cent) (Housing Commission of New South Wales 1946:25). Further, one must acknowledge that the Federal government favoured the preferential granting of home loans to families with children; although it was never actually expressed as a distinct policy from the central bank, it was certainly a part of the political rhetoric throughout the 1950s and early 1960s.

Women's access to employment, transportation, leisure activities and social services within the urban environment is critically connected to their domestic role and the support by the patriarchal state given to that role in urban and social planning. In a major study of the journey to work in Sydney, Manning has shown that 'despite the apparent similarity in the overall availability of local employment for men and women, the travel patterns of the two sexes are quite different' (Manning 1978:78). In general, it was found that women travel shorter distances to work owing to a preference by married women for reduced time spent in travelling. The lower income received by women leads to inability to pay for speedy travel, with more reliance on walking and bus modes (see Manning 1978:80). Manning further claims that such transport preferences by women 'implies that they choose nearer jobs than men at some sacrifice of the range of choices' (Manning 1978:90). Studies of working-class women in Melbourne support this tendency for married women, in particular, to prefer work close to home (Bryson and Thompson 1972:56; Gepp 1968). More importantly, Bryson and Thompson's study shows that the reduced mobility of full-time working mothers and the availability of industrial work close to home resulted in a much greater proportion of factory work among this group as compared to single girls who were more concentrated in office work and who had wider geographic mobility (Table 15.2).

Table 15.2 Occupations of daughters and mothers working full time in Newtown, 1966

	Daughters %	**Mothers %**
Industrial	33.3	50.0
Service	—	8.1
Sales	11.9	10.8
Office work	50.0	27.0
Professional	4.8	4.1
	100.0	100.0

Source: Bryson and Thompson 1972:57

More specific studies in the United States and France (the Paris region) support the theory that women choose to restrict the time spent on the journey to work in response to domestic responsibilities. In addition, research in the United States (Wekerle 1980:106) suggests that such choice increases the 'accessibility costs' of gaining employment and urban services, while the Paris study (Fodor 1978:463, 481) suggests that women are subject to daily problems in co-ordinating commuting time and work hours with the operational hours of child-care centres.

It is obvious that access to transport and consequent questions of equity have an important relationship with the spatial allocation of the centres of production and consumption; this is particularly important when considering the changes wrought by corporate capitalism to the built environment in the post-war years. Changes in the production locus of the city have resulted in the decline of central-city manufacturing and the rise of peripherally-located industrial estates, although some space-efficient enterprises such as printing, clothing, footwear and jewellery have remained in the city (Neutze 1977:98). Associated with this trend has also been the rise in employment in office industries, particularly the female-dominated clerical positions (Neutze, 1977:101).

Aided by the Cumberland County Plan, whose zoning provisions precluded substantial expansion of industry in the inner areas of the city, central-area factory jobs fell from 168 000 (67.7 per cent of metropolitan jobs) in 1945 to 149 800 (45.4 per cent of metropolitan jobs) in 1961 (Alexander 1981*a*:152). Certainly, the Plan was successful in meeting its objective of a more equal distribution of jobs in relation to residences. Alexander (1981*a*:153) shows that 'the ratio of manufacturing jobs to resident manufacturing workers increased in all of the designated suburban areas with the notable exception of the fringe district of Baulkham Hills-Blacktown where a good deal of greater-than-expected population increase occurred'. Unfortunately, such statistical information of employment-residence correlation has only been compiled in aggregate terms; there are no figures available for female workers. All indications are that the situation for women workers was very different from that of male workers. Manning's work clearly shows that, in general, female workers have shorter journeys to work and are more captive public-transport users than men; yet the trend was clearly for female job opportunities to grow faster in the city centre. Further, Black (1978:123) showed that the suburbanisation of factory jobs benefitted the motorist to a greater degree than the user of public transport. The effects for women are clear — those women who wished to work close to home in the suburban districts were restricted in their job-search area and range of employment, since traditional female areas were increasing in the city centre and restricted car access meant that many could not take advantage of manufacturing decentralisation. For many women who moved out to the western suburbs from the slum-clearance schemes, such movement in the early years presented immense difficulties, particularly in respect to access to the traditional outwork of the clothing industry.

Such spatial changes in production and its effects on the female labour force were recognised in the Cumberland County Council Plan (1948:95). While it did not specifically isolate the more general effects of the changing pattern of urbanisation on women (for example, it did not include gender differences in its important statistical analysis of the employment/living/working relationship (Cumberland County Council Plan 1948:44)), it did encourage decentralisation of factory employment partially on the basis of attracting married women to the labour-scarce paid economy. It specifically stated that conditions of employment must be made attractive for women (Cumberland County Council Plan 1948:62). Although not entering the debate regarding how such attractiveness was to be achieved, the Plan boldly advocated community-support services such as community centres, kindergartens and local health centres. Such facilities, together with a neighbourhood base for planning and a commitment to more circumferential transport services, would have increased the access of suburban inhabitants, particularly women, to urban services previously concentrated in the city centre. For the woman who was solely restricted to the domestic situation, transport access may well have been one of deprivation. The diminishing importance of public transport in the post-war years and the rise of mass motor car ownership (Spearritt 1978*a*:168), affected the mobility of women and their access to urban services markedly. First, although it can be claimed that the motor car can operate to increase access by enabling more direct cross-suburban travel in comparison to the city-centred public transport system, initially it operated to decrease transport access for women, particularly since most women during the 1950s did not drive. More generally, accessibility to motor car use has been shown to contain great disparities among men and women, different age groups and different physically-handicapped groups (Morris 1982:21).

Car ownership further encouraged a greater dispersal of residential settlement, often without any other mode of transport provided to service such settlements. The early sites for the New South Wales Housing Commission's buildings at Granville and Westmead were criticised for their lack of public transport. The Granville development was two miles from the nearest rail station and half-a-mile from the nearest bus service (*Sydney Morning Herald*, August 15 1944:2). Further, for a large part of the suburban population, railway access was inconvenient for work and leisure journeys. New suburban developments were mainly serviced by private bus companies since the Department of Government Transport did not consider extension into new suburbs an economic proposition. The lack of feeder-bus services and the infrequency of private-bus services—at best they ran once an hour—further decreased alternative transport services (Jeans and M. Logan 1961:39). According to many women living in the Bankstown area, it was easier to walk, even if it did take much longer and restricted the area to a two-to-three mile radius (Allport 1980).

Even if women did drive, they did not necessarily have access to the car to assist in the purchase of shopping. Jeans and M. Logan (1961:39) quote the example of the Seven Hills shopping centre which, at the start of the 1960s, had a large surplus of parking space and drew its trade from an area in which people walked or rode in buses. Nor did they have personal mobility, as the one-car household had to service the transport needs of all household members including children's leisure needs. It is clear from the numerous studies quoted by Manning (1981) that one of the basic assumptions of modern urban design—all adults have a car and children will be able to use motor transport for all trips apart from the journey to school—has resulted in considerable inequities in transport access, particularly in the one-car household. It is important to note that many leisure developments catering for children were built on low-level land, unusable for residential development and were not conveniently located for transport routes. Further, the numbers of children involved at any one time was often not sufficient for private bus services to cater to such areas. Consequently, children needed to be transported both to after-school leisure activities and to weekend engagements. Thus, women's access to car transport had to fit in with the primary need for the wage earner to get to work, the hours of various urban services, such as baby health centres, doctors, dentists, shopping complexes and libraries, the arrival home of children from school and the need for leisure transport by these children.

Harman (1983*b*) argues that changes in consumption and social reproduction have meant that transport access for the suburban woman has become more important as consumption has become more socialised. Using the work of Mullins (1981) and Pringle (1983), she notes that shifts away from the self-sufficient domestic economy, 'the demise of the Australian urban vegetable garden, fowl run, fruit trees, and "do-it-yourself" skills in home repair, cooking and sewing' have resulted in an increase in the number and frequency of trips necessary to service the home. Reductions in home-delivery services, home visits by doctors, the decline of the cornerstore and the growth of car-oriented supermarket complexes further increase the number of trips or vary multi-purpose trips. For the woman without a car, and perhaps accompanied by one or two pre-school children, such shopping expeditions can become a nightmare—her work not only involves an increased physical load to carry but also child supervision in the shopping complex and on the journey home. Pringle believes that this takes up a much higher proportion of women's time than it used to and argues that the widening of women's consumption activities is a result of production being gradually removed from home. Further, the development of capitalist markets after the war 'depended on the promotion of consumption as a "way of life" and the superiority (and relative cheapness) of the "bought" over the home-made' (Pringle 1983:12). The organisation of selling also acted to increase the labour and hours necessary to acquire household goods and services. By 1961–62 while self-service establishments constituted only 16 per cent of retail outlets, they held 71 per cent of the grocery trade (Johnston and Rimmer 1969:41). Certainly, as Dyer (1979:2) notes, it is useful to list the regular visitors to a suburban home in 1938 and notice how few have survived—icemen, roaming vendors of fresh food (butcher, greengrocer, grocer, rabbito), bottle-o, rag-and-bone-men, woodmen, clothes-prop men, rent and insurance collectors.

While Harman and Pringle provide analyses which are particularly perceptive, the actual timing of the process deserves more subtle analysis. Many home delivery services had been severely curtailed during the war, a fact Mary Ryan continually bemoaned; yet these were an important part of life in the pre-shop Housing Commission areas, particularly the temporary settlements. It is a contention of this chapter that the developments Harman and Pringle refer to did not permeate the lives of the majority of suburban women, particularly those in the fast-growing outer municipalities, until the 1960s. The picture that emerges from the Bankstown study was that housework, including the production of home-consumed goods,. was still heavily labour-intensive until the 1960s and that the self-sufficient domestic economy was still strongly aided by the home-centredness found in many studies of suburban households.

Nonetheless, it is true that in the building of shopping centres on housing estates by the New South Wales Housing Commission, such centres were often inconveniently located for many with little transport access. The commission did not permit the building of isolated corner shops; it favoured the small grouping of shops usually located in the centre of the estate, as at Lalor Park (Jeans and M. Logan 1961:46). In some of the larger centres, such as Ermington or Villawood, a large shopping centre was built which attracted chain stores which, with cheaper prices, offered some advantages to outweigh the transport difficulties. More often than not, only a small number of shops was provided 'in small blocks unattractive to the chain-store group but sufficiently concentrated to make the shopping trip inconveniently long for many people on the estate' (Jeans and M. Logan 1961:43).

It is a pity that the corner-shop development was halted during the late 1950s for, as Dyer (1979:30) notes, such cornershops provided an important social outlet for housewives. It also meant a particularly disconcerting experience for women who had moved from the inner-city areas, where they were dependent on the local network for friendship, support and short-term financing for household expenditure, and where shopping was part of that intimate and familiar network (see Tennant 1959; also Park 1949; Connell and Irving 1980:298–300).

Access to transport also affects access to other urban services such as health care, educational resources and leisure facilities. In both the CHC's Final Report and the Cumberland Plan, emphasis was placed on the necessity for localised and decentralised health-care systems. The Cumberland Plan proposed that each neighbourhood would have clinic services and that, in addition to expansion of existing hospitals, new district hospitals of 200 beds would be built in centres such as

Fairfield, Bankstown, Sutherland and Hurstville. These district hospitals were to be supported by outpatient, ambulance and welfare services (Cumberland County Council 1948:117, 179–80). While each of the twenty district centres nominated in the plan was to have a district hospital, only five such centres contained a hospital by 1975 (Alexander 1981*a*:163).

Certainly, there was a political commitment to the decentralisation of hospital and medical services; yet Donald (1981) argues that centralisation is still the major problem facing the Health Commission and that the voluntary board of management system and the lack of a research and planning division in the Hospitals Commission, were the principal reasons for the failure of the decentralisation proposals. The voluntary board of management system required that before a hospital could be available, the time-consuming process of arousing public interest, petitioning the government and overseeing the construction process had to take place. Donald (1981:78) correctly argues that such a process was difficult in new settlement areas and that uncertainty about the continuing availability of finance for major capital works during the 1950s excerbated the situation.

Perhaps most crucial to all suburban women was the overcentralisation of obstetric and paediatric services. The bulk of the demand for these services after the war lay in the newly-developed suburbs. Overwhelmingly, settlement in those areas came from the newly-married young people providing the baby boom noted by demographers of the period (Jeans and M. Logan 1961:31). Yet most women from these suburbs travelled to the city centre to have their babies in the specialist hospitals clustered there, necessitating long journeys for family or friends visiting; the situation had not changed by 1974 as Table 15.3 illustrates.

Table 15.3 Supply of gynaecologists, obstetricians and paediatricians by region; Sydney metropolitan area 1974

Region	**Gynaecologists and obstetricians per 100 000 women aged 15–44**	**Paediatricians per 100 000 persons aged less than 6 years**
Central	88	168
Northern	11	18
Western	13	5
South-western	20	2
Southern	10	13
Inner-western	37	23
Sydney metropolitan area	37	33

Source: Donald 1981:69

Such a pattern indicates that long journeys were required not only for the birth of the child, but for ante-natal care, examinations after birth, and for specialist attention for children. In addition, although the Baby Health Centre movement did receive impetus from the reconstruction planning debate, the opening of new centres did not keep pace with population increases. By 1954, compared with the county average, there were at least half as many babies again to each baby health centre in the Fairfield, Liverpool and Ryde districts and twice as many in Blacktown and Hornsby (Jeans and M. Logan 1961:40).

This lack of health services in suburban areas was compounded by the low level of expenditure by the local governments on health in areas which in fact required rather high levels of expenditure due to the lack of proper sewers (Jeans and M. Logan 1961:40). The dependence on tin-pans and septics throughout the 1950s and part of the 1960s often created additional work for the household, particularly in low-lying areas in the wet weather. With the lack of kerbs and guttering in most of the suburbs and the poor state of the roads, many of the residents spent large sections of their time 'clearing street and road gutters, tending incinerators, carting rubbish, disinfecting, maintaining or repairing inefficient lavatories' (Brennan 1965:304). With husbands at work, many of these tasks had to be undertaken by the women.

These patterns of access to urban services and resources such as employment, transport, sewerage and health need also to be paralleled with studies on access to educational resources and leisure facilities in order to review fully existing concepts of spatial inequality in terms of gender and the circumstances surrounding the domestic relations of production. Black's (1978) study of comparative accessibility in different Sydney suburbs showed that within the acceptable range of a bus journey, many areas still lacked jobs, and medical and recreational facilities. On the other hand, primary schools and high schools were reasonably distributed within walking or bus journey (Manning 1981:52). It seems that the provisions of educational facilities was considered a high priority by residents of new areas. Many women who did not work in the paid workforce expended a great deal of energy into community pressure campaigns for a new primary school or district high school and the reaction by the authorities often meant quick success (Kelly 1957:402–3). They were, however, slower to react with the provision of leisure facilities. In 1944, the State government began subsidising local libraries. By June 1947, sixty local councils had adopted the Act, forty-seven libraries were in operation, of which eight were in Sydney and the suburbs. By June 1952, there were still only twenty-four municipal libraries in the metropolitan area while the number of councils stood at forty (New South Wales Statistical Register 1948 and 1953). The Cumberland Plan suggested that each district centre should have a theatre assembly hall, a large central library supporting smaller neighbourhood libraries and a district exhibition hall for art and museum exhibitions and lectures (Cumberland County Council 1948:177).

The community-centre scheme, which had offered so much and had been greeted so enthusiastically during the war, did not prove feasible in the outer suburbs. The only evidence of a community centre being built in Sydney during this period was the one at Castlecrag, an area settled by highly-motivated middle-class professionals who were able to assist in the financing of the centre. Undoubtedly, it was the high cost of such centres which deterred local councils from building the centres themselves. The financial base of local councils in the outer suburban areas was restricted by low land values and their failure to borrow to finance infrastructure building. Similarly, the State government was hamstrung by its inability to continue financing the capital works necessary for the social infrastructure of metropolitan growth; community-service schemes, while theoretically necessary, were placed low on the agenda of both State and Federal governments. Further, Menzies had made it quite clear in 1951 that the Cumberland Planning Scheme could not expect financial support from the Commonwealth.

Intimately related to the question of access to urban services (as central components of the domestic relations of production) are the effects of housing, tenure types, architectural practices and zoning policies on housework and child-care. Zoning in particular, often limits the location of child-care centres and commercial establishments which could act to make aspects of housework such as laundering more communal. Further, council ordinances and local government regulations often hinder the development of residential areas which are not based on the nuclear family. Building ordinances, if enforced, restrict communal living and only recently has legislation in New South Wales been amended to allow for extension of domestic homes by 'granny flats'.

Housework and child-care during the 1950s was essentially the sole preserve of women. The availability of overtime in the labour-scarce economy, meant that men were absent from the home for long hours. Even traditional men's duties in child-care, such as the discipline of male children, fell to the women. Further, many of these households were building their own homes and the extra earnings achieved through overtime were channelled into the building programme. Little money was available for the purchase of labour-saving household equipment envisaged by the CHC. Many of the residents of the newly developed Bankstown area stated that the purchase of washing machines, electric refrigerators and floor polishers was delayed until the beginning of the 1960s. Women still used copper boilers for washing, although electrically powered, and spent one day a week on their knees polishing the bright, wooden floors. On wet days, the women would need to dig makeshift drains to divert water in low-lying areas, and in their spare time (although few could remember having any) they harassed authorities for the establishment of schools, proper roads, effective street lighting and the improvement of local transport facilities (Allport 1980).

Perhaps most alienating of all was the attitude of the local community towards those rehoused in commission areas. Since the men were away so long at paid workplaces, it was the women who had to cope with the refusal of credit by local business, the cries of 'slum kids' at the local school, the cool reception at local church services and the paternalistic visits of commission welfare officers. Such communities were a far cry from those envisaged by the CHC.

Section VI:
Housing, wealth and speculation

Chapter 16
The ideology of home ownership

Jim Kemeny

One of the most powerful and pervasive social and political ideologies in Australia today is the belief in home-ownership. This finds expression in the enshrinement of home-ownership as 'The Great Australian Dream' and, superficially at least, lends considerable credence to the political rhetoric of a 'property-owning democracy'. Yet, strangely enough, not all capitalistic societies place such great stress on home-ownership as a form of tenure. Indeed, a number of societies which are considerably more wealthy than Australia have among the lowest home-ownership rates in the world (notably Sweden, West Germany and Switzerland), and even the United States and Canada, with their longer-established immigrant populations, both have lower home-ownership rates than Australia (United Nations 1974: Tables 182 and 198).

How then did Australia become such a home-ownership oriented society? This discussion will focus on two related aspects. First, it will be argued that home-ownership did not spread 'naturally' but was to a large extent engineered over a period of time, and that governmental sponsorship of home-ownership in preference to other housing strategies played an important part in determining Australia's modern tenure structure. Second, some of the ideological and political considerations underpinning the sponsorship of home-ownership will be examined. In particular, it will be argued that home-ownership as a form of tenure has close affinity with a range of conservative political beliefs, and that these played a major part in motivating politicians to promote a policy of sponsoring home-ownership.

The spread of home-ownership as an important form of tenure in Australia was not something which just happened as the expression of the preference of the Australian people within a free system of choice. Essentially, it required the diversion of resources for new building away from investor landlords and towards the private individual. Such a strategy became feasible in the first half of the twentieth century as a result of the general shift of investment which was occurring then in all capitalist societies away from less profitable forms of investment, including the construction of rental accommodation and towards expanding new industrial investment. The problem

This chapter is based on an article which appeared in *Arena* No. 46, 1977 and is published here by kind permission of the Editors.

in Australia, as well as in other capitalist societies, was what should take the place of private investment in rental accommodation. In some societies, notably Sweden, the solution chosen was to expand governmental investment in housing by providing non-subsidised housing (in competition, as it were, with private investor landlords), while providing various forms of aid to investors to build and to maintain rental accommodation. As a result of this strategy, the standard of rental accommodation in Sweden was maintained and a wholesale switch to home-ownership prevented.

The Swedish strategy was clearly motivated by political considerations, since the Social Democrats, who came to power in 1932, have always considered home-ownership as an obstacle to social equality and the equitable distribution of social welfare, in contrast to their political opponents on the Right who have always favoured home-ownership. The situation in Australia has been fundamentally different and the opposite strategy has been pursued to that in Sweden. The problem appeared fairly intractable, since in order to extend home-ownership it was necessary to increase dramatically the number of home-owners among working-class households whose ability to obtain credit was necessarily limited. The solution to this problem lay in making potential buyers more competitive than investor landlords, and had two aspects. The first was to set up, encourage and subsidise the complex economic infrastructure of lending for home-purchase which exists today. This involved subsidising savings banks and building societies for purposes of making loans available for home-purchase, guaranteeing mortgages for home-purchasers and other measures which attempted to divert funds into the owner-occupier sector, so as to make borrowing for home-ownership more widely possible and institutionalised as a normal means of obtaining housing.

This is not the place for a detailed description of the vast political programmes instituted at State and Federal levels to achieve this end. In South Australia some of the principal measures included the *Advances for Homes Act* of 1928 by which the State Bank was funded to make loans available for home-purchase, the *Mortgagors Relief Act* of 1931 and its various updating amendments to lengthen the repayment of loans, the *Building Societies Act* of 1941 and its various updating amendments guaranteeing bank loans for home-purchase. Even the setting-up of the South Australian Housing Trust in 1936 had a provision in it for the sale of homes to tenants or those who would be eligible to be tenants.

The second was to subsidise directly home-owners in competition with investor landlords by means of both tax exemptions and direct cash subsidies and other grants. Perhaps the most important single tax-exemption for owner-occupiers is that from tax on imputed rent, which the Federal government's *Report on Housing* estimates as costing the Treasury no less than $500 million in 1974-75 (Australian Priorities Review Staff 1976:14). This, and the failure to tax capital gains on owner-occupied property, represent exemptions which landlords are not allowed in a number of other countries, notably Sweden and West Germany. These, together with the array of other exemptions and deductions, as well as various direct cash grants (such as the subsidy of one-third of the deposit saved on a home), represent a formidable armoury of weapons to encourage the growth of an owner-occupier sector at the expense of a renting sector.

Curiously, all these measures did nothing to raise the proportion of home-owners in Australia between 1921 and 1947, and in metropolitan urban areas the home-ownership rate remained at around 45 per cent throughout this period (ABS 1938:365; 1951:566). The switch to home-ownership was sudden and dramatic and in the seven years from 1947 to 1954, the home-ownership rate increased by no less than 15 per cent to reach 61 per cent in metropolitan areas and 63 per cent in Australia as a whole. There are several reasons why this should have occurred when it did. The financial infrastructure for private borrowing had become well-established by the late 1940s, but it would appear that the immediate reasons were the increasing prosperity at that time, the post-war immigration boom, and the acute housing shortage, which combined to produce the circumstances for the demise of investor landlordism and the conversion of Australia to a home-owning society.

Of major importance in this switch to home-ownership was one political act which, interestingly enough, was not aimed directly at encouraging home-ownership. This was the *Landlord and Tenant Act*, a war-time measure which was renewed annually throughout this period to control rents. It must have been clear that such legislation could only restrict the building of rental accommodation at a time when housing was in acutely short supply, and at least one factor in determining the support which the measure received was the strongly-held conviction that home-ownership should be encouraged at the expense of landlordism. As one South Australian politician put it:

> I am not interested in people who invest money with a view to letting homes. I say that the individual has a right to own his own home and that the government should be the only institution to build homes as an investment. (South Australian House of Assembly 1950:867)

Hill (1959:6–7) argues that this legislation enacted by the States was the single most important factor in causing the switch to home-ownership, and that not only was there virtually no new rental accommodation built between 1947 and 1954, but no less than 90 000 rental houses — or one-sixth of the privately owned rental stock — were sold for owner-occupation.

The virtual demise of investor landlordism in Australia has had far-reaching consequences, since it has facilitated the maintenance of home-ownership as the principal form of tenure. It has already been noted that in Sweden governmental strategy had been both to supplement and support existing investor landlords. This had enabled the Swedish government to control rent levels, facilitate the guarantee of security of tenure and set high maintenance and repair standards, since the government as a major landlord can effectively act in the market, and more important, existing investor landlords are more or less prevented from selling out due to the lack of an expanding home-ownership market. The demise of investor landlordism in Australia was therefore an important preliminary to increasing home-ownership.

However, it has not meant that the private rental sector is disappearing. Rather, it has involved a shift from investor landlordism to small-scale amateur landlordism, resulting from the tendency among owner-occupiers to invest in second houses to provide a supplementary income in later life. Such landlordism is necessary to cater for two different groups: those whose incomes are so low as to preclude absolutely the possibility of buying a home, and young single people or newly-married couples who are saving for a deposit. The difficulty in controlling such a rental sector by means of legislation is in marked contrast to the situation resulting from the Swedish strategy, as the Federal government's *Report on Housing* implies (Australian Priorities Review Staff 1976:84). The resulting insecurity of tenure and poor maintenance standards, as well as landlord interference in tenant autonomy, means that renting ceases to be an attractive proposition. British experience in controlling tenancies, where research shows that small-scale landlordism predominates, had resulted either in the withdrawal of rental accommodation from the market or else wholesale evasion of the law by both landlords and tenants (Cullingworth 1963:Chapter 5; Greve 1965).

The resulting tenure balance in Australia has been a mixture of about two-thirds of households owning their homes and the rest either renting privately or else renting subsidised welfare housing provided by the State Housing Trusts. This balance is comparable to that which exists in other societies which have opted for home-ownership, notably Britain and the United States and contrasts with Sweden, where instead of providing welfare housing, rent subsidies are paid to the poorer households. Such a strategy would be ineffective in Australia since, as we have seen, there is no way to control effectively rent levels to prevent landlords from raising rents. Opting for welfare housing therefore supplements very well the emphasis on home-ownership, though one consequence is the division of tenure forms on a class basis.

Before going on to consider some of the ideological and political motivations of the sponsorship of home-ownership in Australia, it may be instructive to consider some implications of the policy for the distribution of wealth. The total costs of the policy to the State and Federal governments have been extremely high over the decades, though it is not possible to quantify this with any accuracy. In tax deductions and exemptions to owner-occupiers alone, the amount probably exceeds a thousand million dollars a year, almost enough to pay for the running of Medibank. If we add to this the cash grants and other measures, then it can be seen that the amount spent on home-ownership represents a major and open-ended commitment which makes home-ownership one of the most important welfare sectors in Australia today. Such welfare is, as might be expected, disproportionately spent on the higher socio-economic groups. Those to benefit most from the land tax and rates deductions, for example, are those whose incomes range from 125 per cent to 200 per cent more than the incomes of university professors (Australian Priorities Review Staff 1976: Table 2). In its first full year Medibank [forerunner to Medicare] cost about $1340 millions (1975–76). In 1974–75 the three main tax deductions and exemptions to owner-occupiers cost the government about $740 millions, not including estate duty exemptions, pensions exemptions and a number of other minor items (Australian Priorities Review Staff 1976:14.)

Data from Britain and the United States show a similar picture. Relief for owner-occupiers from tax amounted in 1970–71 to almost 300 million pounds, and the subsidy per mortgaged house sixty pounds a year and rising rapidly, while the subsidy per council house was forty pounds a year and falling. For the same period, one United States estimate suggests that housing subsidies for households with incomes above US$20 000 were at least four times higher than for households with incomes below US$3000 (Dolbeare 1974). In Britain, recent figures show that about 80 per cent of professionals as against 20 per cent of unskilled manual workers are owner-occupiers (Thompson 1975:17; F.Berry 1974:130–1). Subsidies to owner-occupiers in the form of tax exemptions not granted to investors amounted in 1966 to about US$7000 millions (Aaron 1972:55).

There are, therefore, far-reaching consequences, both political and social, of the governmental sponsorship of home-ownership. The fact that home-ownership has tended to be most enthusiastically promoted by the more conservative political parties in a number of countries such as Britain, Australia and Sweden reflects a close affinity between the lifestyle and values associated with home-ownership, such as thrift, self-help, the ownership of property, and independence, and conservative political and social principles. In Australia, the Liberal Party has always been more firmly committed to promoting home-ownership than the Labor Party. Indeed, even as late as 1945 a prominent Labor Minister, Mr Dedman, argued against Liberal Party legislative programmes which '... were deliberately designed to place the workers in a position in which they would have a vested interest in the continuance of capitalism' (Australian Parliament 1945:6265).

In spite of such opposition within the Labor Party, it is important not to overlook the fact that at both State and Federal levels the Labor Party has both continued and instigated policies which effectively support home-ownership, it has not officially opposed home-ownership and has sometimes strongly encouraged it. Overt political arguments in favour of home-ownership have in fact been the exception rather than the rule. Interestingly, some of these came to the surface at just the time when home-ownership was spreading rapidly, in the late 1940s and early 1950s. This can be understood in large part in terms of the context of the Cold War, at a time when anti-communist hysteria was at its height. The Menzies election victory of 1949, based largely on a platform of anti-communism, including promises to instigate a political purge of public employees and to proscribe the Communist Party, was just the most dramatic and overtly political manifestation of this phenomenon. During this time, a number of politicians expressed anxiety about the industrial and political allegiance of the working classes to the capitalist system in Australia, and the extension of home-ownership to the ordinary working man was seen as one major antidote against communism, by giving him a stake in the system.

The overtly class expression of this may be savoured from speeches and statements by prominent politicians. See the speeches by the Premier and Deputy Premier of Queensland in 1953 and 1954 cited in Jones (1972:120). See also, the statement by the Federal President of the Liberal Party, R. G. Casey in *The Advertiser* (Adelaide) Tuesday, 1 March 1949:2 and the speech by D. E. Costa in the House of Representatives on the second reading of the loan (Housing) Bill (1952) (Australian Parliament 1952:2354). See also speech by J. F. Gaha in the House of Representatives on the second reading of the Commonwealth and State Housing Agreement Bill (1945) (Australian Parliament 1945:6275). For a further discussion of this see Kemeny (1981 and 1983).

Such explicit political justifications of the extension of home-ownership were largely manifestations of the particular political atmosphere at the time, and it would be a mistake to see the home-ownership policies of the various governments as being justified in these terms. The general—though as noted earlier, by no means complete—political consensus was that home-ownership was a good thing, and in normal times there was no need to appeal to partisan motives. The eulogies on home-ownership which were delivered in political debates are well exemplified by the speech made in 1943 by the Premier of Victoria, Mr Dunstan, when moving the second reading of the *Housing Bill* in the Victorian House of Assembly:

> I know of no saying with more significance and real wealth of meaning than 'an Englishman's home is his castle'. Pride of ownership, security of tenure, sanctuary and contentment, are all bound up in that expressive phrase. Invariably, the man who owns his home is an exemplary citizen. His outlook on life is immediately changed from the moment when the first nail is driven into the structure that is eventually to become 'his castle'. In reality, it is a symbol of achievement, purpose, industry and thrift. The home

owner feels that he has a stake in the country, and that he has something worth working for, living for, fighting for; something he has never had in the past, something that he has to look forward to in the future... The fact that a man owns his own home gives him a sense of added responsibility, an urge to improve the locality in which the house is situated... The value of housing schemes for the people cannot, therefore, be measured in ordinary terms of pounds, shillings and pence. The indirect benefits far outweigh any direct monetary loss that might be entailed.

I consider that any government that weighs the cost on the scales of profit and loss is losing sight of the things that really count in the long run—the chief of which is the fostering of a contented and happy people. (Victorian Parliament 1943:1522)

The fact that there was a general political consensus on the preference for home-ownership is not to say that there were not political motivations for its sponsorship. Besides the rather more general conservative motives—the encouragement of thrift, pride of ownership, and individual responsibility which home-ownership was seen to entail—it is possible to point to two rather less obvious factors, both of which derive from the nature of home-ownership as a form of tenure.

One of the curious effects of home-ownership is that whereas people who pay rent for housing as they use it, people who own pay for a lifetime of housing in advance, either all at once or, more usually, by means of a mortgage which is re-paid over a period usually not exceeding twenty-five years or so. Home-ownership therefore has the effect of radically re-distributing expenditure on accommodation so that the heaviest burden falls on the young and the lightest on the old. Because housing is such an expensive item in household expenditure, such a re-distribution is of major importance. House-purchases account for several thousand million dollars a year in Australia (ABS 1976). British data show that median mortgage repayments are twice as high as rents, and that this is true among home-owners in all socio-economic groups (Thompson 1975:159).

This has two important political consequences, which have been clearly understood by legislators. The first is that it helps to give substance to the commitment of young people to the system by placing them into a form of tenure in which they must work hard both to save an initial deposit and to keep up mortgage re-payments. The stress by politicians on the incentive provided by home-ownership and the sense of responsibility which it engenders is therefore not just moral but also material. The sociological implications of this, particularly for lower-income earners, has been well expressed by Levison in the United States context:

Many workers, in the elation of the first days after their honeymoon, lock themselves into a lifetime of debt when they buy a house and furniture to add to the payments they are already making on

> their car. From then on, their freedom to travel or try a new job, or just engage in a range of activities outside work is taken from them by the structure of debt in which they are enmeshed.
>
> For some the house becomes a focus of attention—the single symbol of affluence amid the daily life of severe economic pressure. It is this that explains the sometimes irrational fury with which workers react to threats to their neighbourhood or home. It is not simply a piece of property, but something which has absorbed so much of their income, so many hours of work, and closed out so many alternatives, that losing it is like making all the sacrifices futile. (Levison 1974:105–6)

Second is the effect of home-ownership on old age. As the Henderson Commission of *Inquiry on Poverty in Australia* showed, the incidence of poverty among the aged is very much greater among renters than owners (Commission of Inquiry into Poverty 1976:24). Home-ownership therefore acts as a source of self-help to cater for old age, which alleviates a category of poverty which the government might otherwise have to deal with directly, and it is clear that politicians at the State and Federal levels have been aware of this as one advantage of sponsoring home-ownership (Australian Parliament 1945:284; 1952:6258; South Australian House of Assembly 1953:1064; Kemeny 1983).

The political implications of the dominance of one form of tenure rather than another in a society are therefore far-reaching. However, in closing this discussion it is important to stress that political factors are only one aspect of the question of tenure in a society and it is clear that other aspects, such as lifestyles and values concerning ownership, play at least a part in determining the relative balance of different forms of tenure. Nevertheless, the political history of home-ownership and the wider political, economic and social ramifications of the spread of home-ownership have been neglected, and much more needs to be done to complete our understanding of the processes involved here. Given the importance of home-ownership in Australia, this is one field which deserves much more attention than it has received so far.

Chapter 17
Housing — an investment for all

Hugh Stretton

This chapter is an edited version of a paper presented to the National Housing Conference in Sydney in September 1982. We have retained the spoken word style because we believe its message is thereby conveyed with the original freshness and urgency — Editors.

When you consider the central concerns of this conference you may well think the subject is not investment 'for all', it's investment for a minority: the 15 or 20 per cent of Australians who are facing actual housing hardship.

Their troubles would certainly justify a conference. Perhaps a keynote speech should begin by reminding you who they are: young families with children and only one breadwinner; households depending on welfare incomes with no breadwinner; single parents and their children; many of the 20 per cent of age pensioners who do not own their houses; many Aborigines; people in outer suburbs short of services; people in mining and refining towns short of houses; and so on. Or — to identify them not by who they are but by what they put up with — people who want to buy houses but cannot; people who did lately buy houses but cannot keep up their payments; people with low incomes paying as much as half of their incomes in rent; People who want public housing but cannot get it, or not when they need it or where they need it; the 70 per cent or so of renters who would rather be owners; the 70 per cent or so of caravan-dwellers who would rather be in houses; old men wanting cheap beds; teenagers away from home wanting cheap beds; women and children needing refuge, especially in the many country districts that do not have any shelters, and so on. And do not forget the other kind of 'housing hardship' — the tens of thousands of unemployed building tradesmen and suppliers, and their dependants.

A keynote speech could detail all that. It could be studded with heart-rending case studies. Then it could list some of the policy options that have been proposed for dealing with each housing sector and each type of housing hardship. If the speaker was not a rabble-rouser, but a responsible type, he might cost each of the policy options. Then he might propose a selection, a package of reforms, costing perhaps $600 or $800 million a year, as a reasonable programme, which our rich but compassionate country might be asked to pay for; a moderate self-sacrifice by the well-off majority to help the poor minority through the present bad times. If the case studies in that sort of keynote speech were vivid and the speaker's concern was infectious, and the proposed reforms were moderate and practical, then we might all be persuaded that the social gain would be worth the economic cost; the sacrifice would be worthwhile.

There are three reasons for *not* offering you that particular keynote speech. First, it is unnecessary—everybody knows where the current housing hardships are. Second, most of you do not need persuading—this is a conference of the already-convinced, the persuad*ers*. Third, the simplest objection to that particular keynote speech is that a main part of its message is wrong. The idea that better housing is a social good with heavy economic costs is the main *hindrance* to better housing policies and performance.

But a lot of people do see the issue in that way, that is, they see better housing as a social good with serious economic costs (of course, there are also people—critics of suburbia and the house-and-garden way of life—who see better housing as a social *evil* with serious economic costs). But sticking to people who see housing as a good, they tend to be troubled by two large questions. First, Joe and Joanna Citizen have a strong market preference for owning a generous spread of house and garden. Is that preference worth what it costs the national economy—and what it therefore costs Joe and Joanna themselves—in the long run? Second, when he has got his own house, and his mortgage round his neck like a millstone, how much more can we then expect Joe Citizen to sacrifice—in personal taxation and extra inflation and lost economic growth—as the price of supplying yet more housing to the old and the poor and the single parents and all the other suffering folk who cannot afford to buy or rent for themselves?

Faced with those questions, hard-headed Treasury economists do not think we can afford much of either kind of self-indulgence. Soft-hearted types like you and me may think the house-and-garden is worth its costs, and we may favour some further sacrifices to house the minorities who cannot afford to house themselves properly.

The theme of this keynote address is that both those judgements are wrong. The understanding of the options is wrong. If it is sensibly managed, housing investment need not hinder economic growth, it can help. Greater housing equality need not have costs in efficiency, it can positively improve national productive efficiency. Reformed housing finance need not fuel inflation, it can restrain it. And far from waiting for economic recovery before we can afford better housing policies, we should be using bigger allocations to housing as aids to recovery and economic growth.

So I am afraid this is not the inspirational kind of keynote address, it is an economics lecture. It is meant to clear away some obstructions, to encourage confidence in more ambitious housing policies. Policies which may look like charitable aids for the 10 or 20 per cent of people in actual housing hardship, but may also be, as the title suggests, 'investment for all'. I will try to persuade any of you who still need persuasion that many productive housing policies, which you and I already recognise as valuable *social* policies, can also be productive *economic* policies.

I am sorry that most of what you are about to hear is not new. It has been said often enough before. It just has not been believed or acted on often enough before. So it needs saying again, however painful economics lectures are.

Themes

I have six themes. First, housing is productive capital. Second, it can aid economic recovery and growth. Third, market forces do not make efficient allocations to housing; some public aid and management are also needed. Fourth, our present managers do not understand the markets. Treasury views of the housing and capital markets, and the neoclassical economic theories which shape those views, are the main hindrances to good housing policy and performance. Fifth, inflation and some changing international financial conditions create a special need to reform the management of our capital market. Finally, reform is possible.

There will not be time to do more than state the arguments baldly.

Housing is productive capital

I will not labour this familiar theme but as long as our economic authorities go on ignoring it we have to go on repeating it. Depending how you choose to measure it, somewhere between 33 and 45 per cent of our material goods and services are produced in households, or by other unpaid labour in other co-operative organisations. That output is likely to go on increasing in volume and importance. Whether or not we are in for substantial technological unemployment, we certainly face shorter hours of paid work, longer education and longer retirement, and altogether more leisure. The capital resources of household and neighbourhood and voluntary association seem likely to be more important than ever. So we need appropriate allocation of capital between households and other productive users.

Housing and economic growth

Housing investment can help recovery and economic growth — but only if government acts to ensure more of it than market forces alone would provide.

If housing is left to the market in developed or developing economic systems, it commonly gets 2.5 or 3 per cent of national product; and about 50 per cent of households get to own their houses. But for housing to do its best for national economic growth, you need higher rates than those. Fortunately it is easy for government by one means or another to raise housing investment to 5 or 6 per cent of national product, and to extend home-ownership to 70 or 75 per cent of households. And the ownership could go to 85 per cent or so if we extended it, as we easily could, to all the households who say they want it and would willingly pay 15 to 20 per cent of income to get it.

Why is high housing investment an aid to economic growth? I mean both kinds of growth—in the domestic productivity which the national accounts do not measure, and the commercial productivity which they do. There are a number of reasons, which apply in different porportions in different historical cases. The house-building industry can be a stable, long-term-reliable one, while at the same time running with extreme competitive efficiency. It can be efficient with a range of firms from national to one-man, with easy entry and ample opportunities for individual enterprise. The industry is naturally protected, needing no tariffs or quotas to keep it stable. It is not directly vulnerable to external prices or markets. Its import component is modest, and can be further reduced if necessary. Because many import components of houses are luxuries, the effect of import restrictions is usually to *reduce* costs. Directing resources to lower-income home-buyers will also reduce the import bill.

It is a labour-intensive industry employing a mix of skilled, semi-skilled and unskilled labour. It employs them mostly in districts where they live or want to live. For marginal home-buyers and home-improvers there is flexibility between paid and do-it-yourself (DIY) labour. These characteristics make it a specially helpful growth industry for countries with steady urban growth from net immigration, or population drift from country to town.

House building has quite a good employment multiplier. For every worker it employs directly, it employs about one more indirectly. There are some further benefits to the economy as a whole, in *saving*, *work incentives* and *capital growth*.

Saving

If there is continuing visible improvement in everyone's chances of better housing and of home ownership, then the nation saves more than it otherwise would; sometimes by working more than it otherwise would. People will save for housing what they would not save for anything else. The institutions which mind their savings lend for housing but also lend to other industries. So there's more of *both* housing *and* industrial capital-formation than there would otherwise be.

Work incentives

Industrial peace and low labour-turnover are widely believed to be helped by good housing with fair costs and secure tenures. The same housing conditions may help the political and social stability which attract investment. It used to be thought that home-ownership anchored labour unhelpfully, and that extreme labour mobility would help economic growth. All the fast-growing and industrially peaceful economies of recent decades point to the opposite effect.

Capital growth

Housing lasts longer than most fixed capital. So allocating (say) 25 per cent of capital formation to housing will make housing 40 per cent of the capital stock over time. Generous housing also attracts spending to other domestic capital—'consumer durables', DIY equipment, productive gardens, etc. So allocations to housing can have a double multiplier effect, especially on domestic and DIY productivity, which may be increasingly important in an age of increasing unemployment and leisure.

To set against those useful effects there are two bad ones, one more preventable than the other. In Australia, housing development has been allowed to inflate urban land prices harmfully in some cities. That is preventable where governments want to prevent it—and the preventive measures include more housing supply, not less. Second, the industry employs many more men than women. That could probably be modified a bit, but in practice perhaps not very much. Though the industry offers women less than their share of employment, it may be argued that it offers them more than a half share of its other benefits.

For the foregoing reasons a big housing industry should theoretically be a big help to economic growth. And in practice, it almost invariably has been. Australia comes near to being the main exception, through the post-war decades we managed to combine quite high housing investment with quite slow economic growth. Let's look at half-a-dozen other national economic performances through those same years.

The British performance through the 'Keynesian' years 1945–70 is not much praised. Housing did not get a very high proportion of national product. Nevertheless, those years saw the most sustained public housing programme in British history; it built more than half of the houses built, and took the public share of housing from below 15 to above 30 per cent. Meanwhile tax and other aids to home purchase took home-ownership up from 40 to 50 per cent of households, and 70 per cent of non-government houses. Meanwhile the general economic performance may have been poor compared with Germany or Japan, but it was nevertheless the best in modern British history; the fastest sustained growth for more than a hundred years, the highest employment ever.

Now look at the celebrated 'economic miracles' of those years: Sweden, West Germany, Holland, Japan, Hong Kong and Singapore. It would take too long to read out the relevant statistics. But—give or take some variations here and there—they can be simply summarised: those countries directed to housing construction about twice the resources that market forces alone would have done; and *while* doing that, and partly *by* doing that, they led the world in economic growth. To put it comparatively, they at least doubled the British allocation of capital to housing, and at least doubled the British rate of growth. There were some years when Singapore and Hong Kong managed to chalk up the highest allocations to housing ever recorded anywhere, together with the fastest economic growth ever recorded anywhere.

In all those cases, it took government action as well as market forces to achieve the high rate of house-building. Some of it, as in the early years of the German recovery, was to replace housing destroyed in war. But most of it had no such special stimulus. It was voluntary policy; a social choice to make a revolution in the quantity and quality of the people's housing, especially the worker's and poorer people's housing.

Two questions about that. First, does it mean that governments were diverting, to housing, resources which the people themselves would have preferred to spend on other things? No, there is overwhelming political and economic evidence that the people wanted the housing and were happy to pay for it. But to get it they needed government aids—that is, they had to pay part of the price collectively—because, for reasons I'll come to in a minute, it's in the nature of the relevant capital and housing markets that if they're left to themselves they cannot and do not make efficient allocations to housing; they cannot and do not allocate capital between housing and other uses in the most productive way.

Second, was the housing performance of those countries an effect rather than a cause of economic growth—a social luxury they could afford *after* they had made their miracles with other industries? No; everywhere except Japan the housing programmes were committed early after the Second World War (or in Singapore, after independence) and acted as initiators of growth. Construction accelerated before, or with other industries, and created significant amounts of the demand to which other industries responded. The housing programmes were agents of growth at least as much as they were effects of it. Even the Japanese exception is instructive. Japan did make its big housing run comparatively late, after it had established a high rate of industrial growth. But when the special housing effort came it did no harm to the continuing economic miracle—through the 1950s when Japan was building seven or eight houses per year per 1000 of population and through the 1960s and early 1970s when the rate nearly doubled to twelve or thirteen per 1000, the rate of economic growth was about the same; the accelerated housing programme did nothing to slow it.

In Germany, with war losses of housing to replace, the big housing programme started early and helped to lead the industrial recovery.

For a quarter of a century Germany built twice the houses per head that Britain did and averaged about twice the British rate of economic growth. The market did not do that. Of ten million houses built in West Germany between 1950 and 1970, a third were built by the non-profit sector and another third had some sort of public subsidy. This is how the British economist Barbara Ward summed up the lessons of the German performance and it can serve as the summary of my second theme:

> ... the Germans have proved that if a resourceful and hard-working people devote a steady five or six per cent of their gross national product to housing a vast transformation can be achieved in only two decades. Nor can anyone, following the growth of the German economy through the same period, argue that the priority for housing has acted as much of a drag on other sectors. On the contrary, the very steadiness and comprehensiveness of the program has been an important stimulus to the rest of the economy ... If wealthy industrialised countries want to give their citizens decent homes, they can. If they do not, the will is absent and the first need is not new building codes or new industrialised construction systems or yet another redistribution of responsibility ... It is a political conversion, a change of heart. (B. Ward 1976:110–11)

So much for that theme. A stimulated, government-aided housing programme has everywhere proved to be an active aid to economic growth. In capitalist countries in the last half-century there has rarely been any sustained above-average growth without such a programme.

Why the market needs help

If housing is productive capital and a proven aid to economic growth, why does sufficient supply of housing not come naturally in a market way, in response to consumer demand?

There are two basic reasons. Here there's only time to state them baldly.

First, remember why we expect markets to get the consumers what they want. In an ideal capitalist system industries attract capital because they can use it profitably. The profits are what attract the capital. In theory the most profitable uses are the most productive ones; their profits allow them to bid capital away from less profitable uses: so capital gets allocated in due proportion to the most productive set of uses. If and when capitalism is efficient and responsive to consumers' preferences, that's the fundamental reason why.

But that principle does not *and cannot* — even in theory — apply to the allocation of capital to housing. Although housing is a main part of the fixed capital for a third or more of our economic output, that third of our output does not sell for money: *so it cannot be the money returns from the use of the capital that pay for the capital.* The household has to bid for and pay for its housing capital with some other resource altogether — typically with wages earned in some other industry altogether. The breadwinner's productivity *in that other industry* determines what housing capital, and therefore domestic productivity, his household can have.

So, there are two inefficiencies. When households compete with one another for shares of the available housing finance, there is no reason to expect that market competition will direct the capital to the household that can use it most productively. An inactive old couple, if they're rich, may get resources which an industrious but poorer family of ten could make ten times as productive. And when households compete for resources against commercial and industrial investors, there is no reason whatever to expect that the most productive user will get the capital. The classical link between market allocation and efficient use — the most basic capitalist efficiency — simply is not there.

That is a first market failure. There is a second one. The competitors for a house or a housing loan are not always rival households. Sometimes the competitors are a household and a landlord-investor. If the household wins the competition it will occupy the house as an owner. If the landlord gets the house the household will have to occupy it as tenant. So whoever wins the market competition for the capital, the household will pay for the capital, either through loan repayments or through rents which finance the landlord's loan repayments; the main issue in the market competition is whether the occupier of the house will buy the capital for himself, or for the landlord. But if he buys it for the landlord it will cost him much, much more; he'll go on paying long after the house is paid for and debt-free. There is no reason at all, either in theory or in practice, to expect that the revenue in the landlord's hands will be put to more productive uses, nationally speaking, than it would have been if it had been in the household's hands. Meanwhile the landlord — if it is a loan he has won — may well provide less productive housing than the household would have provided for itself. He may restrict the tenant's uses of the house. He may build flats instead of houses-with-gardens; landlord-investors have scarcely ever built new homes-in-gardens for rent to family households.

So in principle, over time, the household can pay more for that house than the landlord will pay for it, or alternatively it can get better housing for its money than the landlord will provide. That has to be so, or the landlord would not be in the business. So efficient allocation, for the most productive use of the resource, would give the resource to the household. Tax treatment which disadvantages landlords and deters them from bidding for the resource is likely to increase productive efficiency, not reduce it. But if you leave the business to the market — which in practice means leaving it to the people who manage the financial institutions — the institutions will often give the loan to the landlord-investor, for a variety of (mostly bad) reasons. When that happens — when a landlord-investor manages to get between the moneylender and a household which would prefer to own if it had the choice — then the market is positively inefficient. It is likely to provide less housing for more money; to reduce household productivity, to reduce the society's overall rate of saving and capital formation and to increase inequalities of wealth and spendable income. (But it's the only kind of housing investment that many orthodox economists will define as productive at all!)

Professional errors

That introduces my fourth theme: the Treasury view of housing investment, and the neoclassical economic theory that underlies it, are wrong. I mean technically wrong, wrong about what causes what.

There is not time here for any thorough account of the reasons why the orthodox neoclassical models do not fit the housing or capital markets. All I can do is list, shortly, some of the policy mistakes that flow from those mistaken theoretical beliefs. 'They' means most neoclassical economists, including most of our Treasury economists, most of the time. Of course there are many individual exceptions and variations.

Consumer sovereignty

'They' argue that consumers decide how to divide their spending between housing and other things. Those who want a lot of house spend a lot of money on it, those who put higher value on other things will choose less housing at lower cost. That is sometimes true. It can be true when buyers choose which house to buy. It can be true as renters choose which house to rent. But it is *not* true when people are choosing whether to buy or rent. It is not true for two reasons: first, buying requires some heavy saving first and it is hard to pay your current housing costs *and* save. Second — and fatally for any 'market efficiency' — the better options do not cost more, they cost less. Over household life, buying a house can leave you as much as 50 per cent better off in assets and spendable income than renting the same house will leave you. Whether you manage to get a cheap good option (say, buying a house and garden) or an expensive bad option (say, renting a less good house throughout your household-life) is not determined by what you, the customer, are willing to spend. It is determined partly by your income and inheritance and rather more, for many households, by institutional policies about the conditions and repayment profiles of housing loans. So there is plenty of vicious-circle causation which has none at all of the logical efficiency of those orthodox economic models. Once driven to pay a high rent to a landlord, the household loses its capacity to save a purchase deposit.

The higher the rent, the harder it is ever to become an owner. The dearer the bad option, the less chance there is of ever switching to the cheaper, better option. This is what orthodox thinkers call consumer sovereignty.

Directing welfare housing accurately to those in most need of it

To do that, Treasury thinkers have succeeded in reversing the two central principles of Curtin's and Menzies' housing policies: the Curtin principle of cost-renting and the Menzies principle of rental-purchase which made so many public housing customers into home-owners. Roughly speaking, Whitlam reversed the Menzies policy and Fraser has reversed the Curtin policy. Their advisers reasoned that home-owners stay too long in their Housing Commission houses, and so do people enjoying low-cost rents. So: abolish rental purchase sales, and raise rents to market levels, and you'll drive out the well-off who can afford to fend for themselves on the open market, vacate the houses for those in greater need, and generally accelerate the turnover of public housing.

Wrong. The rental-purchasers used to sell their houses and pay out their contracts after seven years or so in most cases. They got deposits to buy private housing, the Housing Commissions got cash to replace in part the lost houses. (Some States failed to replace the houses they sold with comparable houses in comparable locations; that was a bad mistake, but it does not make a case against rental-purchase). The vital effect of no-deposit rental purchase is that—with no subsidy from anyone—it allows the household to house itself and save simultaneously—and in seven or ten years, that is the gateway out of public housing altogether. When we abolish that rental-purchase option, the same tenant occupies the same house as tenant. But now his saving has to be done *on top of* his rental-housing cost. It is that much harder, that much slower. He is there for longer. Now 'jack up' his rent to market levels and you can soak up and destroy *all* his saving capacity. You have not driven him out of public housing, *you have imprisoned him in it.* If the Curtin-Menzies policies had continued, most of the 'generation of 1972' would be out as owner-occupiers by now, vacating their public housing, or a cash equivalent of it, for needier customers. But step by step the Whitlam-Fraser policies—the restriction then abolition of rental-purchase sales, the reduced supply of public-housing capital, the advance to market rents—have achieved effects precisely opposite, in very many cases, to those incompetent Treasury expectations. They have *slowed* the turnover of public housing, *reduced* the available vacancies, *lengthened* the waiting lists and the waiting times for many of the people in genuine need.

Next, *the tax treatment of landlords, owner-occupiers and renters*: Some orthodox thinkers would like neutral tax treatment of landlords and owner-occupiers, including generous depreciation allowances to encourage more landlord investment in housing. I have suggested earlier why I think that is mistaken; investors in luxury markets can well afford the taxes, and in mass housing markets discouraging professional landlords does more to improve housing supply than to reduce it.

There is more heat about the taxation of owner-occupiers. Most orthodox economists would like to income-tax home-owners, first on the income with which they pay their mortgage interest, and then on an imaginary or 'imputed' rent of their owner-occupied houses. There is an equitable case for doing that if you focus *only* on the differential tax treatment of owner-occupers and tenants. But Patricia Apps (1973*b*) has shown what is wrong with focusing on that relation alone. If housing is productive capital, one should also compare its tax treatment with the tax treatment of other productive capital — in this case, the tax treatment of commercial and industrial land and buildings. When a business uses real estate we do not make it pay its mortgage loan interest or its rent out of taxed income; both are deductible expenses. So — first — if we tax home buyers and owners as the economists want us to do, we will discriminate in favour of commercial capital and against domestic capital, without regard for their comparative productivity or capacities to pay. Even on neoclassical principles that must be expected to distort the allocation of capital and reduce the national product. Second, if we want to combine equal tax treatment of commercial and domestic capital with equal tax treatment of home-owners and renters, we should allow renters (or perhaps defined categories of bona-fide renters) to subtract the rent they pay from their taxable incomes, just as we allow business renters to do.

Rent control

All economics textbooks condemn rent controls. Not just Treasury economists, but according to a recent American survey 98 per cent of all economics graduates, believe that rent controls do nothing but harm, even to the tenants they are supposed to protect. Rent controls (they say) reduce the return to housing investment. That deters investors and reduces the supply of new housing. The shortage drives prices and rents up, by black-market payments where necessary, above the levels that would have prevailed without the controls.

Wrong. What rent controls chiefly do is three things. They usually protect the tenants they are meant to protect, which usually (though not invariably) reduces inequalities of income. They often deter landlords from a little of the maintenance they might otherwise do — and many poor tenants prefer that to being done up and priced out. But above all they deter landlord-investors from bidding for available housing finance and available houses. That leaves more *finance* for households wanting to build or buy, and more *houses and building resources* for them; so they get more for less than they otherwise would. That has a number of effects. It takes more households out of private renting, thus easing, not increasing, the pressure on rents. It may often also happen that the improved possibility of buying gives people more *incentive* to save, while the controlled rents leave them more *capacity* to save — which allows even more of them eventually to build or buy.

So the conventional wisdom may apply to the few cash investors, with no need to borrow, who build new low-cost housing within the means of working-class and welfare tenants. But those are very, very few.

Meanwhile, the net effect of rent controls in Australian conditions, if they are sensibly applied, is likely to be lower housing rents and prices, more saving, more home-ownership, and quite probably more housing overall — the reverse of every orthodox expectation.

Finally, there is the role of housing in the national economy as a whole: the relation of housing investment to growth, employment and inflation.

Growth and employment

When the Treasury says — as I am told unreliably that it says — 'When we say housing investment diverts resources away from growth we are not talking theory, we are talking facts', they are actually talking nonsense. Theory, practice and all historical and contemporary experience say that an assisted level — an above-market level — of housing investment is not merely a powerful aid to economic growth, it has usually been a necessary condition of it

Inflation

Once again I can only state baldly a theme that has been argued at length in other places. It concerns our institutional management of borrowing and lending in conditions of inflation. When serious inflation sets in, lenders and borrowers face a basic question: to protect lenders from loss, should they specify the capital they lend in the traditional way in nominal money terms? If they do that, they will have to try to cope with inflation by adding the rate of inflation to the rate of interest. With long-term loans, like most housing loans, that has the dramatic effect of requiring much bigger repayments, not just of nominal money but of real purchasing power, through the early years of the loan. Many home-buyers and others who need to repay evenly over time from wage or small business incomes cannot make those high early repayments, so many are excluded from borrowing. For a number of reasons that way of adapting the capital market to inflation distorts the market systematically. It discriminates against most long-term borrowers, and against those who need level schedules of real repayment. The general effect is to favour old businesses against new ones, big firms against small ones, business borrowers against home-buyers, and richer home-buyers against poorer ones, often including childless home-buyers against those with young children.

The alternative way to adapt to inflation is to index it into the capital debts so that they maintain real value over time. Interest rates can then stay as low as they do in stable conditions, and debts can be repaid by level repayments over long terms. Home-buyers and small businesses can benefit greatly from that — and so can government. From 1945 to about 1970 our public housing programme nearly-enough paid its way. The tenants' regular rents repaid the government's loans, and, incidentally, purchased a massive capital asset for the taxpayers, who did at least as well out of the business as the tenants did. But with the inflation of the 1970s, tenants' rents could nowhere near cover the massive early loan repayments that were required by the inflation-plus interest rates. Perceiving a need for large (though short-term) subsidies, government proceeded to cut the business down.

Government and banks and other financial institutions can respond to inflation in one of three general ways. They can add the rate of inflation to the interest rate. They can index it into the capital sums lent and borrowed. Or they can do both: they can run a 'dual flow' capital market which offers terms of both kinds and as borrowers and lenders go for the terms they prefer, interest rates and/or regulation can adjust the volumes of the two flows. That third option has its risks and difficulties, but I believe it is workable and the most efficient and equitable of the options.

The first of those options — the system we have now — is very harmful to the housing business and its potential role in economic recovery. I think it is also on balance strongly inflationary. It has depressing effects on investment but those inflation-plus interest rates get built into a great many prices.

This whole capital mistake about the management of debts under inflation comes from some mixture of institutional inertia and class war. There is no rationale for it in neoclassical economic theory. Where the theory itself threatens to do most damage is in inspiring and now implementing the Campbell Report (Committee of Inquiry into the Australian Financial System 1981). I think that report is terrible for a dozen reasons, but at present it is appropriate to stick to the housing reasons. There are two main housing reasons. First, the open competition for resources which is recommended by those who would deregulate our financial system is not the way to get efficient allocation between housing and other uses, or between household and household, for reasons I suggested earlier. It will get less and dearer finance for housing and hand it to richer rather than poorer households. But—second—housing finance will become more variable and unstable, as a residual effect of exposing our capital market to international movements in the defenceless way the deregulators recommend. The international financial system is running nearly out of control. It contains rising proportions of mobile rentier funds, and also of slosh money: proceeds of oil, governmental, criminal and other super-profits, sloshing around the world looking for speculative gains or, with increasing desperation, for safe places and safe uses. Too much of it has been accepted on imprudent terms by the western banking system, and on-lent to Third World and East-European countries with no real prospects of productive use or punctual debt-service. To choose this historical time for Australia to expose itself to that system, with faith that is regulated by some efficient hidden hand, seems to me to be quite lunatic. But that is what we are doing and it is chiefly bad economic theory that has persuaded our masters to do it.

Housing will be one of the worst sufferers. None of our carefully-detailed schemes to help particular groups who face housing hardship, or our schemes to restore workable systems of mortgage lending and repayment for the majority of home-buyers, can be relied on to work as planned if the national supply of financial capital is fluctuating, vulnerable and beyond any reliable stablising control or policy direction.

Reform is possible

What could government do instead? To create the economic conditions for successful housing policies, I think it would have to reverse course in one radical—but also quite conservative—way. We need a boundaried financial system, one which can trade funds with the outside world but which is insulated from fund movements that we do not want. That is not frightening, except to professors; it calls for modern replacements for the exchange and foreign investment controls we managed without too much trouble for a quarter of a century.

Within our own capital market, we could return most of the business to the traditional institutions. It would then be intelligent and efficient to positively scandalise the professors by doing three other things, of which the first two are reassuringly conservative: impose some appropriate equivalent of the sixty or forty rules on the major institutions including insurers, superannuators and other institutional investors as well as banks; control housing interest rates, with attention to market conditions but with the general purpose of keeping the rates as low as practicable; offer capital-indexed as well as interest-indexed-terms in the savings and housing sectors, and anywhere else there proves to be market demand for both. That is not a housing policy. But some such basic economic conditions seem to me to be necessary conditions for any general national success with housing.

Conclusion

That is the end of this economics lecture. To sum it up: housing is productive capital; high housing investment, as long as people want the housing, can aid economic recovery and growth. It can also help us to adapt well to the current directions of technological and economic change. But market forces cannot and do not make efficient allocations to housing. Some public aids and some public investment are also needed.

Of course, it is possible to devise bad public aids to housing, and bad public housing investments. But as long as we stick to good ones, we must not be put off by orthodox economists who think that all market controls and public investments are intrinsically inefficient. Applied to capital markets and to housing markets, those neoclassical economic models are systematically, reliably wrong.

Author's postscript, 1986

The text is as it was delivered in September 1982, in the last year of the Fraser government. The succeeding Labor government has surprised and distressed its supporters by deregulating the financial system and raising real interest rates sky-high, with the effects predicted above.

Chapter 18
Housing policy, planning practice

Ross King

From an account of the housing boom of the 1950s and 1960s in Australia, and of the subsequent crisis, it is argued that housing-related monetary and fiscal policy is to be conceptualised as addressing the conditions necessary for the extraction of 'absolute rent' (in the Marxian classification of ground rent), while urban planning practice is to be understood as necessarily supporting the creation and maintenance of a system of differentiated submarkets, as a condition for the realisation of 'monopoly rents'. The persisting housing crisis following 1973 in Australia — to be understood as a local effect of the 'second global crisis of capitalism' — relates to a breakdown in the mechanisms of monetary and fiscal policy that underpinned the 1950s and 1960s investment boom. That breakdown seriously eroded the previous capacity of the housing sector to provide opportunities for profitable investment; accordingly, urban planning is now required to ensure such opportunities, by guaranteeing a more differentiated submarket structure for uneven development and devaluation/revaluation, but with seriously regressive equity effects.

Investment and progress, 1945–73

Any consideration of the role of housing investment in a capitalist society is likely to lead to the conclusion that, from the point of view of capital, it serves three overriding functions:

- to ensure demand for the expanding production of industrial capital, and thereby a continuing basis for capital accumulation;
- to ensure reproduction of the capital-labour relationship, specifically by aiding the reproduction of a population with requisite skills and levels of social and geographical mobility (and under this function might be subsumed the provision of shelter);
- to stabilise the conflicts inherent in the capital-labour relationship by shifting the focus of working-class concerns from issues of production to those of consumption — from the workplace to the home.

It may also serve the 'false' function of providing a temporary outlet, in speculative as distinct from productive investment, for capital over-accumulated elsewhere — in what Harvey (1981 and 1982) terms the 'primary circuit' of capital (industrial production) or in other sectors of the built environment or 'secondary circuit' (for example, commercial property).

The progress of housing production and consumption in Australia in the post-1945 economic boom reflected the imperatives of these functions, as well as the shifts in class formation over the period — the post-war baby boom, the waves of overseas migration, increases in real wages, etc. Four aspects of the progress warrant comment.

The investment boom and the triumph of the owner-occupiers

The advance towards universal home-ownership — the elusive myth of 'a property-owning democracy' — seemed spectacularly sustained. In 1947 some 40 per cent of Sydney households had been owner-occupiers, and by 1971 it was 66 per cent; in Melbourne the shift was from 46 per cent to 70 per cent. More significantly, by the 1970s around 90 per cent of households with married heads (that is, couples, families) had achieved owner-occupancy by the time the head was in his forties (ABS 1979).

The prospect of home-ownership had been crucial in sustaining requisite demand necessary for the expansion of profitable investment in housing in the 1950s and 1960s. Enabling that investment had been the increases in real wages (relative to inflation, average earnings by 1973 were 1.74 times their level of 1953) and, especially, artificially low interest rates on housing loans to owner-occupiers (but not to investors in rental stock). The role of interest rates has at times been complex: in the immediate post-war years the Federally-planned investment boom in housing failed to materialise until, in 1949, inflation rose substantially above the prevailing housing interest rates simultaneously with the removal of some war-time controls; prices for existing houses rose dramatically (in Melbourne by an estimated 28 per cent in 1949, and 48 per cent in 1950), as purchasers were effectively paid to borrow; profit margins for new production rose accordingly, investment was switched into the housing sector, and the golden age had begun.

The advance of suburbia

Lending was directed mainly towards purchasers of new detached houses on allotments of around 0.1 hectare, generally in newly-developing suburbs. With the increasing availability of cars in the 1950s and 1960s, and falling motoring costs relative to wages, new submarkets could be profitably developed beyond the old radial public transport systems that had previously structured the cities. The effect of suburban expansion — and of larger and better-designed houses — was to trigger demand for building materials, cars, white-goods, furnishings, energy, etc., and thereby to guarantee the domestic markets essential to the industrial expansion of the 1950s and 1960s.

By the 1960s, the children of the post-war baby boom were entering the workforce in a period of rapidly-rising youth wages; household formation rates were historically very high, and the result was unprecedented opportunities for new investment in flats, generally in *inner* suburbs (much of whose old, existing dwelling stock had been fortuitously devalued through the lending policies of previous decades). It is worth noting Hugo's (1979) observation that the number of households with heads aged *under twenty-five years* increased by an average 9.7 per cent per annum between 1961 and 1966 in Australia, rising to 10.6 per cent per annum between 1966 and 1971. Subsequently the rate fell to around 2 per cent annually between 1971 and 1976, and the flats boom ended. Its place however was taken by a quite extraordinary boom in new house construction—so the very large body of households with heads *twenty-five to thirty-four years* increased by nearly 6 per cent annually between 1966 and 1971, and by around 4.4 per cent from 1971 to 1976, before that boom too ended.

Residential differentiation and relative disadvantage

In common with most communities in most countries, the distribution of the population to the dwelling stock in Australian cities is very differentiated in terms of socio-economic status (and, by implication, social class), household structure and ethnic composition. Harvey (1975) has argued that this internal differentiation provides a system of 'distinctive milieus for social interaction from which individuals to a considerable degree derive their values, expectations, consumption habits, market capacities and states of consciousness' (1975:362), that the differentiation is thereby crucial to the reproduction of requisite variety in the population and of the social relationships between classes, and that it is largely instrumental in structuring social mobility. Differentiated neighbourhoods also provide the focus for 'community consciousness' and community-based political action, which increasingly replaces 'class consciousness' as the locus of social conflict (1975:364–5). With the rapid expansion of the Australian cities, the less-rapid departure of once-resident doctors, lawyers, school teachers and the like from working-class suburbs, and the quite slowly increasing concentration of the ownership of capital (other than housing capital), residential differentiation and its concomitant spatial inequalities increased.

Besides its role in structuring consumption and reproduction and in re-focusing social conflict, Harvey (1974) argues that residential differentiation serves a further crucial function, in structuring geographically distinctive housing submarkets. These provide the opportunity for differential, and uneven, investment and disinvestment in housing, and so for the extraction of what Harvey terms class-monopoly rent — the rent where a class of owners are willing to release the resources under their control 'only if they receive a positive return above some arbitrary level' (1974:241; see also, N. Smith 1982). Class-monopoly rent is probably best seen as a case of 'monopoly rent', in Marx's classification of ground rent (to which we shall subsequently return).

So residential differentiation can be seen as necessary to the realisation of monopoly rents; monopoly rent provides the necessary incentive structure for the urbanisation process to proceed; and many aspects of community conflict in an urban society are to be interpreted as a manifestation of class struggle — between classes of providers and classes of consumers — around the realisation of monopoly rent. Clearly the lending practices of the 1950s and 1960s, favouring some submarkets over others, were significant in this process; so was urban planning with its enthusiastic adoption of zoning to fragment residential areas, and green belts and other practices to maintain relative scarcity and hence requisite profit margins.

The role of public policy

Four areas of public policy were especially instrumental in this progress of housing production and consumption (and segregation) in the 1950s and 1960s. First, monetary policy was used explicitly to encourage home-ownership, more circumspectly to control the level of investment in owner-occupied housing as a Keynesian counter-cyclical economic regulator; the principal device was central-bank controls over savings-bank mortgage interest rates. By the end of the 1960s the low-interest-rate policy was failing however.

Second, taxation policy favoured investment in owner-occupied housing. Since 1923 there has been no tax on the imputed rent from owner-occupier housing capital in Australia; whereas renters pay for their housing from their post-tax income, owner occupiers pay from their *pre*-tax income for that component of their housing represented by their own equity in the dwelling (it is paid of course in the form of foregone interest on their invested capital). For the component represented by *borrowed* capital, they pay mortgage interest, and this certainly does come from post-tax income. This advantage to owner-occupiers was relatively unimportant while marginal tax rates were low; however, like interest rates, these also rose during the 1950s and 1960s; in 1949–50 the marginal tax rate for male average earnings was 15 per cent, by 1959–60 it was 20.6 per cent and by 1969–70, 32.9 per cent.

Third, there has been a substantial programme of Federally-funded, State-administered housing assistance since 1945. The first Commonwealth-State Housing Agreement (CSHA), in 1945, was intended to produce a public rental sector whose low rents — suppressed by the device of publicly-subsidised, long-term (fifty-three years) financing—could ultimately undermine an allegedly extortionate private-rental sector. (It was an era when most Australian households were renters.) The purity of the plan was relaxed in 1951, then in 1956 abandoned for the orthodoxy of an emphasis on assistance to lower-income *purchasers*. Subsequent CSHAs maintained the orthodoxy; in 1964 assistance was extended more generally to first-home buyers, through a Home Savings Grant Scheme; and from that time, the only significant unassisted group has been private-sector renters (revealed in the 1975 Poverty Inquiry to be the poorest group in the community).

Finally there has been land use planning, and investment in social infrastructure—transport services, education facilities, public utilities, etc.—fragmenting housing markets, supporting the production of inequalities between the resulting submarkets, and maintaining requisite scarcity.

Global crisis and housing crisis, 1973–80s

The economic boom of the 1950s and 1960s was 'global', in that it occurred in all the advanced capitalist societies. Also global was the over-accumulation that accompanied it—capital accumulated in the primary circuit (that is, industrial production) faced declining opportunities for its profitable investment in that circuit. Australian resources developments were suddenly attractive to the new Eurodollars market, as well as to domestic capital, and so the 1960s minerals boom was under way, reaching its apotheosis in the Poseidon adventure and debacle of 1968. Thence, from 1969, speculative capital increasingly chased commercial property, and the Australian property boom had begun, effectively ending—also in some chaos—in 1973 (Daly, 1982; Chapter 19 in this volume).

Somewhat lagging the boom of speculative investment in commercial property came one of speculation in land for housing development. A number of factors were involved in this switching of capital to the housing sector. First, from 1967 there was the burgeoning of demand for new houses in new suburbs, attributable partly to the post-war baby boom and partly to the suburbanisation of the migrants of the 1950s and 1960s, and referred to previously. In 1972–73 there were some 170 500 dwelling commencements in Australia—double the number of ten years previously. Growth in demand for new land seemed limitless, so did opportunities for speculation; the banks, insurance companies and finance companies lent generously for land speculation, and many also engaged in it directly.

Second, from 1973 until 1977 the speculation was fuelled and profits underpinned by State investment, ostensibly to create a land bank with which to suppress prices, but in fact mismanaged and corrupted, especially in Victoria (Troy 1978; Sandercock 1979; 1983*c*).

Third, with the onset of high interest rates in the early 1970s and therefore high holding charges, many speculators and developers began to falter during 1973; prospects looked better in the first half of 1974, but then began the collapses and receiverships. From around 1973, borrowing conditions for households were increasingly liberalised to enable them to purchase the over-supplied land and houses: the financial institutions, especially the banks, attempted a series of rapid rescues by shifting debts from shaky—and uninsureable—firms (often their own subsidiaries!) to households whose mortgages would be insureable. The main liberalisations were acceptance of a household's second income, or even the promise of *future* income, in determining ability to repay a housing loan.

Fourth, the ultimate enticement to purchase was the negative *real* interest rates from 1973; in that year, although savings-bank interest on first-mortgage housing loans was 7.75 per cent, the rate of inflation measured by the consumer price index (CPI) was 9.4 per cent, so the real interest rate was minus 1.65 per cent. In 1974 it was minus 4.6 per cent, then minus 6.1 per cent in 1975, minus 5.0 per cent in 1976 and minus 1.8 per cent in 1977. Thereafter they were positive again.

A consequence of the switching of capital to the housing sector—and a necessary condition for its continuation—was rapid escalation in the price of residential allotments, especially in the major cities. In Sydney, median land prices rose 218 per cent between January 1968 and January 1974, from $5810 to $18 500; in Melbourne the rise was 238 per cent, from $3850 to $13 000 (Australian Department of Urban and Regional Development 1974). Consumer prices generally rose 51 per cent over that period. House prices—more correctly, house-and-land prices—likewise boomed; in Sydney the most dramatic increases began in 1972, in Melbourne a year later. The estimated mean rate of house-price increase in Melbourne was 26 per cent in 1973 and 31 per cent in 1974; it continued generally ahead of inflation in 1975, 1976 and 1977, and thereafter *fell* relative to inflation. Over the five years from the end of 1972 to the end of 1977, the mean rate of house-price increase in Melbourne was 153 per cent, whereas the increase in consumer prices was 86 per cent. However over the next five years, from the end of 1977 to 1982, the rate of house price increase was 29 per cent against an increase in consumer prices of 55 per cent.

The social consequences of these extraordinary events were unprecedented and quite catastrophic; four aspects of them especially warrant discussion.

Affordability crisis

The savings banks have been the major lenders for owner-occupier housing in Australia, and on the basis of their conditions we can estimate an 'affordable' house price for any year, as the price that could be paid for a dwelling by a household on a single income equal to male average earnings, borrowing at prevailing savings-bank interest rates, with the loan limited so that repayments computed on monthly rests over a twenty-five year term would not exceed 20 per cent of pre-tax income and the total loan would not exceed 80 per cent of the value of the property (with the remaining 20 per cent 'deposit' together with transaction charges covered from the household's savings). Such an 'average' household purchasing in such an 'average' way could historically have afforded around 70 per cent of Melbourne's houses sold in each year, and a somewhat higher proportion of its flats (estimated from the individual property records of the Victorian Valuer-General's Office). Certainly there were disruptions but they were usually short-lived and the previous 'equilibrium' restored: after the 1930s Depression by rising wages, lower interest rates and stagnating house prices; after the extraordinary house-price boom of 1949 and 1950 (when the proportion of affordable dwellings fell to an estimated 56 per cent), by the wage inflation of 1951 and 1952; after monetary policy restrictions of 1961, by a drop in house prices in 1962. In that context, the price rises of 1973 and 1974, coinciding with high nominal interest rates (though apparently triggered by negative *real* rates), must be deemed catastrophic—in 1973, affordability fell to 40 per cent and in 1974 to 14 per cent. Further, the effect on affordability seems to have been permanent—although the affordable proportion of houses sold in 1980 had risen to 34 per cent, by 1982 it had fallen again to 18 per cent.

If we alter the above assumption of 'affordability' to consider the situation of a two-income household (specifically by augmenting the borrowed capital by an assumed second-mortgage loan over five years, serviced by a spouse's income with repayments equal to 50 per cent of average earnings), then we find that the proportions of dwellings affordable after 1974 are closer to the longer-term 'equilibrium' levels. It is certainly significant that, between the 1976 and 1981 Censuses, owner-occupancy in Melbourne actually increased (from 69.6 to 70.9 per cent); so, presumably, did the dependence on two incomes.

The conclusions to be drawn from this are:

- first, that Melbourne (and Sydney) house prices in 1973 and 1974 simply rose to soak up the additional capital suddenly switched into home purchase, through the device of lenders redefining the borrowing capacity of households, apparently with the objective of resolving a crisis of over-investment by firms in new land and housing;
- second, that the lenders did *not* thereafter return to the previous definition of borrowing capacity.

The paradox is that after 1977 house prices fell relative to inflation, but affordability did not return to the old equilibrium position.

Disinvestment crisis

The substantial rises in house prices relative to inflation during the 1950s, 1960s and 1970s (and the less substantial rises in flat prices) provided the incentive for considerable investment in rental housing —which in turn further fed the price rises! *Over*-investment tended to suppress rents, though this seemed to matter little—in the Australian taxation system, a landlord's rental income was taxed but not his capital gains, so that rents did not *need* to rise precisely because house prices did rise. So in Melbourne, for example, advertised house rents relative to male average earnings fell from 39 per cent in 1972 to 32 per cent in 1977; for flats the fall was from 25 to 20 per cent.

With the market stagnation after 1977 and the consequent end of capital gains *generally* (though not, as we shall see, in all submarkets), the incentive to rental investment also ended. Disinvestment was manifested in a number of ways. New production, which had peaked nationally at 170 500 commencements in 1972–73, slumped to around 119 000 by the end of the decade; more significantly, output of flats and other medium-density dwellings halved from 48 000 in 1972–73 to 24 400 in 1978–79; and both rental investment and demographic factors (the decline in household formation previously attributable to the post-war baby boom) were instrumental in the slump. Both new and existing blocks of flats were increasingly subdivided in ownership by the device of 'strata titling', thereby facilitating their sale for owner-occupancy, or for more 'portable', short-term investment. (Rental housing investment was increasingly affected by the volatility developing in capital markets both globally and locally in the late-1970s, with the growing demand for short-term, often quite speculative, investment. Certainly strata-titling facilitated portability, though the uncertainty of capital gains after 1977 seriously reduced the attraction of housing even as a medium-term investment.) The private-rental sector became extraordinarily tight, with the vacancy rate (that is, the proportion of dwellings vacant) virtually disappearing, and (in Melbourne) rents finally rising relative to average earnings after 1977. Changes to residential tenancy laws in a number of States, to 'improve' the situation of renters *vis-a-vis* that of their landlords (see Berry 1983*c*) only compounded the problem.

Welfare housing crisis

The increasing effect of the affordability crisis in excluding lower-income households from owner-occupancy, and the tightening rental market, led, in the late-1970s, to a dramatic lengthening of waiting lists in the relatively small public-rental sector (in 1981 it accommodated 4.9 per cent of households nationally). Further, the waiting lists were increasingly dominated by statutory-income recipients, and especially by lone-parent families; 'public housing' increasingly became 'welfare housing'.

Residential differentiation, and redistribution crisis

The overall devaluation of housing capital in Melbourne after 1977, reflected in the average rate of house-price increase being substantially below the rate of more general inflation, was far from uniform in its effects on the differentiated submarkets of the city. Whereas the average rate for the market as a whole was 29 per cent over the five years from the end of 1977 to the end of 1982 (against a 55 per cent rise in consumer prices generally), in the outer-bayside municipalities it was 23 per cent, in the outer north, 19 per cent and in the outer west, 16 per cent. By contrast, in the generally affluent, middle-class suburbs of the middle-ring east (Hawthorn, Kew, Malvern, Camberwell), the mean price rise was 82 per cent; and in the equally favoured middle-ring bayside (Brighton, Sandringham), it was 94 per cent. Certainly there had been differential shifts in house prices previously. Over the fifteen years from the end of 1962 to the end of 1977, for example, the mean metropolitan increase was 461 per cent, but consistently higher was that in the gentrifying inner city, the favoured middle-ring east, the outer north-east (at the boom of the middle-class escape from the city), the outer bayside (making its fall from grace after 1977 all the more significant), and the middle-ring north (possibly reflecting the role of Southern European migrants in regenerating the stock). These shifts however were nowhere near as dramatic as those following 1977.

These more recent changes would seem to represent first, the general devaluation of housing capital mentioned above, second, a refocusing of attention *away* from the previously favoured outskirts of the city, especially in the north-east and outer bayside, and third, a re-focusing *towards* the higher status middle-ring east, the middle-ring south and the middle-ring bayside. It is important to see these re-evaluations in the light of the expansion of unemployment (to around 11 per cent of the workforce by 1981, in some parts of the city), of the affordability crisis affecting the vast proportion of the population on average earnings or worse, but also of the expansion of the professional workforce (among males, from 9.4 per cent of the metropolitan workforce in 1966 to 13.7 per cent in 1981) and the consequent competition from that expanding class for the residential milieus traditionally seen as most effectively guaranteeing their reproduction. Shifts in class formation underlay the creation of significant new opportunities for profitable investment in housing (and, as we shall see, urban planning practice underpinned the submarket structure necessary for the realisation of those opportunities).

The post-1977 price shifts had two crucially-important consequences. First they accelerated the relegation of lower-income groups from the previously somewhat heterogeneous inner and middle-ring east, south and bayside suburbs. The working-class submarkets in these areas had generally been characterised by pockets of smaller dwellings, frequently Victorian, and by the 1950s fairly delapidated. They supplied cheap housing opportunities for (mainly Southern European) migrants in the 1950s and 1960s; but by the 1960s, with the expansion of the professional and managerial groups, they were also gentrifying. The differential price changes after 1977 added compulsion to the process. Whereas in 1972 some 61 per cent of houses sold in the metropolitan area as a whole would have been affordable (using the previous definition of affordability), by 1982 the proportion was 18 per cent; but in the inner suburbs the decline was from 72 per cent to 15 per cent, in the middle-ring south from 55 per cent to zero, in the middle-ring east 40 per cent to zero, and in the middle-ring bayside from 60 per cent to zero. The working class had lost its traditional milieus and submarkets, and Melbourne—like Sydney and Adelaide—was effectively turning inside-out.

The second effect of the price shifts was to redistribute wealth; two examples will illustrate the scale of the redistribution. Devaluation in the separate house submarkets of the outer-bayside Mordialloc, Chelsea, Frankston and Mornington municipalities, from 1978 to 1982, imposed total capital losses estimated at $895 million (in 1982 dollars), or around $21 300 per dwelling. On the other hand, revaluation in the separate house submarkets of *middle-ring* bayside Brighton and Sandringham, over the same period, bestowed estimated capital gains of $443 million, or some $23 100 per dwelling.

A strong case is to be made for the argument that the urban housing market is the principal mechanism for the redistribution of wealth in Australia—it is certainly so in Melbourne. The main redistributions are from renters to landlords and, especially since 1977, from generally working-class owner-occupiers in less convenient, working-class suburbs to generally more affluent owner-occupiers in inner or more traditionally middle-class areas.

The failure of housing policy

To understand something of these extraordinary market shifts since 1973—hence something of the causes and effects of the housing crisis as a local manifestation of the 'second global crisis of capitalism' (Harvey 1981)—it is useful first to understand the conceptually-distinct components of house price, and to explore the conditions necessary to support these components. What 'causes' prices to rise or fall?

The Marxian argument is that 'ground rent' can have three components (and, of course, house price is simply the capitalisation of improved ground rent) (Harvey 1982:330–72; Saunders 1981:234–7;

Badcock 1984:80–4). *Absolute rent* arises from the ability of landowners as a class to extract rent from even the most marginal of land; landowners can withhold some of the more fertile land from productive use, and all rents in a particular region or submarket can thereby be jacked up. *Differential rent* derives from the greater profits flowing from lower production costs associated with more fertile and better-located land (with lower transport costs), when compared with those of the most marginal land. It can take two forms: it can arise from some relatively permanent feature (say, better accessibility), or alternatively from the differential application of capital (fertiliser on rural land, house improvements on urban). It should be obvious that the second form tends to transform into the first. Finally, *monopoly rent* is extracted when a producer holds some monopoly position that enables excessive profits; the excess is simply creamed off as a monopoly rent, and excessive profits reduced to average profits.

The house-price booms of 1949–50 and 1973–74 in Melbourne represent increases in ground rent that were *general* across the urban housing market, and not restricted to specific submarkets. It seems, therefore, that they must be conceptualised as shifts in absolute rent (they are certainly not to be seen as changes in monopoly or differential rent).

There were however, significant differences between these two events. The 1949–50 boom had the effect of increasing speculator-developers' profits from investment in housing and hence the incentive to invest in new housing production; it thereby created the conditions for enhanced consumption of other production from industrial capital, resolving a crisis ultimately located in the area of consumption. In 1973–74, on the other hand, the shift in absolute rent may be seen as somewhat incidental to the resolution of a crisis immediately located in consumption (excess housing production had to be exchanged and consumed) and ultimately in over-accumulation in the global economy (with consequent speculative over-investment in the Australian urban housing and land markets). The price rises were more an outcome of a mechanism—for transferring debts from speculator-developers to consumers and for soaking up excess capital—than they were an integral part of the mechanism. In 1949–50 they *were* integral to the mechanism. Also, in contrast to the earlier case, the effects of the price rises in Sydney and Melbourne were somewhat catastrophic. The first was to postpone the inevitable devaluation of housing capital, and to transfer its effects from some firms to most households—from speculator-developers to 'speculator-consumers'! Second, they triggered the new local crisis in distribution and consumption of housing, manifesting itself in the persisting problems of affordability and disinvestment from rental housing. Third, higher current housing costs eroded households' discretionary income, and hence demand for other goods and services, *including manufacturing output*. The institutions of finance capital had significantly redistributed consumer demand, in contradiction with their own longer-term interests. And fourth, because absolute rent had been pushed to an apparent affordability barrier, the opportunity to use shifts in absolute rent to provide outlets for over-accumulated finance capital had been significantly impaired, if not destroyed.

This last consequence is crucially important. Housing policy, as a Keynesian counter-cyclical regulator, was by the 1980s in some difficulty. No doubt, new demand (and higher prices and profit margins) could be triggered by suppressing interest rates on borrowings, as in the 1950s and 1960s; but in the post-1983 regime of finance market de-regulation, such a reversion is scarcely feasible. More direct subsidies are possible, of course, and had indeed been used in the Fraser Coalition government's scheme for tax deductibility of mortgage-interest payments in 1982, and in the Hawke Labor government's system of grants to first-home buyers in 1983. Each of these had observable effects on demand and on prices overall (therefore on absolute rent), with consequential benefits to existing owners and incentives to new investment. However all such schemes ultimately confront 'the fiscal crisis of the state' (J. O'Connor 1973). Likewise, governments can increase direct expenditures on new welfare housing programmes (as was done by newly-elected Labor governments in New South Wales in the latter 1970s, in Victoria in 1982, and Federally in 1983); these are *not* likely to have effects on absolute rents, and so their benefits can probably be contained to their intended recipients; but like the less-targetted subsidies, they too confront the apparently increasing fiscal constraints on state action.

Ultimately then, the tinkerings of housing policy are ineffectual; absolute rent has been pushed to an affordability barrier, and no solution to the housing crisis is feasible prior to the devaluation of fixed capital in housing that would represent a significant reduction in absolute rent. And while that devaluation proceeds — slowly, so it seems from the evidence of the early 1980s — the ability of the housing sector (of the secondary circuit of capital) to provide an outlet for capital over-accumulated in the primary circuit, is severely constrained.

The success of planning practice

Clearly, however, this constraint is not total. As we have seen, the post-1977 devaluation was decidedly uneven, and judicious investment — in submarkets where values were appreciating rather than depreciating — could have paid handsomely. As an example, if a landlord had invested in inner-suburban flats in Melbourne at the end of 1977, with 10 per cent equity in the properties and the rest borrowed at trading-bank terms, and if he had received an average rental and used 'negative gearing' to offset current-account losses against other income for tax purposes, and if he were taxed at the marginal rate for twice male average earnings, his capital gains would still have yielded him an average net return, during the next five years, of 19 per cent per annum *over inflation*—certainly less than the 39 per cent obtainable in the same submarket in the previous five years, but better than the 5 per cent per annum *below* the rate of inflation available from similar investment in the rental flat market in the outer suburbs!

It seems that the extraordinarily differentiated shifts in prices and rates of return after 1977 are to be conceptualised as shifts in monopoly rent (or class-monopoly rent as theorised in Harvey 1974, and described previously). And it seems that urban planning practice has been crucial in maintaining the differentiation of submarkets, in guaranteeing boundaries and requisite scarcity in some submarkets, and in ensuring controlled expansion of others where the invasions create new opportunities for speculator-developers. A single example can illustrate the innovatory skill of the planners. Amendment 224 to the Melbourne Metropolitan Planning Scheme, in 1983, introduced a system of urban conservation areas fragmenting the old, historic inner suburbs into:

- designated areas where conservation controls could ensure protection from deleterious intrusions, enhance amenity, stimulate further gentrification by the expanding professional and managerial classes, and hence enable monopoly rent to be extracted;
- a reduced range of areas where commercial and higher-density residential investment would be channelled, again facilitating monopoly rent.

So everyone benefits, except lower-income renters whose domain those suburbs have traditionally been.

As the realisation of absolute rent seems to be dependent on the support of finance capital and of the monetary and fiscal policies that comprise 'housing' policy in Australia, so is the extraction of monopoly rent apparently dependent on the residential differentiation of the city and on the urban planning practice that supports it. Indeed it could be argued that to support the creation and sustaining of housing submarkets is the essential role of urban planning practice in a market economy, and that in a crisis of housing affordability and disinvestment, that role becomes crucially important to the requisite switching of investment between the primary and the secondary circuits of capital, and so to economic growth and expansion. However the role also highlights the fundamental contradiction between planning ideology (to do with social equity, participatory democracy, etc.) and planning practice (directed to the necessary conditions for capitalist investment).

Resolutions

An attempt to resolve these contradictions inhering in housing policy and planning practice must be left to another paper. Let it suffice to say that it needs to address:

- the taxation system that sustains the present inequalities of payment for housing use;
- the gross spatial inequalities in social investment that underlie unequal life-prospects and the present residential differentiation of the city;
- the housing-related constraints on production in the household sector, especially by the under-employed, and thereby on transformations in the mode of production, exchange, consumption and reproduction.

Chapter 19
Speculators and the games people play

Maurie Daly

Capitalism is an insidious disease, and the distinction between activities which are considered useful, normal, or even honourable, and those which are in some way reprehensible, is often one of degree rather than of kind. The question of land speculation falls into this category. Speculators were universally condemned during the 1973 land boom, yet they acted according to the same logic which made a person choose a finance company debenture or a building-society share over a savings-bank account. John Paterson (1974:31) wrote in 1974 that 'it would be quite incorrect to suggest that speculative activity was the sole or even the principal cause of the rise in residential values over the past few years, but speculative holders have profited hugely'. The corporate activities of finance institutions and developers, the macro-economic policies of governments, the effects of bad or inadequate planning, the impact of servicing costs, the increase of population and wealth: these were the ultimate sources of the increases in land prices, and speculators were beneficiaries of the process. Speculators became particularly significant at the peak of the boom, in 1973 and 1974, and their activities sharply accelerated the general trend of rising prices. One of the social consequences of speculator's activities was to help push prices beyond the reach of young people and poor people, but they acted according to the logic of capitalism, and capitalism does not have a social conscience. According to that logic, the high profits of speculators from land dealings were accompanied by higher levels of risk and, for the vengeful, the crash of 1974 apportioned losses to speculators in accordance with the risks they had taken. By then, however, the damage to city and community had been done.

The speculators in property were simply reacting to the accepted beliefs about what were reasonable investments in the early 1970s. The gospel of *Phillip's Sensible Talk to Those in Search of Wealth* received an enthusiastic, evangelical revival some eighty-seven years after its publication. There were modern counterparts where it was proclaimed that 'fabulous wealth is possible from sound Real Estate investment, and is available even to those with the most modest savings'. Land values had been rising consistently in Australia since Sydney Cove was first discovered. 'There is no ceiling to Real Estate

Based on Daly, M. (1982) Chapter 4 in *Sydney Boom, Sydney Bust*, and published here by kind permission of George Allen & Unwin

Values. It is a story not often told but incredible in its unlimited potential for accumulating wealth' (Johnson 1970). As inflation reached 12 per cent in 1973, Drayman and Associates gave the sound advice of letting 'inflation work for you. Land can be reserved today at a fixed price and be purchased in the future when you know positively how much profit you can make' (*Australian Financial Review* 1973). In 1974, the year of the crash, a property reporter affirmed that 'of all the investment opportunities, including Commonwealth Bonds and BHP shares, nothing could be a safer investment than property' (*Australian Financial Review* 1974*a*). Land values had been increasing more rapidly than wages, profits and the general cost of living.

The distorting effect of such preaching infected almost all groups in society. Two professional groups in particular, accountants and valuers, stood in a bad light at the end of the boom. One particular aspect affecting both development and finance companies was the proper evaluation of the worth of the properties held. The discrepancies between the book values and the realisable values of property of the failed companies was so great as to cast severe doubts on the competence of the profession which was ultimately responsible: the valuers.

In 1974, in his report to the General Council of the Valuers Association, the President of the Association stated: 'the services of the professional valuer have never been needed more by the public' because of inflation, unprecedented activity in the real-estate market, and new legislation which had been introduced to control land use (*The Valuer* 1974). The plea came too late. By 1974 valuers had failed the public. This is not to assert that all or even most valuers were negligent, but sufficient anomalies did exist for them to receive some of the blame for the runaway prices.

Consulting valuers played a key role because financiers generally used their valuations to judge the merit of prospective loans; very few finance companies had a valuing staff of their own. Those active in developing or selling land always knew the 'right' valuer to get the valuation they required, and they were adroit at playing valuers off against each other to obtain a satisfactory valuation. Stories of 'soft' valuations and contradictory valuations were legion, but difficult to document. Two examples given by Corbett in Brisbane give sufficient indication of the general trend (*The Developer* 1974). A piece of real estate thirteen kilometres from Brisbane was valued by one firm of valuers at $730 000; the same plot was estimated, a few months later, to be worth $2.9 million, although there had been no development of the land nor any zoning change. Corbett's second example referred to two valuations of the same Brisbane land made on the same day; one valuer priced the land at $3 million and the other at $1.5 million.

The ability of companies and individuals to manipulate valuations was quickly realised and used, in the first place by operators who wanted to make full use of the liberal flow of funds coming out of the finance houses, and who were pressed by competitors into accepting the high selling prices of the vendors. Financiers were equally guilty in not investigating such deals properly. Second, companies undertook fairly frequent revaluations of their stocks of land to raise the book values of their assets, thus helping to boost share prices, to attract debenture capital, or to effect easier loans for new projects. Third, dealers used the weak valuation system, and the indiscriminate pursuit of larger shares of the market by the financiers, to expand their operations as cheaply as possible. The weakness was that many valuations were based on the last, and silliest, sale rather than on the prospective return on funds.

A single developer could easily lever up the price of properties in a area simply by purchasing several of them. Each new sale would push the price of land higher, but because the activity of the developer was usually taken as a sign of competence, he would have no problem in finding the finance for each new venture, and the terms on which he borrowed would improve with smaller deposits and lower interest rates. Some developers found that they could then have their original property revalued at a much higher price, obtaining a refinancing deal which effectively meant that they obtained 100 or 120 per cent finance. Using the weak valuation system and playing off one finance company against another, such a 'developer' could expand into a substantial property owner on the slimmest of capital bases. At the end of the boom finance companies were embarrassed to discover how several companies might be thus owed large sums of money by the one operator who had no prospect of repaying his loans.

By 1973 valuers seemed to have little to fear in adopting recent sales as the real basis of their valuations because prices had persisted in steep upward climb for five or six years, and both clients and financiers appeared to be satisfied with the system. As well, the valuers worked on a commission basis and higher valuations certainly did not reduce their take-home pay.

Some valuers, and it was probably only a very small proportion of the profession, were ingenuous in their valuations, but the real blame lay with the individuals and companies who used and manipulated their results. Corporate chicanery became a feature of the boom years. Finance companies, for example, set up development companies in which they had less than a 50 per cent interest and whose operations never appeared in their consolidated results. The remaining interest might be held by a nominee company whose ownership and origins would be untraceable. There might in fact be several companies set up to help shift money, land or options to generate the greatest profit, and neither through the names of the companies, nor the shareholdings (which would be changed frequently), nor the directorship (which would also change often) could any association with a finance company or a developer be discovered. The company might take an option over land which had a relatively low valuation by putting down a deposit borrowed from the finance company at low interest rates. Elaborate plans for the development of the land, zoning changes acquired through bribery and other forms of inducement, and soft valuations would be employed to push up the value of the land. The option might then be sold at a handsome profit, or perhaps exercised and the land itself would be resold profitably (*Australian Financial Review* 1974*b*).

There were numerous variations on the theme. If a property was put up for sale for $200 000, an Australian company with an associated office in Port Vila might have taken out an option on the land for $2000. The Vila Company might then have sold the option to an associated company in Britain, America, Switzerland, or even Australia, but the associations would not be obvious or even traceable. If the option were sold for one million dollars and development costs came to $1.2 million, the company could avoid taxes and effectively write off the development costs.

Other profit-raising ventures were possible without resorting to the exotica of overseas tax havens. Companies were sometimes fleeced by their own employees or even their own directors. Some employees bought up parcels of land in a particular area through dummy companies and then, using all the tricks of valuation, would bring the fact of rising prices in that area to the notice of the employers. The development company might then purchase the land from the dummy companies. There were instances of the directors of one of the largest developer-finance companies in Australia (now defunct) employing the same methods to retail land to their own companies, and in the process to enlarge their personal fortunes.

Another method of boosting sales, and the price of land, was for an agent or a company to sell a parcel of land to a buyer at a specified price, and to guarantee its resale within a nominated period for a specified minimum profit. The process could be repeated several times as very large areas were progressively broken down into smaller blocks, the guaranteed price emerging out of the added value placed on smaller lots and the upward trend in values generated by the number of sales. One of the largest developers in eastern Australia guaranteed their clients an increase of 150 per cent in the value of their land over four years.

The recycling of sales by companies or their representatives descended to the level of the individual lot. Salesmen for development companies formed their own dummy companies to which they signed over a proportion of an estate before the land went to the market. If there was interest in those lots at the sale, the salesman would confess that the desired blocks were sold, would promise to try and renegotiate a further sale in the interest of the inquiring party, but naturally at a higher price. Several settlements would then take place on the same day with the salesman, via his dummy company, reaping the immediate, forced profits.

Flabby valuations, unprincipled individuals and weak corporate laws were unnecessary, but expected, forces on top of the inflationary pressures of the system itself. It did not stop there, because government at both State and local levels became involved. Allegations concerning the associations of members of the Askin government, and specific attacks on members of the Queensland and Victorian governments were made about land dealings, bribery, and decisions made in developers' favour (*Australian Financial Review* 1979). Stories about corruption at the level of local government were commonplace, but difficult to substantiate. Allegations extended all the way up from building inspectors who gave certain clients special consideration, to engineers and town planners who approved suspect plans or rezoning, to councillors who at times sat as representatives of specific business interests (Sandercock 1977:41).

Legislation was gradually introduced to try to combat some of the practices carried out by unscrupulous land dealers. In 1964, the Land Vendors Act was introduced to counter problems arising out of term sales of land. Prior to the Act, vendors could sell land on extended terms with the purchaser receiving the title only after all payments had been made. Dishonest developers could abscond with their money after payments had been made and the purchaser could not get ownership of their land; the extent of one such scandal in Yagoona prompted the legislation. The new Act was only partly successful. It deprived developers of useful working capital, and to get around its restrictions many developers set up a financial arm, or formed an association with a financier, so that the usual 10 per cent deposit became part of a loan from a finance company to be paid off over several years.

The Land Vendors Act of 1964 prohibited term sales of land in a subdivision of five or more lots unless the linen plan of subdivision had been approved by council and a trustee appointed. During the boom, much land was pre-sold prior to a developer's receiving approval. The developer would accept deposits from buyers even though it might be from six months to two years before approval was granted. This helped the developer build up working capital but it also opened the door to speculators. Because of the requirements imposed by councils on the Registrar-General, the purchaser at times found that the lot he gained title to was not the lot he had originally seen, and often the time taken to gain approval was so great that it caused financial loss and inconvenience. If the developer failed to complete the subdivision, the buyer ran the risk of losing his deposit, and the crash of 1974 saw many in that situation. Some developers mortgaged their lands, and if the mortgagor had exercised its power of sale before the purchaser had completed the final payment, he or she would forfeit their interest in the land. Buyers found that the simple term 'contract' could assume many different guises, and in situations where the vendor's solicitor was used to set up the contract, the vendor sometimes found that the contract afforded no protection.

When the 10 per cent deposit had been paid, some contracts provided the vendor or purchaser the right to withdraw unless the plan of subdivision was approved by council within eighteen months of the date of contract. Developers therefore could use the deposited money for eighteen months, make no real approaches to council and simply refund the deposits at the end of the eighteen months. In a rising market, the developer might not have wanted immediate approval and, after refunding the deposits, might have placed the land back on the market at a higher price. In both situations the developer had the use of interest-free sums of many thousands of dollars for a period.

Few of the miscreants were even brought to trial because of weakness in the law. One exception was Ruru Pty Ltd whose principals in April 1980 were charged with thirty-nine offences of making false entries and fraudulently misapplying cheques. Deposits of $240 000 had been paid on forty-five blocks of land at Doonside and the contracts of sale stated that if the purchasers did not receive their titles within twelve months the deposits would be refunded. Not one person got his block back, and no one received his deposit back, the Crown alleged.

In the turmoil of the boom, it is not surprising to find that one of the commonest complaints against developers concerned false representation and promises. Such promises usually involved matters such as the availability of sewerage or other services, or the provision of finance or title deeds. Since many were verbal promises, it was extremely difficult for purchasers to prosecute the developer or agent. One prosecution did proceed. Roger Matson was sentenced to thirteen years jail on 22 February 1980, for nineteen convictions of false pretences. Matson had received a total of $500 000 from between 500 and 600 people for worthless title deeds, and he then went into voluntary liquidation to the tune of $900 000.

Syndication was another area which became open to abuse during the boom. Syndication implied a situation where land was owned by a number of co-owners according to some mutual agreement which gave occupational rights to each individual tenant-in-common. On 22 February 1980, injunctions were made against Robert Sterling Pty Ltd under the Trade Practices Act in connection with 256 contracts for land investments made with the company; it was alleged that the buyers believed they were obtaining exclusive possession of the land when in fact they were purchasing an interest as a tenant-in-common. The company became insolvent in July 1978, and most of the investors lost all their money. Another aspect of syndication was the joining together of investors to finance speculative dealings in land or buildings. Money would be raised from the public to be invested on a syndicated basis, and the prospect of raising such money was clearly related to the assets of the companies involved. In September 1974, the Intercontinental Development Corporation Pty Ltd and the Liberty Mortgage Underwriters (ACT) Pty Ltd collapsed and a liquidator was appointed. These were syndicated companies which placed a value of $2 367 250 on their fifteen properties which included land, factories and home-units; the liquidator valued them at $1 820 850. The chairman and managing director was sentenced to fourteen years jail for fraud, and one of the directors was sentenced to twelve months periodic detention.

Another activity which became notorious because of its effects on the public was 'gazumping': a practice in which the vendor of land or a house received a number of deposits but did not enter into a binding contract with any of the depositors. Purchasers were usually lured into a false sense of security because the deposit was called a holding deposit. In fact, it had no legal status. Vendors who collected several such deposits effectively entered into an auction with a number of potential buyers. Gazumping was a product of boom conditions for land during the 1969 to 1974 period; these conditions returned with a vengence in 1979-80 when a shortage of houses and a quantity of investment money combined to push up prices. To combat the practice the New South Wales government announced in April 1980 a plan for a twenty-one-day freeze after a deposit had been paid, and during that period neither buyer nor seller would be able to withdraw from the sale.

Term sales, false promotions, syndication and gazumping were of such an order in the 1970s that the State government set up a committee 'to Consider Sharp Practices in Relation to Land Development' in 1976–77. Its report led to the tabling of the Land Sales (Amendment) Bill, 1979, designed to circumvent abuses in those areas.

Another approach to curbing the excesses of the land market was for the government to enter the market-place directly and to try to provide land on fairer, more reasonable terms. The genesis of this approach arose out of the concern of the Housing Commission of New South Wales in finding land for welfare housing. In its *Annual Report* of 1969–70 and of 1970–71, the Housing Commission had noted the 'considerable difficulty' it was having in securing adequate reserves of land. The commission established its own Land Branch and began in earnest to built up its land bank, spending $4376 million in 1970 and 1971 to acquire 382 hectares. In 1972, expenditure on unserviced land increased to $10 058 million with 2030 hectares being purchased, and in 1973 a further $21 184 million was spent to acquire 7181 hectares of land. In 1974, the commission bought 551 hectares of unserviced land for $19 051 million, but outlaid a further $14 876 million on other land acquisitions.

The Housing Commission had wide powers of resumption and, with the competition the boom created, it had to use them broadly: in 60 per cent of all purchases of raw land between 1972 and 1974. Some acquisitions of the Housing Commission were made on very favourable terms. In South Penrith in 1973, it paid $12 115 per hectare for 519.6 hectares of land at the same time as Cambridge Credit purchased the nearby 251.4 hectare St Clair estate for $29 764 per hectare. In general, however, the Housing Commission, with its late start in buying land and its restricted resources, found difficulty in competing with developers and was limited to the more marginal areas until 1974.

The crash brought an abrupt change of attitude; beleaguered developers were most anxious to off-load supplies of land to the commission but they were forced to accept lower prices. In April 1974, the Housing Commission resumed 11.7 hectares of land held by Parkes Developments. It offered Parkes $19 760 per hectare; Parkes demanded $34 580 and the matter was settled out of court for $24 983 per hectare. The commission purchased the Cambridge Credit St Clair estate for $21 867 per hectare.

Great expectations were held for the policies of land banking. The idea had a long history, going back in practical form to at least the 1920s and being adopted in Denmark, Norway, Finland, Great Britain, The Netherlands, Germany, Austria, Poland, Czechoslovakia, Switzerland, Italy, France and Spain. The idea was for the government to purchase quantities of land either to help improve housing conditions or to help control supply, and hence, the price of land. If the government land bank was sufficiently large it would remove speculative profits from the land it sold; and through economies of purchasing costs, holding costs and servicing costs it would reduce the absolute price of land. The so-called stabilised value would be much below that of the market value in a system without land banking, and the community would be thus able to recoup part of the unearned increment (Troy 1978:31). After protracted negotiations, the New South Wales government finally responded to Federal government initiatives in establishing an Urban Lands Council to receive money from the Federal government; in 1975, this provided $13.55 million for land acquisition and development. The political composition of both State and Federal governments had changed by 1976, resulting in a diminution of Federal money and the translation of the Urban Lands Council into a Lands Commission along the lines first proposed by the Federal Labor government. Between 1974 and 1976, 716 hectares of urban land were acquired at a cost of $9.22 million and by the end of 1977, 320 lots had been developed and twenty-six sold.

It is difficult to judge the effect of the Lands Commission on prices. The recession which began about 1975 and the collapse of the land boom reduced the supply of developed land in Sydney. In 1975 it was estimated that there were 12 000 vacant residential lots in Sydney but the Lands Commission estimated that the number had fallen to 9000 by mid-1978. It proposed to top up supply for the financial year 1978-79 by releasing 2100 blocks on to the market in the western areas of Campbelltown, Penrith, St Marys, Werrington and Fairfield. Blocks at Campbelltown averaged $10 500 which compared favourably to prices before the establishment of the commission and to the general level of inflation for the period. The period 1975 to 1979 was one of recession, however, and the real test of the commission's approach to the management of the urban land market will come when the recession has finished. By the end of 1980, the Lands Commission had spent $54.7 million, with the sum for land acquisitions arising from $9.3 million in 1979 to $12.3 in 1980. By 1980, the commission had purchased 11 196 hectares which would yield 15 500 lots.

In August 1985, the New South Wales commission ceased to exist as a separate entity, it was amalgamated into the Department of Housing. During the recessionary years of 1982 and 1983 there were may who blamed the sluggishness of the land market on Landcom and who suggested that the commission possessed unfair advantages over private developers. There were others who said that Landcom had failed to provide community facilities and that its activities were equivalent to those of the developers which it replaced. Landcom adopted an aggressive attitude in the market and in 1983-84 achieved record sales of 3500 lots. In 1984-85 sales fell 26 per cent while the value of stockpiled developed land grew by 137 per cent. Undeveloped holdings rose by 26 per cent so that the total value of land held by Landcom rose to $113.5 million. Total sales in 1984-85 were $57.5 million. In 1984-85 cash-in-bank deposits were reduced by a third the level of the preceeding year. The commercial nature of Landcom's position and its reliance on borrowed funds have made it operate in a manner very similar to the private development companies. Consequently, the organisation which was meant to help iron out the severe fluctuations in the supply of land has itself become victim of general market forces.

In his introduction to the report of the task force of the Australian Insitute of Urban Studies into the price of land, Professor Gates (1973:2) wrote:

> The task force did not set out to look for villians or bogey men. If it had, indeed, it may well not have found any. The trouble is not that there are bad men but that there are inadequate institutions.

Inadequate institutions there certainly were: inadequate planning to ensure a reasonable supply of land and a rapid-enough transit of development applications; inadequate control both of, and by, the finance institutions to prevent the flame of growth turning into a conflagration; inadequate accounting, management, and forward-planning by development companies; and inadequate interest, and understanding, and concern for the social consequences on the part of governments.

But Professor Gates was too kind. Such shortcomings were seized upon by men capable of devious designs and unscrupulous enough to reap their ill-gotten profits out of the lunacy of the land boom. At the end of it all the city had sprawled even further; services were even more inadequate; the young and the poor were relatively worse-off; investment funds which might have been put into production or socially useful activities had been dissipated; and millions of dollars of small investors' funds had been lost as sharks and charlatans grew rich.

Section VII:
The future

Chapter 20
Increasing urban efficiency and equity

Clive Beed

In the early chapters of *Melbourne's Development and Planning* (Beed 1981), many suggestions were mooted to increase efficiency and/or equity but which involve significant changes from existing urban organisation and which would take a long time to work themselves out. For example, it was argued that the full benefits of mass public transport, such as electric trains, trams and buses, and of walking and cycling requires radically-changed land use patterns. One of these possibilities is a restructuring of existing settlement and a linear extrusion for new settlement to generate a denser city. As another example, a denser city may be a prerequisite for overcoming some of the undesirable effects of structural unemployment. Encouraging any of these changes would require changed forms of decision-making for land use. Prevailing land use decision-making modes encourage low-density settlement. Many of the proposals to mitigate inefficiencies and inequities in the production of new residential land demand a radically-altered decision-making context. All of these policy suggestions differ dramatically from prevailing trends and few market influences can be discerned which are working in their direction.

Changing urban structure

In a general sense, the above suggestions do tie in with each other because they require a changed city form which could be achieved only by stronger public control over land use. One model of changed urban structure directed to these ends is the spatial consolidation, concentration or 'densification' of large Australian cities which is often thought to be capable of increasing efficiency. Since it is the antithesis of suburbanisation, the cost items in the balance sheet could decline (see Beed 1981:Figure 5.6).

Since settlement densities would be higher than prevailing outer-suburban norms, public-utility costs could fall. Higher densities increase the chances for public transport to compete with private transport so that total transport costs, especially social and energy costs, may go down. With the same effects, opportunities for private non-motor transport (walking and cycling) would be enhanced. If all this eventuated, less land would be consumed by transport. As higher-density buildings can be more energy-efficient than lower-density ones, built-form energy costs may abate. Since people would live and work closer together, less land would be used by buildings; more green space could be preserved, natural urban creek valleys disturbed less, more untouched landscape kept for recreation in the city, more urban forests planted.

People living, working and recreating closer together conjures up ideas of a more socially-interactive lifestyle in which some of the isolation and alienation costs of suburbanisation might be reduced. If they wanted to, people may find it easier to become more communally and politically involved. In addition, if there is a relation between urban density and the generation of service jobs, less unemployment may persist in the transition to a post-industrial economic structure. Since all of these things would be happening closer to each other, the spatial distribution of net benefits could become more equitable. To a greater degree than now, more people would be able to participate and enjoy the net benefits; no longer would car ownership be as necessary to achieve the fruits of big city life.

Of course, some of the present benefits of living in large Australian cities could diminish. For example, opportunities for living with generous private indoor and outdoor space could wane. The remainder of this chapter explores the question of whether it is possible to reduce costs through urban consolidation without restricting too severely the presently perceived benefits of low-density outer-suburban settlement.

The dual approach to changing urban structure

Moving toward a denser city need not depend only on maintaining population and socio-economic activity in the existing inner city. Density could be increased by encouraging consolidation in the outer suburbs through the development of nodes similar in character to those in the inner city. The aim of this approach would be to achieve comparable, albeit lower access benefits to those generated in the inner city, but at lower cost because the communicating population would be closer. These nodes would be developed in the already built-up area, as the Melbourne Metropolitan Board of Works (MMBW), proposed with activity centres in its 1980 Metropolitan Strategy (see also Bunker Chapter 10 in this volume).

A consolidation policy along these lines, with policy directed mainly at the outer rather than the inner suburbs was one of the four strategic alternatives put up by the MMBW in 1979–80. Since this strategy—'Suburbanised Growth'—did not direct policy at the inner city it meant 'an increased dispersal of activities from the central and inner areas' to suburban locations. Suburbanised Growth encompassed a number of variants; one was a 'strong multi-nodal city' but even this involved 'the deliberate shift of emphasis and activities away from Central Melbourne' (MMBW 1980:27). A strategy in this direction had the strength that it conformed with the trend to outer-suburban living. It would make workplaces and other services more accessible to outer-suburban population just as suburbanisation does now. The MMBW cited the Conservation of Urban Energy (CUE) group's 1979 'Cluster-and-Connect' Strategy as an example of Suburbanised Growth. This was incorrect: the CUE did 'not propose either decline of the central city area' as in Suburbanised Growth, 'nor a grossly over-concentrated central area' as in Centralised Growth (CUE 1979:4).

From available evidence, it is difficult to determine whether higher net benefits would be achieved by inner or outer consolidation in fostering a more dense city. In terms of coping with the effects of structural change, for example, 'it is not possible at this stage to determine with any degree of accuracy... the precise pattern of concentration which would most facilitate this (for example, close to the CBD or in nodes along radial public transport links)' (Little and Carter 1979:xii). In adopting a staged approach toward a more dense city, it does seem likely that the drawing power of the inner city would overwhelm that of outer-suburban nodes for a long time. The inner city attracts the greatest number and diversity of trip purposes and the various programmes would be likely to increase people and goods flows to the area (Beed 1981:Chapter 7). If policy were directed to spatial consolidation, the benefits of the inner city would be worth retaining. Some of these benefits accrue to low-income people. In addition, it is possible that the qualities of a centralised lifestyle would be more acceptable in the city as a whole by building on the model that has long existed in the inner city; 'the probability that the process could filter out to suburban nodes would seem greater' (Little and Carter 1979:195). This suggests that inner nodes should be fostered initially.

Yet, policy which sought *only* to maintain or increase population and socio-economic activity in the inner city implies massive commuting to the inner city until sufficient outer-suburban residents moved inward to live in the inner city. In the interim, which might be a number of generations, the high flows of people from spatially-dispersed outer suburbs to a consolidating inner city imply a high reliance on private motor transport. In the same way as now, public transport would not be able to compete effectively with private motor transport for passenger/goods pick-up or delivery in the low-density outer suburbs. Certainly, the competitiveness of public transport would improve because of high people-flows to the small inner area but its edge may be too marginal for significance. In any case, the likelihood is that more people would travel to the inner suburbs by both public *and* private transport. Indeed, in one modelled effect of this strategy, public-transport use overall decreased slightly because public road transport became even more disadvantaged than now (MMBW 1979*c*:i). Continuing high reliance on private motor transport would mean high social costs (congestion, air and noise pollution, accidents and social disruption), high resource costs, including energy, and much motor trip-making. For those who worked in the inner city, long journeys to and from work, even by public transport, would be necessary. These effects would last for generations, given the present overwhelming importance of the outer suburbs for residential settlement.

In a scenario of consolidation directed only at the inner city, the trend to public transport and non-motor private transport would accelerate only as people moved their homes to the inner suburbs where their jobs and other amenities were. This development would require extensive redirection in national, State and local government policy (Beed 1981:Chapter 7). Even if they recognised the advantages of inner-city living, it is uncertan how many existing suburbanites would prefer an inner-suburban residence. Probably the greatest hope would lie in newly-forming households although some established household types, such as some of the elderly, may be willing to trade down in space, provided satisfactory accommodation and social environments could be created in the inner city. However, this readjustment would take many years and the results may not be certain, although the tendency to smaller households would be in its favour. During this interim, influences would persist against the centralisation of population and economic activity. The orientation to private transport among those remaining in the outer suburbs would encourage the suburbanisation of population and economic activity. A contradiction would materialise if new economic activity and population were not retained in, or attracted to, the inner suburbs on the scale necessary to foster consolidation.

These considerations were another reason why the MMBW rejected its 'Centralised Growth' option in 1980. Orienting policy to the inner city would leave untouched the majority of population and socio-economic activity which occurs in the outer suburbs. Enormous numbers of workers would continue to make long work-journeys to the inner city; social costs from this transport would remain high in the inner suburbs; a high reliance would persist on private transport in the outer suburbs. On the other hand, the strategy of trying only to encourage consolidation in the outer suburbs—'Suburbanised Growth'—was rejected also by the MMBW in 1980. The weaknesses of this strategy were the run-down in benefits from the inner city and an increasing dependence on private transport. Fostering nodes or activity centres near the periphery of settlement would stimulate car-based suburbanisation which the MMBW was anxious to avoid.

Greater efficiency and equity may be achieved by influencing the majority of population which lives in, and the socio-economic activity which occurs in, the outer suburbs, through fostering consolidation in *both* outer and inner areas. While maintaining, and even increasing, inner population and economic activity is essential, much population and activity would persist in the outer area, at least in the foreseeable future. Since population agglomerations may generate some of their own employment demand in the post-industrial society, it seems equitable to provide the outer-population remnant, whether it be a majority or not, with possibilities for generating suitable employment. Although the gross benefits of this process would probably be smaller than those created in the inner area (for example, there would probably be less employment choice), they could be generated at proportionately lower cost through the reduced need for motor travel. By this means, it may be possible to reduce the difference in the magnitude of net benefits between inner and outer nodes. It could be that for the city as a whole, similar benefits would accrue but be more equitably spread by encouraging nodes of activity throughout the city.

This suggestion does imply a need to maintain critical spatial balance between nodes in the inner and outer suburbs. Achievement and maintenance of the planned drawing-power of each node would be crucial. This would require efficient communication between each node so that the system of nodes could function more readily as an integrated whole. For example, it may be decided that the inner-city nodes should have the major drawing power over some time period. If this was the intention, it would be important to ensure that people could have convenient access by public transport to the inner nodes. Thus, locating nodes at major public-transport interchanges would be important to preserve connectivity between nodes.

Nodal development means the conscious agglomeration of people-attracting facilities. Socio-economic activity has suburbanised with a high incidence of dispersion in Melbourne (Beed 1981:Chapter 5). Compared with the inner city, accessibilities to and densities of urban facilities are very low in the outer area. The resulting outer pattern resembles a scatter of 'confetti along main roads' (Stretton 1976:225). In this *ad hoc*, random layout, 'all the advantages of concentration are lost — the association of lunchtime shopping with offices, the ability to walk from one appointment to another, the opportunity to concentrate public-transport services on a high-density node' (Jay 1978:71). By reducing these disadvantages of suburbanisation, nodal development aims to generate at least the existing level of benefits in the city, but at lower cost. It is even possible that gross benefits may increase because more people would have a chance of interacting with a greater range of urban amenities. For example, if a suburban mother without a car travelled to a node which included shops, recreational, educational, child-care and other personal services all within walking distance of each other, she could utilise a number of these services. If the woman wanted a job and it was located in the node too, she could take it; it would be good if the day nursery and primary school were in the node as well. Today, the typical situation confronting the outer-suburban woman is that amenities are so separate from each other that they can be reached only by a car or by a long public transport journey. In a nodal layout, non-working teenagers could more easily get to their favourite haunts—eating places, discos, sports clubs, library and schools—if they were located together in the node. Their greater patronage of these facilities would generate enhanced benefits, some of which would accrue to themselves and some to others.

Mixed land use

The proposed content and benefits from nodal development do not differ in degree from current patterns where many incipient nodes exist, but they do differ in kind. Current suburban centres in the outer suburbs emphasise retail activity, but greater benefits and reduced travel costs could be achieved by grouping a far greater range of functions. Some of the post-war suburban shopping centres seemed to have been planned with this possibility in mind. Rentable office space is usually available in these centres, and theatres or auditoriums may be provided. Occasional provision is made for children's recreation in school holidays while art exhibitions are held periodically. The *ideal* would be to locate together at the public-transport interchange, major employment, retail, educational, recreational and administrative functions, especially those which drew or sought to draw large numbers of people to them. This idealised content of nodal development is not vastly different from a current description of Melbourne's inner area, although the spatial mix of activities in the outer suburbs would need to be planned on different criteria from those now prevailing. One similarity is that nodes imply a diverse mixture of land use to allow for convenient interaction between different activities. Single-purpose zoning is inconsistent with nodal development for which heavier reliance would have to be placed on performance standards (Beed 1981:Chapter 6). Activities would need to be permitted in nodes as long as they did not produce specified adverse environmental effects like noise, odour above certain levels.

Mixed land uses, which are a vital consideration in nodes, are not compatible with the typical effects produced by the private land market. Usually, particular land uses become dominant at particular locations as they outbid less profitable activities for desirable sites (Richardson 1978). For example, offices dominate in the present CBD; retailing dominates at ground-floor level in current suburban 'nodes'. In these suburban centres, non-commercial activity like elderly-citizens' clubs or municipal libraries may be pushed to less accessible sites or try to save space by occupying unsuitably small areas. Residential land uses are usually pushed right out of these centres. The necessary mixture of activities which planned nodes require will not materialise by relying on the private rent-paying ability of land users as the main criterion of land use determination. Indeed, the profitability which determines rent-paying ability need have little relevance to social benefit which is the objective of nodal development. Programming land use change to meet broad urban social and transport objectives would require a public leasehold system of land use in which public decision-making replaced the private market and passive constraints set by land use zoning.

Hierarchy of nodes

It is unlikely that resources would exist to establish enough major nodes to ensure that all city dwellers had equal and convenient access to one. It would be impossible physically and undesirable aesthetically to have everyone living within convenient distance of a major node, whether the node was in the inner suburbs or not. A hierarchy of nodes would be required, even within the inner suburbs, having similar interrelationships to those described above.

Various models of this can be constructed. At the lowest level of the hierarchy, for example, a few minutes walk or bike ride on a 'slow way' (Duek-Cohen 1975:86) might take people to a local mixed business/bus stop/bike hire/meeting place, located in one building which might be an existing house. This is the 'neighbourhood house' idea in one Melbourne model of this process (White et al. 1978:146). If people continued to live at prevailing residential densities (that is, from fifteen to forty persons per hectare) and if the maximum tolerable walking distance to the neighbourhood centre was 705 metres, then between 3000 and 7000 persons could walk to the centre (Loder and Bayly 1978:49). A few more minutes bike ride or bus trip might lead to the next nodal level in the hierarchy, the 'local focus' (White et al. 1978:148) which would include a greater range of functions: more shops, a health clinic, larger meeting spaces, some compatible employment etc. The major node, the 'district' or 'sector' centre might not be reached until the third or fourth level in the hierarchy (Thomson 1978:265).

It is not feasible to specify the detailed content of each hierarchical level in this system of nodes. The content could only be worked out in practice and may well differ between nodes at one hierarchical level. The Conservation of Urban Energy Group in Melbourne worked out, for one municipality, the location and content of the two lowest-level nodes and the transport organisation to serve them (CUE 1979; 1982). This was a valuable exercise and its implementation possibilities were examined by the MMBW (1985).

Self-containment of nodes

Nodes would not be able to function as self-contained entities or provide exclusive employment for those living closest to them. Planning to equate the number of jobs in a node with the number of workers living in the surrounding residential area would not eliminate commuting to other nodes. Indeed, planning to match the skills, experience and tastes of surrounding residential workers with the characteristics of jobs in a node would be a task hardly worth pursuing and of impossible complexity. In terms of aggregate job numbers, it so happens that there is plenty of scope currently for local employment in large Australian cities. Looking only at the relation between total job-numbers and resident workers in a three-kilometre radius for each part of the city, two-thirds of Sydney workers could work locally. This measure takes no account of the suitability of jobs by occupation, skills, experience or taste so that less than one-third of Sydney workers do work locally (Manning 1978:66). Thus, while there is some scope for reducing the total length of work-trips through increasing suburban accessibilities to jobs in nodes, the limitations must be held in mind. Commuting between nodes would not be eliminated, although improving local job-accessibility would decrease the number of very long work-trips (Black 1977:195).

As long as nodes contained a wide range of functions, the number and length of motor trips for other purposes might be reduced. Trips to shop, school, health services and urban recreation are currently more localised than trips to work; 'most children go to nearby schools, residents shop in the nearest suburban or district centres, and... many leisure, social, recreational journeys and trips for medical and personal business reasons are made to nearby activity centres' (Black 1977:197). By rearranging land uses, it is probable that an increased proportion of these needs could be met with fewer motor trips. Admittedly, a number of trips for these purposes are performed currently as part of the work trip; that is, commuters shop or drop children at school on their way to work. Accordingly, possibilities of reducing the number of motor trips for other purposes should not be exaggerated. Nevertheless, many of the extra trips are made *because* of current land use layouts; because shops and jobs are not located at the one place, workers are encouraged to make a motor trip to get to the shop. Of course, car trips to other nodes would still be necessary for visits to more specialised functions, such as tertiary educational institutions. Although these may be more intermittent in nature than inter-nodal work trips and undertaken more in off-peak times, the necessity for efficient public transport connectivity between nodes for both work and non-work trips is clear. A failure to recognise the necessary interrelations between the component parts of cities has lead to false expectations about possibilities of nodal self-containment.

Urban structure and social interaction

It might be thought that a more socially-interactive lifestyle would be one of the effects of a nodal configuration. The idea of a greater proportion of the city's population interacting over less space does conjure up visions of a more co-operative lifestyle. Some of this anticipation derives from the common criticism of the intensely privatised nature of Australian urban society, especially in suburbia. Residents in the outer suburbs are often thought to be isolated and alienated from each other, especially if they are housewives who have to stay at home all day. Putting people-attracting activities in nodes of varying function in a hierarchical arrangement is thought to be one way of reducing personal loneliness in large Australian cities.

While there are elements of validity in this belief, it can be exaggerated both in its description and explanation of the *status quo* and in the effects that nodes could have. There is evidence which suggests that a comparison of inner and outer-suburban lifestyles does not reveal significant differences in isolation due solely to variation in densities (Beed 1981:Chapter 5). A housewife in an inner-suburban flat can be just as lonely as one in an outer-suburban villa. Moreover, not all stay-at-home women see themselves as isolated. Perhaps around a half of full-time Australian big-city housewives do not feel lonely; they report the availability of little time in the day to socialise outside their homes even if physical distance were not a problem. Thus, in a small survey in Thomastown, a northern fringe suburb of Melbourne, 55 per cent of the housewives interviewed said that they did not feel isolated (Wearing and Wearing 1973:19–20). In a large Melbourne-wide survey of women, 50 per cent reported that they had only one or two hours available to themselves each day after the essential chores were done (Australian Department of Tourism and Recreation 1975:27).

While some loneliness may be generated in the outer areas of large Australian cities through the poor physical access that exists to urban facilities, some can be generated also from other conditions of life affecting those who stay at home all day. For example, it can arise because of the distribution of tasks within households. Since women have been culturally attuned to do most of the housework and child rearing, some loneliness can arise from the solitary nature of these activities in the nuclear family. Indeed, by becoming completely subordinate to the needs of the household and occupying most of their time with household tasks, these women may not even perceive their situation as lonely. Thus, in another Melbourne survey, only 17 per cent of housewives would have gone out more if household help had been available (Scott and U'Ren 1962:48).

Even if the lowest-level node in the hierarchy, the neighbourhood house, were only a few minutes walk away, it is possible that a majority of full-time housewives may not visit it regularly. On the other hand, the figures above show that the other half of full-time housewives do feel lonely at times and had more than two hours free every day. Their patronage of a neighbourhood house may be more regular. Moreover, the presence of the house would be likely to have an educative effect on the housewives who did not see themselves as lonely. Since the house would be the local transport junction, both for public motor and non-motor private transport, increasing numbers of people would become familiar with its functions. Not only would the house provide a centre for social interaction, but it could offer, as some do now, other services like child-minding and food ordering which could help relieve the burden of household chores. The house might also offer commercial services like cleaning and cooking which would have the potential for relieving the housewife even more. However, unless the house offered the housewife satisfying recreation or paid work in lieu of the time she saved, she may persist in performing the many solitary tasks of housework herself.

Thus, while nodal development has the potential for relieving suburban isolation, many factors additional to the convenient physical presence of a node are necessary to increase social interaction. Nodes are a necessary condition for increasing social interaction, but they are not a sufficient condition; anticipating a large increase in interaction because of their mere presence is to commit the fallacy of physical determinism. Equally crucial to encouraging social interaction, assuming this is a desirable objective, would be the provision of adequate private indoor and outdoor space in people's homes and a diversity of functions available at nodes.

Table 20.1 is one suggested schema for a range of functions in the three lowest-level nodes in the hierarchy, the private dwelling, the neighbourhood house and the local focus, based on the CUE approach which seeks to integrate physical and social criteria (White et al. 1978:154–5). This is quite different from the range of functions in the present centres of agglomeration in large Australian cities, and from the role and locations of present neighbourhood houses (for example, Community Child Care 1980:18ff). Not only does it depend on a hierarchical arrangement inter-connected by the transport system, but each node in the hierarchy, except the private dwelling, encompasses a far wider range of functions than exists now. Centres which attract people now do so mainly because they revolve around the exchange of commercial goods and services; shopping is the predominant interactive function outside the home, although it has important recreational aspects. The range of functions besides shops and commercial offices in present urban and suburban centres is quite narrow. To provide people with opportunities for more interaction, especially for those who do not possess the money or inclination to *buy* sociability, a much more diverse range of non-commercial and self-help functions would need to be accommodated in nodes. Needless to say, this is unlikely to occur where the private rent-paying ability of land users determines the functions in today's centres in Australian cities.

Concentrating non-residential activity at nodes provides only the potential for social interaction. Constructing some medium-density residential accommodation in nodes only provides this possibility also.

Table 20.1 Functions for three lowest levels in nodal hierarchy

Private dwelling	**Neighbourhood house**	**Local focus**
Sleeping		Higher-density dwellings, temporary hostel accomodation
Cooking, eating	Snacks, occasional meal	Restaurants
Child nurturing	Child minding and socialisation, playgroup	Kindergarten, creche, primary and secondary school
Reading, listening to music	Library	Library
Other private recreation, creative hobbies	Passive indoor games, workshops	Swimming pool, indoor recreation centre, workshops, exhibition centre
Private gardening	Common plots	Parks
Home maintenance	Workshop	Indoor recreation centre, workshops
Car, bicycle maintenance	Workshop	Indoor recreation centre, garages
Washing clothes	Laundromat	Laundromat
Private study	Tutoring, notices	Learning exchange, adult education centre
Televiewing	Video-recorder, films	Theatres, meeting rooms
Talking, thinking, worship	Meetings, discussions	Theatres, meeting rooms churches
	First aid post	Health centre
		Government services, e.g., home help, elderly citizens' club, employment register, post office
	Corner shop	Commercial services, e.g., bank, insurance, convenience shops, offices, hotel
	Dial-a-bus stop, bike hire	Dial-a-bus stop, priority lane bus stop, railway station, tram stop, bike hire

Source: Adapted from White et al. 1978:154–5

Appropriate dwelling design can serve as the basis from which social interaction can develop. For example, single or two-storey medium-density houses sited in small culs-de-sac and grouped around pedestrian pathways away from motor traffic can generate more social interaction between people than conventional low-density housing (for example, Mercer 1975:Chapter 4). However, these are only possibilities; although people may live closer together, they would not necessarily want neighbours as friends. On the basis of present experience, there are few indications that residents in medium-density housing constitute a more tightly-knit, friendly group than those in conventional low-density housing. In a Melbourne survey of medium-density residents, similar majorities of occupants did not regularly visit or participate in activities with neighbours as for two typical low-density estates surveyed (Foddy and Reid 1976:32). Again, this is a conclusion made on the basis of present land use configurations where medium-density housing has not been part of nodal development. However, the point remains that physical propinquity is only one factor encouraging interaction between people. Probably of greater importance in friendship formation is homogeneity between people in their interests, values and backgrounds.

It must be emphasised that nodal development is not being advocated here as a solution to alleged urban social problems, whether they be personal alienation, loneliness or lack of face-to-face contact. It is too simplistic to slip into the fallacy of physical determinism and assume that because communal facilities are provided in urban nodes, people will flock to them and be cured of their psychological traumas. Additional socio-economic intervention would be required if boredom, unemployment, divorce and loneliness were to be tackled effectively. The effects on people of the processes examined here must not be overstated. Sole causality cannot be attributed to the built urban environment. Having said that, it is equally important to recognise that spatial structure and organisation do play an important part in personal contentment.

Urban structure and community control

There is a strong implication in the preceding argument that the private sector would be unable to take the initiative in encouraging a consolidated nodal pattern. Earlier chapters of *Melbourne's Development and Planning* (Beed 1981) described the ways in which private interests both encouraged and responded to particular stimuli to produce prevailing land use and transport choices in large Australian cities. In many ways, a nodal configuration has quite different needs from those of the *status quo*. Transport choices would have to be biased to public motor and non-motor private modes. Land use activities of appropriate content would have to occur at particular locations. Once the minimal quantity and quality of activities existed at nodes, change could occur only within the confines of a city-wide plan. Interrelations between nodes in the hierarchy could exist only in relation to the city plan. Most of these requirements are not consistent with the process of private landowners determining the uses of their land in accordance with their own assessments of private benefits and costs.

Consciously fostering nodal development to increase consolidation and enhance social efficiency and equity would not be able to rely mainly on the market test of allocating sites to the highest bidders. 'The market for property' as 'the most important in allocating activities and land uses to locations' (Neutze 1978:21) means than the relative wealth of bidders and their estimated future private returns determine the uses to which land is put. Despite Neutze's claim, it is not necessarily 'in the best interest of a city that a site should be used for the purpose for which it is most valuable' (Neutze 1978:20) where 'most valuable' can be expressed only through the highest private bids for a site. In the CBDs of the Australian capitals, high-rise office blocks are pushing out other land uses; in the inner suburbs, higher-income immigrants are displacing lower-income residents precisely through this process (Daly 1982; W.S. Logan 1985). While the private returns to the owners of these sites are probably higher than they could get from alternative land uses, it is likely that social optimality requires a greater mix of less-profitable functions. The more relevant test is land use which yields the highest *social* return; this need have little relation to the value of a site to its private owner.

Nodes in the manner advocated here are unlikely to take root in the present socio-institutional context where private entrepreneurs, guided mainly by private benefits and costs, take the major land use initiatives on the basis of development rights accruing to the highest bidder. Where the private rent-paying ability of land determines its ultimate use, non-commercial activities will rarely rub shoulders with the commercial, even in the absence of zoning regulations; where competition between users of land determines land use, a narrow range of land uses will usually be produced at any one location. Where the sum of individual private land use plans constitute the development path for a city, a pre-arranged land use configuration is unlikely to come about. While initiatives for development come mainly from private entrepreneurs, long delays will occur in the co-ordination and installation of public urban services. While development does not proceed outward in orderly spatial sequence, amenity inputs cannot be programmed. The orderly expansion of a city is not compatible with a situation where developers offer land on the market where and when they can (or are prepared to) buy it. Typically, new residential estates are too small to be co-ordinated with the growth of jobs in a locality, which are not planned anyway. Few obligations exist for employers to consider the effects their location decisions might have on the work-journeys of potential employees. Residential development usually proceeds far faster than the availability of jobs, recreation, health, education, welfare and public transport services in a locality. While private transport remains the dominate transport mode, the potential for this co-ordination and consolidated development will be undermined. While governments oversee these processes in the direction of maintaining current trends, nodal development will not occur. In short, the formation of nodes in the manner advocated here, to achieve a more consolidated city, is not compatible with the effects of contemporary Australian capitalism on large cities (Beed 1984).

This is not to suppose that no moves in the direction of increasing urban efficiency and equity can be achieved in the context of Australian capitalism. For example, much valuable work has been accomplished with neighbourhood houses and their potential role in an integrated land use-transport social configuration can be recognised (Social Alternatives for Melbourne Collective 1985). Nor is it true to suppose that only governments can take the necessary action. Local initiative and experiment are crucial elements of the model proposed here. While governments have to exercise policy 'downward' local initiative has to proceed 'upward'. A mutual interrelation between government policy and 'people power' is necessary if urban efficiency and equity are to be increased. This does presuppose change in a variety of formal arrangements to bring people closer to effective political power. For example, representation in local government may need to be on the basis of regular turnover of councillors from neighbourhood houses or street meetings. Of course, there are signs of this process under way. For example, many local councils use the voluntary expertise of motivated local residents, even on a formal basis. At the same time, the contemporary contribution of sporadic urban social movements to bringing about change in the Australian big city should not be exaggerated. Given the limits to urban change set by the capitalist mode of production, urban planning in Australia has been susceptible to urban social protest, but more so to the needs of capitalism.

Melbourne's Development and Planning (Beed 1981), examined the empirical context within which urban planning has operated in Melbourne since the Second World War. In general, the overall picture was of processes influenced and/or caused by market forces acting within broad constraints set by the state. The state has acted to adjust or change these processes only to the extent that they have not contradicted or undermined the conditions necessary for the maintenance of the capitalist mode of production. It has not always been easy to see what these conditions are in the contemporary Australian urban context. For instance, one question investigated was whether surburbanisation or consolidation is more in conformity with the present requirements of Australian capitalism. A tentative conclusion was that suburbanisation has served the needs of capitalism up to now. But it would be unwise to predict with certainty the continuation of the tendency. It may be that the spatial needs of post-industrial capitalism in which service or tertiary employment dominates, are not oriented as strongly to the continuation of suburbanisation. If this is so, the power of the state will be utilised by dominant sections of the capitalist class to dampen suburbanisation in large Australian cities. Prediction of these future developments is fraught with uncertainty. Rather than predictions, the analysis has attempted to show that government and state power has not been used since the Second World War in large Australian cities to contradict processes largely determined by market forces. Usually, market influences and government policy have reinforced each other.

While these market forces have taken the ostensible form of being the expression of consumer preference, their content has reflected more the constraints within which consumers have been able to operate. The property relations governing capitalist society have left residents in the large Australian city relatively little room to manoeuvre. Even against their personal wills, consumers have been forced to the private car as public transport has deteriorated, they have been forced to the outer suburbs in land-extensive housing, they have not been able to afford to live in the inner city. The 'market', as the chief guide in these decisions, has reflected the unequal ownership and control of urban resources which is intrinsic to the capitalist mode of production.

Chapter 21
Towards qualitatively new forms of state intervention

Blair Badcock

The dimensions of structural change

In the mid-1970s the growing pains that we normally associate with fluctuations in the business cycle were replaced by economic turbulence of a magnitude last experienced by the advanced capitalist economies during the 1929–35 Depression. Radical (Castells 1980; J.O'Connor 1984) and moderate political economists (Heilbroner 1980) concur in the view that a structural crisis in capitalism is under way that will inflict changes of seismic magnitude upon the economies of countries like the United States, Britain and Australia. External shocks to the international monetary system (the collapse of the United States dollar as the currency standard; the resetting of crude oil prices by OPEC in 1974 and 1979; stagflation; the Third World debt crises) were accompanied in turn by the election in Australia (1975), Britain (1979), and the United States (1981) of three governments whose conservative complexion and contractionary monetary policies aggravated the downturn, and added substantially to the chronically high structural unemployment created by the 'de-industrialisation' already under way within the manufacturing sectors of the advanced capitalist economies.

Undoubtedly the most traumatic effect of the convulsion of capital during the last decade (see Badcock 1984:150–8) has been the restructuring forced upon the manufacturing sector within the advanced economies. In particular, labour-replacing technology and the competition of the newly-industrialising countries (South Korea, Taiwan, Singapore, Hong Kong) have decimated the manufacturing workforce in advanced capitalist economies. 'Between 1975 and 1982, jobs in Europe's industry fell by a tenth. The whirlwind was especially fierce in Britain which lost almost a quarter of its industrial jobs between 1979 and 1983 (Thomas 1985*a*:223). On the other hand, while plant closures and layoffs in United States manufacturing accelerated during the recession in 1981–82, by 1984 the recovery had stimulated new investment in manufacturing so that the pick-up in aggregate output, investment and employment levels (but least of all in the hard-hit durable goods sector) led some conservative United States

A version of this chapter, written before the change of Federal government in Australia in March 1983, first appeared in Badcock, B. A. (1984) *Unfairly Structured Cities*, pp 330–8. This is a revised version of that chapter and is published here by kind permission of Basil Blackwell.

economists to condemn the use of the term 'de-industrialisation' as a misnomer (Weidenbaum and Athey 1985). Bluestone's (1984) response is that the analysis of aggregates masks the sectoral and regional unevenness of the dislocation occurring in manufacturing. For those groups of workers and communities displaced or discarded by structural change, and not yet re-absorbed in expanding sectors of the economy, the phenomenon of 'de-industrialisation' is a reality. Indeed, a Bureau of Labour Statistics survey of 5.1 million United States workers displaced between 1979–84 revealed that 25 per cent were still looking for work and that 15 per cent had left the workforce; but of the re-employed workers, 45 per cent were earning less in their new job, while over 10 per cent had to settle for part-time work (reported in *Economic Impact* 1985:72).

The impact of the structural transformation of capital is intrinsically selective and uneven. By the early 1980s the tendencies peculiar to this present round of structural adjustment were beginning to emerge in a detectable form (see Gershuny and Miles 1983; or Massey 1983). Arguably, this time round the sectoral and geographical effects are more pronounced because technological displacement and technologically-based job-expansion coincide only minimally in both a sectoral and spatial sense. At the risk of oversimplifying the end result of a very complex matrix of processes, *to date* most of the labour displacement has taken place in the manufacturing sector, while through the 1970s employment in the services sector expanded at an annual average rate of 2.5 per cent in the member countries of the OECD (Thomas 1985*a*:224). This has been associated, in turn, with the decline of inner-city districts within the 'rustbelts' of the United States and Britain — the areas with the relict technology, rundown infrastructure and lowest levels of productivity, or the single-industry towns (Wollongong, Consett, Akron). Thus while no region within the British space-economy has escaped unscathed (Table 21.1), manufacturing in the West Midlands, which was close to the top of the regional earnings league in the 1960s, has been devastated. In thirty-two months, between 1981 and 1983, 156 000 jobs were lost (300 000 in all since 1980) in the region, with more than 85 per cent from engineering and metal fabrication. By 1985, with unemployment in the West Midlands at 17 per cent, in ten Birmingham wards it was more than 30 per cent, and in three it was over 40 per cent (including the Handsworth district which was at the hub of the urban riots in October, 1985). In Australia, cities like Wollongong, Newcastle and Whyalla have borne the brunt of restructuring in the Australian steel, coal and metal-trades industries: following the loss of over 100 000 manufacturing jobs nationally between June 1982 and June 1983, unemployment peaked at 21 000 (21 per cent of the workforce) in Wollongong (Sandercock and Melser 1985:123; see also, Schultz 1985). The suburbs of Warilla, Cringilla, Warrawong, and Berkeley, where unemployment levels exceeded 25 per cent in November 1984, concentrate young manual workers and their families living in Housing Commission homes.

Table 21.1 The impact of de-industrialisation in selected British regions

	Unemployment (August 1985)		
	Number	**Percentage of workforce**	**Vacant factory floor space (million sq. metres)**
North-west	436 500	15.7	2.15
W. Midlands	347 800	15.4	1.87
North-east	229 100	18.2	1.01
Scotland	337 200	14.9	0.20
South-west	201 900	11.8	0.08
Wales	175 000	16.4	0.33

Source: based on UK Department of Employment statistics published in *The Observer* 29 September 1985:33.

The experience is radically different in the 'sunbelt' regions of the United States and Britain. New growth areas in California and the southern States in the United States, and along the M4 corridor in the south of England, have captured a disproportionate share of the employment growth; not only in the 'high-tech' and defence industries, but also in the business, professional and government services. Saxenian (1983) has estimated that 25 000 new jobs were created yearly during the 1970s in the Santa Clara Valley ('Silicon Valley'), to the south of San Francisco. Now, with approximately one-third of the workforce employed by 700 electronics companies, 'Silicon Valley' boasts one of the wealthiest communities in the United States (however, the assembly workers employed in the production of semiconductors cannot afford to reside locally). While the development of the British 'sunbelt' which stretches in an arc from Bristol to Cambridge, lags well behind its United States counterparts in the 'high-tech' sector—perhaps 20 000 jobs have been created in the private sector for the whole of Berkshire (Breheny et al. 1983:65)—it has benefitted from the national programme of office decentralisation.

Lastly, structural readjustment threatens to produce echelons of human 'left-overs' who, despite a return to economic growth, will be excluded from the labour market because they live in a depressed region, lack appropriate skills or have not had the opportunity to retrain. Currently, young people, married mothers (who constitute the bulk of the 'hidden unemployed'), and members of ethnic minorities are grossly over-represented within the ranks of the unemployed. In the seven major OECD countries, youth unemployment stood at 17 per cent in 1983, with Italy (32 per cent), Britain (23 per cent), and Australia (22 per cent) well above the group average. A common feature of unemployment trends is the length of time labour-market casualties are spending locked out of work; in many European countries and Australia, young people and adults out of work for over a year comprise between 60 and 80 per cent of all unemployment

(OECD, reported in the *International Herald Tribune* September 24 1985:11).

Technological displacement and the adaptability of the state

There was an element of mimicry in the initial reaction of governments in the United States, Britain, and Australia to the economic downturn in the mid-1970s. Monetarist doctrine, which had been dusted off and polished up by a number of neo-conservative economists teaching in the universities, was adopted as a talisman by the Thatcher, Reagan and Fraser governments. The fashionable view was that the welfare state was in a crisis because collective social expenditure had risen to the point where it exceeded the capacity of the economy to fund it. The prescription for dealing with stagflation entailed a number of measures that would re-ignite depressed economies via the supply side: government spending had to be lowered to the point where national deficits were no longer inflationary; the tax burden needed reducing so that a greater share of company profits was available for new investment; institutional rigidities obstructing the free movement of capital and labour needed dismantling. There was little recognition of the structural dimension of unemployment: redundancy was a necessary, if painful, concomitant of the cyclical downturn and contractionary monetary policies. With the defeat of inflation and the resurgence of economic growth, unemployment would decline again to acceptable levels. In the meantime, in order to bring some respectability to the numbers on the dole, governments of all political hues — including the first Hawke government in Australia — cobbled together 'make-work' schemes '... as a panic reaction to an essentially temporary unemployment crisis' (Thomas 1985*a*:263)

With the advantage of hindsight a number of lessons can be drawn from the neo-conservative strategy for managing an unstable economy. First, monetarism (especially Reaganomics) has been discredited in large part — clearly the 5.5 million jobs generated in the United States during the eighteen-month surge in 1983–84 was due as much to the huge budget deficit (over US$200 billion in the 1985 fiscal year) as to the flexibility of the United States labour market. Second, although the Thatcher government's strategy is still premised upon this assumption, and while it has also influenced policy in Australia in the last decade, 'there is no evidence that countries with high (or rapidly rising) government spending or tax shares have performed any worse in this time in economic growth, inflation or unemployment' (Saunders 1985:13). Kuttner's (1981) analysis of the French, West German, Swedish, Japanese, United States and British economies during the 1970s also shows that 'the better economic performers among western countries include the more egalitarian ones'.

In the United States, Britain, and Australia the ideological antipathy held by conservatives towards the concept of welfare has checked one of the few areas of employment growth. According to Thomas (1985*a*: 224);

> [a] closer look at the 1970s shows, perhaps surprisingly, that in most countries most new service jobs were generated in welfare. In the United States, for instance, jobs in social services grew in percentage terms more than in any other service sector in the economy to 1984. Britain was a major exception. Between 1976 and 1982, we had the lowest percentage increase in welfare jobs of any OECD country except Australia. Between 1979 and 1982, we were unique in seeing a decline in jobs in general government (central government, health and local authorities). Nonetheless, as a sector of the British economy, it did better than most.

In one respect the approach adopted by Britain's Conservative government has proved itself inherently contradictory: the stubborn refusal to countenance even mildly stimulatory policies has led to a massive escalation in the social security bill (up 30 per cent in real terms in the last six years). With 3.34 million workers, or 13.8 per cent of the workforce, out of work in late-1985, the direct cost of unemployment benefits had risen to 7.5 billion pounds, not to mention the rise in the number of poorly-paid households drawing supplementary benefits (Jacobs 1985). By way of contrast, 'In Europe the degree of consensus on the need for high levels of welfare spending has scarcely altered. In no European country is there a leading politician who shares Mrs. Thatcher's sharp critique of welfarism' (Walker 1984:25). Indeed, even in Denmark and Sweden, for all the signs of an incipient 'tax revolt' in the late 1970s, 'there's been a settling back both in politics and social administration in the mid-1980s to the high-spending collectivist traditions of Scandinavia' (Walker 1984: 25).

The third 'lesson' from the past decade has come with the realisation that, 'An economy that grows in a time of industry rationalisation and rapid technological innovation, when labour is being widely displaced by capital, need not generate many new jobs' (Windschuttle 1984:6). Belatedly, compared with the reaction of governments in western Europe, political parties in the United Kingdom, the United States, and Australia are beginning to come to terms with the fact that unemployment in the 1980s is as much structural as cyclical in its origins, and that the prospects for a return to full employment in the next decade, or indeed within the next generation, are not encouraging. The Hawke Labor government found to its dismay that in the twelve months to June 1984, with the best economic performance recorded in the last twenty-five years (a 10 per cent jump in the rate of growth), the Australian economy only created enough 'real' full-time jobs to absorb new entrants to the labour market (Windschuttle 1984:6). And despite the range of job-creation programmes that are now in place in most industrialised countries (Thomas 1985*b*), the OECD prediction is for 31.5 million jobless in the second half of 1986 in the twenty-four member states. As Thomas (1985*a*: 223) points out, 'industrialised countries in the west would have to create 20,000 more jobs than they are losing, every day for five years, if unemployment is to return to its 1979 level'. The pessimism surrounding job creation in the future stems from a number of studies that have endeavoured to assess the impact of new technology upon employment, both in terms of its potential for creating and destroying work. Although the estimates vary according to the underlying assumptions about the growth of the labour supply and the technical sophistication of robots, for example, there is broad agreement about the trend to a significant *net* reduction in the global employment levels found in the advanced capitalist economies (see Maud 1984; Weiss 1983). In the United States, Ayres and Miller (1983), and Rumberger (1984) working with Leven at Stanford, agree that by 2020, or thereabouts, all the tasks currently performed by machine operators in American manufacturing industry will have been automated. Ayres and Miller (1983:52) suggest that the impact of office automation over the same period may well be more dramatic than the introduction of robots in manufacturing, and the study by Gershuny and Miles (1983) of the impact of the new information technologies upon the service sector tends to bear that out.

In the face of this bleak picture some futurologists look to the fecundity of 'high-tech' fields like computer software, biogenetics, robotics and photovoltaics to offset the displacement of labour occurring elsewhere in the economy (see *The Economist* 1984). Certainly the software and semi-conductor sectors posted impressive rates of growth in the United States, even in the midst of the recession in the early-1980s. However, some estimates carefully prepared for the United States economy by Markusen (1983:20) indicate that only about 600 000 extra jobs will be available in the 'sunrise' industries by 1990, representing a doubling of the level in 1982–83. This is due in part to the growing tendency for the high-technology sector in the United States to automate and internalise its own production. In 1983, the *Multinational Monitor* reported that over 40 per cent of the workers employed by six of the largest semi-conductor producers in Silicon Valley worked in assembly plants located overseas (Shorrock 1983). Consequently, the United States Bureau of Labor Statistics concludes that the contribution of high technology to the creation of new jobs will probably peak at about 3 per cent. This is consistent with the forecast of Rumberger (1984) and Leven, who anticipate that between 1978 and 1990 the United States economy will absorb three times the number of workers in building maintenance (600 000) than in systems analysis (200 000), and over five times the number in the fast-foods industry (800 000) as in computer programming (150 000).

It is this trend to a two-tier wage structure that leads Bluestone and Harrison (1982) to ponder the political and economic ramifications of a bisected labour force, especially with the growing prospect that the low wage sector will expand much more quickly than jobs for technicians, engineers, and professionals between now and the end of the century.

Towards qualitatively new forms of state intervention

It is the readiness to try something new in the wake of technological change and labour-shedding that distinguishes the governments of western Europe from those of Britain, the United States and Australia. The European social democracies have not escaped the restructuring of capital underway at present. But because they have central planning machinery, manpower policies, and adequate income-support programmes in place, they are better equipped to spread the social and economic costs of dislocation more equitably than governments in the United Kingdom, the United States, or Australia. Also,

> there is more and more discussion in Europe on the need for 'structural' adjustments to solve the problem of unemployment—meaning what to do about declining industries, regions of poverty, and neglected segments of the population. Since these are problems that cannot be solved quickly, there is correspondingly a growing belief that Europe's unemployment is a long-term problem, requiring fundamental institutional changes, even if no one can produce the specifications for them yet. (Chamberlain 1980:18)

Part of the challenge facing the state is to anticipate, rather than engaging in a delayed reaction to the restructuring of capital. At the very least, the state should be endeavouring to channel structural change in socially desirable directions. Here we are not alone in assuming that the economic conditions that lie ahead under advanced, or possibly, late capitalism will demand more rather than less state intervention: 'One widely-shared conviction is that in the future governments will necessarily play a more active economic role, presumably directing corporate activities more definitively than is now the case' (Chamberlain 1980:36; see also Hodgson 1984).

How should the state respond to the 'crisis' of capital? (Bearing in mind that not only is capital a 'moving target', but that the capitalist system has proved remarkably adaptable and resilient over several centuries.) The intention here is not really to draw up a blueprint, but simply to point to some of the reforms and adjustments that are necessary if the state is to come to grips with the inevitability of restructuring, and in the process achieve a morally defensible social order. If capital is to be made to serve the interests of society as a whole within the advanced capitalist economies then the state will need to engage in some form of indicative planning and co-ordination and dispense with the adversarial system of market relations. States must also install proper manpower policies, transfer an equitable share of the economic surplus and national wealth to those persons denied the opportunity to participate in its creation, and regain the initiative in urban and regional development. The proposals below have been drafted primarily with the Australian scene in mind. It should also be said that the type of social transformation that these reforms presage could be exceedingly painful for vested interests on both sides of the class divide. To complicate the task further, experience in western Europe shows that political expediency operates far too often to prejudice the success of some of the reforms proposed. Indeed one perspective holds that:

> a capitalism forced by political pressure to produce full employment with high levels of resource and capacity use is a capitalism facing a fundamental challenge to its underlying relations. Full employment is inimical to capitalism because of the shift in the balance of class power required by a prolonged absence of unemployment (Dow 1984:14).

Short of adopting such a defeatist position, there would appear to be few realistic alternatives in the long-run for the Australian economy to what we are proposing. By this account, the throwback in the mid-1970s to monetarism and libertarian values will be judged an aberration in the tortuous but inexorable passage from capitalism to a benign form of democratic socialism.

National economic planning

The cultivation of clichés about capitalism versus socialism remains one of the most disabling cankers of economic and political life in Britain, the United States and Australia. It is the innate conservatism of these property-owning democracies based upon outmoded and simplistic dichotomies of this kind that has forestalled the setting in place of an indicative plan for national economic development (though a short-lived attempt was made by the Conservatives in Britain during the mid-1960s with a National Economic Development Council). The post-war record of governments, more so in Australia and the United States than in Britain, is one of *ad hoc*, reactive, incrementalist policy-making. Yet, ironically, the modern corporation is a tightly-structured organisation that co-ordinates all facets of its activity and leaves nothing to chance—that is, the whims of the private market. In reality, economic development is no longer achieved simply via the process of market adjustment but through a combination of state intervention, and the political and other activities of large and powerful corporations and unions (Hodgson 1984:182). There is a case for increasing the element of central planning in Australia to buttress vital sectors of the economy which at present are exposed to the restructuring of capital. A start was made by the Hawke government in the mid-1980s with policies that at least attempt to guide, if not replace, the market determination of the country's industrial structure (the Steel Plan and the rationalisation of the car industry); but what is missing is overall co-ordination of the various sectors.

It is not only social democracies like Sweden and West Germany that owe their post-war prosperity to national economic planning (after all the United States made it a condition of Marshall Plan assistance!), but also avowedly 'free enterprise' states like Gaullist France, Japan and Singapore. By allocating capital to high-priority sectors and locations in accordance with national economic development goals, Japan, West Germany, and Gaullist France maintained significantly higher rates of economic growth throughout the 1960s and 1970s than Britain or even the United States. In Japan the Ministry of International Trade and Industry (MITI) uses 'administrative guidance' to bring about structural adjustment within the Japanese economy. An important element in several of these frameworks is access to investment capital outside the private banking sector. In France, where most of the banks are nationalised, credit allocation serves national planning objectives. Alternatively, in some countries socialised savings constitute an important source of new capital. Sweden uses its social security savings accumulated on behalf of future pensioners in this way. In Singapore the Central Provident Fund has played a vital part in the island-state's economic-growth miracle.

Lastly, there are compelling reasons for the Australian government to develop the institutions and the industrial policies that would aid local manufacturers to counteract the practices designed to freeze Australia and other 'branch-plant' economies out of international trade. Increasingly, it is the competition between industry policies that is the main feature of world trade:

> Japan, so often held up as a model of competitive virtue, has constructed its own comparative advantage by blocking manufactured imports and putting resources into selected growth industries. In this process, the Ministry for International Trade and Industry has taken a key role in moulding business decisions through an intimate relationship with the business community. (Ewer 1985:29)

In Australia, government should be insisting on the addition of value by processing more locally-sourced materials like wood-chip, liquified gas, and alumina. As a case in point, instead of setting up an aluminium fabrication and semi-fabrication industry in Australia, Comalco recently spent one hundred million dollars securing access to the Japanese market. The agreement, which includes a thirty-year contract to supply aluminium to Showa Aluminium Industries of Japan, may be a sound strategic decision for Comalco as a primary producer but it effectively means that Australia forfeits the right to develop a significant processing and fabrication industry of its own.

Negotiating a truce between capital and labour

Since the present author wrote that, 'The future of effective indicative planning will remain in the balance so long as Australia persists with an adversarial system of industrial relations' (Badcock 1984:332), Australia has enjoyed a three-year truce between business and labour in the form of a wages Accord. Government-supervised wage indexation has dampened down the escalating wages bill of employers and helped to underpin the living standards of those in the workforce. In addition, the creation of the Económic Planning Advisory Council (EPAC) has brought together the major class groupings and representatives of State and local government, and welfare organisations, in an effort to involve them in the formulation of government policy. While these represent significant developments (though the Accord is especially fragile), they cannot be expected to allay the ingrained mistrust that characterises industrial relations in a time of great uncertainty.

Faults lie with both sides. In Australia, management seldom takes employees into its confidence when it is planning production or new investment, let alone making provision for representation on the board. Thus at the same time as it was threatening to halt the production of steel in Australia, BHP calmly announced that it had outlaid US$2400 million to purchase the mining conglomerate, Utah International. Eventually, in the process of reducing the steel division workforce by 12 000 workers, BHP's executives 'were certainly found wanting, with no commitment to real consultation' (Schultz 1985: 217). By way of contrast, when it became obvious that Sweden's three steelworks could not all continue to function profitably, the Swedish government insisted that the three enterprises (one state-owned, two privately) co-ordinate their restructuring plans and develop programmes to ease the smooth transfer of workers to other employment. The restructuring was obviously resisted by Swedish steelworkers and was not without its share of anxiety and social dislocation; but, as Schultz (1985:216–17) points out, 'This was a far cry from the shock of *ad hoc* restructuring that occurred in Australia'. For its part, organised labour now possesses monopolistic powers that are every bit as formidable as the corporations, especially when they are exercised in strategic sectors of the economy. The alienation and cynicism felt by much of the Australian workforce is reflected in the level of industrial disputes: in 1974 6.29 million days were lost because of strikes and in 1981, 4.19 million days, but in 1982, with the recession biting, this level fell to 1.83 million days. Compare this combative atmosphere with West Germany, Norway and Austria where trade-union and employer representatives directly participate in the process of income and prices determination via specialised technical and contact committees (Chamberlain 1980:169–82). Moreover, in order to secure their interests in economic stabilisation, governments furnish the forecasts of expected performance which are taken as an agreed basis for negotiating non-inflationary wage settlements. This is considered to be an essential prelude by the trade union movement to greater worker-participation and eventual industrial democracy.

Manpower planning and job creation (or rationing)

The threat to a continuity of full employment as we have known it in the advanced capitalist economies necessitates a radical rethinking of the work ethos. The social changes that this will force may well be as profound as those that occurred with industrial urbanisation in the mid-nineteenth century. Clearly all governments are going to have to combat structural unemployment on several fronts. Because the conservative regimes in Britain, the United States and Australia did not begin to take 'de-industrialisation' seriously until they were confronted with the reality of jobless growth in the mid-1980s, the initial commitment to manpower planning, retraining and job creation programmes was half-hearted. The direct and calculable expense of unemployment has only just begun to dawn upon their Treasuries; as yet the 'opportunity costs' of 'lost' demand, ill-health, and the added pressures upon social security and public housing have scarcely figured in the debate (Merritt 1982:150–4). Some time ago now, the social democracies in western Europe began to look beyond one-off, short-term labour-absorbing community projects and capital works such as the construction of public housing and transport infrastructure (which figured so prominently in the economic rebound experienced in Australia in the mid-1980s).

Before governments have to resort to the rationing of work there are a number of avenues still open for absorbing more labour. First, contrary to present policy in Britain, the United States and Australia, personal services in medicine, education, recreation and leisure can be expanded. It is the failure to acknowledge the multiplier effects of public-sector employment that has perpetuated the misguided notion, in the face of the long-run structural shift to a services-based economy, that employees of the state are non-productive. Second, many governments have adopted a combination of measures designed to keep young people out of the real labour market for as long as possible. These measures include raising the school-leaving age (up from fourteen to eighteen years in Belgium in 1983), guarantees of work experience for the long-term unemployed (the Swedish Youth Employment Law), and various vocational training schemes (West Germany's apprenticeship system, though stretched by youth unemployment levels, still provides the best model). Finally, in 1984–85, both the British and Australian governments made a serious commitment to providing young school leavers with appropriate skills. As experience shows in several European countries, the trainees still have to compete for too few jobs at the end of their courses; nonetheless, according to a persistent critic of the Labor government's approach to unemployment, Australia's youth training scheme, 'if administered properly, promises an alternative route into the workforce for a significant number of young people' (Windschuttle 1985:23). A third group of measures that have been adopted by several European governments, and are discussed in some detail by Thomas (1985*b*), includes: a shorter working week (Belgium and Eire have been particularly innovative); government-subsidised 'career breaks' in conjunction with job-sharing (Holland has created 100 000 jobs this way); early retirement (West Germany, France and Italy now have early retirement legislation); and, of course, beefed-up community job-creation programmes, which steer the long-term unemployed into socially useful work (France, West Germany, Denmark, Sweden, and Italy have been joined by Britain, with its Community Programme, and Australia in this).

Revamping redistribution

The collective sense of compassion which underlay the steady expansion of the welfare state in the good times after the war was one of the first casualties of the economic downturn in the mid-1970s. Paradoxically, as privation and hardship mounted, conservative governments in the United Kingdom, United States, and Australia set about lowering the welfare 'burden'. The Reagan administration's attempts to reduce social spending have been so systematic and (potentially) severe that even Republicans in the House of Representatives and Congress have blocked certain budgetary proposals each year (Piven and Cloward 1982). Midway through 1985, the Social Services Secretary in the Thatcher government tabled a Green Paper containing a series of 'reforms' designed to yield savings in the order of five billion pounds (Jacobs 1985:26). The Green Paper mounts a comprehensive attack against the founding principles of the welfare state (universality and contributory insurance) by replacing them with selectivity (means-tested benefits), privatisation (of the earning-related pension scheme, or SERPS), and regressiveness. Irrespective of the fate of the Green Paper:

> Since 1979, 8.2 billion pounds has been cut, in real terms, from the social security incomes of the poorest 15 per cent of the population, while tax cuts have furnished an extra 6 billion to those on higher pay, including 2.6 billion to income earners above 20,000 pounds a year. (The British average wage is about 8,000 pounds.) (Jacobs 1985:26)

In Australia, it is fair to say that the 'retreat from the welfare state' ceased with the election of the Hawke Labor government in 1983 (Graycar 1983); however, when faced with the challenge of overhauling the taxation system and breaking down the concentration of private wealth, the government displayed a penchant for vacillation and timidity not traditionally associated with a reformist party. Pleasing pressure groups and holding the 'middle ground' electorally, extracts a price.

Unfortunately, the effect of the present reward structure is to heap the costs of structural change almost entirely upon those who are locked out of the workplace. With progressively fewer workers directly engaged in manufacturing, and maybe even in office functions, there will be irresistable pressure to redistribute more generously the surplus generated by industrial technology. The assumption is that Australia is sufficiently well-endowed with resources to support all members of society with status and dignity. Though a redistribution of productive capacity is taking place at present between countries, it is conceivable that in the immediate future automation will cancel out the advantages of low-wage regions in all but a few product areas. If investment in new technology is based upon a system of asset-sharing in industry, then workers in manufacturing are capable of generating enough wealth to support members of the community dependent upon a social wage—in much the same way that a miniscule agricultural workforce is now capable of feeding and clothing the non-farm population in the advanced capitalist economies. The case for increased redistribution between full-time workers and the workless is placed in a better perspective when it is realised that in Australia in the last fifteen years, for every 100 workers, the number of people receiving social allowances of some kind has doubled from twenty to forty. A guaranteed minimum income for workers for whom there is no work may well be the price the community has to pay for political and social stability.

Regaining the initiative in urban and regional development

A long-term goal of a national development plan would be the smoothing out, within reason, of the gross regional imbalances that arise if capital is given *carte blanche* by the state to invest and disinvest where it will. There should be a role for regional policy in Australia, if only to harness local development initiatives selectively, as is now chiefly the case in Britain (Hamilton 1985). In Australia, at a minimum, this would require the establishment of a policy unit by Federal government charged with mapping out the broad contours of a balanced space-economy, taking into account the existing distribution of natural and human resources. Then, as a matter of some urgency, governmental assistance would be provided, consistent with national planning objectives, to local and regional capitals that are being forced to close down their operations or regroup in response to the worldwide appropriation of space by transnational corporations. Foreign investment would also be supervised much more closely and, if need be, subjected to controls and sanctions of various kinds (cf. the Norwegian government's enlightened custody of its North Sea oil reserves). Also, the co-ordination of resource allocation and the setting of priorities in Australian urban and regional development would help to counteract the perennial distortion to the national space-economy that results from internecine rivalry, not only between the States, but between capital cities as well. Certainly the arguments for 'flagging' the unintended consequences of public policy for cities and regions remain just as potent as they were in the days of DURD (the Department of Urban and Regional Development) in the early 1970s.

Second, a regional planning framework for Australia 'may be the best way of ensuring wide community involvement in economic planning issues' (Sandercock 1982:31). This could be accomplished by extending some of the Whitlam government's initiatives, such as the regional councils for social development, so long as the tendency to over-centralisation were avoided. With such a framework in place communities like Wollongong and Whyalla would have been much better equipped to monitor and prepare for structural adjustment. And in areas of rapid growth, the success of bodies like the Western Sydney Regional Organisation of Councils in attracting both private and government grants should speak for itself.

Third, all governments are going to have to grapple more conscientiously with the looming problem of regional disaffection and grievance within urban communities. The recent rioting in Tottenham and Handsworth merely serves to remind the Conservatives in Britain that they ignore the recommendations of the Scarman Inquiry at their peril. Following the riots in twenty British cities in 1981 Lord Scarman was commissioned by the Conservative government to uncover the causes of violence. In his report he painted a depressing picture of inner-city life (see Harrison 1983), and recommended a programme of positive discrimination to ameliorate the appalling housing conditions and unacceptable unemployment rates suffered by Britain's two million black and Asian residents. Many local social movements may or may not have a class/racial/gender dimension; nevertheless, with the global reshuffling of industrial capital the reality of the 'throwaway' region or community is upon us. Because of the constraints that operate it is wrong to assume, as many labour economists seem to, that workers discarded by capital are free to move to areas that offer better prospects: housing may be impossible to sell; the person may be one of several workers in the household; the redundant worker may have a few or inappropriate skills; school leavers without work depend upon their parents for sustenance. Those people immobilised by circumstance, and jobless for long periods, cannot be expected to put up indefinitely with impoverished, nondescript and desolate residential environments. One would have thought that, if for no other reason than their own peace of mind, the political and economic powerbrokers would be working to dissipate the sense of despair, alienation, and mounting hostility felt by the victims of industrial change. When workers spent most of their working life in a factory, down the mine, or on the land, they were less concerned about living spaces bereft of amenities. One of the real challenges ahead of advanced capitalist societies, and not just their urban and social planners, is to create the conditions and opportunities that will give as much meaning as possible to the daily lives of people out of work within cities.

Concluding prognosis

It has been intimated above that real headway in the search for solutions to problems found in captialist cities and regions will not be made unless governments adopt a broadly-based strategy that addresses structural change in its entirety. There is a body of opinion which holds that such an approach would help in the long run to prevent the formation of the conditions that the urban aid programmes of the 1960s and 1970s were supposed to cure. While that remains a moot point, there is no doubt that there will be a continuing need for the routine management of cities and the strategic planning of urban development.

A few final observations based upon the Australian scene should suffice to illustrate the range of problems and processes that are likely to require the intervention of urban and regional planners. First, despite the change in tempo now that the long boom of the 1950s and 1960s is behind us, property capital will continue to redevelop and refurbish undercapitalised segments of the built environment. (The need to monitor and regulate urban property development will not diminish.) Second, disinvestment leaves behind an environment to be cleaned up, vacant structures to be re-utilised, and throws out a challenge to planners to participate in community economic development (Sarkissian 1983). Third, there is good reason for believing that the imminent scarcity of motoring fuel may force some fairly significant structural adjustments in the organisation of cities. For example, part-sufficiency in petroleum is in doubt beyond 1990 in both the United Kingdom and Australia. The outermost zones of Australian cities that were purpose-built around the private automobile definitely lack the structural adaptability of the inner area; or for that matter, of the compact British city with its well-developed public transport system. The strong government support that is now being given at the State level in Australia to urban consolidation reflects the growing concern that poor, jobless households will be stranded by fuel shortages on the outskirts of Australia's largest cities.

The ageing of the Australian population, with the added presence of a permanent pool of unemployed workers, will, in time, necessitate a thorough revision of government policies in relation to collective consumption, especially public housing and urban redevelopment. As the demand for housing assistance creeps upward, the Commonwealth may have to consider broadening the grants to the States so that, in turn, those local-government councils that are willing can also supply housing services (as they do in Britain). This raises the final question about the state's future role in reproducing the labour force and the most efficacious use of collective facilities. The notion of education for life without work will not only change the nature of schooling, but it must force educational planners radically to alter the place of school facilities within the Australian urban setting. As well as becoming a genuine hub of community life in the cities, educational infrastructure and resources will have to be freely accessible to students and non-students, and workers and non-workers alike.

Conclusion

Chapter 22

Planning practice and social theory: a guide to further reading

Margo Huxley

The material presented in this book of readings has covered a diverse range of issues and has attempted to indicate the sorts of knowledge urban planners need in order to respond to changing social and economic conditions. We make no apology for the fact that I believe that the most relevant knowledge for planners must be derived from social theory and political economy. It is only when based on an awareness of the socio-economic implications of the role and outcomes of planning practice that traditional approaches to statutory control or civic design can become more responsive to the real social needs for planning.

Thus, understanding and improving practice certainly requires at least an adequate empirical knowledge of that practice, but that in turn must be informed by a dialectically-derived relationship with theory. The intention here is to sketch, in barest outline, the major contours of the social theories which might best inform a deeper understanding of planning practice in Australia. In so doing, I introduce further readings for those interested in pursuing such a project and shall set out six broadly interrelated areas:

- planning and the capitalist mode of production;
- class forces and groups in capitalist social formations;
- structure, agency and 'locale';
- the conceptualisation of the state and its role;
- urbanisation under capitalism;
- planning theory and planning practice.

The coverage of these fields is necessarily somewhat arbitrary and truncated and can only serve to hint at the complexity of the subject matter (a fuller review of some of this literature may be found in Huxley and McLoughlin 1985).

Planning and the capitalist mode of production

For those who wish to have a deeper understanding of the whole question of the mode of production, particularly the evolution of the current phase of global capitalism, excellent collected readings are available from Schwartz (1977), and Barratt Brown (1985). There are also monographs by Mandel (1975), Wallerstein (1979; 1983) and Amin (1976). Fine and Harris (1979) and Fine (1982) also provide excellent summaries, while Giddens (1981*a*) has produced a penetrating 'critique of historical materialism'.

Other writers link the mode of production more or less directly to questions of urbanisation (for example, Castells 1977; Gordon 1977; Edel 1981; Fainstein and Fainstein 1982). Outstanding among these is the evolving work of David Harvey (for example, 1973; 1974; 1978*a*; 1981*a* and 1982). There is a subsidiary debate which relates to the formation of 'world cities' in the context of global capital movements and the operation of transnational corporations (TNCs)—see for instance, Cohen (1981), Friedman and Wolff (1982), Soja et al. (1983) and Chase-Dunn (1984).

These works provide a starting point for achieving a historical awareness of the development in Australia of the capitalist mode of production. All colonial settler societies have imported a mode of production as it existed at a particular time. In the case of Australia, this was the British version of late-mercantile/early-industrial capitalism of the eighteenth and nineteenth centuries, in which the role of the colony was largely to export raw materials, import appropriate technologies and to repatriate to Britain the greater proportion of the surpluses generated. It is then necessary to trace how the early colonial cities gradually transformed into centres of wealth-production in their own right, especially through protected manufacturing industries, and how British hegemony gradually gave way to United States, and latterly Asian, economic domination.

In my opinion, the best long-term historical account is that offered by Berry (1983*a*; 1984; also Chapter 3 in this volume). Other excellent accounts of the economic and social history of the country and more recent developments are to be found in Glynn (1970), Forster (1970), and Catley and McFarlane (1981). The essential points for planners to grasp in this area are the historical and contemporary origins, destinations and modes of capital investment (and disinvestment) including the mechanisms and results of switching of investment (for example, Taylor and Thrift 1982). These processes must be understood in terms of sectors (for example, extractive, manufacturing, services) and in terms of spatial locations—the geography of investment in which capital is 'the architect of spatial structures' (Badcock 1984:Part II; see also Stilwell 1980).

Public and private investments alike have switched at certain historical periods between rural and urban sectors and locations, from manufacturing to services, from both of these to the built environment (see Harvey 1982); and within the built environment, between speculative office building in the central business district and suburban commercial and housing developments (Daly 1982; Chapter 19 in this volume; also Berry Chapter 3 in this volume). In recent years, it has become more than ever necessary for planners to understand the global organisation of production, exchange and the division of labour, especially the role of the giant TNCs and how their activities are shaping Australian cities and regions; see particularly the work of Crough, Stilwell, Wheelwright and the TNC Research Project at Sydney University. For further references see Huxley and McLoughlin (1985:Chapters 5 and 6) and Badcock (1984).

Class forces and groups in capitalist social formations

Even though it can be argued forcefully, on both theoretical and empirical lines, that the role of capital is crucial in shaping economic and spatial development, it is simplistic to see capital as the sole determinant of such developments. To do so is to deny the economic significance of class contradictions or seriously to underestimate the roles of class fractions, community, bureaucratic and other groups with specific interests. Their interactions or struggles play prominent parts in the urbanisation process under capitalism and a more powerful understanding of societal change can be obtained from their examination (Giddens 1979; 1984).

Those who would like to take their studies of class and other forces further might begin with the classic texts by Westergaard and Resler (1975), Poulantzàs (1975), several by Giddens (1979; 1981*a*; 1981*b*; 1982) and the collection of readings edited by Giddens and Held (1982). The edited collection by Pickvance (1976), as well as Simmie (1974), Harloe (1977), Harloe and Lebas (1981), Cox and Johnston (1982) and Blowers et al. (1982), are more specifically concerned with 'urban social movements' as first defined by Castells (1977), and which Dunleavy (1980) and Saunders (1981) have sought to refine and extend. Castells' more recent work such as *The City and the Grassroots* (1983) moves away from economistic structural definitions of urban social movements towards an examination of the human and cultural motivations involved in the defence of place (see also Castells 1984). (The concept of 'locale' as defined by Giddens will be discussed in the next section of this chapter.)

The foundations for an understanding of the dynamics of class forces and interest groups in Australia have already been laid. Good background texts on 'class structure in Australian history' are those by Connell (1977) and Connell and Irving (1980) and a standard sociological approach to Australian cities is to be found in Kilmartin, Thorns and Burke (1985). Most contemporary Australian writers emphasise the need for an understanding of class and other conflicts in explaining social and urban change. This is true of the overall approach of Sandercock and Berry (1983), of Stilwell (1980; 1983; and Chapter 4 in this volume) and of Alexander (Chapter 8 in this volume).

Detailed studies of urban protest movements, often involving temporary and somewhat unlikely alliances, include those by Roddewig (1978) on the role of the Builders Labourers' Federation in alliance with residents to impose 'green bans' on what were judged to be unacceptable developments, and Jakubowicz (1973; 1984) on the 'saving' of Woolloomooloo from redevelopment. Mullins (1977; 1979*b*; 1982) has documented localised 'urban social movements' against freeway proposals in Brisbane. The most detailed accounts of struggles and alliances, involving different sections of the community, of capital and parts of the bureaucracy, all with different stakes to be defended and games to be played are those offered by W. S. Logan (1985; and Chapter 9 in this volume) on the 'power play' surrounding the control of central and inner Melbourne in the last fifteen years. The collection by Halligan and Paris (1984) includes a useful introduction to the study of urban politics and many excellent contributions to the Australian literature on this subject.

The current economic recession has meant considerable hardship and social dislocation for workers in places like Wollongong, Sydney, Melbourne and Adelaide (see Badcock 1984; and Chapter 21 in this volume). A good introduction to the urban and regional implications of economic restructuring can be found in Stilwell with illuminating contributions from Larcombe (Stilwell 1980:Chapter 9). Sandercock and Melser (1985) and Schultz (1985) have also addressed the problems of the unemployed in single-industry towns such as Wollongong. Work such as this will become increasingly important to planners as capital-switching and the restructuring of global capitalism continues to be manifested at the local level, and the 'unwaged' seek the means to survive; see, for example, writings on the informal and domestic economy such as Gershuny (1978; 1983), Pahl (1981) and Gershuny and Miles (1983).

A grouping that has become the focus of particularly active study is that of women. Feminist studies emphasise that the interactions between class and gender are not reducible to simplistic economic categories (Hartman 1979; MacKinnon 1982; Alford 1984; Burton 1985). The study of gender and space represents an acknowledgement of the differential impacts that urban form can have on men and women (Hanson and Hanson 1980; Markusen 1980; Saegert 1980).

Dolores Hayden (1982; 1984) is one of the pioneers in the examination of the relationship between built form and patriarchal social relations, and special issues of the *International Journal of Urban and Regional Research* (1978), *Signs* (1980), *Heresies II* (1981) and *Built Environment* (1984) also explore this field.

In the Australian context, Encel et al. (1974) provide an early study of women in Australian society, Connell (1983) examines the relationships between class, sex and culture, and Cass (1978) makes valuable contributions to the theorisation of consumption and the political economy of housework. Manning (1978) and Howe and O'Connor (1982) examine the differences between journey-to-work patterns for men and women; Young (1980) continues the revealing exposition of women's daily lives by time-budget surveys; Game and Pringle (1979) examine the role of suburban consumerism in reinforcing socially-created conceptions of sexuality; and Pringle (1983) looks at 'women and consumer capitalism'. Baldock and Cass' (1983) edited collection on 'women, social welfare and the state' is an extremely useful and comprehensive overview of gender and class issues in public policy.

E. Harman's (1983*b*) 'capitalism, patriarchy and the city' is a critique of both traditional and feminist approaches. 'By not taking greater account of the specific nature of the corporate city, feminist urban theory remains one step behind macro-social changes, while tendencies associated with economic restructuring, energy crises and neo-conservatism threaten to put them still further behind' (1983*b*: 105). Feminist theory and research stand out as requiring further attention in order that implications for economic and social theory in general, as well as for urban research in particular, can be more clearly articulated.

Structure, agency and 'locale'

A major theme in social theory is the relationship between the individual's freedom to act and the constraining framework of social structure. One of the most persistent criticisms of 'vulgar' and structuralist versions of Marxist theory is that they present deterministic views of the inevitable unfolding of history driven by class conflict under the capitalist mode of production. Human agency and individual motivations appear to have no influence over the outcomes of structural contradictions (for an example of this type of critique see W.S. Logan Chapter 9 in this volume). Studies of social processes and behaviour, organisational structure or political and bureaucratic decision-making on the other hand, often produce accounts of voluntaristic human action devoid of the constraining and explanatory significance of the wider social structure.

For more than a decade, Anthony Giddens has been prominent in the exploration of the relationship between the theoretical economic categories of 'capital' and 'labour' and groupings in capitalist formations. His work has examined class theories (1981*b*), the relationship between individual action and the structuration of society (1979; 1981*a*; 1984), and 'time, space, social change' (1979:Chapter 6). His work has influenced not only reassessments of structuralist theories but also the focus of organisational studies. Many such studies are now attempting to place bureaucratic activity (such as planning) into a wider context by examining the structural constraints on the 'action space' of individuals, and individuals' ability to influence structure (see, for example, Benson 1977; Ranson et al. 1980; Wilmoth 1986).

Of particular importance for the study or urbanisation (and planning) is the linking of the structure/agency interaction to considerations of time and space. Radical geographers such as Soja (1980),

Peet (1981), Thrift (1983) and Gregory and Urry (1985) have produced reconceptualisations of 'space' and 'place' as integral not only to the operations of capital (see also Harvey 1982 and N. Smith, 1984), but as essential components of social action. These reconceptualisations have been applied to studies of the differential impacts of industrial restructuring and unemployment across different localities (Urry 1981; Cooke 1983*a*; Massey 1984; see also Cooke 1984, for an examination of the relationship between class, gender and locality).

Giddens (1979) has used the term 'locale' to capture the interrelationship between structure/agency and time/space. Locale is 'place' as a spatial parameter and a physical environment, mobilised as a part of social interaction over time (1979:206). Pahl (1984) also explores the historical and social dimensions of the creation of locale in his study of the Isle of Sheppey, while Friedmann (in Bluestone and Harrison 1982:20; 1985) characterises the difference between 'life space' and 'economic space' as a significant factor in the urbanisation process.

The idea that defence of locale is at the basis of urban social movements and influential in shaping the form of urbanisation in particular societies is central to Castells' (1983) *City and the Grassroots* and to his later explorations of the interpretations of space, technological change and society (Castells 1985). His *Space and Society: Managing the New Historical Relationships* (1984) is of particular interest to planners.

The conceptualisation of the state and its role

Since we link planning to urbanisation and the state, it is necessary to acknowledge the range of views on how the modern state may be conceptualised. This is extremely important, for different theories of the state lead to markedly different conceptualisations of planning and its practice. Theories of the state are many and complex and I am unable to do them justice in the short space available here. State theory has been usefully summarised by Jessop (1982), Clark and Dear (1981), Badcock (1984:Chapter 3), Stilwell (1980; and Chapter 4 of this volume) and especially in an Australian context, by Head (1983:Chapter 2) The recent collection edited by McLennan et al. (1984) and the work of Clark and Dear (1984) pursue the study of the state in greater depth. In addition, the evolution of the debate about the conception of the state can better be appreciated by a reading of seminal texts such as Poulantzas (1969), Miliband (1973), J. O'Connor (1973), Offe (1975; 1984) and Habermas (1976).

For our purposes, the most useful theory of the state approximates most closely to what is called 'materialist theory' (Clark and Dear 1981:56–60). In this, prominence is given to the antagonism between capital and labour. The economic and political spheres are interrelated, principally due to the tendency of the rate of profit to fall (economic crisis) being made into a state (political) responsibility. However, there is no reason why resultant state interventions must necessarily be in the interests of capital and indeed there is a wealth of empirical evidence to show that this is not the case (see, for example, Stilwell, Chapter 4 in this volume). The materialist approach regards the state's role as crisis management under the influence of changing balances in class and other social forces, including the interests of state bureaucrats themselves (see W.S. Logan, Chapter 9 in this volume). This emphasis on changing balances necessarily introduces a historical dimension to the analysis. Such a framework makes possible a much fuller conceptualisation of urban change, the planning apparatus and the role of the planner.

In studying the role of planning, or the actions of any state bureaucracy, it is necessary to conceptualise the constraints placed on individual action by the structure of the organisation and of the wider society in which it operates. At the same time, individual actions and decisions by bureaucrats are not always demonstrably the direct result of pressure from capital, labour or interest groups. As shown in the previous section, structure and agency are in dialectical interaction and a full analysis of 'the state' must take this into account (see Giddens 1979; 1981*a*; 1984; M.P. Smith 1984; and Wilmoth 1986). In this way we can study the sorts of 'games people play' such as described by Maurie Daly (Chapter 19 in this volume) and Bill Logan (Chapter 9 in this volume) while acknowledging the structural influences on the outcomes.

The theoretical and empirical relationship between the overall state apparatus and what is known as the 'local state' has been the subject of many investigations. They range from Cynthia Cockburn's (1977) *The Local State* which characterises local government as merely the local branch of the central state, to Peter Saunders' (1981) *Social Theory and the Urban Question* in which local government is depicted as having relatively autonomous control over local matters of social consumption in response to local competitive politics, while central or regional government retains control over productive infrastructure in response to corporate modes of politics. Summaries of the various approaches to the local/central debate can be found in Saunders (1979; 1981), the special issue of *Environment and Planning A* (Vol. 13, No. 10, 1981), Johnston (1982) and Clark and Dear (1984).

The work on central/local state relations is a clear example of an area of theoretical and empirical inquiry that has been developed in the United States and the United Kingdom and should not be uncritically applied to the Australian federal system (see Saunders 1984). It is particularly important that the study of planning in Australia should be founded in a theory and analysis of the state apparatus that captures the historical dimensions of its specific institutional context.

Urbanisation under capitalism

The foregoing discussion points to the need for a conceptual framework which addresses the question of how the total built form is produced by the interactions (sometimes collaborative, more often conflictual) of capital, labour and the state and various empirically identifiable 'fractions' of each. We must also identify the power relations involved in this process of interaction and how these evolve, shift and change over time. But at the higher level of generality, we are trying to investigate the relations between social processes and the production of built form as they unfold, interactively and temporally.

This overall process of the production of the built form is by no means a smoothly-functioning process (Dear and Scott 1981:1). First and foremost, urbanisation under capitalism embodies a specific form of the overarching contradictions inherent in that particular mode of production. The most important contradictions in the capitalist urbanisation process arise from the continuing tensions between the essentially private motivation to develop land to further profitable accumulation (whether directly through the extraction of rent or indirectly to provide the physical basis for production and exchange) and the public responsibilities for the conditions of continuing profitable accumulation (for example, provision of infrastructure, correction of market failures, taking responsibility for negative externalities, especially by means of urban planning) and dealing with important matters of social consumption (Saunders 1981). Struggles for comparative locational advantage lie at the heart of the private calculus behind developmental decisions, and the outcomes of this struggle, in terms of the extraction of land rents, are capitalised into the prices of land and buildings. The state and the various sections of its apparatus are involved in this struggle in at least two ways, both as landowners and developers in their own right, with their own locational and developmental calculus and more generally as mediators and arbitrators in the whole fabric of the 'urban land nexus' (Scott 1980).

This inherent contradiction can be seen as a continuing tendency towards crisis which is by no means dampened homeostatically to ensure unstable equilibrium (as traditional urban theory would suggest) nor managed with constant capability by the state and its planning arm (as Habermas (1976), might suggest). There is clear empirical evidence which indicates that these inherent contradictions produce a build-up of tension resulting in periodic crises (Scott and Roweis 1977). These appear, historically, as moments of major dysfunction in the urban system which are the spatial manifestations of crises of accumulation (and associated legitimation, rationality and fiscal crises). Urban crises are compounded by the very slow rate of convertibility of the built environment and it is this phenomenon above all which gives the study of urbanisation its particular quality and interest (Scott 1980; Dear and Scott 1981:Chapter 1; Harvey 1982).

Those who wish to take their studies of urbanisation beyond the level aimed at in this book should read the indispensable collections by Dear and Scott (1981) and M.P. Smith (1984) and the monographs by Castells (1977; 1983), Saunders (1979; 1981), Broadbent (1977), Bassett and Short (1980), Pahl (1975) and above all, Harvey (1982) and N. Smith (1984). Pickvance (1980) has provided a pertinent summary of the links to be made between 'theories of the state and theories of urban crisis'. Studies drawing on various perspectives on Australian experience include Neutze (1977; 1978), Stilwell (1980), Burnley (1980; 1982), M. Logan et al. (1981), Linge and McKay (1981), Maher (1982*a*) Sandercock and Berry (1983), Badcock (1984) and Berry (1984).

Writers who detail the process of land development include Ambrose and Colenutt (1975) and Massey and Catalano (1978) in the United Kingdom, Form (1972) and Feagan (1982) in the United States and Sandercock (1977; 1979) and Troy ((1978) in Australia. Scott (1980) and Roweis and Scott (1981) attempt more theorised accounts of land development in general.

Planning theory and planning practice

I will not rehearse in detail here the substance/procedure/systems debates over the theory and conduct of planning which characterised the writings of the 1960s and 1970s since most students will be all too familiar with them. Instead we shall concentrate on the development of inquiry into planning since the late-1970s.

Since the publication of Scott and Roweis' (1977) pathbreaking reappraisal of planning theory and practice there have been two main strands to the scholarly exploration of urban planning theory. The first seeks to derive planning out of the need for state regulation of the anarchic relations of the 'urban land nexus' and capitalist urbanisation processes (Scott 1980; Roweis and Scott 1981; Jensen-Butler 1983). This approach regards the professional ideology of traditional land use planning, developed from public health regulations and civic design, as being a mystification of the real purpose of planning to provide the conditions for profitable private accumulation (Harvey 1978*b*; Kirk 1980).

The second strand of theorising about planning draws on Habermas' ideas of 'distortion-free communication' and the state's role in legitimating capitalist economic and social relations through its 'global planning' functions (Habermas 1976). Writers such as Kemp (1980; 1982), and Forester (1983; 1984) contend that the 'professional mediation' by planners in 'territorial politics' (Roweis 1983) allows them to initiate participatory and mutual-learning strategies which can ultimately lead to alternative forms of social organisation.

Neither of these developing theorisations is entirely satisfactory, for while the first 'capital-logic' style approach appears too limiting and deterministic, the second 'empanicipatory' strand runs the risk of lapsing into idealistic voluntarism (Jensen-Butler 1983).

Another theoretical approach of relevance to planning has been the resurgence of interest in the 'agency' of bureaucratic actors in the context of the 'structure' of the state and capitalist society which has led to a reassessment of Pahl's (1975) notion of 'gatekeepers' or 'urban managers'. It is now generally acknowledged that Pahl's original formulation gave too much weight to the ability of bureaucrats to act autonomously in making allocational decisions, but the urban managerialist thesis is still of relevance when studying bureaucratic actions and their effects on the distribution of urban resources. Williams (1978; 1982) and Leonard (1982) have both proposed modified approaches to urban managerialism and examined the possibility (or otherwise) of a *rapprochement* between Marxism and Weberianism.

As Chris Paris and Peter Williams (Chapter 7 in this volume) point out, planning is neither merely ideology nor all-powerful, it is not monolithic nor inevitable, but it exists and does have effects. Any theory of planning must acknowledge the constraints on planning practice arising from particular historic circumstances of a given social formation and at the same time recognise the opportunities available for individual or 'professional' action within those constraints. Overviews of developments in planning theory can be found in Burchell and Sternleib (1978), Healey et al. (1982), Paris (1982) and Cooke (1983*b*).

Empirical studies of planning can also be grouped under two broad headings: those of planning processes and procedures and those of planning outcomes (Kilmartin, Huxley and McLoughlin 1985).

Examinations of day-to-day planning practice in the United Kingdom have included McLoughlin (1973*a*; 1973*b*), Underwood (1981) and Healey (1983). Critical appraisals of planning practice and its basis in conventional geographic and statistical analysis can be found in Sayer (1979*a*; 1979*b*), and the professional formation and social underpinnings of planners' assumptions are studied by Cullen and Knox (1981), Knox and Cullen (1981) and McLoughlin (1983*a*), as well as Marcuse (1976) in the United States. McAuslan (1980) has produced a pioneering critique of *The Ideologies of Planning Law*.

Recent and valuable texts concentrating on the particularly British 'inner city' analysis-and-policy syndrome include Hall (1981), Lawless (1979) and Rees and Lambert (1985). Piven (1975) has examined the work of the radical Cleveland planners in the United States.

The assessment of the actual outcomes of land use planning is an extremely difficult task since it requires the researcher to isolate the effects attributable to planning actions from those of the myriad of public and private influences on the use of land. Examples of planning outcomes in response to urban crises of accumulation have been given by Scott and Roweis (1977), such as the rebuilding of Paris by

Haussmann under Napoleon III and the English *Public Health Act* of 1875. But such dramatic 'cause-and-effect' connections are exceptional and generally the pressures that produce changes in the built environment attributable to planning are more diffuse.

Eric Reade (1982) has pointed to methods by which the *physical* effects of land use planning must be guaged before its *social and economic* effects can be assessed. Hall et al. (1973) massive examination of the 'containment of urban England' is the most comprehensive documentation of the outcomes of planning to date. Their findings—that in the main, land use planning has regressive distributional effects—have been echoed by other researchers, both in the United Kingdom and the United States (for example, Simmie 1974; Broadbent 1977; Fincher 1981; Wolch and Gabriel 1981; Herzog 1983). There is also a growing body of work on the regressive effects that the outcomes of conventional planning have on women (Breugel and Kay 1975; Markusen 1980; Wekerle et al. 1980).

Such findings do not automatically reinforce the view that planning operates at the behest of property capital, but rather indicate the *contingency* of planning outcomes; if planning has regressive effects, it should also be able to have progressive ones (Fainstein and Fainstein 1979, Forester 1984). But further complicating the picture of planning outcomes is the fact that the education and professional formation of planners often leads to (somewhat confused) perceptions of the 'problem-solution' relationship which may produce policies that are in the interests of no one group in society (see, for example, McLoughlin 1983*b*, Sandercock 1983*a*, T. Logan, forthcoming).

In terms of the practice and outcomes of planning, much less work has been done in the Australian context than in the northern hemisphere. Many of the relevant studies have already been referred to in Chapter 1 and we will not repeat them here. Additional references include Harrison (1978), T. Logan and Ogilvy (1981), T. Logan (1984) and Alexander (1985) on the operation of the formal planning system in Australia; Butlin (1976), Paterson et al. (1976) and Adrian (1984) on the outcomes and unintended consequences of state intervention in the urban process; Kelleher (1981) and Auster (1985) on planning law; Minnery (1985) on planners' role conflicts and Nittim (1975), T. Logan (1976), and Ferrier (1976; 1978) on women and planning.

Conclusion

I hope that the foregoing cursory glance at social theory will not only act as a guide to further reading, but also serve to indicate areas for future research and theorisation in the field of Australian urban studies and urban planning.

In the light of the contributions to this book, urban planning as an aspect of the role of the state in capitalist urbanisation provides a rich vein of study. For instance, how do we explain the massive growth of state bureaucratic agencies in Australia which would appear to be far beyond anything required by the hypothesised 'needs' of capital? On the other hand, how would an 'urban managerialist' analysis account for the primacy of private land development and speculation in Australian urban processes in the face of such large public organisations for 'intervention' and 'allocation'?

Within the state apparatus itself, how is it that planning—partly based on the imported ideologies and mechanisms of the (historically) much stronger British system—is relatively weak compared with agencies concerned with transport, infrastructure or housing? And within the planning function, what is the relationship between the day-to-day control functions and incremental *ad hoc* changes to the regulations and large-scale changes to plans and policies and their implementation? What is the relationship between such large and small-scale changes and pressures from capital, labour, interest groups or planners themselves?

In a period of economic restructuring and the transformation of the global operations of capital such questions will become increasingly important. The relationship between local control and participation and regional/national economic policies will be crucial in determining the ability of planners to respond to real local needs, rather than reinforcing existing spatial and distributional inequalities.

The contributions to this book do, I believe, reflect a realist spirit in looking at what *can* be done under specific conditions and what *should* be done to improve our cities. Towards this end, Australian urban planning needs to become much more self-reflective than it has been in the past and at the same time to be critically aware of the substantive matters such as land development, economic restructuring, the role of the state, class structuration and social equity which lie at the heart of its practice.

References

Aaron, R. E. (1972) *Shelter and Subsidies: Who Benefits from the Federal Housing Subsidies?*, The Brookings Institution, Washington DC.

Adrian, C. (1984) 'Canberra: myth versus reality', *Urban Policy and Research*, 2, (4):3–10.

Adrian, C. and Stimson, R. (1984), *Capital City Impacts and Local Investment in Australia*, AIUS Publication No. 20, Canberra.

Alexander, I. (1979) *Office Location and Public Policy*, Longman, London.

—— (1981*a*) 'Post-war metropolitan planning: goals and realities', in Troy, P. N. (ed.).

—— (1981*b*) 'Conflict and confusion in planning: recent experience in Australian city centres', *Polis*, 8 (2):24–8.

—— (1982*a*) Land use and transport planning in Australian cities: an overview. Paper presented at a Conference on Urban Problems and Policies in Germany and Australia, Australian National University, 30 August-1 September.

—— (1982*b*) 'Office suburbanisation: a new era?', in Cardew, R., Langdale, J. V. and Rich, D. C. (eds).

—— (1985) 'Does central Perth have a future?', *Urban Policy and Research*, 3 (2):16–24.

Alexander, I. and Dawson, J. (1979) 'Suburbanisation of retail sales and employment in Australian cities', *Australian Geographical Studies*, 17:76–83.

Alford, J. (1978) 'Australian labour, multinationals and the Asia-Pacific region', *Journal of Australian Political Economy*, 6:4–23.

Alford, K. (1984) *Production or Reproduction?* Oxford University Press, Melbourne.

Allport, C. (1980) Interviews by Carolyn Allport with residents at Revesby, Chester Hill and Bankstown, (NSW), January-July.

—— (1983) 'Women and suburban housing: post-war planning in Sydney, 1943–1961', in Williams P. (ed.).

Ambrose, P. and Colenutt, B. (1975) *The Property Machine*, Penguin, Harmondsworth, UK.

Amin, S. (1976) *Unequal Development*, Harvester, Brighton, UK.

Apps, P. (1973*a*) 'A critique of urban planning: directions for research', *Royal Australian Planning Institute Journal*, 11, (1):8–15.

—— (1973*b*) Tenure, real housing costs and house price inflation. Paper No. 5, School of Architecture, University of Sydney.

Archer, R. W. (1980) 'Planning for housing research and urban consolidation', in *Planning for Urban Consolidation*, Planning Research Centre, University of Sydney.

Aungeles, S. (1979) 'The social consequences of industrial development and decline', *Journal of Australian Political Economy*, 4:38–53.

Auster, M. (1985) 'Plans as policy, or plans as law', *Urban Policy and Research*, 3, (1):13–15.

Australian Bureau of Statistics (ABS) (1938) *Official Yearbook of Australia*, No. 31, Australian Government Publishing Service (AGPS), Canberra.

—— (1951) *Official Year Book of Australia*, No. 38, AGPS, Canberra.

—— (1976) *Housing Finance for Owner Occupation; October, November and December 1975*, AGPS, Canberra.

—— (1979) *Survey of Home Rental and Ownership*, Catalogue No. 8710.0, AGPS, Canberra.

—— (1981) *The Labour Force, Australia, June 1981*, Document 6203.0, AGPS, Canberra.

—— (1982*a*) *Internal Migration, Australia*, AGPS, Canberra.

—— (1982*b*) *Building Activity, Australia*, AGPS, Canberra.

Australian Committee on Decentralisation (1972) *Report of the Committee of Commonwealth/State Officers on Decentralisation*, AGPS, Canberra.

Australian Council on Population and Ethnic Affairs (1983) *Population Report No. 7: Population Change 1976–81*, AGPS, Canberra.

Australian Department of Employment and Youth Affairs (1981) *Monthly Review of the Employment Situation*, AGPS, Canberra.

Australian Department of Immigration and Ethnic Affairs (1985) *Australia's Population Trends and Prospects 1984*, AGPS, Canberra.

Australian Department of Labour (1975) 'Female employment in four urban centres', in Nilord, J. R. and Isaacs, J. E. (eds), *Australian Labour Economics Readings*, new edn., Sun Books, Melbourne.

Australian Department of Tourism and Recreation (1975) *Leisure: An Inappropriate Concept for Women?*, AGPS, Canberra.

Australian Department of the Treasury (1945) Letter to the Director-General, Post-War Reconstruction, 24/6145, Australian Archives CP 43/1, 43/101; CP 44/1, 44,333.

Australian Department of Urban and Regional Development (1972–75) *Annual Reports*, AGPS, Canberra.

—— (1974) *Urban Land Prices 1968–1974*, AGPS, Canberra.

Australian Institute of Urban Studies (AIUS) (1980) *Managing the Eighties*, AIUS, Canberra.

Australian National Commission for UNESCO (1978) *Urban Management Processes*, AGPS, Canberra.

Australian Parliament (1945) (House of Representatives) *Parliamentary Debates*, (Hansard) Vol. 185, AGPS, Canberra.

—— (1952) (House of Representatives) *Parliamentary Debates*, (Hansard), Vol. 219, AGPS, Canberra.

Australian Population and Immigration Council (1980) *Population Report 4*, Department of Immigration of Ethnic Affairs, Canberra.

Australian Priorities Review Staff (1976) *Report on Housing, August 1975*, AGPS, Canberra.

Ayers, R. N. and Miller, S. M. (1983) 'Robotic realities: near-term prospects and problems', *Annals of the American Academy of Political and Social Sciences*, 470:28–55.

Badcock, B. A. (1973) 'The residential structure of metropolitan Sydney', *Australian Geographical Studies*, 11 (1):1–27.

—— (1984) *Unfairly Structured Cities*, Basil Blackwell, Oxford.

Badcock, B. A. and Urlich-Cloher D. (1978) *Low-Rent Boarding and Lodging Accommodation in the City of Adelaide*, City of Adelaide Planning Commission, Adelaide.

—— (1981) 'Neighbourhood change in inner Adelaide, 1966–76', *Urban Studies* 18:41–65.

Baldock, C. and Cass, B. (eds) (1983) *Women, Social Welfare and the State in Australia*, George Allen & Unwin, Sydney.

Barratt Brown M. (ed.) (1985) *Models of Political Economy*, Penguin, Harmondsworth, UK.

Barrett, B. (1971) *The Inner Suburbs: The Evolution of an Industrial Area*, Melbourne University Press, Melbourne.

Bassett, K. and Short, J. R. (1980) *Housing and Residential Structure: Alternative Approaches*, Routledge & Kegan Paul, London.

Becker, J. F. (1977) *Marxian Political Economy*, Cambridge University Press, Cambridge.

Beed, C. S. (1981) *Melbourne's Development and Planning*, Clewara Press, Melbourne.

—— (1984) 'Suburbanization and Australian capitalism', *Polis*, 11:27–31.

Beed, C. S., Andrews, J., Moriarty, P. and Lacey, G. (1983) 'A cost-benefit analysis of increased investment in Melbourne's public transport system', *Urban Policy and Research*, 1 (2):2–10.

Beed, C. S. and Moriarty, P. (1985) A proposed land-use transport strategy for Melbourne. Proceedings of the SAANZ Conference, Brisbane, September.

Bell, M. (1983) Forecasting and urban programming in South Australia. Paper presented to the seminar on 'Forecasting and Urban Programming', Victorian Public Service Board, Melbourne.

Benson, J. (1977) 'Organisations: a dialectical view', *Administrative Science Quarterly* 22, (1).

Beresford, M. and Kerr, P. (1980) 'A turning point for Australian capitalism', in Wheelwright E. and Buckley K. (eds), *Essays in the Political Economy of Australian Capitalism*, Vol. 4, ANZ Book Co., Sydney.

Berry, F. (1974) *Housing; The Great British Failure*, Charles Knight, London.

Berry, M. (1983*a*) 'The Australian city in history: critique and renewal', in Sandercock and Berry.

—— (1983*b*) 'Whose city? The forgotten tenant', in Sandercock and Berry.

—— (1983*c*) 'Tenant politics', in Sandercock and Berry.

—— (1984) 'The political economy of Australian urbanisation', *Progress in Planning*, 22:1–83.

Berry, M. and Huxley, M. (1985) Property development, capital switching and state intervention: studies of Melbourne, Australia. Paper presented to International Sociological Association Urban and Regional Development Research Committee Conference, University of Hong Kong, 14–20 August.

Black, J. (1976) 'Australian land use transport studies', in Webb, G. R and McMaster, J. C. (eds) *Australian Transport Economics*, ANZ Book Co., Sydney.

—— (1977) *Public Inconvenience: Access and Travel in Sydney Suburbs*, ANU Urban Research Unit, Canberra.

—— (1978) Changes to employment accessibility in Sydney. Papers of the Regional Science Association, Australia and New Zealand Section.

Blowers, A., Brook, C., Dunleavy, P. and McDowell, L. (eds) (1982) *Urban Change and Conflict: An Interdisciplinary Reader*, Harper & Row, with the Open University Press, London.

Bluestone, B. (1984) 'Is deindustrialisation a myth? Capital mobility versus absorptive capacity in the US economy', *Annals of the American Academy of Political and Social Sciences*, 475:34–51.

Bluestone, B. and Harrison, B. (1982) *The Deindustrialisation of America: Plant Closings, Community Development and the Dismantling of Basic Industry*, Basic Books, New York.

Boddy, M. (1981) 'Inner cities: keeping the lid on?', *Progress in Human Geography*, 5:599–604.

Boehm, E. (1979) *Twentieth Century Economic Development in Australia*, 2nd edn, Longman Cheshire, Melbourne.

Bolton, G. C. (1972) *A Fine Country to Starve In*, University of Western Australia Press, Nedlands.

—— (1981) 'From Cinderella to Charles Court: the making of the State of Excitement', in Harman, E. and Head, B. (eds).

Booth, D. R. (1970) *An analysis of private land-use controls and private cities as systems to produce public goods*, Ph. D thesis, UCLA, University of Michigan, Ann Arbor, Michigan.

Bowman, M. (1978) *Local Government in the Australian States: An Urban Paper*, AGPS, Canberra.

—— (1979) *Australian Approaches to Environmental Management: The Response of State Planning*, Environmental Law Reform Group, Hobart.

Bracken, I. (1982) 'New directions in key activity forecasting', *Town Planning Review*, 53:51–64.

Breheny, M. J. and Roberts, A. J. (1978) 'An integrated forecasting system for structure planning', *Town planning Review*, 49:306–18.

—— (1980) 'Forecasting methodologies in strategic planning: a review', *Papers of the Regional Science Association*, 44:75–89.

Breheny, M. J., Cheshire, P. and Langridge, R. (1983) 'The anatomy of job creation? Industrial change in Britain's M4 corridor', *Built Environment*, 9(1):61–73.

Brennan, T. (1965) 'Urban communities', in Davis, A. and Encel, S. (eds) *Australian Society*, F. W. Cheshire, Melbourne.

Breugel, I. and Kay, A. (1975) 'Women and planning', *Architectural Design*, August:499–500.

Broadbent, T. A. (1977) *Planning and Profit in the Urban Economy*, Methuen, London.

Brown, A.J. and Sherrard, H.M. (1951) *Town and Country Planning*, 1st edn, Angus & Robertson, Sydney.

Brown, J. (1981) 'Infrastructure policies in the Pilbara', in Harman, E. and Head, B. (eds).

Bryson, L. and Thompson, F. (1972) *An Australian Newtown: Life and Leadership in a New Housing Suburb*, Penguin, Ringwood, Victoria.

Built Environment (1984) Women and the Environment 10:1.

Bunker, R.C. (1965) 'Australia since the War: a study of economic growth and physical planning', *Town Planning Review*, 35:311–28.

—— (1971) *Town and Country or City and Region?*, Melbourne University Press, Melbourne.

—— (1983) *Urban Consolidation: The Experience of Sydney, Melbourne and Adelaide*, AIUS, Canberra.

—— (1985) 'Urban consolidation and Australian cities', *Built Environment* 11(2):83–96.

Bunker, R.C. and Orchard, L. (1982) *Urban Consolidation in Adelaide*, AIUS, Canberra.

Burchell, R. and Sternlieb, G. (eds) (1978) *Planning Theory in the 1980s: A Search for Future Directions*, Centre for Urban policy Research, Rutgers University.

Burnley, I.H. (ed.) (1974) *Urbanisation in Australia: The Post-War Experience*, Cambridge University Press, Cambridge.

—— (1976) *The Social Environment*, McGraw Hill, Sydney.

—— (1980) *The Australian Urban System*, Longman Cheshire, Melbourne.

—— (1981) 'Italian settlement in Sydney', *Australian Geographical Studies*, 19 (2):177–94.

—— (1982) *Population, Society and Environment in Australia: A Spatial and Temporal View*, Shillington House, Melbourne.

Burnley, I.H., Pryor, R. and Rowland, D. (eds) (1980) *Mobility and Community Change in Australia*, University of Queensland Press, St Lucia.

Burnley, I.H. and Walker, S.R. (1982) 'Unemployment in metropolitan Sydney', in Cardew et al. (eds).

Burr, K. (1982) Melbourne Metropolitan Planning Scheme Amendment 150. Delegation and separation of matters of metropolitan and local significance. Unpublished paper, MMBW, Melbourne.

Burton, C. (1985) *Subordination: Feminism and Social Theory*, George Allen & Unwin, Sydney.

Butlin, N.G. (ed.) (1976) *Sydney's Environmental Amenity 1970–1975*, ANU Press, Canberra.

Carchedi, G. (1977) *On the Economic Identification of Social Class*, Routledge & Kegan Paul, London.

Cardew, R.V. (1980) 'Flats in Sydney: the thirty per cent solution', in Roe J. (ed.) *Twentieth Century Sydney*, Hale & Iremonger, Sydney.

—— (1982) 'Comparative costs of urban consolidation: inner and outer', in Sandercock, L. (ed.) *Urban Consolidation: The Equity Issue*, Centre for Environmental and Urban Studies, Macquarie University, Sydney.

Cardew, R.V., Langdale, J.C. and Rich, D.C. (eds) (1982) *Why Cities Change*, George Allen & Unwin, Sydney.

Carlton Association (1969) *Housing and Survival in Carlton*, Carlton Association, Melbourne.

—— (1972*a*) *Urban Renewal in Carlton: An Analysis*, Carlton Association, Melbourne.

—— (1972*b*) *Freeway Crisis*, Carlton Association, Melbourne.

—— (1972*c*) *Carlton Plan: A Strategic Policy*, Carlton Association, Melbourne.

Carter, R.A. (1980) Will the strategy work? Urban Land Institute Forum, Melbourne.

—— (1982) 'The effect of proposed district centres on Melbourne's central business district', *Urban Policy and Research*, 1(1):2–7.

Cass, B. 1978) 'Women's place in the class structure', in Wheelwright E.L. and Buckley K. (eds) *Essays in the political Economy of Australian Capitalism*, Vol. 3, ANZ Book Co., Sydney.

Castells, M. (1977) *The Urban Question*, Edward Arnold, London (originally published in 1972 as *La Question Urbaine*).

—— (1978) *City, Class and Power*, Macmillan, London.

—— (1980) 'Cities and regions beyond the crisis: invitation to a debate', *International Journal of Urban and Regional Research*, 4(1):127–9.

—— (1983) *The City and the Grassroots*, Edward Arnold, London.

—— (1984) 'Space and society: managing the new historical relationships', in Smith M. P. (ed.)

—— (ed.) (1985) *High Technology, Space and Society*, Sage Publications, Beverley Hills.

Catley, R. and McFarlane, B. (1974) *From Tweedledum to Tweedledee*, ANZ Book Co., Sydney.

—— (1981) *Australian Capitalism in Boom and Depression*, Alternative Publishing Cooperative, Chippendale, NSW.

Centre for Urban Research and Action (CURA) (1977) *The Displaced: A Study of Housing Conflict in Melbourne's Inner City*, CURA, Melbourne.

Chadwick, G. F. (1971) *A Systems View of Planning*, Pergamon, Oxford.

Chamberlain, N. W. (1980) *Forces of Change in Western Europe*, McGraw-Hill, New York.

Chase-Dunn, C. (1984) 'Urbanisation in the World-System; new directions for research', in Smith M. P. (ed.).

Cheshire, P. C. (1979) 'Spatial unemployment and inequality', in Bowers J. K. (ed.) *Inflation, Development and Integration: Essays in Honour of A. J. Brown*, Leeds University Press, Leeds.

City of Hobart (1968) *Fringe Area Land Use Survey*, The City Council, Hobart.

—— (1972) *Battery Point Planning Scheme*, The City Council, Hobart.

—— (1976) *City of Hobart Draft Planning Scheme*, The City Council, Hobart.

—— (1977) *Battery Point Planning Scheme*, The City Council, Hobart.

City of Perth (1971) *City of Perth Planning Scheme Part I: Scheme of Proposals*, City Council Planning Department, Perth.

—— (1982) *Local Open Space in the Perth Metropolitan Region*, The City Council Planning Department, Perth.

City of Sydney (1974) *City of Sydney Strategic Plan*, the City Council and Urban Systems Corporation, Sydney.

Clark, G. and Dear, M. (1981) 'The state in capitalism and the capitalist state', in Dear, M. and Scott, A. J. (eds).

—— (1984) *State Apparatus: Structures and Language of Legitimacy*, George Allen & Unwin, Hemel Hempstead, UK, and Boston, Massachusetts.

Clarke, G. (1970) 'Urban Australia', in Davies, A. F. and Encel, S. (eds) *Australian Society: A Sociological Introduction*, 2nd edn, Longman Cheshire, Melbourne.

Coates, B. (1979) Allocation policy and practice of the South Australian Housing Trust in metropolitan Adelaide. Unpublished Master of Urban and Regional Planning thesis, University of Adelaide.

Cockburn, C. (1977) *The Local State*, Pluto Press, London.

Cohen, R. (1981) 'The new international division of labour, multinational corporations and urban hierarchy', in Dear M. and Scott A. J. (eds).

Colenutt, R. (1976) 'The political economy of the property market', *Antipode*, 8:24–30.

Collins, J. (1975) 'The political economy of post-war immigration', in Wheelwright, E. L. and Buckley, K. (eds) *Essays in the Political Economy of Australian Capitalism*, Vol. 1, ANZ Book Co., Sydney.

Commission of Enquiry into Poverty (1976) (The 'Henderson Report') *Poverty in Australia — First Main Report, April 1975*, AGPS, Canberra.

Committee of Inquiry into the Australian Financial System (1981) (The 'Campbell Report') *Final Report*, AGPS, Canberra.

Commonwealth Housing Commission (1944) *Final Report*, Government Printer, Sydney.

Community Child Care (CCC) (1980) 'Neighbourhood children's centres', *Ripple*, September.

Community Facilities Committee (1944) *First Report*, Department of Post-War Reconstruction, Canberra.

Compton, R. and Gubbay, J. (1977) *Economy and Class Structure*, Macmillan, Basingstoke, UK.

Connell, R. W. (1977) *Ruling Class, Ruling Culture*, Cambridge University Press, Melbourne.

—— (1983) *Which Way is Up? Essays on Sex, Class and Culture*, George Allen & Unwin, Sydney.

Connell, R.W. and Irving, T.H. (1980) *Class Structure in Australian History*, Longman Cheshire, Melbourne.

Conservation Council of Victoria et al. (1983) *Steps Towards a Better Melbourne: A Community View*, Melbourne.

Conservation of Urban Energy Group (CUE) (1979) *Proposals for Energy Conservation: Nunawading Municipality as a Case Study*, CUE, Melbourne.

—— (CUE) (1982) *Nunawading Energy Study*, CUE, Melbourne.

Cook, F.C. (1945) *City of Hobart Plan*, The City Council, Hobart.

Cooke, P. (1983*a*) 'Regional restructuring: class politics and popular protest in South Wales', *Environment and Planning D: Society and Space*, 1, (3):265–281.

—— (1983*b*) *Theories of Planning and Spatial Development*, Hutchinson, London.

—— (1984) 'Region, class and gender: a European comparison', *Progress in Planning*, 22:85–146.

Copithorne, L. (1980) *Natural Resources and Regional Disparities*, Economic Council of Canada, Ottawa.

Coughlan, W.G. (1957) 'Marriage breakdown', in Elkan, A.P. (ed.) *Marriage and the Family in Australia*, Angus & Robertson, Sydney.

Court, C.W. (1978) The road back to world recovery. Speech to the International Union of Young Presidents' Organisation, Sydney.

—— (1980) Fight for the future. Address to the Australian Mining Industry Council, Canberra, 9 May.

Cowan, R.S. (1974) 'A case study of technological and social change: the washing machine and the working wife', in Hartinan, M. and Banner, L.W. (eds) *Clio's Consciousness Raised*, Harper & Row, New York.

Cowen, Z. (1966) 'Some political and legal aspects of urban redevelopment in Australia', *Australian Journal of Public Administration*, 25:55–67.

Cox, K.R. and Johnston, R.J. (eds) (1982) *Conflict, Politics and the Urban Scene*, Longman, London.

Crough, G. and Wheelwright, E.L. (1982) *Australia — A Client State*, Penguin, Ringwood, Victoria.

Crow, R. and Crow, M. (1969–72) *Plan for Melbourne Parts 1-3*, Communist Party of Australia, Melbourne.

CUE *see* Conservation of Urban Energy Group.

Cullen, J. and Knox, P. (1981) '"The triumph of the eunuch": planners, urban managers and the suppression of political opposition', *Urban Affairs Quarterly*, 17, (2):149–72.

Cullingworth, J.B. (1963) *Housing in Transition*, Heinemann, London.

Cumberland County Council (1948) *Report on the Planning Scheme for the County of Cumberland, New South Wales*, Government Printer, Sydney.

CURA (1977) *see* Centre for Urban Research and Action.

Daly, M.T. (1982) *Sydney Boom, Sydney Bust*, George Allen & Unwin, Sydney.

—— (1984) 'The revolution in international capital markets: urban growth and Australian cities', *Environment and Planning*, A, 16:1003–20.

—— (1985) Australian urban development in the international context. Paper presented to the ANZAAS Conference, Monash University, Melbourne, 22–29 August.

—— (forthcoming) 'Capital cities', in Jeans, D. (ed.) *Australia: Society and Space*.

Daly, M.T. and Paris, C. (1985) From the General to the Particular: global economic restructuring and local housing crises in New South Wales. Paper presented to the International Sociological Association, Urban and Regional Development Research Committee, University of Hong Kong, 14–20 August.

Davidoff, L., L'Esperance, J. and Newby, H. (1976) 'Landscape with Figures: home and community in English society', in Mitchell, J. and Dakley, A. (eds) *The Rights and Wrongs of Women*, Penguin, Harmondsworth, UK.

Davidoff, P. and Reiner, T. (1962) 'A choice theory of planning', *Journal of the American Institute of Planners*, 28 (2):103–15.

Davies, J.G. (1972) *The Evangelistic Bureaucrat*, Tavistock, London.

Davison, G. (1970) 'Public utilities and the expansion of Melbourne in the 1880s', *Australian History Review*, 10 (2):169–89.

Dear, M. and Scott, A.J. (eds) (1981) *Urbanization and Urban Planning in Capitalist Society*, Methuen, London.

Denman, D.R. (1978) *The Place of Property*, Geographical Publications, Berkhampstead, UK.

Dick, J. (1982) 'Energy policy and the resources boom', *Ekstasis*, 26:8–12.

Dobinson, K. (1982) Transport conservation and the multi-nodal city. Paper presented at the 52nd ANZAAS Conference, Macquarie University, Sydney.

Dolbeare, C.N. (1974) 'The housing statement: a lack of welfare in the welfare state', *Dissent*, (Fall):534–41.

Donald, O.D. (1981) 'Medical services', in Troy, P.N. (ed.).

Donnison, D.V. and Soto, P. (1980) *The Good City*, Heinemann, London.

Dow, G. (1984) 'The case for corporatism', *Australian Society*, 3 (5):14–16.

Dresser, M. (1978) 'Review of "Landscape with Figures"', *International Journal of Urban and Regional Research*, 2:558–63.

Duek-Cohen, E. (1975) 'Slow ways' in cities. Paper to Australian Institute of Engineers Conference, Melbourne.

Dunleavy, P. (1980) *Urban Political Analysis*, Macmillan, London.

Dyer, S.W. (1979) Ordinary suburban thoughts. Paper presented to the 'Wrong Way-Go Back' Conference, Sydney University, 8–9 February.

Economist, The (1984) 'Jobs and Technology', March 24, 290 (7334):71–2.

Edel, M. (1981) 'Capitalism, accumulation and the explanation of urban phenomena', in Dear M. and Scott A. (eds).

Edgington, D.W. (1983) Coping with Japan: the geography of Japanese transnational corporations in Australia. Paper presented to Melbourne Urban and Regional Studies Seminar, Monash University, Melbourne, November.

Encel, S., MacKenzie, N., and Tebbutt, M. (1974) *Women and Society: An Australian Study*, Cheshire, Melbourne.

Environment and Planning A (1981) The State, The Law and the Spatial Sciences (special issue) 13, 10.

Evans, A.W. and Beed, C.S. (1986) 'Transport costs and urban property values in the 1970s', *Urban Studies*, 23.

Eversley, D. (1973) *The Planner in Society*, Faber & Faber, London.

Ewer, P. (1985) 'Vital policy issue still simmering', *Australian Society*, 4, (9): 27–9.

Fainstein, N. and Fainstein, S. (1979) 'New debates in urban planning: the impact of Marxist theory within the United States', *International Journal of Urban and Regional Research*, 3 (3):381–403. Reprinted in Paris, C. (ed.) (1982):147–73.

—— (eds) (1982) *Urban Policy under Capitalism*, Sage Publications, Beverley Hills.

Fagan, R., McKay, J. and Linge, G.J.R. (1981) 'Structural change: the international and national context', in Linge, G.J.R. and McKay, J. (eds).

Faludi, A. (1973) *Planning Theory*, Pergamon, Oxford.

Feagan, J. (1982) 'Urban real estate speculation in the United States: implications for social science and urban planning', *International Journal of Urban and Regional Research*, 6, (1):35–60.

Feldman, M.M.A. (1977) 'A contribution to the critique of urban political economy: the journey to work', *Antipode*, 9:30–50.

Ferrier, M. (1976) 'Women post-Stretton', *Royal Australian Planning Institute Journal*, 14 (3/4):52.

—— (1978) 'Women and Planning', *Australian Planner*, 18(3):12.

Fincher, R. (1981) 'Local implementation strategies in the urban built environment', *Environment and Planning*, A 13:1233–1252.

Fine, B. (1982) *Theories of the Capitalist Economy*, Edward Arnold, London.

Fine, B. and Harris, L. (1979) *Re-reading Capital*, Macmillan, London.

Fisher, P. (1974) 'How the trendy twees replaced the blue collars and ethnics', *National Times*, 14 January:13.

Foddy, W.H. and Reid, B. (1976) *Multi-Own-Your-Own Unit Residential Complexes*, Monash University, Melbourne.

Fodor, R. (1978) 'Day care policy in France and its consequences for women: a study of the metropolitan Paris region', *International Journal of Urban and Regional Research*, 2:463–81.

Fogg, A. (1974) *Australian Town Planning Law: Uniformity and Change*, University of Queensland Press (for AIUS), St Lucia.

Forester, J. (1983) 'The geography of planning practice', *Environment and Planning D: Society and Space*, 1:163:180.

—— (1984) 'Lest planning be seen as a tool ...', *Built Environment*, 10, (2):124–31.

Form, W. (1972) 'The place of social structure in the determination of land use', in Stewart M. (ed.) *The City: Problems of Planning*, Penguin, Harmondsworth, UK.

Forster, C. A. (ed.) (1970) *Australian Economic Development in the Twentieth Century*, George Allen & Unwin, Sydney.

—— (1974) 'The journey to work and a satellite town: the cautionary example of Elizabeth', *Australian Geographical Studies*, 12:3–26.

—— (1977) An atlas of employment in greater Adelaide. *Working Paper*, 18, Flinders University National Institute of Labour Studies, Adelaide.

—— (1978) 'Accessibility to employment and the journey to work in metropolitan Adelaide', Australia and New Zealand Regional Science Association Proceedings: 145–55.

—— (1983*a*) 'Spatial organisation and local unemployment rates in metropolitan Adelaide: significant issue or spatial fetish?' *Australian Geographical Studies*, 21:33–48.

—— (1983 *b*) 'Unemployment in the cities', *Geographical Education*, 4, 131–40.

—— (1984) 'Adelaide: a social atlas', in *Atlas of Population and Housing, 1981 Census*, Vol. 5, Division of National Mapping and Australian Bureau of Statistics, AGPS, Canberra.

Frank, A. G. (1969) *Capitalism and Underdevelopment in Latin America*, Modern Reader Paperbacks, New York and London.

Friedman, M. (1962) *Capitalism and Freedom*, University of Chicago Press, Chicago.

Friedmann, J. (1985) 'Transactive planning and life space: Forum interview', *Urban Policy and Research*, 3, (3):37–40.

Friedmann, J. and Wolff, G. (1982) 'World City formation: and agenda for research and action', *International Journal of Urban and Regional Research*, 6:308:344.

Froebel, H., Heinrichs, H. and Kreye, C. (1979) *The New International Division of Labour*, Cambridge University Press, London.

Fry, E. C. (1978) 'The growth of Sydney', in McCarty J.W. and Schedvin, C. B. (eds) *Australian Capital Cities*, Sydney University Press, Sydney.

Galbraith, J. K. (1974) *Economics and the Public Purpose*, Andre Deutsch, London.

Galligan, B. (1981) Federalism and resource development. Paper presented at 'State, Capital and Labour' Conference, Murdoch University, Western Australia.

Gamarnikow, E. (1978) 'Introduction to "Women in the City"', *International Journal of Urban and Regional Research*, 2:390–403.

Gamble, A. and Walton, P. (1976) *Capitalism in Crisis: Inflation and the State*, Macmillan, London.

Game, A. and Pringle, R. (1979) 'Sexuality and the suburban dream', *Australian and New Zealand Journal of Sociology*, 15 (2):4–15.

Gates, R. (1973) *The Price of Land in Australian Cities*, AIUS, Canberra.

Gepp, H. (1968) 'A note on working issues', in *Married Women in Industry: Three Surveys*, Department of Labour and National Service, Melbourne.

Gershuny, J. (1978) *After Industrial Society? The Emerging Self-service Economy*, Macmillan, London.

—— (1983) *Social Innovation and the Division of Labour*, Oxford University Press, Oxford.

Gershuny, J. and Miles, I. D. (1983) *The New Service Economy: The Transformation of Employment in Industrial Societies*, Frances Pinter, London.

Gibson, K. D. (1984) 'Industrial reorganisation and local production in Australia, 1860–1982: an historical materialist analysis', *Australian Geographical Studies*, 22:221–42.

Gibson, K. D. and Horvath, R.J. (1983) 'Global capital and the restructuring crisis in Australian manufacturing', *Economic Geography*, 59(2):178–99.

Giddens, A. (1979) *Central Problems in Social Theory*, Macmillan, London.

—— (1981*a*) *A Contemporary Critique of Historical Materialism*. Edward Arnold, London.
—— (1981*b*) *The Class Structure of the Advanced Societies*, 2nd edn, Hutchinson, London.
—— (1982) *Sociology: A Brief but Critical Introduction*, Macmillan, London.
—— (1984) *The Constitution of Society: Outline of the Theory of Structuration*, Polity Press, Cambridge.
Giddens, A. and Held, D. (eds) (1982) *Classes, Power and Conflict: Classical and Contemporary Debates*, Macmillan, London.
Glyn, A. and Sutcliffe, R. (1972) *British Capitalism, Workers and the Profit Squeeze*, Penguin, Harmondsworth, UK.
Glynn, S. (1970) *Urbanisation in Australian History*, Nelson, Sydney.
Gordon, D. (1977) 'Capitalism and the roots of the urban crisis', in Alcaly R.E. and Mermelstein D. (eds) *The Fiscal Crisis of American Cities*, Vintage Books, New York.
Gough, I. (1979) *The Political Economy of the Welfare State*, Macmillan, London.
Graham, R.J. (1981*a*) Dilemmas of local government planning and land use change: the case of Hobart, Planning Research Centre, University of Sydney.
—— (1981*b*) 'Intrinsic inequalities of land use planning', *Royal Australian Planning Insitute Journal*, 19(4):139–40.
Graycar, A. (ed.) (1983) *Retreat from the Welfare State: Australian Social Policy in the 1980s*, George Allen & Unwin, Sydney.
Gregory D. and Urry J. (eds) (1985) *Social Relations and Spatial Structures*, Macmillan, London.
Gregory, R. (1976) 'Some implications of the growth of the mineral sector', *Australian Journal of Agricultural Economy*, 20 (2):63–76.
Greve, J. (1965) 'Private landlords in England', *Occasional Papers in Social Administration No 16*, Bell, London.
Groenewegen, P.D. (1976*a*) 'Fraser and the New Federalism', *Arena*, 42.
—— (1976*b*) The Taxable Capacity of Local Government in New South Wales, *Research Monograph* 13. Centre for Research on Federal Financial Relations, ANU, Canberra.
—— (1979) *Public Finance in Australia*, Prentice-Hall, Sydney.
Habermas, J. (1976) *Legitimation Crisis*, Heinemann, London.
Hall, P. (ed.) (1981) *The Inner City in Context*, Heinemann (for SSRC), London.
Hall, P., Thomas, R., Gracey, H. and Drewett, R. (1973) *The Containment of Urban England*, (2 vols) George Allen & Unwin, London.
Halligan, J. and Paris, C. (eds) (1984) *Australian Urban Politics: Critical Perspectives*, Longman Cheshire, Melbourne.
Hamilton, A. (1985) 'Regional aid', *The Observer* London, September 29:33–6.
Hamnett, C. (1979) 'Area-based explanations: a critical appraisal', in Herbert, D.T. and Smith, D.M. (eds) *Social Problems in the City: Geographical Perspectives*, Oxford University Press, Oxford.
Hanson, S. and Hanson, P. (1980) 'Gender and urban activity patterns in Uppsala, Sweden', *Geographical Review*, 70:291–299.
Hardin, G. (1977) *The Limits of Altruism*, Indiana University Press, Bloomington.
Harloe, M. (ed.) (1977) *Captive Cities: Studies in the Political Economy of Cities and Regions*, John Wiley & Sons, London.
—— (1978) Urban change and conflict. *Conference Paper* 19, Centre for Environmental Studies, London.
Harloe, M. and Lebas, E. (eds) (1981) *City, Class and Capital: New Developments in the Political Economy of Cities and Regions*, Edward Arnold, London.
Harman, E. (1981*a*) 'Mining and the manufacturing sectors in Western Australia', in Harman, E. and Head, B. (eds).
—— (1981*b*) 'Ideology and mineral development in Western Australia 1960–1980', in Harman, E. and Head, B. (eds).
—— (1983*a*) 'The city, the state and resource development in Western Australia', in Williams, P. (ed.).
—— (1983*b*) 'Capitalism, patriarchy and the city', in Baldcock, C. and Cass, B. (eds).
—— (1985) Government business in Western Australia 1983–85: legal and political aspects of the new hybrid enterprises. Paper presented to the Annual Conference of the Australian Political Studies Association, Adelaide, 28–30 August.

Harman, E. and Head, B. (eds) (1982) *State, Capital and Resources in the North and West of Australia*, University of Western Australia Press, Nedlands.

Harman, F. (1981) 'Resource development and personal income levels', in Harman, E. and Head, B. (eds).

Harris, C. and Dixon, K. (1978) *Regional Planning in New South Wales and Victoria since 1944*, Centre for Research on Federal Financial Relations, ANU, Canberra.

Harrison, P. (1974) 'Planning the metropolitan areas', in I. H. Burnley (ed.).

____ (1978) 'City planning', in Scott, p. (ed.). *Australian Cities and Public Policy*, Georgian House, Melbourne.

Harrison P. (1983) *Inside the Inner City: Life under the Cutting Edge*, Pelican Books, Bungay, UK.

Hartman H. (1979) 'The unhappy marriage of Marxism and feminism: towards a more progressive union', *Capital and Class*, 8:1–33.

Harvey, D. (1973) *Social Justice and the City*, Edward Arnold, London.

____ (1974) 'Class-monopoly rent, finance capital and the urban revolution', *Regional Studies*, 8 (3):239–55.

____ (1975) 'Class structure in a capitalist society and the theory of residential differentiation', in Peel, R., Chisholm, M. and Haggett, P. (eds) *Progress in Physical and Human Geography: Bristol Today*, Heinemann, London.

____ (1978*a*) 'Labour, capital and class struggle around the built environment in advanced capitalist societies', in Cox, K. (ed.). Reprinted in Giddens, A. and Held, D. (eds) (1982):Chapter 26.

____ (1978*b*) 'On planning the ideology of planning', in Burchell, R. and G. Sternleib, G. (eds).

____ (1981) 'The urban process under capitalism: a framework for analysis', in Dear, M. and Scott, A.J. (eds). Reprinted from *International Journal of Urban and Regional Research*, (1978) 2 (1):101–131.

____ (1982) *The Limits to Capital*, Basil Blackwell, Oxford.

Hayden, D. (1982) *The Grand Domestic Revolution: A History of Feminist Designs for American Houses, Neighbourhoods and Cities*, MIT Press, Cambridge, Massachusetts.

____ (1984) *Redesigning the American Dream: The Future of Housing, Work and Family Life*, W. W. Norton & Co., New York.

Head, B. (1983) 'State and economy: theories and problems', in Head, B. (ed.).

____ (ed.) (1983) *State and Economy in Australia*, Oxford University Press, Melbourne.

Healey, P. (1983) *Local Plans in British Land Use Planning*, Pergamon, Oxford.

Healey, P. and Underwood, J. (1977) The organisational work of planning departments in the London Boroughs. *Conference Paper* 18, Centre for Environmental Studies, London.

Healey, P., McDougall, G. and Thomas, M. (eds) (1982) *Planning Theory: Prospects for the 1980s*, Pergamon, Oxford.

Heilbroner, R. L. (1980) *The Worldly Philosphers*, 5th edn, Simon & Schuster, New York.

Heresies II (1981) Making Room: Women and Architecture (special issue) 3,3.

Herzog, L. (1983) 'Politics and the role of the state in land use change: a report from San Diego, California', *International Journal of Urban and Regional Research*, 7, (1):92–113.

Hill, M. R. (1959) *Housing Finance in Australia 1945–56*, Melbourne University Press, Melbourne.

Hodgkinson, A. (1980) 'Structural change in the world aluminium industry and the implications for Australia', *Journal of Australian Political Economy*, 9, November.

Hodgson, G. (1984) *The Democratic Economy: A New Look at Planning, Markets and Power*, Pelican Books, Bungay, UK.

Holland, S. (1975) *The Socialist Challenge*, Quartet Books, London.

Horvath, R.J. and Tait, D. (1984) *Sydney: A Social Atlas*, National Mapping Service, Canberra.

Housing Commission of New South Wales, (1943) *Annual Report*, Government Printer, Sydney.

____ (1946) *Annual Report*, Government Printer, Sydney.

Howard, E. (1902) *Garden Cities of Tomorrow*, Faber & Faber, London (reprinted 1960).

Howe, A. and O'Connor, K. (1982) 'Travel to work and labour force participation of men and women in an Australian metropolitan area', *The Professional Geographer*, 34:20.

Hugo, G. (1979) 'Some demographic factors influencing recent demand for housing in Australia', *Australian Quarterly*, 51 (4):4–25.

Hugo, G. and Smailes, P. (1985) 'Urban-rural migration in Australia: a process view of the turnaround', *Journal of Rural Studies*, 1(1):11–30.

Huxley, M. and McLoughlin, J. B. (1985) 'The New Urban Studies Literature: a review with special reference to Australia', *Progress in Planning*, 24 (3):162–245.

Indicative Planning Council for the Housing Industry (1980) *Report on Multi-Unit Dwelling Development in Australia*, IPC, Canberra.

—— (1981) *Report for 1981/2 to 1983/4*, AGPS, Canberra.

International Journal of Urban and Regional Research (1978) Women and the City (special issue), 2, (2).

Jacobs, M. (1985) 'Thatcher's bomb under the welfare state', *Australian Society*, 4(9):24–6.

Jackson, R. V. (1977) *Australian Economic Development in the Nineteenth Century*, ANU Press, Canberra.

Jakubowicz, A. (1973) 'Towards a sociology of the city: or the city game', *Australian and New Zealand Journal of Sociology*, 9 (2):58–65.

—— (1984) 'The Green Bans movement: urban struggle and class politics', in Halligan, J. and Paris, C. (eds).

Jarvie, W. (1981) Internal migration and structural change: some preliminary observations. Paper to the Pacific Regional Science Conference, Queensland, August 16–20.

—— (1984) The turnaround in Australia: changes in inter-regional migration 1966–71 to 1971–76. Unpublished Ph.D thesis, Flinders University, Adelaide.

Jay, C. (1978) *Towards Urban Strategies for Australia*, AIUS, Canberra.

Jeans, D. and Logan, M. (1961) 'The problems of growth in Sydney's new suburbs', *Australian Journal of Social Issues*, 1 (1):29–48.

Jeans, D. and Spearritt, P. (1981) *The Open Air Museum*, George Allen & Unwin, Sydney.

Jensen-Butler, C. (1983) 'A materialist basis for planning theory and practice: comments on papers by Roweis and by Forester', *Environment and Planning D: Society and Space*, 1:469–479.

Jessop, R. (1982) *The Capitalist State*, Martin Robertson, Oxford.

Johnson, F. (1970) *How to Get Real Estate Rich*, Rydge, Sydney.

Johnston, R. J. (1982) *Geography and the State*, Macmillan, London.

Johnston, R. J. and Rimmer, P. J. (1969) *Retailing in Melbourne*, Department of Human Geography Publication H9/3, ANU, Canberra.

Jones, E. and Stilwell, F. J. B. (1983) 'When is an urban problem not an urban problem', in Williams P. (ed.).

Jones, M. A. (1972) *Housing and Poverty in Australia*, Melbourne University Press, Melbourne.

—— (1977) *Organisational and Social Planning in Australian Local Government*, Heinemann, Melbourne.

Joy, S. (1977) Criteria and criticisms. Paper presented to the 48th ANZAAS Congress, Melbourne. Reprinted in Seddon G. (ed. 1978) *Urbanisation*, Centre for Environment Studies, Melbourne University.

Katznelson, I. (1981) *City Trenches*, Pantheon Books, New York.

Keating, M. (1978) 'Economic Planning', in Troy, P. N. (ed.) *Federal Power in Australia's Cities*, Hale & Iremonger, Sydney.

Keegan, D. (1985) 'Urban sprawl drains tax coffers', *The Weekend Australian*, August 10–11:9.

Kelleher, L. (1981) 'How appeals subvert plans,' *Royal Australian Planning Institute Journal*, 19(3):109–11.

Kelly, G. (1957) 'Portrait of a new community', *Meanjin*, 16 (4):399–407.

Kemeny, J. (1978) 'Home ownership and finance capital', *Journal of Australian Political Economy*, 3:89–97.

—— (1981) *The Myth of Home Ownership*, Routledge & Kegan Paul, London.

—— (1983) *The Great Australian Nightmare*, Georgian House, Melbourne.

Kemp, R. (1980) 'Planning, legitimation and the development of nuclear energy: a critical theoretic analysis of the Windscale Inquiry', *International Journal of Urban and Regional Research*, 4:350–371.

—— (1982) 'Critical Planning Theory—review and critique', in P. Healey et al. (eds).

Kendig, H. (1979) *New Life for Old Suburbs*, George Allen & Unwin, Sydney.

—— (1981) *Buying and Renting: Household Moves in Adelaide*, AIUS, Canberra.

Kilmartin, L. and Thorns, D. (1978) *Cities Unlimited: The Sociology of Urban Development in Australia and New Zealand*, George Allen & Unwin, Sydney.

Kilmartin, L., Thorns, D. and Burke, T. (1985) *Social Theory and the Australian City*, George Allen & Unwin, Sydney.

Kilmartin, L., Huxley, M. and McLoughlin, J.B. (1985) 'Towards a sociology of Australian town planning', School of Environmental Planning, University of Melbourne.

King, R. (1980) Interest rates, energy and house prices: some aspects of the Melbourne housing market, 1966–80, Centre for Environmental Studies, University of Melbourne.

Kirk, G. (1980) *Urban Planning in Capitalist Society*, Croom Helm, London.

Knox, P. and Cullen, J. (1981) 'Planners as urban managers: an exploration of the attitudes and self-image of senior British planners', *Environment and Planning A*, 13:885–898.

Kuttner, B. (1981) 'Growth with equity', *Working Papers Magazine*, 8 (5):32–43.

Labor Resource Centre (1978) *Employment Bulletin*, 2(3) (April).

Lansdown, R. B. (1977) 'The issue of national settlement policy', *Australian Quarterly*, (March).

Larcombe, G. (1980) 'The political economy of Newcastle', in Stilwell, F. J. B.: Chapter 9.

Lawrence, R. J. (1972) 'Social welfare and urban growth', in Parker, R. S. and Troy, P. N. (eds) *The Politics of Urban Growth*, ANU Press, Canberra.

Lawless, P. (1979) *Urban Deprivation and Government Initiative*, Faber & Faber, London.

Layman, L. (1981) 'Changing resource development policy in Western Australia, 1830–1860s,' in Harman, E. and Head, B. (eds).

Leonard, S. (1982) 'Urban managerialism: a period of transition?', *Progress in Human Geography*, 6, (2):190–215.

Levison, A. (1974) *The Working Class Majority*, Coward, McCarn and Gerghegar, New York.

Linge, G. J. R. (1975) 'The forging of an industrial nation: manufacturing in Australia 1788–1913', in Powell, M. J. and Williams, M. (eds) *Australian Space, Australian Time*, Oxford University Press, Melbourne.

—— (1979) 'Australian manufacturing in recession: a review of the spatial implications', *Environment and Planning A*, 11:1405–30.

Linge, G. J. R. and McKay, J. (eds) (1981) *Structural Change in Australia: some spatial and organisational responses*, ANU Press, Canberra.

Lipsey, R. (1979) 'World Inflation', *Economic Record*, 55:283–96.

Little, F. M. (1977) *Socio-economic Implications of Urban Development*, MMBW, Melbourne.

Little, F. M. and Carter, R. A (1979) *Urban Development, Economic Development and Growth*, MMBW, Melbourne.

Lloyd, C. and Troy, P. N. (1981) *Innovation and Reaction: the life and death of the Federal Department of Urban and Regional Development*, George Allen & Unwin, Sydney.

Loder and Bayly (1978) *Subregional Structure: a Study of its Influence on Public Transport and Car Usage*, MMBW, Melbourne.

Logan, M. I. (1977) Regional Implications. Paper presented to the 48th ANZAAS Congress, Melbourne. Reprinted in Seddon, G. (ed. 1978) *Urbanisation*, Centre for Environmental Studies, The University of Melbourne.

—— (1978) 'Regional policy', in Scott P. (ed.) *Australian Cities and Public Policy*, Georgian House, Melbourne.

—— (1984) 'Manufacturing decentralisation in the Sydney metropolitan area', *Economic Geography*, 40(2):151–62.

Logan, M. I., Maher, C. A., McKay, J and Humphreys, J. S. (1975) *Urban and Regional Australia: Analysis and Policy Issues*, Sorrett Publishing Pty, Malvern, Victoria.

Logan, M. I., Whitelaw, J. S. and McKay, J. (1981) *Urbanisation: The Australian Experience*, Shillington House, Melbourne.

Logan, T. (1976) 'Decentralists forget jobs for the girls', *Royal Australian Planning Institute Journal*, July/October:42.

—— (1979) 'Recent directions of regional policy in Australia', *Regional Studies*, 13 (2):153–60.

—— (1981) *Urban and Regional Planning in Victoria*, Shillington House, Melbourne.

—— (1984) 'Urban and regional planning in a federal system: New South Wales and Victoria', *Environment and Planning A*, 16:1041–54.

—— (forthcoming 1986) 'A critical examination of Melbourne's District Centre Policy', *Urban Policy and Research.*

Logan, T. and Ogilvy, E. (1981) 'The statutory planning framework', in Troy, P.N. (ed.).

Logan, W. S. (1978) 'Post-convergence political geography: death or transfiguration?', *Monash Publications in Geography*, 18, Monash University, Melbourne.

—— (1982) 'Gentrification in inner Melbourne: problems of analysis', *Australian Geographical Studies*, 20:65–95.

—— (1985) *The Gentrification of Inner Melbourne*, Queensland University Press, St Lucia.

Lojkine, J. (1976) 'Contribution to a Marxist theory of urbanisation', in Pickvance, C. (ed.).

Low, N.P. and Power, J. M. (1984) 'Policy systems in an Australian metropolitan region: political and economic determinants of change in Victoria', *Progress in Planning*, 22:97–173.

Lyne, J. (1974) *Greater Melbourne*, Cambridge University Press, Melbourne.

McAuslan, P. (1980) *The Ideologies of Planning Law*, Pergamon, Oxford.

McCarty, J. W. (1978) 'Australian capital cities in the nineteenth century', in McCarty, J. W. and Schedvin, C. B. (eds) *Australian Capital Cities*, Sydney University Press, Sydney.

McKay, J. and Whitelaw, J. S. (1978) 'Internal migration and the Australian urban system', *Progress in Planning*, 10:1–83.

McKeon, R. (1982) Patterns of regional development and an examination of possible indicators of regional difficulties. Paper to Department of Geography, ANU, Canberra, 17 February.

MacKinnon C. (1982) 'Feminism, Marxism and the State: an agenda for theory', *Signs*, 7, (3):515–544.

McLennan, G., Held, D. and Hall, S. (eds) (1984) *The Idea of the Modern State*, Open University Press, Milton Keynes, UK.

McLoughlin, J.B. (1969) *Urban and Regional Planning: A Systems Approach*, Faber & Faber, London.

—— (1973*a*) *Control and Urban Planning*, Faber & Faber, London.

—— (1973*b*) 'The future of the planning profession', in Cowan, P. (ed.) *The Future of Planning*, Heinemann, London.

—— (1983*a*) 'The crisis in British planning education and research', in Williams, P. (ed.).

—— (1983*b*) 'Planning education and research in Australia', *Urban Policy and Research*, 1 (4):16–21.

Maher, C. A. (1976) The changing residential functions of the inner city: an Australian example. Paper presented to Urban Research Unit seminar, on 'The Inner City', ANU, Canberra.

—— (1982*a*) *Australian Cities in Transition*, Shillington House, Melbourne.

—— (1982*b*) 'Population turnover and spatial change in Melbourne, Australia', *Urban Geography*, 3 (3):249–57.

—— (1984) *Residential Mobility within Australian Cities*, Census Monograph, Catalogue No. 3410.0, AGPS, Canberra.

—— (1985) 'The changing character of Australian urban growth', *Built Environment*, 11 (2):69–82.

____ (forthcoming) Internal migration and metropolitan development in Australia. Proceedings of the Regional Science Conference, Melbourne, December, 1984.

____ (forthcoming) Macro-economic forces and urbanisation in Australia. Proceedings of the International Geographical Union Commission on National Settlement Systems, Pisa, August 1984.

Maher, C. A., O'Connor, K. and Logan, M. I. (1981) 'Employment opportunities', in Troy, P. N. (ed.).

Maher, C. A., Goodman, A. and Savage, R. (1985) Population mobility within Australia's metropolitan areas, 1976–81. *Working Paper No 5, 1981 Internal Migration Study*, Department of Immigration and Ethnic Affairs and Department of Geography, Monash University, Melbourne.

Mandel, E. (1975) *Late Capitalism*, New Left Books, London.

Manning, I. (1973) *Municipal Finance and Income Distribution in Sydney*, ANU Urban Research Unit, Canberra.

____ (1978) *The Journey to Work*, George Allen & Unwin, Sydney.

____ (1981) 'Traffic and local planning', in Troy, P. N. (ed.).

____ (1984) *Beyond Walking Distance*, ANU Press, Canberra.

Marcuse, P. (1976) 'Professional ethics and beyond: values in planning', *Journal of the American Institute of Planners*, 43, (3):264–74.

Markusen, A. R. (1980) 'City spatial structure, women's household work and national urban policy', *Signs*, 5(3) supplement:23–44.

____ (1983) 'High-tech jobs, markets and economic development prospects: evidence from California', *Built Environment*, 9(1):18–27.

Massey, D. (1983) 'The shape of things to come', *Marxism Today*, 27(4):18–27.

____ (1984) *Spatial Divisions of Labour*, Macmillan, London.

Massey, D. and Catalano, A. (1978) *Capital and Land: Landownership by Capital in Great Britain*, Edward Arnold, London.

Matwitjiw, P. (1985) *Atlas of Youth Unemployment, 1981*, Australian Institute of Multicultural Affairs, Melbourne.

Maud, R. (1984) 'The chip and capitalism', *Australian Society*, 3(10) 16–18.

May, R.J. (1971) *Financing the Small States in Australian Federalism*, Oxford University Press, Melbourne.

Melbourne and Metropolitan Board of Works (MMBW) (1954) *Melbourne Metropolitan Planning Scheme*, Melbourne.

____ (1967) *The Future Growth of Melbourne*, Melbourne.

____ (1971) *Planning Policies for the Melbourne Metropolitan Region*, Melbourne.

____ (1977) *Melbourne's Inner Area: A Position Statement*, Melbourne.

____ (1979*a*) *The Challenge of Change*, Melbourne.

____ (1979*b*) *Alternative Strategies for Metropolitan Melbourne*, Melbourne.

____ (1979*c*) *Some Transport Implications of Containment*, Melbourne.

____ (1980) *Metropolitan Strategy*, Melbourne.

____ (1981) *Metropolitan Strategy Implementation*, Melbourne.

____ (1982) *Dual Occupancy*, Planning Guideline No. 1, Melbourne.

____ (1985) *The Implementation of the Cluster-and-Connect Model in Nunawading*, Melbourne.

Mercer, C. (1975) *Living in Cities*, Penguin, Harmondsworth, UK.

Merrett, D.J. (1977) 'Australian capital cities in the twentieth century', *Monash Papers in Economic History 4*, Monash University, Melbourne.

Merritt, G. (1982) *World Out of Work*, Collins, London.

Metcalf, D. and Richardson, R. (1976) 'Unemployment in London', in Worswick, D. (ed.) *The Concept and Measurement of Involuntary Unemployment*, George Allen & Unwin, London.

Miliband, R. (1973) *The State in Capitalist Society*, Quartet Books, London, (first published by Weidenfeld & Nicholson, London, 1969).

Mingione, E. (1981) *Social Conflict and the City*, Basil Blackwell, Oxford.

Minnery, J. (1985) 'Urban planners and role conflicts', *Urban Policy and Research*, 3, (1):25–30.

MMBW *see* Melbourne and Metropolitan Board of Works.

Moltoch, H. (1976) 'The city as a growth machine: toward a political economy of place', *American Journal of Sociology*, 8:309–32.

Morgan, J. (1983) The spatial distribution of recorded and hidden unemployment in the Adelaide Statistical Division. Unpublished B. A. Hons Thesis, Flinders University, Adelaide.

Moriarty, P. and Beed, C. S. (1985) 'Effects of changing land use and modal split in Melbourne', *Urban Policy and Research*, 3(3):2–10.

Morris, J. (1981) 'Urban public transport', in Troy, P. N. (ed.).

Mowbray, M. (1982) 'Rates, roads, rubbish and redistribution: the politics of local taxation', *Journal of Australian Political Economy*, 11:73–88. *See also* Halligan J. and Paris C. (eds) (1984): Chapter 6.

Muller, R. (1979) 'National economic growth and stabilisation policy: the challenge of our post-market economy', *Occasional Paper 3*, Transnational Corporations Research Project, Faculty of Economics, University of Sydney.

Mullins, P. (1977) 'The social base, stake and urban effects of a Brisbane urban social movement', *Australian and New Zealand Journal of Sociology*, 13(1):29–35.

—— (1979*a*) 'Australian's sunbelt migration: the recent growth of Brisbane and the Moreton Bay region', *Journal of Australian Political Economy*, 5:17–32.

—— (1979*b*) 'The struggle against Brisbane freeways: 1966–74', *International Journal of Urban and Regional Research*, 3(4):342–52.

—— (1980) 'Australian urbanisation and Queensland's underdevelopment: a first empirical statement', *International Journal of Urban and Regional Research*, 4(2):212–38.

—— (1981) 'Theoretical perspectives on Australian urbanisation: I. material components in the reproduction of Australian labour power', *Australia and New Zealand Journal of Sociology*, 17(1):65–76.

—— (1982) 'The "middle class" and the inner city', *Journal of Australian Political Economy*, 11:44–58.

Myrdal, G. (1963) *Economic Theory and Underdeveloped Regions*, Methuen, London.

Neutze, M. (1965) *Economic Policy and the Size of Cities*, ANU Press, Canberra.

—— (1977) *Urban Development in Australia*, 1st edn, George Allen & Unwin, Sydney.

—— (1978) *Australian Urban Policy*, George Allen & Unwin, Sydney.

—— (1981*a*) *Urban Development in Australia*, 2nd edn, George Allen & Unwin, Sydney.

—— (1981*b*) 'Housing', in Troy, P. (ed.).

—— (1982) 'Urban planning, policy and management', *Australian Journal of Public Administration*, XLI(2):145–58.

Newman, P. (1981) 'Energy and urban form', *Royal Australian Planning Institute Journal*, 19:35–7.

Newman, P. and Kenworthy, T. (1979) *Urban Density: Understanding the Trends*, Murdoch University Press, Perth.

—— (1981) 'Public and private transport in Australian cities: an analysis of existing patterns and their energy implications', *Transport Policy and Decision-Making*, 1:133–48.

New South Wales Planning and Environment Commission (1980) Sydney's Inner Areas, *Working Paper*, P. E. C., Sydney.

New South Wales Department of Environment and Planning (1981) *The Environmental Planning and Assessment Act, 1979: A Guide for Local Government*, Department of Environment and Planning, Sydney.

—— (1982) *Residential Development Standards, Technical Bulletin*, 15, Department of Environment and Planning, Sydney.

—— (1984) *Planning Issues in the Sydney Region: Urban Consolidation*, Department of Environment and Planning, Sydney.

New South Wales, Government of (1957) *Official Yearbook*, Government Printer, Sydney.

New South Wales Planning Authority (1968) *Sydney Region Outline Plan*, State Planning Authority, Sydney.

Nittim, Z. (1975) 'How ya gonna keep 'em down on the farm?', in *The Gilded Cage*, W E L, Sydney.

Norman, P. (1975) 'Managerialism: review of recent work', in Harloe, M. (ed.) *Proceedings of the Conference on Urban Change and Conflict*, Centre for Environmental Studies, London.

O'Connor, J. (1973) *The Fiscal Crisis of the State*, St Martin's Press, New York.

—— (1984) *Accumulation Crisis*, Basil Blackwell, Oxford.

O'Connor, K. F. (1978) 'The journey to work of inner city residents in Melbourne, 1966 and 1971', *Australian Geographical Studies*, 16:73–81.

—— (1979) 'Discussion Paper', in Carter, R. A. (ed.) *The Role of Urban Development in National Economic Development—Conference Proceedings*, University of Melbourne.

—— (1984) 'Urban and regional change in Australia: an empirical introduction', *Environment and Planning A*, 16:993–1002.

O'Connor, K. and Maher, C. A. (1979) 'Change in the spatial structure of a metropolitan region: work-residence relationships in Melbourne 1961–71', *Regional Studies*, 13:361–80.

Offe, C. (1975) 'The theory of the capitalist state and the problem of policy formation', in Lindberg, R., Alford, C., Crouch, C., and Offe C. (eds) *Stress and Contradiction in Modern Capitalism: Public Policy and the Theory of the State*, Lexington Books, Massachusetts.

—— (1984) *Contradictions of the Welfare State*, Hutchinson, London.

Okun, A. (1975) *Equality and Efficiency: The Big Trade-Off*, Brookings Institution, Washington DC.

O'Leary, G. and McEachern D. (1980) 'Capitalist recession and industrialisation in the Third World: reflections on the Warren thesis', *Journal of Australian Political Economy*, 7:86–104.

Pahl. R. E. (1970) *Whose city?*, 1st edn, Longman, Harlow, UK.

—— (1973) 'Cities Symposium: a comment', *Australia and New Zealand Journal of Sociology*, 9(3):20–22.

—— (1975) *Whose City?*, 2nd edn, Penguin, Harmondsworth, UK.

—— (1977) 'Managers, technical experts and the state', in Harloe, M. (ed.).

—— (1981) 'Employment, work and the domestic division of labour', in Harloe, M. and Lebas, E. (eds).

—— (1984) *Divisions of Labour*, Basil Blackwell, Oxford.

Paris, C. (ed.) (1982) *Critical Readings in Planning Theory*, Pergamon, Oxford.

Paris, C. and Williams, P. (1984) 'Planning, urban crisis and urban management', *Journal of Australian Political Economy*, 16:67–73.

Park, R. (1949) *Poor Man's Orange*, Angus & Robertson, Sydney.

Parkin, A. (1979) 'Cities without politics', *Politics*, 16:291–4.

—— (1982) *Governing the Cities: The Australian Experience in Perspective*, Macmillan, Melbourne.

Parkin, F. (1972) *Class, Inequality and Political Order*, Paladin, London.

Paterson, J. (1975) 'Unobtrusive measures: their nature and utility for architects', in Lang J., Burnette C, Moleske W. and Vacation D. (eds) *Designing for Human Behaviour*, Dowden, Hutchinson & Ross, Stroudsburg.

Paterson, J. (1974) *Melbourne Metropolitan Residential Land Study*, AIUS, Melbourne.

—— (1978) 'Urban management: the Australian context', in Australian National Commission for UNESCO, *Urban Management Processes*, AGPS, Canberra.

—— (1980) 'Urban Consolidation: lovelier the second time around?', in Archer R. W. (ed.) *Planning for Urban Consolidation*, Planning Research Centre, University of Sydney.

Paterson, J., Yencken, D. and Gunn, G. (1976) *A Mansion or No House*, Urban Development Institute of Australia, Melbourne.

Patience, A. and Head, B. (eds) (1979) *From Whitlam to Fraser*, Oxford University Press, Melbourne.

Peet, R. (1981) 'Spatial dialectics and Marxist geography', *Progress in Human Geography*, 5:105–10.

Perry, D. and Watkins, A. (1978) Contemporary dimensions of uneven urban development: a research report. Paper presented to the Ninth World Congress of the International Sociological Association, Urban and Regional Development Research Committee, Uppsala, Sweden.

Pickvance, C. (ed.) (1976) *Urban Sociology: Critical Essays*, Tavistock, London.

—— (1980) 'Theories of the state and theories of urban crisis', in McNall, S. and Howe, G. (eds) *Current Perspectives in Social Theory*, Vol. 1, Jai Press, Greenwich, Connecticut.

Piven, F. F. (1975) 'Planners and class interests', *Journal of the American Institute of Planners*, 41, (5):308–310.

Piven, F. F. and Cloward, R. (1982) *The New Class War: Reagan's Attack on the Welfare State*, Basic Books, New York.

Poulantzas, N. (1969) 'The problem of the capitalist state', *New Left Review*, 58:67–78.

—— (1973) *Political Power and Social Classes*, New Left Books, London.

—— (1975) *Classes in Contemporary Capitalism*, New Left Books, London.

Power, J. (1970) 'Town planning and politics', *Australian Planning Institute Journal*, 8(2):33–7.

Power, J., Wettenhall, R. and Halligan, J. (eds) (1981) *Local Government Systems in Australia*, AGPS, Canberra.

Price, C. (1970) 'Immigrants', in Davies, A. F. and Encel, S. (eds) *Australian Society: A Sociological Introduction*, Longman Cheshire, Melbourne.

Pringle, R. (1983) 'Women and consumer capitalism', in Baldock, C. and Cass, B. (eds).

Ranson, S., Hinings, B. and Greenwood, R. (1980) 'The structuring of organisational structures', *Administrative Science Quarterly*, 25, (1).

Ravenscroft, M. (1943) 'The housing problem', *Social Horizons*, July.

Reade, E. (1982) 'The effects of town and country planning in Britain' in *Urban Change and Conflict* (a second level course: Unit 23), the Open University Press, Milton Keynes, UK.

Reed, A. and Wilmoth, D. (1983) The New South Wales Development Program. Paper presented to the Seminar on 'Forecasting and Urban Programming', Victoria Public Service Board, Melbourne.

Rees, G. and Lambert, J. (1985) *Cities in Crisis*, Edward Arnold, London.

Relph, E. (1976) *Place and Placelessness*, Pion, London.

Rex, J. and Moore, R. (1967) *Race, Community and Conflict*, Oxford University Press, London.

Richardson, H. (1978) *Urban Economics*, Dryden Press, Hinsdale.

Rimmer, P. (1969) *Manufacturing in Melbourne*, ANU Press, Canberra.

Roddewig, R. J. (1978) *Green Bans: The Birth of Australian Environmental Politics*, Hale & Iremonger, Sydney.

Robins, P. A.. (1981) 'The regional impact of structural change in Australian manufacturing industry: the case of South Australia', in Linge, G. J. R. and McKay, J. (eds).

Robson, J. (1979) 'Technological change and unemployment in the 1980s', *Journal of Australian Political Economy*, 5:56–72.

Rose, A. J. (1966) 'Dissent from down under: metropolitan primacy as the normal state', *Pacific Viewpoint*, 7:1–27.

Roweis, S. (1983) 'Urban planning as professional mediation of territorial politics', *Environment and Planning D: Society and Space*, 1:139–62.

Roweis, S. and Scott, A. J. (1981) 'The urban land question', in Dear, M. and Scott, A. J. (eds).

Rumberger, R. (1984) The potential impact of technology on the skill requirements for future jobs. Paper presented to the US-Australian Joint Seminar, Monash University, Melbourne.

Ryan, M. (1943/4) Unpublished diaries (held by the family).

Saegert, S. (1980) 'Masculine cities and feminine suburbs: polarised ideas, contradictory realities', *Signs*, 5(3) supplement:96–111.

Sams, D. and Beed, C. S. (1984) 'Changes in self-containment within Melbourne 1966–1981', *Urban Policy and Research*, 2(3):15–25.

Sandercock, L. (1977) *Cities for Sale: Property, Politics and Urban Planning in Australia*, Melbourne University Press, Melbourne (first published by Heinemann, 1975).

—— (1979) *The Land Racket*, Silverfish Press, Melbourne.

—— (1982) From physical determinism to political economy: the new agenda for planners. Paper presented to the 52nd ANZAAS Congress, Macquarie University, Sydney.

—— (1982) 'Democratic socialism and the challenge of social democracy', in Evans G. and Reeves J. (eds) *Socialist Principles and Parliamentary Government*, Drummond, Melbourne.

—— (1983*a*) 'Urban studies in Australia: producing planners or educating urbanists?', in Murray-Smith S. (ed.) *Melbourne Studies in Education 1982*, Melbourne University Press, Melbourne.

—— (1983*b*) 'A socialist city in a capitalist society?', in Sandercock L. and Berry M.

—— (1983*c*) 'Politics and land deals: the case of Melbourne', in Sandercock and Berry.

—— (1983*d*) 'Educating planners: from physical determinism to economic crisis', in Sandercock L. and Berry M. (eds).

—— (1983*e*) 'Urban policy: from Whitlam to Fraser', in Sandercock L. and Berry M.J.

—— (1984) 'Planners, planning policy and recession', in Eade R. and Eccles D. (eds) *Planning in a Recession*, Footscray Institute of Technology, Melbourne.

Sandercock, L. and Berry, M. (1983) *Urban Political Economy: The Australian Case*, George Allen & Unwin, Sydney.

Sandercock, L. and Melser, P. (1985) 'Like a building condemned: planning in an old industrial region', *Built Environment*, 11(2):120–31.

Sarkissian, W. (1983) *Employment Creation through Community Economic Development: Selected Readings*, Social Impacts Publications, Sydney.

Saunders, P. (1979) *Urban Politics: A Sociological Interpretation*, Penguin, Harmondsworth, UK.

—— (1981) *Social Theory and the Urban Question*, Hutchinson, London.

—— (1983) 'On the shoulders of which giant? The case for Weberian political analysis', in Williams, P. (ed.).

—— (1984) 'The crisis of local government in Melbourne: the sacking of the City Council', in Halligan J. and Paris C. (eds).

—— (1985) 'Is small better?' *Australian Society*, 4(9):11–4.

Saxenian, A. (1983) 'The genesis of silicon valley', *Built Environment*, 9(1):7–17.

Sayer, R.A. (1979*a*) 'A critique of urban modelling', *Progress in Planning*, 6:187:254.

—— (1979*b*) 'Understanding urban models versus understanding cities', *Environment and Planning A*, 11:853–862.

Schwartz, J. (ed.) (1977) *The Subtle Anatomy of Capitalism*, Goodyear Publishing Co., Santa Monica.

Schultz, J. (1985) *Steel City Blues: The Human Cost of Industrial Crisis*, Penguin, Ringwood, Victoria.

Scott, A.J. (1980) *The Urban Land Nexus and the State*, Pion, London.

Scott, A.J. and Roweis, S.T. (1977) 'Urban planning in theory and practice: a reappraisal', *Environment and Planning A*, 10:1097–1119.

Scott, D. and U'Ren, J. (1962) *Leisure*, Cheshire, Melbourne.

Shorrock, T. (1983) 'Atari moves to Asia', *Multinational Monitor*, 5 (4):11–13.

Signs (1980) Women and the American City (special supplement) 5, (3).

Simmie, J. (1974) *Citizens in Conflict: The Sociology of Town Planning*, Hutchinson, London.

Simsion, D.W. (1979) The role of the regional authority in implementing change. Paper presented to the Urban Development Industries Association Congress, Melbourne.

Smith, M.P. (ed.) (1984) *Cities in Transformation: Class, Capital and the State*, Sage Publications, Beverley Hills.

Smith, N. (1982) 'Gentrification and uneven development', *Economic Geography*, 58 (2):139–55.

—— (1984) *Uneven Development: Nature, Capital and the Production of Space*, Basil Blackwell, Oxford.

Smith, V.L. (1980) 'Experiments with a decentralised mechanism for public goods decisions', *American Economic Review*, 70:584–99.

Socialist Alternative Melbourne Collective (SAMC) (1985) *Make Melbourne Marvellous*, Communist Party of Australia, Melbourne.

Soja, E.W. (1980) 'The socio-spatial dialectic', *Annals of the American Association of Geographers*, 70, (2):207–225.

Soja, E.W., Morales, R. and Wolff, G. (1983) 'Urban Restructuring: an analysis of social and spatial change in Los Angeles', *Economic Geography*, 59(2):195–230.

Solomon, R.J. (1976) *Urbanisation: The Evolution of an Australian Capital*, Angus & Robertson, Sydney.

South Australian Department of Urban and Regional Affairs (1980) *Energy and Land Use*, Report prepared by Travers Morgan and Partners, Adelaide.

South Australian House of Assembly (1950) *South Australian Official Reports of the Parliamentary Debates*, (Hansard), Government Printer, Adelaide.

—— (1953) *South Australian Official Reports of the Parliamentary Debates*, (Hansard), Government Printer, Adelaide.

South Australian Housing Trust (1981) *Annual Report: Year Ending 30 June 1981*, Government Printer, Adelaide.

Spearritt, P. (1974) 'The Kindergarten Movement', in Edgar, D.E. (ed.) *Social Change in Australia: Readings in Sociology*, Cheshire, Melbourne.

—— (1978*a*) *Sydney Since the Twenties*, Hale & Iremonger, Sydney.

—— (1978*b*) 'Public transport versus the car: what price survival?' *Current Affairs Bulletin*, 58:4–15.

—— (1984) 'The privatisation of Australian transport', in Halligan, J. and Paris, C. (eds).

Stevenson, G. (1977) *Mineral Resources and Australian Federalism*, Centre for Research on Federal Financial Relations, ANU, Canberra.

Stilwell, F.J.B. (1974*a*) 'Economic factors and the growth of cities', in Burnley, I.H. (ed.).

—— (1974*b*) *Australian Urban and Regional Development*, ANZ Book Company, Sydney.

—— (1976) 'Inequality in wealth and income in Australia', in Wheelwright E.L. and Stilwell, F.J.B. (eds).

—— (1980) *Economic Crisis, Cities and Regions*, Pergamon Press Australia, Sydney.

—— (1983) 'State and capital in urban and regional development', in Head, B. (ed.).

Stilwell, F.J.B. and Hardwick, J.M. (1973) Introduction to Regional Development in Australia. Department of Town and Country Planning, University of Sydney.

Stimson, R. (1982) *The Australian City: A Welfare Geography*, Longman Cheshire, Melbourne.

Stretton, H. (1970) *Ideas for Australian Cities*, 1st edn, The Author, Adelaide.

—— (1972) 'Planning to break the rules', *Royal Australian Planning Institute Journal*, 10(4):135–9.

—— (1974) *Housing and Government*, The Boyer Lectures, Australian Broadcasting Commission, Sydney.

—— (1975) *Ideas for Australian Cities*, 2nd edn, Georgian House, Melbourne.

—— (1976) *Capitalism, Socialism and the Environment*, Cambridge University Press, Cambridge.

—— (1978) *Urban Planning in Rich and Poor Countries*, Oxford University Press, Melbourne.

Stricker, P. and Sheehan, P. (1981) *Hidden Unemployment: The Australian Experience*, Institute of Applied Economic and Social Research, University of Melbourne.

Sutcliffe, A. (1981) *Towards the Planned City*, Basil Blackwell, Oxford.

Szelenyi, I. (1977) Class analysis and beyond: further dilemmas for the new urban sociology. School of Social Sciences, Flinders University, Adelaide.

—— (1981) 'The relative autonomy of the state or state mode of production', in Dear, M.J. and Scott, A.J. (eds).

Tasmania, Government of (1962) *Local Government Act*, Government Printer, Hobart.

—— (1978) *Building Regulations*, Government Printer, Hobart.

Taylor, M. and Thrift, N. (1982) *The Geography of Multinationals: Studies in the Spatial Development and Economic Consequences of Multinational Corporations*, Croom Helm, London.

Tennant, K. (1959) *Foveaux*, Angus & Robertson, Sydney.

Theophanous, A. (1980) *Australian Democracy in Crisis*, Oxford University Press, Melbourne.

Thomas, D. (1985*a*) 'Taking the measure of unemployment', *New Society*, 72, 1168: 223–5.

—— (1985*b*) 'Learning about job creation', *New Society*, 72, 1169:62–3.

Thompson, E.J. (ed.) (1975) *Social Trends. No. 6*, HMSO, London.

Thomson, J. M. (1978) *Great Cities and their Traffic*, Penguin, Harmondsworth, U.K.

Thrift, N. (1979) 'Unemployment in the inner city: urban problem or structural imperative? A review of the British experience', in Herbert, D. T. and Johnston, R.J. (eds) *Geography and the Urban Environment: Progress in Research and Applications*, Vol. II, Wiley, Chichester.

—— (1983) 'On the determination of social action in space and time', *Environment and Planning D: Society and Space*, 1, (1):23–57.

Timlin, J. (1974) 'Megacorp and Westernport Bay', in Dempsey, R. (ed.) *The Politics of Finding Out: Environmental Problems in Australia*, Longman Cheshire, Melbourne.

Timms, D. (1971) *The Urban Mosaic: Towards a Theory of Residential Differentiation*, Cambridge University Press, Cambridge.

Troy, P. N. (1978) *A Fair Price*, Hale & Iremonger, Sydney.

—— (ed 1981) *Equity in the City*, George Allen & Unwin, Sydney.

UK Department of the Environment (1977) *Inner Area Studies: Liverpool, Birmingham and Lambeth: Summaries of Consultant's Final Reports*, HMSO, London.

Underwood, J. (1981) 'Development Control: a case study of discretion in action', in Barrett, S. and Fudge, C. (eds) *Policy and Action*, Metheun, London.

United Nations (1974) *United Nations Statistical Yearbook 1973*, Department of Economic and Social Affairs, Statistical Office, New York.

Urban Systems Corporation (1974) *The City of Adelaide Plan*, Urban Systems Corporation Pty Ltd, Sydney.

Urry, J. (1981) 'Localities, regions and social class', *International Journal of Urban and Regional Research*, 5:455–474.

US Department of Housing and Urban Development (1980) *Urban Infill: The Literature*, US Government Printing Office, Washington DC.

Uthwatt, Mr Justice (1942) (The 'Uthwatt Report') *Report of the Expert Committee on Compensation and Betterment*, HMSO, London.

Vanek, J. (1974) 'Time spent in housework', *Scientific American*, November: 116–20.

Victoria, Government of (1978) (The 'Darvall Report') *Report of the Board of Inquiry into the MMBW*, Government Printer, Melbourne.

—— (1979) (The 'Bains Report') *Report of the Board of Review of the Role, Structure and Administration of Local Government in Victoria*, Government Printer, Melbourne.

—— (1984) *Victoria—The Next Step: Economic Initiatives and Opportunities for the 1980s*, Government Printer, Melbourne.

Victorian Parliament (1943) (House of Assembly) *Parliamentary Debates*, (Hansard), Vol. 216, Government Printer, Melbourne.

Vipond, J. (1980*a*) 'The impact of high unemployment in areas within Sydney', *Journal of Industrial Relations*, 23:326–41.

—— (1980*b*) 'Intra-urban unemployment differentials in Sydney', *Urban Studies*, 17:131–8.

—— (1981*a*) 'Changes in unemployment differentials in Sydney 1947–76', *Australian Geographical Studies*, 19:67–77.

—— (1981*b*) What can we do? Policy options on unemployment. Paper presented to the AIUS seminar 'Unemployment in the Cities', Adelaide, September.

—— (1982) *The Suburban Unemployed*, Centre for Applied Economic Research, University of New South Wales, Kensington, NSW.

Walker, D. (1978) 'Two sources of uneven development under advanced capitalism: spatial differentiation and capital mobility', *Review of Radical Political Economy*, 10 (3):28–38.

—— (1984) 'Euro-trends', *New Society*, 67, 1102:25–6.

Wallerstein, E. (1979) *The Capitalist World-Economy*, Cambridge University Press, Cambridge.

—— (1983) *Historical Capitalism*, Verso, London.

Wanna, J. (1980) 'The economic development of South Australia: a Marxist analysis', *Journal of Australian Political Economy*, 9:3–24.

Ward, B. (1976) *The Home of Man*, Andre Deutsch, London.

Ward, C. (1973) *Anarchy in Action*, Allen & Unwin, London.

Warren, B. (1973) 'Implementation and capitalist industrialisation', *New Left Review*, 81:112–41.

—— (1978) 'The post-war experience of the Third World', *Journal of Australian Political Economy*, 3:3–24.

Watts, H. W. and Rees, A. (1977) *The New Jersey Income Maintenance Experiment. Vol II, Labour Supply Responses*, Academic Press, New York.

Wearing, R. J. and Wearing, A. J. (1973) *Housewives in a New Suburb*, AIUS, Canberra.

Weidenbaum, M. L. and Athey, M. J. (1985) 'Revival of the "rust belt"', *Economic Impact*, 50(2):59–67.

Weiss, M. A. (1983) 'High-technology industries and the future of employment', *Built Environment*, 9(1):51–60.

Wekerle, G. (1980) 'Women in the urban environment', *Signs*, 5(3):188–214.

Wekerle, G., Peterson, R. and Morley, D. (1980) *New Space for Women*, Westview Press, Boulder, Colorado.

Westergaard, J. and Resler, H. (1975) *Class in a Capitalist Society*, Heinemann, London.

Western Australia, Department of Community Welfare (1981) *Emergency Assistance*, A Department Paper, Government Printer, Perth.

Western Australia, Department of Industrial Development and Commerce (1981) *Manufacturing Industry in Western Australia*, Government Printer, Perth.

Western Australia, Department of Resources Development (1980) *Major Development Project Impact Study: Economic Impact of the Western Australian Alumina Industry*, Government Printer, Perth.

Western Australia, Department of Town Planning (1982) *Resource Development and Urban Planning in Western Australia*, (Planning Ministers Conference, 18/19 February), Government Printer, Perth.

Wheelwright, E. L. (1980) 'Cheap labour havens and de-industrialisation', in Crough, G., Wheelwright, E. L. and Wilshire, E. (eds) *Australia and World Capitalism*, Penguin, Ringwood, Victoria.

Wheelwright, E. L. and Stilwell, F. J. B. (eds) (1976) *Readings in Political Economy*, (2 vols), ANZ Book Co., Sydney.

White, D. et al. (1978) *Seeds for Change: Creatively Confronting the Energy Crisis*, CUE, Patchwork Press, Melbourne.

Whitelaw, J. S. and Maher, C. A. (forthcoming) 'A tale of few cities: urbanisation in a constrained environment', in Heathcote, L. (ed.) (title to be announced), Academy of Social Science, Canberra.

Wilenski, P. (1978) 'New South Wales', in Australian National Commission for Unesco, *Urban Management Processes*, AGPS, Canberra.

Williams, P. (1976) Change in an urban area: the role of institutions in the process of gentrification in inner London. Unpublished Ph.D thesis, University of Reading, U.K.

—— (1978) 'Urban managerialism: a concept of relevance', *Area*, 10:236–40.

—— (1982) 'Restructuring urban managerialism: towards a political economy of urban allocation', *Environment and Planning A*, 14:95–105.

—— (ed.) (1983) *Social Process and the City*, George Allen & Unwin, Sydney.

—— (ed.) (1984) *Conflict and Development*, George Allen & Unwin, Sydney.

Wilmoth, D. (1977) National Urban Planning in Australia: a critique of the Labor years 1972–5. Paper presented to the Union of Radical Political Economists, California.

—— (1982) 'Urban consolidation and social equity', in Sandercock, L. (ed.) *Urban Consolidation: The Equity Issue*, Centre for Environmental and Urban Studies, Macquarie University, Sydney.

—— (1986) 'Structure and agency in the formation of national urban policy in the U.S.A.', *Progress in Planning*, 25, (2).

Wilson, R. K. (1980) *Australia's Resources and their Development*, University of Sydney Press, Sydney.

Windschuttle, K. (1981) 'Unemployment — no end in sight', *Australian Quarterly*, 53:167–76.

—— (1984) 'Make jobs, not work', *Australian Society*, 3 (9):6–7.

—— (1985) 'Jobs for the young', *Australian Society*, 4 (9):21–3.

Winston, D. (1961) 'Urban structure and future growth', *Journal of the Australian Planning Institute*, 13:24–9.

Wolch, J. and Gabriel, S. (1981) 'Local land-development policies and housing values', *Environment and Planning A*, 13:1253–1276.

Wright, E. O. (1976) 'Class boundaries in the advanced capitalist societies', *New Left Review*, 98:3–41.

Young, S. (1980) '... you can't be in two places at once ...', *Social Alternatives*, 1, (8):17–22.

Index